The Phenomenology of Everyday Life presents results deriving from a rigorous qualitative approach to the psychological study of everyday human activities and experiences. This approach is grounded in the philosophical traditions of existentialism and phenomenology and employs dialogue as its major method of inquiry. The reasons for these choices are not arbitrary; all derive from the view that a proper study of human events must be framed in terms of a philosophy explicitly developed to encompass human activities. In addition, such events can properly be investigated only on the basis of a method sensitive enough to articulate the nuances of human experience and reflection. In this latter regard, it is important to note that insights deriving from literature and the humanities are equally revealing of the human world as those deriving from experimental psychology, biology, or medicine. The purpose of the present work is not to replace scientific observation with humanistic analysis but to provide an additional perspective on significant human questions.

The Phenomenology of Everyday Life

The Phenomenology of Everyday Life

HOWARD R. POLLIO
University of Tennessee

TRACY B. HENLEY
Mississippi State University

CRAIG J. THOMPSON
University of Wisconsin

with

James Barrell	Elizabeth Myers
Marilyn Dapkus Chapman	Bethany Nowell
Bruce Erdmann	Katherine Parks
Laurel Goodrich	Lawrence Ross
Michael Hawthorne	Bruce Seidner
Jean Hunt	John Shell
Randy Lang	Abi Sills-Lang
William MacGillivray	John Sproule

CAMBRIDGE
UNIVERSITY PRESS

PUBLISHED BY THE PRESS SYNDICATE OF THE UNIVERSITY OF
CAMBRIDGE
The Pitt Building, Trumpington Street, Cambridge CB2 1RP, United Kingdom

CAMBRIDGE UNIVERSITY PRESS
The Edinburgh Building, Cambridge CB2 2RU, United Kingdom
40 West 20th Street, New York, NY 10011-4211, USA
10 Stamford Road, Oakleigh, Melbourne 3166, Australia

First published 1997

Printed in the United States of America

Typeset in Times Roman

Library of Congress Cataloging-in-Publication Data
Pollio, Howard R.
The phenomenology of everyday life / Howard R. Pollio, Tracy
Henley, Craig J. Thompson with James Barrell . . . [et al.].
p.   cm.
ISBN 0-521-46205-3 (hardcover)
1. Phenomenological psychology.   I. Henley, Tracy B.
II. Thompson, Craig J.   III. Title.
BF204.5.P65   1997
150.19'2 – dc21   96–40020
                                                          CIP

*A catalog record for this book is available from
the British Library.*

ISBN 0–521–46205–3   hardback

Contents

Preface

The purpose of *The Phenomenology of Everyday Life* is to describe an alternative approach to the psychological study of everyday human activities and experiences. This approach is grounded in the philosophical traditions of existentialism and phenomenology and employs dialogue as its major method of inquiry. The reasons for these choices are not arbitrary: Both derive from the view that a proper study of human events must be framed in terms of a philosophy explicitly developed to encompass human activities. In addition, such events must be investigated on the basis of a method sensitive enough to articulate the nuances of human experience and reflection. It is important to point out, in this latter regard, that insights deriving from literature and the humanities are equally revealing of the human world as those deriving from experimental psychology, biology, or medicine. Language, whether in dialogue or drama, is never beside the point in human life.

As we hope subsequent chapters will demonstrate, our purpose is not to replace scientific observation with humanistic analysis but to provide an additional perspective on significant human questions. If we are to be successful in interesting colleagues in this endeavor, the work must be both relevant and rigorous: relevant to the everyday concerns of human existence and rigorous enough to pass critical evaluation by colleagues more comfortable with regression equations than thematic analysis. Thus the challenge is twofold: (1) to suggest new topics for research that will be recognized as significant by the empirical researcher as well as the clinical practitioner; and (2) to describe our procedures with sufficient clarity and precision to allow for public scrutiny of their utility and rigor.

To meet these goals, our present book begins with an introduction to existential and phenomenological philosophy. The intent here is not to say anything philosophically new but to present certain implications of this tradition for psychology. Although a number of significant philosophers are presented (i.e., Heidegger, Sartre, Buber, etc.), the most important position for our work is the more psychologically oriented one developed by Merleau-Ponty. Using his approach, in combination with the psychological perspectives provided by Gestalt Psychology and the continuingly contemporary William James, we seek to provide in Chapter 1 a clear and useful description of what philosophers call *consciousness*, which we term, more conservatively, *human experience.*

Chapter 2 presents details of the general methodological procedure used in each of the subsequent content chapters: the phenomenological interview. Although it is possible to situate this procedure in terms of either dialogic (Buber) or hermeneutic (Gadamer) contexts, it also may be characterized as a rigorous version of the clinical interview familiar to practitioners. One major difference between the two is that phenomenological interviewing always has its primary focus on the phenomena being discussed rather than on the person discussing it. In addition, the interviewer's concern is radically descriptive, and not ameliorative in nature, and thematic analysis takes place both within the unfolding dialogue and in a special postinterview setting known as the *interpretative group.* A final difference between clinical and phenomenological interviewing is that interpretation is never inferential in phenomenological research but always seeks to remain at the level of the dialogue itself.

With philosophical and methodological commitments in place, Chapters 3, 4, and 5 explore the major existential grounds brought to light by existential-phenomenological philosophy. As befits an overriding concern with the philosophy of Merleau-Ponty, the first of these chapters deals with the human experience of the human body. Chapter 4 also has clear philosophical roots (in this case to Bergson, Husserl, and Heidegger) and concerns the human experience of time. Finally, Chapter 5 deals with the human experience of other people; here, as before, there are phenomenological (Schultz) and existential commitments (Buber, Sartre). Although each chapter is sensitive to its philosophical origins, the thematic descriptions are empirical in nature and in no way limited by prior philosophical argument. Our descriptions always derive from our interviews and never from our theoretical or philosophical commitments, no matter how significant these were for contextualizing the research initially.

The third major section of this text concerns selected topics from everyday life. Within this set of five chapters, three deal primarily with interpersonal relationships (feeling alone, making amends, and love and loving), one with the experience of falling apart, and one with the meaning of death in the context of life. In each chapter, an intellectual debt is acknowledged not only to existential philosophy and Gestalt psychology but also to psychoanalysis and empirical social psychology. It is in these chapters, perhaps more than in previous ones, that the clinical origins and implications of the present approach may be seen most clearly.

The final chapter, as is the case with final chapters, is meant to convince the reader once more that there are distinct benefits to be derived from an empirical existential-phenomenological approach to psychology. Within this context, Chapter 11 discusses issues such as the relationship of behavior to experience, the existential meaning of reductionism, the nature of consciousness, the conceptual and empirical status of the concept of self, and, finally, the need for both qualitative and quantitative research methodologies. The purpose is to summarize what has gone before and to make a final attempt at describing a radically empirical approach to the topic of human experience that derives at least as much from humanistic sources as from more strictly scientific ones.

At this point, a question may arise as to the intended audience. The answer is a simple one: anyone interested in obtaining a clear and comprehensive description of someone else's experience. Although the area of clinical psychology comes easily to mind, so too do the related disciplines of social work, nursing, and education. Certain nontherapeutic contexts also suggest themselves in which the professional consultant seeks to discover the wishes and needs of a client – that is, seeks "to understand other minds." Included in this group are research and practice deriving from business, marketing, architecture, and law. Finally, we hope that more research-oriented colleagues in anthropology, sociology, and social psychology will find both our methods and our findings of interest. Perhaps even a philosopher or two might be interested – if only to see what we have done with a significant line of contemporary philosophical thought.

The title page of this text lists sixteen different names in addition to the authors. Although some of these individuals conducted the research on which specific chapters are based, some did not. Who, then, are these individuals, and how did they get on the title page? Basically, these good folks formed the core of individuals attending the Wednesday Night Seminar Group during that period of time when the present set of ideas and methods were being developed. Each of these friends and colleagues was instrumental in shaping the overall approach articulated in the present book, and each contributed not only clinical and research expertise but also ongoing personal support. Each also wrote his or her dissertation on a topic initially proposed at one Wednesday Night Seminar and interpreted in the course of many subsequent Wednesday Night Seminar meetings. This book is as much the product of group process as it is of individual researchers working on individual problems. So as not to have the various chapters appear to be separable elements of a patchwork quilt, however, the final text was written in a single style to provide for a continuity of voice.

This, then, is what *The Phenomenology of Everyday Life* is about and how it got that way. It is truly a collaborative effort that evolved over the course of the past decade. During this period, everyone participating in this work experienced a certain excitement and a certain awe as various projects were completed; we can only hope that some of these feelings have made their way onto the printed page and will serve to interest other colleagues in pursuing a dialogic approach to the study of human experience.

Howard R. Pollio, Knoxville, Tennessee
Tracy B. Henley, Starkville, Mississippi
Craig J. Thompson, Madison, Wisconsin

PART I

Existential Phenomenology and the Science of Psychology

1

The Nature of Human Experience

In the beginning of his classic monograph, "A Stroll through the Worlds of Animals and Men" (1934/1957), the European naturalist Jakob von Uexkull invited his readers to "blow, in fancy, a soap bubble around each creature to represent its own world, filled with the perceptions it alone knows.... Through the bubble we see ... the world as it appears to the animal (itself), not as it appears to us. This we may call the *phenomenal world* or the *self world* of the animal." Von Uexkell then went on to suggest that for many biologists these worlds will be invisible because of a prior commitment to conceptualizing animal life in purely mechanical terms. He advises us, as enlightened readers, to regard all animals, the human being included, not as machinelike objects but as subjects who live in their unique worlds that are as "manifold as the animals themselves."

Von Uexkull was not the only one of psychology's ancestors to call for a nonmechanistic and phenomenal view of human and animal life. A few years earlier, William James (1890) had written about the uniqueness of human perception, specifically in regard to four different Americans traveling in Europe:

One ... will bring home only picturesque impressions – costumes and colors, parks and views and works of architecture, pictures and structures. To another, all this will be non-existent; and distances and prices, population and drainage arrangements, door and window fastenings, and other useful statistics will take their place. A third will give a rich account of the theaters, restaurants, and public balls, and naught besides; whilst the fourth will perhaps have been so wrapped in his own subjective broodings as to tell little more than a few names of places. (James, 1890, pp. 286–287)

For two separate observers, concerned with two separate species and two separate realms, the significance of phenomenal experience was recognized early on as an important psychological issue, and from our present vantage point in the twentieth century, we must wonder why psychology chose not

3

to follow their direction. Although part of the answer surely has to do with the fact that phenomenal experience could not easily be turned into directly observable behavior, a potentially more significant reason seems to be that there was no way in which early psychology could conceptualize "phenomenal" except as "subjective" – that is, as in opposition to "objective." What this means is that human experience was considered as equivalent to the Mind of Cartesian philosophy (i.e., as both a valid mode of understanding and as a questionable topic for empirical study). When early psychology did study "mental" phenomena, the resulting introspectionist psychology could only describe them in terms of atomistic content bearing little relationship to what was usually meant by Mind both in philosophy and in everyday life.

Although such a state of affairs prevailed in American psychology, European philosophy (not to mention more esoteric and even less well-known Eastern theologies and philosophies) had developed or was developing approaches to human experience in which consciousness was viewed as neither self-sufficient nor as located in the unreachable interior of a thinking subject but, rather, as a relationship between the living subject and his or her world. This position, which in Western philosophy derives from Kant, gave rise both to a philosophy of consciousness known as *phenomenology* and to a psychology of perception known as *Gestalt*. Although it is true that certain aspects of Gestalt psychology ultimately did affect American psychology, it is equally true that early phenomenology had far less impact largely because it seemed more concerned with foundational issues in philosophy than with psychological aspects of human life. This view of phenomenology began to change, however, once it was explicitly joined to a philosophy of existence – initially by Heidegger (1927/1962) and more recently by Merleau-Ponty (1945/1962) – to yield the contemporary postition known as *existential phenomenology*.

What is the nature of this philosophy that enables it to hold out the promise of allowing psychology to consider a multiplicity of first-person perspectives without resorting either to an inappropriate mentalism or solipsism? As its name suggests, it is a combination of two philosophies, one concerned with a certain perspective on human existence and the other with a certain mode of investigating that existence. This combination is the result of neither convenience nor historical accident; rather, both philosophies derive from a common interest in human experiences in the world of everyday human life. This interest does not view experience (or consciousness, in more technical terms) as a consequence of some internal set of events such as mind or brain but as a relationship between people and their world, whether the world at that moment consists of other people, nature, time, one's own body, personal or philosophical ideas, or whatever. What is sought by both existentialism and phenomenology is a rigorous description of human life as it is lived and reflected upon in all of its first-person concreteness, urgency, and ambiguity. For existential-phenomenology, the world is to be lived and described, not explained.

Although existentialism began somewhat earlier than phenomenology, it was not until the advent of phenomenology that existentialism was provided with a method appropriate to its concerns. If existentialism begins with Kierkegaard in the mid-nineteenth century, and phenomenology with Husserl at the end of the same century, it is not until Heidegger that the two are combined into a single project – that of describing everyday human existence in uniquely human ways. Unfortunately for psychology, Heidegger is among the most philosophical of philosophers, and it remained for Merleau-Ponty to cast psychological insight and empirical research into a philosophical system more congenial to a psychological study of human existence. Indeed, the early Merleau-Ponty (1942/1963, 1945/ 1962) derived much of his inspiration, not to mention empirical support, from the work of Gestalt psychologists such as Köhler, Wertheimer, and Goldstein. If scientific psychology is to take an existential phenomenological turn, it must be grounded in the philosophy of Merleau-Ponty and only secondarily in Heidegger, Husserl, and Kierkegaard, however significant they may be to Merleau-Ponty's own thought.

At the center of Merleau-Ponty's philosophy, and of crucial importance for psychology, is his description of the "lived body." This concept is meant to provide a way of overcoming Cartesian dualism, especially as it manifests itself in certain current behavioral and cognitive approaches to psychology. There seems to be no more significant problem than that of providing a coherent way of dealing with the fact that human beings both have a body and are a body. The positions usually taken in psychology either assume a physical monism (as, for example, Skinner) or seek transformational relations to mediate between the world of events physically construed and the meaning of these events for some mental process (as, for example, early cognitive psychology). Most psychologists no longer worry about dualism but seem content to view it as a problem that time and biology will solve.

Probably the major problem to any position other than a dualistic one is that the human body, as an object of perception by any competent observer, has a clear boundary between "It" and everything else. The human body maintains its boundary for perception whether we move, sit still, type, or watch a movie. It is recognizable as a well-defined entity when we or someone else views it in a mirror, photograph, or videotape. We even see our body as a well-bounded object in dreams or fantasies. Observers such as physicians or physiologists also view the body as a bounded object; they, however, also are allowed to examine the body's contents – its internal organs, muscles, bones, and connecting tissue – and the idea of the body as anything other than a well-defined biophysical entity capable of containing other well-defined biophysical entities seems counter not only to common perception and imagination but to medical science as well. Everywhere we turn we are struck by the materiality and boundedness of the human body; our own, and those of other people.

There are, however, times when the bodily contour seems not only less well-defined but even problematic, and these times are most apparent when we change from a third- to a first-person perspective on the body. All of the self-evident evidence for the body as a distinct object derives from a third-person perspective – that is, when I look at my body in a photograph or mirror or more imaginatively in day or night dreams. It also occurs when I, as either physiologist, physician, or just plain person-watcher, consider the body of some other person from an outside (third-person) perspective. My body or someone else's body is well defined only when considered from the point of view of an outsider – that is, from a third-person perspective.

Adopting a first-person perspective changes radically the experience of my body as defined by a single, distinct contour. If I extend the possibility of a similar change in experience when you consider your body from your own first-person perspective, we both should become much less comfortable with a description of the body in which it is characterized as an object. The body, which a moment ago from a third-person perspective was so stable, coherent, and unequivocal, no longer seems from a first-person perspective to end at the tips of my toes, nose, fingertips, and head. Rather, it has become a less distinct and more mobile event that sometimes resides in the natural world in the form of a rock, tree, or animal; at other times, in some aspect of the human world such as a person, book, or building; and at still other times, in some personal past in the form of an idea or memory, or, right now, in some object with which I am involved such as a pen or typewriter. Except for the case where I am directly aware of my body, my usual experience is that I am least aware of my body as an entity and most aware of some aspect of the world that has called to me. This class of personal experiences is described in the philosophical literature by the concept of intentionality, a concept very much at the heart of an existential-phenomenological approach to human existence and one of the defining properties of human experiencing.

Characteristics of Human Experience

Intentionality

The concept of intentionality, first introduced to modern phenomenology by Brentano and Husserl, is meant to capture the descriptive insight that "every experience has its reference or direction toward what is experienced, and, contrarily, every experienced phenomenon refers to or reflects a mode of expression to which it is present" (Ihde, 1979, pp. 42–44). Within philosophy, intentionality is taken to imply that experience and world co-constitute one another for some person. It is extremely important for psychology, however, to note explicitly that intentionality is not an intellectual process connecting a thinking subject with a world outside its ken; rather, intentionality is meant to emphasize that human experience is continuously directed toward a world that it never possesses in its entirety but toward which it is always directed.

Intentionality, as the phenomenologist uses the term, is also not to be confused with the more common concept of intention. When a person says "I intend to do . . . ," the implication is that the person has a plan or preset agenda to carry out. Intentionality, on the other hand, is a basic structure of human existence that captures the fact that human beings are fundamentally related to the contexts in which they live or, more philosophically, that all being is to be understood as "being-in-the-world." Intention describes one mental state among many; intentionality describes a basic configuration of person and world.

A simple example should serve to clarify the difference. Imagine that Person *A* makes a statement which Person *B* experiences as upsetting. *A* might then say to *B*: "I didn't intend to upset you." What this means is that Person *A* did not make the statement with the explicit plan of upsetting *B*. But what, then, is the *intentionality* of the situation? For *A*, there is the experience of *B*'s being upset; for *B*, there is the experience of the world as upsetting. Intentionality describes the structure of the situation for each participant although the specific natures of their engagement in that situation differ. Situations also may arise with (or without) mental intention; every situation, however, is always characterized by a specific configuration of person/world from the point of view of the person. Even though human beings can and do act without prespecified plans, every situation is intentional (i.e., embodies a relationship between the person and some aspect(s) of his or her present world).

Other implications follow from considering intentionality as the fundamental structure of human experience. One of the more significant is that the experience of myself does not precede my experience of the world – the "You must come before the I," as Nietzsche once remarked. What seems to be the case is that we learn and relearn who we are on the basis of our encounters with objects, ideas, and people – in short, with every different kind of "otherness." The other side of this relational state of affairs is that what we are aware of in a situation reveals something important about who we are. If, for example, we come into a room and notice only the furniture, we are likely a very different person from someone who notices only the people, the food, or the artwork. The objects of our awareness reveal what is noteworthy for us, and if the self comes into being on the basis of its encounters with otherness, what gets noticed in that encounter reveals what that self is like in terms of what is significant for and to us. William James also knew this (see Preface).

What we experience is also never separate from the culture or language in which we live, talk, and act. Our actions – linguistic, conceptual, and otherwise – take on meaning only within some sociolinguistic framework. Although culture is conceived by existential-phenomenological thought as an organized and organizing structure, it is not construed as a causal force. For example, the structure of language does not "cause" us to speak, but if we are to speak, a certain language must be used. As Gadamer (1960/1975) put it, language speaks us as much as we speak it. Culture also is not an encapsulated entity but one that grounds all that we see and do. For one person, going to a local shopping mall may be experienced as an adventure (such as hunting for unadvertised sales); for another, it may be experienced as a laborious chore. The reference of the experience (i.e., going to the mall) and its alternative meanings (adventure or chore) are but two of many culturally given possibilities. Understanding the meaning of some experience requires us to describe the intentional stance (or situated perspective) of the event from the point of view of the experiencing person.

The Intentionality of Human Activity. The description of experience that emerges from an analysis based on the intentionality of experience may seem far removed from human action. Husserl and Merleau-Ponty both identify a type of intentional relationship between person and world – an operative or functional intentionality – that is concerned neither with judgment nor reflection but with action. Merleau-Ponty's analysis of the lived body represents his attempt to describe first-person experiences of human movement (what is usually termed *behavior*) in such a way as not to lead us to conclude that "I am in my body," which is then "In the world," but rather to suggest that "I am in the world" directly. Behavior, for Merleau-Ponty, is a direct relationship between me-in-the-world in much the same way that perception is a direct relationship between me-and-things-in-the-world.

The best presentation of such direct experiences of a lack of separation between me and my world are provided by first-person descriptions of skilled acts by highly practiced individuals such as a professional football player catching a pass or a cold philosopher chopping wood for a winter fire. Pollio (1982) describes the case of one professional football player who notes that when he catches a football he is aware of nothing but, as he put it, "me and the ball." If we attempt to capture the experience of skilled behavior from the first-person perspective of a professional athlete, the event as experienced is remarkably narrow and well described in terms of a direct relationship between the athlete and the ball.

Coaches often describe the athlete's ability as "concentration," but such a description implies that there is some separate *someone* to concentrate, and some separate *something* on which to concentrate, or the more usual categories of mind and body, with mind serving to focus body. The skilled performer did not say "I first decide to blot everything out and pay attention only to the ball." What he said instead is that catching the ball becomes all of the world and that he does what is necessary to achieve this end. In talking about "concentration," the coach speaks from a third-person perspective that sees the movements of the athlete; the athlete speaks from a first-person perspective in which body, will, and outcome are experienced as a single, unified event.

If an athlete's experience is so immediate, how does the world – the game situation – regulate his or her actions? Here there are no sure answers – only a few hints from the German coach/psychologist H. G. Hartgenbusch (1927), who asked athletes to provide first-person descriptions of several different sports. In soccer, for example, Hartgenbusch found that the goalkeeper standing before a rather large goal opening seems to be where the ball is hit more often than should be the case by chance. Hartgenbusch points out that the goalkeeper is the most dominant part of the goal mouth and for the ordinary soccer player serves as an aiming point, a target to be shot at. The expert player has learned to disregard this target point and shoots instead at the open space surrounding the goalkeeper. A good player then, is one who has "learned to reconstruct his field to change the phenomenal center from the goalkeeper to another point in space [and] this [new point] comes to have the same attraction as the goalkeeper had before" (Hartgenbusch, 1927, p. 49).

There are a number of unusual words in this description such as *attraction, phenomenal center*, and *field* which suggest that the first-person world of the athlete is not determined by first looking over the situation, next deciding what to do, and then doing it, but that it all occurs in a more immediate, unreflected, and ongoing way. "As soccer players move toward the goal, they see the playing ground as a field of changing lines whose direction leads toward the goal. . . . When I asked the player what he saw, [he said] I only saw a hole" (Hartgenbusch, 1927, p. 49).

The world of a skilled athlete illustrates the structure of a direct intentional relationship between person and world in a particularly clear way. A second example is provided by the philosopher Ihde (1979) and concerns his experience of chopping wood for a winter fire. In describing this experience, Ihde reports that while chopping he does not pay attention to or think about his experience. Following an earlier description by Merleau-Ponty (1945/1962), the intentional nature of his actions is described in the following terms: "I am outside myself in the world of my project." A different and more differentiated description of this experience is "I-am-in-the-ax-directed-toward-the-wood." Even for a philosopher, thinking and the experience of self are at a minimum during the process of chopping wood, and the focal point of awareness is on the wood to be chopped and not on the self; if the self appears at all, it appears only when the philosopher reflects on the intentional nature of the relationship between him and the wood or when someone else describes observing him chop wood. The first-person world is a relational one in which some aspect of the world is focal and in which the self as a clear and distinct entity appears only to third-person perception or to my own later reflection. Unlike the worlds of reflection and/or third-person perception, first-person experience, even of movement, does not have a constant shape: All that is constant is a focus on some event or situation as it relates to what from other perspectives could be called "me" or "I."

The Intentionality of Human Thinking. Both ordinary perception and skilled behavior reveal that we regularly experience ourselves as directly related not only to the objects of our perception but also to the worlds in which we move. Neither perception nor action separates us from our world even if there are times when we may be uncertain of our perceptions or unsure of our actions. It is only in those cases, in which there is some hesitancy about what we are to do, that we may experience drawing back from the world into the "interior" world of thinking and/or planning. Yet even here, the situation may be described in terms of intentionality, for what now happens is that I am directly aware of ideas and possible situations, and the intentional structure relates what is experienced (an idea) and my mode of experiencing it (thinking about it). Although "what" I experience is now a mental event, and "how" I experience is by thinking, there is still the first-person experience of connection that is as clear and relational in the case of thinking as it was in the case of chopping wood or catching a football. Thinking, as a human event, yields a different experience of "how" the self relates to its objects and/or plans; it does not, however, require a change in the way in which first-person experience is to be described from a first-person point of view (i.e., as intentional).

In discussing this issue, Pollio (1982) wondered if thinking exhibits a vastly different intentional structure from other, more observable, activities such as are usually grouped under the term *behavior*. Somewhat playfully this concern was framed in terms of the following question: "Is thinking about thinking different from just plain thinking?" The answer he gave was as follows: If we are thinking$_1$ about thinking$_2$ the first and second "thinkings" are not the same. The first thinking is a process, something immediate and ongoing; it is what I am doing right now. The second thinking is the object of my present, ongoing activity and is obviously different from the process of thinking itself. In terms of intentionality, thinking$_2$ defines the relational pole of thinking; as such the characteristic pattern for thinking – in this case, thinking$_1$ – is no different from any other human experience, even if its intentional object is thinking itself.

The possibility that we are able to think about anything and everything – thinking, our self, and the natural world included – has been taken by philosophers since Descartes (and before) to endow thinking with some special meaning as *the* fundamental activity defining what it means to be human or, even, what it might mean to exist. As Hazel Barnes (1956) points out in her introduction to *Being and Nothingness*: "The consciousness which says 'I am' is not the consciousness which thinks . . . and Descartes' 'cogito' is not Descartes' thinking; it is Descartes reflecting on the doubting" (p. 11). What a Cartesian approach, and those that derive from it such as much of contemporary cognitive psychology, end up by doing is to separate the (first-person) experience of thinking from the thinking person. Having done this, they are led to describe perception as depending upon the interpretation of a stimulus, and behavior as the output phase of some internal plan developed on the basis of prior or ongoing cognitive activity. For a Cartesian-based psychology, thinking is the connection between perception and action; as such, it serves to remove the person from direct contact with the world and leaves him or her isolated in an internal storehouse of ideas, images, representations, and plans.

While the description of any psychological activity, be it walking, seeing, or thinking, in the form of impersonal third-person processes is extremely significant for contemporary psychology, we must never lose sight of the fact that descriptions provided by scientific analysis always depend upon direct experiences in and of the world that precede their schematization in scientific language. The world of third-person description (and theory) presupposes what it attempts to explain. For example, we must have experienced planning or calculating in a first-person way before we can understand what a computer program is about; we must have moved through space before we can understand what a map or geometry is all about; we must have experienced time well before we can understand what a clock or calendar is about. While the fruits of rational, scientific thought are extremely powerful, it is important to note that they too can be construed in terms of intentional relationships between people and their ideas and concepts. Thinking is an intentional act no less than perceiving or behaving.

Figure/Ground

Perhaps no perceptual demonstration is as familiar as that of the vase and faces figure first introduced to psychology by the Danish psychologist Edgar Rubin. Although textbook writers present this, and other, reversible figures as parlor games only loosely related to significant aspects of perceiving, Rubin used this figure to demonstrate directly the difference between figure and ground. The demonstration is especially powerful if the person pays special attention to his or her experiences of the white area in the figure. For example, when the vase is seen, the white area is experienced as brighter, closer, and better defined; when the faces are seen, the white area loses its thinglike character and becomes dimmer, more poorly defined, and further away. Comparable effects are experienced if the perceiver considers differences in his or her experiences of the black area when two faces are seen in contrast to when the black area serves as background to the perception of a white vase.

　　Observations such as these and others were used by Rubin to define the following properties as characterizing first-person perceptual experiences of figure and ground:

1. The figure appears to have a definite form and a sharp boundary; the ground is less defined and appears more diffuse.
2. The figure is experienced as closer than the ground, which is experienced as behind the figure.
3. The figure is more easily named and/or described than the ground.
4. The figure is experienced as in clearer focus than the ground.

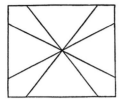

Figure 1.1. Köhler's crosses figure (from Köhler, 1947, p. 107)

While the Rubin figure is extremely well known, we might wonder if figure and ground are experienced as clearly and directly when an unknown object is used. To explore this possibility, Köhler (1947) asked his readers to consider Figure 1.1, which may be seen as a cross with four slender arms running across the figure diagonally or as a different cross consisting of four larger sections. As in the case of the vase and faces, whichever figure appears, appears more compelling and thinglike than the remainder of the figure, which is experienced as less well defined and further from the viewer. When the "other" cross appears, the first one disappears, and the figure now experienced yields all of the same properties as were experienced in regard to the now-absent initial figure.

In addition to providing good first-person demonstrations of figure/ground phenomena, these figures provide compelling first-person examples of the fact that one and the same contour may be experienced as belonging to two different objects. It seems quite clear that the faces and the vase (or the two crosses) cannot exist without one another; in more perceptual terms, the vase depends upon the faces as much as the faces depend upon the vase (the same description also obviously applies to the crosses). It also seems clear that when one of the figures is seen, the other is not. While the two objects co-constitute each other, only one is figural at any one time.

These perceptual demonstrations capture an extremely general aspect of human experience: All objects of experience are experienced only in relation to some less clear part of the total situation serving to situate the focal object. There are no figures by themselves: All figural aspects of (perceptual) experience always emerge against some ground that serves to delineate its specific experiential form – in the case of our perceptual examples, their specific shapes. For this reason, it is never experientially valid to talk of an isolated figure of experience, perceptual or otherwise; rather, we must always talk about the figure/ground structure of experience (note the slash) to emphasize that human experience is a patterned event defined by focal and background aspects.

For the moment, figure/ground has been described by a pair of black and white figures located within line-drawn boxes. If we take the line-drawn box as our figure, however, it is clear that the box will emerge as a figure only against the ground of the page. Moving on, we note that the page may be experienced as figure against the ground of the book, the book against the ground of the desk, the desk against the ground of the floor and wall, the floor and/or wall against the ground of the room, the room against the ground of the apartment, the apartment the building, the building the street, and so on. Whatever we take as figure is always grounded by both a near ground that is directly related to the figure and by a variety of other grounds that serve to provide the core figure/ground event with its initially more vague grounding. This latter set of limits to the core figure/ground pattern is called the *horizon* or sometimes even the *fringe* of experience.

Within phenomenological accounts of perceiving, the concept of horizon is used in a second sense, and this concerns the solidity of objects. Consider the case of some book or other. From where I, as perceiver, now sit, I see only a gray side, the white of some pages about an inch and a half thick, and some words on the spine of the book: B. F. Skinner, *About Behaviorism.* Suppose that I first pick the book up and place its front cover toward me, and then turn it over so that its solid gray back cover now faces me. After each of these changes, some aspect of the book has disappeared from direct view as others have come into view; with each turn, the book presents a new profile to me.

For any careful description of how I perceive an object, it is clear that I am not surprised that the book has many different aspects that are not visible to me at the same time; nor am I surprised by what might be termed an "absence-within-a-presence," say the back of the book, when the front of the book is toward me. Experiences such as these were described by Husserl as the object's inner horizon so as to stress the (experiential) fact that objects usually are not perceived as facades (as they may be in trompe l'oeil paintings) but as having thickness and dimension. Objects that appear always do so as a play of presence and absence-within-presence, and it is the combining of presence and absence-within-presence that yields the more general experience that things exist as objects independent of me in the field "out there."

Thus both the transcendence of the thing and the transcendence of the world is to be found in the sense of presence including the specific absence-in-presence that is the inner horizon of the thing on the one side and the horizon of the world at the limit. The thing as a "whole" always exceeds any manifest vision, just as the world exceeds any perspective upon the world, and I sense this with and not outside experience. (Ihde, 1979, p. 64)

With this more extended description, the power of a figure/ground approach to experience more generally and perceptual experiences more particularly would seem complete. Yet we seem to have left out a significant aspect of the situation – the person for whom the object, event, or idea is figural. The concept of intentionality has already dealt with this issue, since experience is always structured as a relation between some experiencer and something experienced. Transposing this insight to the language of figure/ground, part of the ground for any figure is the person for whom it is figural. Under this rendering, the concept of figure/ground implies that the personal perspective is, itself, always a significant aspect to what is perceived. When we consider perceptual experience more completely from the side of the person, it is clear that all experience, perceiving included, is always situated (i.e., contextualized in some ground). The existential concept that applies here is that being is never isolated from the world but is always experienced as in-the-world.

The existential-phenomenological concept of being-in-the-world is surprisingly similar to that of current behavioral thought, which construes behavior not as mechanical action but as interbehavior – that is, as an interaction between some specific organism in some specific environment. Although it is difficult for a phenomenological approach to psychology to accept all of the implications of this position – for example, its emphasis on a third-person description of "organisms" and "environments" – it does offer a view of behavior as necessarily taking place within a specific situational ground. To control behavior, the interbehaviorist advises us to do something with and to the ground within which behavior takes place, and this advice emerges as good sense from both the phenomenologist and the behaviorist.

The situatedness of human experiences, however, requires us to emphasize not only that there is a situation but that the situation is significant only in the unique way it is experienced by the person. While a third-person description offers a reasonable starting point – the person in some specific situation – only a first-person perspective requires us to specify which aspects of the situation are significant (i.e., to change a third-person into a first-person description). Person and situation mutually co-constitute each other, and it is always the relevance of the situation to me that is crucial in its role as ground for my experience and/or behavior.

The focal event in any experience is thus grounded by two different sets of events: (1) by the multiple grounds surrounding it as object; and (2) by the multiple grounds surrounding the person, including his or her experiences of the present situation, the language he or she speaks, the culture in which he or she lives, and so on. The facts of figure/ground lead us to view the focus of experience – the figural event – as comprised of a double figure/ground/horizon pattern, with the focus of experience serving as the nexus connecting the relevant aspect of this dual structure. All experiencing is relational, and the field of experience – the phenomenal field – is grounded as much by the world of nature and things as by those of culture, history, and situation. All events experienced as figural emerge only against the multiple grounds of everyday reality comprised of its worldly and socio-personal aspects.

As in the case of intentionality, the concept of figure/ground provides an additional way of describing behavior-and-experience as separate perspectives that, at the same time, are aspects of a single existence – that of the person in question. Both behavior and experience are field events subject to the figure/ground/horizon structure that is at times made relevant by personal meanings and at other times by the world as now lived. Far from giving a Cartesian view of the body as a distinct thing or of experience as an "internal" event, the perspective provided by integrating figure/ground experiences with those of intentionality yields a coherent pattern in which figural aspects are always experienced as figural in some situation. Personal existence is a grounded perceptual/conceptual event *and* an embodied motor event, with both aspects rooted in a world of everyday reality that each of us lives and thinks about whether we are describing experiences of a reversible figure, the books we read, the nature of our body, or any of the multitude of objects and events present to us in the course of an ordinary day. Figure/ground implies a rootedness to contexts in much the same way as intentionality implies a relatedness to the world in general.

Continuity and Change

The first-person field defined by considerations of intentionality and figure/ground provide a description of human experience that is too much like a thing and too little like a living event. When we consider our own first-person experiences of the world, we are struck by its mobility and change; we seem unable to stay continuously rooted to a single figure, and although each focal event may be accurately described as a coherent, intentional, figure/ground/horizon structure, the fields of our experience come and go in a changing way.

No one has better captured this aspect of human experiencing than William James in his description of the stream of consciousness (e.g., James, 1890). One of the most accessible presentations of the stream of consciousness, provided by James in his *Talks to Teachers* (1899), concerns the experience of attending a lecture:

In most of our fields of consciousness there is a core . . . that is very pronounced. You, for example, now, although you are also thinking and feeling, are getting . . . sensations of my face and figure, and . . . voice. The sensations are the *centre* or *focus*, the thoughts and feelings, the *margin* of your actually present conscious field.

On the other hand, some object of thought, some distant image, may have become the focus of your mental attention even while I am speaking – your mind . . . may have wandered from the lecture; and, my face and voice, although not absolutely vanishing from your conscious field, may have taken up there a very faint and marginal place. Again, some feeling connected with your own body may have passed from a marginal to a focal place, even while I speak.

In the successive mutations of our fields of consciousness, the process by which one dissolves into another is often very gradual . . . sometimes the focus remains but little changed, while the margin alters rapidly . . . sometimes the focus alters, and the margin stays. Sometimes focus and margin change places. Sometimes, again, abrupt alterations of the whole field occur. (pp. 16–17)

Within this single description, James has captured many of the same insights provided to a description of human experience by the principles of intentionality and those of figure/ground, which James renders as *focus* and *margin*. The aspect of James's description that is uniquely emphasized is that of change, with change characterized as "successive mutations" of the phenomenal field that gradually dissolve into one another. To be sure, experiences of change also are captured to some degree in reversible figures as well as in terms of changes in the objects of intentional relatedness; yet it is James who emphasizes this aspect of experience most clearly, not only in terms of his specific descriptions of change but also in terms of the metaphor he chose to use in presenting it to the reader – *the stream of consciousness*.

Although James wavered in considering the stream of consciousness as pertaining to thinking or to more general conscious life, looking at it in either way does little to change its significance for psychology. In both cases, five characteristics define the Jamesian stream:

1. Every event experienced is always experienced by some specific person.
2. Within each person, consciousness is constantly changing.
3. Within each person, consciousness is sensibly continuous.
4. Within each person, consciousness always deals with objects.
5. Within each person, consciousness selects among its objects and events.

James's first point simply tells us that there is always some I who thinks or experiences, never just "thoughts or experiences" by themselves. Thus, any description of consciousness must take the person into account. The Jamesian stream is always "somebody's stream," and it should come as no surprise that James's chapter on this topic in *The Principles of Psychology* (1890) is followed by one on the consciousness of self. For James, the two topics are intimately related, as he notes quite explicitly in his briefer text:

Whatever I may be thinking of, I am always at the same time more or less aware of myself, of my general existence. At the same time it is I who am aware; so that the total self of me, in being as it were duplex, partly known and partly unknown, partly object and partly subject, must have two aspects described in it of which for short-ness we may call the Me and the other the I. (James, 1892, p. 176)

It is not difficult to see James suggesting some concept of intentionality in this quote. The two sides of intentional structure are given by the relation-ship between the object of consciousness (what I am thinking of) and the self (my general existence), in which the I and Me may be viewed as reflections from (and on) the "self's side" of the relationship.

Consciousness as involving both change and continuity is captured in James's second and third points. Indeed, it was James who sometimes compared consciousness to the life of a bird, consisting, as he put it, "of an alternation of flights and perchings." This comparison was meant to empha-size not only that consciousness was continuously changing but that it was experienced as comprised of two different aspects: one concerning content, and the second, transitions between content. Early attempts at describing the flow of consciousness by associationist philosophers (e.g., Hobbes, Locke) and psychologists viewed it as consisting only of "stopping points" such as ideas, words, and images and their interconnections. On this basis, experience was compared not to the "flight and perchings" of some bird but to a train or chain of ideas connected together by prior contiguous occur-rences. Rather than describing human awareness as a train, or even a bird's flight, James's more general image of the stream of consciousness suggests that mental life is continuous and cannot be viewed as a series of separate events loosely articulated on the basis of having occurred together in the past.

Although James frequently used the word *continuous* in describing the stream of consciousness, Natsoulos (1988) points out that he also some-times seemed to describe the stream as discontinuous; as consisting of "pulses" of experience temporally adjacent to one another. Building on Gibson's (1979) analysis, however, Natsoulos agrees with the view of a continuous stream that "proceeds with continually transforming content that includes, more or less specifically, what has preceded and what will follow . . . (the) units of experience are units of intentional content: that of which one is aware" (p. 366).

James's fourth point may be seen as a return to the issue of intentional-ity, this time from the side of the object. For James, an object of consciousness was described as consisting of a relatively clear central aspect known as its *focus* or *core* and a less distinct and sometimes more peripheral aspect known as its *margin* or *fringe*. Such structure not only characterizes objects of thought or imagination but objects of perception as well. The Jamesian stream, thus, is remarkably free of the usual distinction between "internal" and "external" objects, choosing to describe both in similar terms. When the focus/fringe structure is combined with the postulates of change and continuity, consciousness is described as moving among its objects in a number of different ways: Sometimes its focal aspect changes, sometimes its marginal aspects change, and sometimes both change. The tempo of change also is described as varying in rate, sometimes being gradual and sometimes abrupt. An object of consciousness, for James, was never identified as an isolated event only adventitiously connected to other objects; rather, it was more usually described as the central aspect of an interrelated field that varied in its degree of distinctiveness, stability, and centrality for the person whose stream was under consideration.

With this extended notion of an object of consciousness, and its relationship to other aspects of the phenomenal field, it seems clear that certain objects more easily and completely capture the person than others. That is James's fifth point: Not all objects are, or become, focal with equal ease. The successful thinker – the man of genius, as James called him – is one "who will always stick in his bill at the right point and take out the right element – 'reason' if the emergency be theoretical, 'means' if it be practical. ...[This view] suffices to show that Reasoning is but another form of ... selective activity" (1890, p. 287).

Human experience, therefore, always involves a set of more or less distinct possibilities to be selected among. Fortunately, what I select frequently agrees with what you select, and, since we usually name what we select, most people in a given society will agree on what to name and notice or notice and name. Despite such agreement, there is one case in which no two individuals ever select exactly alike. There is, as James said, one "great splitting of the universe made by each of us." In this split, there is almost always one part in which I am more interested. If, along with James, we call these parts *Me* and *Not-Me*, it is obvious that no matter how hard I try, I am never as interested in the Not-Me as in the Me, in the Yours as in the Mine. My Me always stands out against the ground of my Not-Me, which, whether you like it or not, includes You. Fortunately for You, however, you feel the same way about your Me and Not-Me, and both of us must come to recognize that in this case we have split the world in two different places.

The Stream of Consciousness in Literature

James's description of the stream of consciousness should have become a central aspect of psychology. Psychology to his day, however, remains under the sway of an objective (third-person) perspective that has refused to concern itself with an invisible and continually changing event known as *human experience*. For this reason, the most significant intellectual locale in which stream of consciousness thinking took hold was literature, and the 50-year period from 1885 to 1935 saw the major works defining this genre of writing come to light in Europe and the United States. The most significant writers providing clear examples include Marcel Proust in France, James Joyce in Ireland, and William Faulkner in the United States. While other writers also employed this technique as an aspect of style, these three authors are of greatest importance for any psychological attempt to describe conscious experience from the personal point of view.

Proust was the most mannerly of the three. While his theme of human memory and lived time is of significance for any psychological description of experience, Proust's books are written largely in the style of interior monologue, and the sentences rendering remembrances of things past are orderly, even if long and complex. The major way in which Proust describes the past as being recaptured is in terms of an involuntary evocation of a past experience by a present one; thus, a cookie reopens experiences in the early life of his narrator, Marcel. For Proust, the past sometimes overwhelms the present, and the person, vividly and in the present tense, relives that past as a complex combination of then and now. Despite the avowed purpose of providing a faithful rendering of experiences of past interpenetrating present, Proust employs the relatively ordinary prose of grammatical monologue, and the reader ends up with the narrator's mannerly description of the past. In Proust we do not, as promised, reenter the past; rather, we are offered an account of it told by the narrator.

With Faulkner, the reader is more directly in the middle of things, as in the novel *The Sound and the Fury*, which opens with a description of the world by a feebleminded character named Benjy. Benjy's stream is recognizably immature and variable, and sense for the reader is not easy to come by in the early pages of the book. Sentences are short and disconnected as Benjy's stream moves back and forth through the experiences of his life, with the patterns of memory enhanced by objects and words of the present. Other characters are rendered by different streams that serve to define them: Quentin's stream is excitedly adolescent and becomes incoherent during the recollection of a fight in which he fainted; Jason's more orderly stream is closer to an interior monologue as he recalls and thinks about his more seemingly controlled life. The descriptions written by Faulkner present different streams for different characters, and the reader is provided with the confusion, excitement, and ambiguity of a first-person rendition. The stream is more alive and experience-near in Faulkner than in Proust.

Joyce offers the most articulated and far-reaching presentation of stream of consciousness writing. His descriptions range from the experiences of a young child listening to a story in *The Portrait of an Artist as a Young Man* to one presenting a mythic stream of consciousness in *Finnegan's Wake*. Midway between the relatively ordinary events of the *Portrait* and the mythic ones of *Finnegan's Wake* is Joyce's *Ulysses*, a book that depicts a variety of streams ranging from ordinary to mythic. Sometimes events are rendered as an interior monologue in which one sentence slides into another in a somewhat grammatical yet unpredictable way; at other times – in Molly's daydream soliloquy – no punctuation is used as thoughts, images, ideas, and memories jumble together without much in the way of syntactical markers. In most descriptions, however, there is little indication as to what is "in" the person and what is "in" the world; everything that is experienced is written largely in the present tense.

In offering a psychological perspective on these writers, it is important to note that a different grammatical form is used at different times and for different characters: Sometimes an interior monologue is used, and sometimes a disconnected series of words and images is used. Each writer also makes tenuous the separation between the world of the present and that of the past, and descriptions frequently encompass events that derive from both, now present to the person. Tempo is also important as some passages depict a stream of consciousness that is alternately leisurely and rapid whereas other passages structure it in the form of a slowly building climax. Each stream, however, moves at a pace appropriate to protagonist and situation.

In stream of consciousness writing, past, present, and future do not align one after another as clock and calendar suggest they should. The temporal organization of consciousness is content-based, with the character equally involved in the event as it now occurs, as it anticipates a future, and/or as it is foreshadowed by some past event. Certain threads of life – its themes or leitmotifs – tie the present focus to other events and meanings, and no event is unconnected from the rest. At any moment, the stream is of a single piece, and such coherence often defies the grid of rational expectation as well as the linear qualities of ordinary historical, narrative, or clock time.

Each monologue is also written in a distinctive signature, whether of a 33-year-old retarded man/boy (Benjy) or of an artist as a young man, and such uniqueness affords each rendition an ability to provide a singular perspective on narrative events. If there is one aspect to the human world rendered by stream of consciousness technique, it is that of personal perspective. Each character renders the world in unique terms. This is as true for a character in the midst of a myth (Bloom in *Ulysses*) as for one stridently in everyday reality (Jason in *Sound and Fury*). It is at this point that the literature of consciousness connects with the literature of character, for in this mode of writing, personal consciousness *is* character. If we take the lead offered by stream of consciousness novels, William James was quite astute in placing the chapter on self immediately after the one on consciousness.

Human Experience and the Freudian Unconscious

During the same period that Proust, Joyce, and Faulkner were providing literary examples of what everyday human experience was like, Freud and other members of the psychoanalytic school were providing examples of a different type of human experience thought to provide evidence for a special region of the person known as the *unconscious*. Although psychoanalytic writers describe the unconscious in terms of spatial metaphors (i.e., as a place within the person), the experiential facts upon which it depends do not necessarily require such a rendition. We need not postulate a specific location in which to place the unconscious to appreciate the significance in our lives of dreams, slips of the tongue, jokes, myths, free associations, and/ or an inability to recall specific memories.

The major examples offered by Freud in presenting an understanding of the unconscious are those that exemplify the processes of condensation, displacement, and repression. As Freud himself notes, these processes occur not only in neurotic symptoms and dreams but in more ordinary wake-a-day states of consciousness such as are involved in the creation/ appreciation of metaphors, analogies, similes, and puns. We regularly experience condensation by having one word or picture fade into another to create a single image – as in many paintings by Magritte or Dali or in almost any poem from Sappho to Ferlinghetti. Similarly meanings often are "displaced" from one psychological experience to another such that landscapes are sad or joyous, policemen are reacted to as if they were father, and psychotherapists are hated with a passion too powerful for what they and we have experienced during one or more hours sitting together in a darkened room.

Within the psychoanalytic scheme of things, however, such events are primarily significant when in the service of repression – the tendency to locate (more precisely, to push) certain classes of material into the Unconscious – with the facades provided by condensation and displacement serving to prevent the relevant material from becoming present to the person in all of its undeniable significance. While still adhering to Freud's postulate, that such events express one or many meanings for the person, the existential phenomenologist feels less comfortable in postulating a "second thinking subject whose creations are simply received by the first." What remains a more comfortable way of talking about unconscious events is that "the analysis of a given behavior always discovers several layers of signification, each with its own truth and that the phenomenology of possible interpretations is the expression of a mixed life in which every choice always has several meanings, it being impossible to say which of them is the one true one" (Merleau-Ponty, 1970, pp. 49–50).

The phenomenological analysis of the facts on which unconscious processes are based concerns itself with two issues: (1) in order not to think of something fraught with personal significance (i.e., to repress it), the person must be more rather than less aware of it; and (2) unconscious meanings do not reside "in" the person but "in" the dialogue between that person and someone else such as a psychotherapist.

Any analysis of the hypervigilance defining repression must accept the analytic truth that a "repressed" event is important and that the tendency not to experience it directly signifies a continuingly meaningful relation between the event and the person. In one sense, I intend not to be aware of such an event, and to carry through this intention, I must know what I am to avoid if I am to avoid it successfully: I must know where *not* to look, what *not* to think. The husband who is unable to find the book his wife had given him when he was angry with her but who found it when they later were reconciled reveals that he "had not really lost the book, but neither did he know where it was. Everything connected with her (during the time of estrangement) had ceased to exist for him, he had shut it out of his life" (Merleau-Ponty, 1945/1962, p. 162).

Repression and other phenomena used as evidence for the unconscious are understood by the existential psychologist as revealing a special way in which we relate to certain themes and contents in a life (i.e., as revealing a unique intentional stance toward them). It is not that we do not know where the book, memory, or object is; rather, we live a special relationship to them such that we remind ourself strongly of their existence at the same time as we hold them from us. The desire not to be reconciled is achieved by relating to the relevant item in such a way as to guarantee that we will hold on to it without having to recognize its significance. By so doing, we satisfy the double intention of preserving its meaning as symbolizing a situation of personal significance too difficult to confront and too significant to disregard. To avoid something so precisely, I must know what I do not want to know; otherwise I could not avoid it so successfully.

In describing dual intentions of this type, Lyons (1973) talks about the "public secret, that reverberating set of presences each person both hides from the world and shares (with it)." We are able to live in the light of a "public secret" because it is always possible to consider human life from many different perspectives, some of which are not available to the person whose secret it is. Like the human face, which is never directly experienced by any one of us, but which can be seen by almost everyone else (or by our looking at it as if we were someone else), the public secret is something best seen from a perspective impossible to the person. The secret is not locked away so deeply inside of me that I cannot see it, only that I am seldom, if ever, in the right position to see it. Part of what grounds what I am aware of as figure is always destined not to become figural for me unless either I change my perspective or have someone else point it out to me who does not relate to the item or memory with the same double intention of concealing and revealing as I do.

It is largely for this reason that Van den Berg (1961) has noted that the unconscious, if it is to be located anywhere at all, must be located "in" the therapist and not "in" the patient. By this maneuver, Van den Berg suggests that the quality of interaction between patient and therapist provides the proper context within which a therapist may mirror for a patient the dual meaning of the event in question. The unconcealing of such an event takes place in the dialogue between patient and therapist and signifies the closeness of their relationship. By analogy, a person also may be close or far from certain aspects of him or herself in terms of the degree to which dreams and symptoms reveal their concealed meanings to, and for, him or her.

In discussing Van den Berg's approach, Schry (1978) notes that the "unconscious exists as a form or texture of reality between two people, one of whom has an awareness of isolated areas. Since it is the therapist who primarily helps the patient come to realize previously unmentionable ways of being with others, the unconscious is discoverable in the therapist's embodied speaking. Since the goal of psychotherapy was stated as the making conscious of the unconscious, the goal of therapy is a change in the relationship between therapist and patient" (p. 286). This description of the way in which patient and therapist go about revealing incompletely concealed events of a life – its public secrets – implies that one of the major tasks involved in dealing with unconscious material is to recognize its importance and to help the person integrate such material into his or her everyday personal world. While the previously unconscious item no longer is experienced as strange – "why did I have that dream or make that slip of the tongue" – it is now experienced in terms of its significance for the person who, from now on, will have to deal with it in the same way as with other significant aspects of his or her personal world.

Metaphors of Human Experience

From Husserl to Merleau-Ponty, from James to Freud, and from Joyce to Faulkner, the description of human experience has been a major project of twentieth-century intellectual life. In the course of pursuing this project, a number of metaphors have been used to convey the ways in which various thinkers and writers have presented their views, and an examination of these metaphors ought to provide the framework for a more comprehensive description of what has been meant by the term *human experience*. Pollio (1990) has presented a relatively brief list of the major metaphors used by novelists, philosophers, and psychologists in conveying contemporary descriptions of human consciousness.

The first impression that comes from considering this list is that some images, such as field or perspective, are static while others, such as stream or train, are more mobile. Some descriptions focus, as did Köhler, on the structure of the field at a given moment; others, such as those by James, focus on the unity of consciousness in its ongoing movement. These characterizations refer only to relative points of emphasis since James also described the figure/ground structure of experience in terms of his concepts of focus and fringe, and Köhler also described the temporal properties of extended gestalts such as a melody or movement pattern.

A more crucial distinction within the movement-oriented metaphors in Table 1.1 concerns the nature of the movement implied. For example, the train or chain metaphor describes movement as constrained by preexisting connections or links between elements, with the direction and flow largely determined by the nature of these connections. Story and fugue metaphors also constrain the flow of consciousness; in these cases, constraint depends upon the socially recognizable schemas of narrative fiction or musical composition. However loosely organized a symphony or monologue might be, both implicitly accept the directive force of linguistic or musical structure even if the structure is no larger than the coherent word, note, or phrase. Of all the metaphors describing movement and change, only James's metaphor of the stream suggests a style of movement relatively free of specific constraint, even if the constraints implied by narrative, symphony, or soliloquy metaphors are not incompatible with it.

If we return again to the metaphors presented in Table 1.1, a further

Table 1.1. *Major Metaphors Used in the Modern Study of Consciousness*

Metaphor set	Theorist
1. Stream, bird's flight	James
2. Train, chain	Freud, earlier associationist philosophers
3. Symphony, fugue, musical composition	Joyce, Proust, Bergson
4. Monologue, soliloquy, tale, story	Faulkner, Proust
5. State, mode	Academic texts in psychology and psychiatry
6. Level, depth	Joyce, Freud, Jung
7. Field, pattern	Köhler, Merleau-Ponty
8. Horizon, perspective	Husserl, Köhler, Heidegger

From Pollio, 1990.

distinction may be noted in terms of those figures describing consciousness in terms of states and modes, and those describing it in more holistic terms such as horizon or perspective. For the first set of metaphors, it is possible to distinguish among those that simply propose a distinction among states (or modes) and those that suggest a "vertical" organization in which some modes are more (or less) accessible to wake-a-day experience. The double meaning of the word "deep" as in below (away from the surface) and profound (significant) implies a similar vertical organization to the structure of experience.

A linguistic analysis of semantic entailments implied by these eight sets of metaphors provides a good basis on which to develop a general description of first-person experience. To begin, experience is organized and flowing, with some parts clear and with other parts serving to provide momentary contexts to support and define the clear central focus. The central events of experience regularly change, and we experience new organizations without ever losing track of the unity provided by the flow between successive figural events. The rate of change has a personal tempo, although it sometimes changes at a rate faster and sometimes slower than that tempo; language is sometimes figural, as when I search for a word, or serves as a continuing framework in which words cohere to form an interior monologue, a complete phrase, or a rushing flow of words and images only loosely articulated to one another. Sometimes the stream is amenable to language; at other times, it consists of kaleidoscopic images. Sometimes I render its content in words; at other times, the words and phrases are strangely out of tune with what is going on. Sometimes I even seem to require the presence of another person to help me make sense of my experience as my own personal perspective prevents me from experiencing something seen only by the other.

The experience of experience is difficult to capture in a clear way precisely because it refuses to sit still and seems to connect with all sorts of objects and events that are sometimes experienced as in the world, sometimes in me, or sometimes in the space between me and the person with whom I am speaking. The ordinarily well-behaved and clearly defined categories of time, body, world, and social order are continuously changing, even as I change and am being changed. First-person experience does not yield to ordinary categories and concepts nearly as well as that of technical third-person description, and it is no wonder that psychology more frequently chose the third- rather than the first-person view as appropriate to its disciplinary task. Unfortunately, psychology must also confront first-person experience, and when this attempt is made, we are forced to deal with phenomena that yield unambiguous organization and structure only when the flow of experience is stopped. Although such (static) descriptions have value, it is the constantly varying shape of consciousness that demands to be articulated.

A different style of language seems required to capture the mobility and changeability of our day-to-day experiences, and we must try to communicate such experiences in the most accessible of terms. Despite this, the language of our descriptions may sometimes seem unclear, and all we can do is note that ambiguity and uncertainty are themselves aspects of the first-person world. Although we may strive for clarity, we should never be disappointed that our descriptions are more ambiguous than we might hope. Describing the human world on its own terms is at least as demanding as living it in the first place.

2

Dialogue as Method

The Phenomenological Interview

Research begins with a question: In the present case, how can we describe everyday human experience in ways that will be comprehensible, if not necessarily acceptable, to empirically minded social scientists? To accomplish the task of describing what other people are aware of requires a method that accepts, from the very beginning, the perspectival nature of human experience and the fact that different people may be talking about similar experiences when using different words and different experiences when using similar words. The combination of these two concerns yields a determinate method – the phenomenological interview – as an almost inevitable procedure for attaining a rigorous and significant description of the world of everyday human experience as it is lived and described by specific individuals in specific circumstances.

All too often, the use of any method, dialogue included, proscribes in advance what is to be studied and how it is to be studied. There is, however, a different and more positive sense in which method and topic come together, where both mutually select one another. If method and phenomenon arise from common concerns – how the world of everyday human experience is to be described – we have a situation appropriate to the original meaning of the word *method*, a meaning that combines the word *hodos*, a path or way, with the word *meta*, across or beyond. Under this rendering, method is not an algorithmic procedure to be followed mechanically if useful results are to be achieved; rather, method is a way or path toward understanding that is as sensitive to its phenomenon as to its own orderly and self-correcting aspects.

When the description of human experience is at issue, it is necessary to employ a method that is both appropriate to its topic and rigorous in its use. One conclusion that existential phenomenology teaches us about human experience is that it is not a static thing; rather, it is more accurately described as a sensibly changing perspectival relatedness to the

28

conditions, possibilities, and constraints of the world. It is always intensely personal and only infrequently transparent to itself; the meaning of one's experience frequently changes as it is described and/or reflected upon. Since experience is personal, the problem of other minds can be bridged only with the help of some specific other whose experiences are not at issue. The method, or path, that seems natural to attain a proper description of human experience is that of dialogue in which one member of the dialogic pair, normally called the *investigator*, assumes a respectful position vis-à-vis the real expert, the subject, or more appropriately, the co-researcher. In this way, a path toward understanding emerges from the common respect and concern of two people committed to exploring the life world of one of them.

Considered in this way, psychology can no longer only be construed as a psychology of the third person, as natural science methods would have it, or as a psychology of the first person, as early introspectionists and even a Gestalt psychologist or two would have it, but is free to pursue methods of the second person in which dialogue becomes a major method. Although first- and third-person procedures are still relevant as paths toward certain topics and phenomena, second-person procedures are more clearly relevant to the task of describing human experience. Unlike third-person procedures, which yield a psychology of strangers, and first-person procedures, which yield a psychology of solitary individuals, dialogic methods encourage the self and the other (the I and the You) to clarify for each other the meaning of their dialogue as it unfolds between them. Dialogue not only allows the speaker to describe experience; it also requires him or her to clarify its meaning to an involved other and, perhaps, even to realize it for the first time during the conversation itself. At their best, second-person methods will lead to a rigorous psychology that depends upon both the I and the You being satisfied that the experience of some event or phenomenon has been rendered in experience-near terms that can be understood by others not in the original encounter. Such a consequence is to be expected since the meaning of a phenomenological interview emerges only from a dialogue directed by the quest for meaningful description.

The Nature of Phenomenological Interviewing

The descriptive data forming the empirical basis of the present set of studies were gathered by means of phenomenological interviews. Since the goal of any phenomenological interview is to attain a first-person description of some specified domain of experience, with the course of dialogue largely set by the respondent, the interview begins with few prespecified questions concerning the topic: All questions flow from the dialogue as it unfolds rather than having been determined in advance. It is not uncommon for experiences and issues discussed at an earlier stage of the interview to reappear at a later point. An implicit assumption is that central or personally relevant issues will emerge repeatedly throughout the dialogue (Kvale, 1983; Polkinghorne, 1989; Wertz, 1983).

The questions, statements, and summaries used by the interviewer are designed to evoke descriptions, not to confirm theoretical hypotheses. The most useful questions focus on specific experiences described in a full and detailed manner. The interviewer facilitates the dialogue by employing questions such as "What was that like?" or "How did you feel when that happened?" as well as by incorporating the participant's own vernacular when asking follow-up questions. It is typically recommended that "why" questions be avoided when conducting phenomenological interviews (e.g., Thompson, Locander, & Pollio, 1989; Thompson, Henley, & Meguiar, 1989). Such questions often shift the dialogue away from describing an experience to a more abstract, theoretical discussion.

The data arising from the interview is dialogic in the true sense of the term. Within phenomenological methods, interview participants function as co-researchers and not merely as research subjects (Giorgi, 1989). The focus on dialogue arises from the decidedly non-Cartesian orientation of phenomenological research. For the more traditional Cartesian view, the research subject "contains" an internal representation of his/her subjective experiences. The researcher's task then becomes one of externalizing such representations without adding biases or distortions. This view of experience creates three paradoxical outcomes: (1) the researcher's task is defined as giving an external "objective" rendering of a subject's internal "subjective" world; (2) numerous sources of error make the task of giving such description exceedingly difficult, if not impossible; and (3) the presence of the interviewer – necessary for there to be an interview – is often viewed as an intrinsic source of error (Kvale, 1983). Demand effects, which are intrinsic to any social encounter, are assumed to bias the "true" nature of the internal representation – an entity located in mental, rather than social, space.

For this view, any data deriving from self-description are likely to be inaccurate to some degree since subjects cannot help but distort internal representations in the process of translating them into linguistic form. One type of presumed (translation) error occurs when important mental representations are altered by defense mechanisms designed to protect the person from encountering certain impulses. A more serious experimental indictment against interview data is that subjects are incapable of accessing mental representations and, therefore, create "fictional" accounts that at best bear only a vague resemblance to the "true" internal representation (Nisbett & Wilson, 1977).

For these and related methodological concerns, the interview has become a somewhat distrusted method. With the theoretical extreme of behaviorism, subjective experiences were seen as so problematic that only externally visible, quantifiable physical movements were admitted as valid. Some behaviorists, however, did acknowledge the utility of verbal descriptions but only as verbal behavior: Personal reflections were seen as an instrumental response to a reinforcing stimulus, not as a useful description of lived experience (Skinner, 1974). Other objective psychological approaches use subjective self-reports, but only when construed in terms of more explanatory theories such as psychoanalysis (Freud, 1917/1935) or computer-based, information-processing, models (Ericsson & Simon, 1984).

From a phenomenological view, internal representation is a chimeric entity. All knowledge, including self-knowledge, is constructed in social discourse (Berger & Luckmann, 1966; Merleau-Ponty, 1945/1962). The description of an experience as it emerges in a particular context *is* the experience. To proceed otherwise, such as by seeking to capture a more "truthful" version, is to look past the concrete phenomenon at hand in search of an abstract ideal. Considering interview data as necessarily distorted arises from a theoretical way of picturing the world. In this case, the picture is of knowledge existing in some "ideal form," independent of its specific contextual manifestations. Within such a picture, contextual specifications are "errors" that obscure the true nature of the phenomenon. The "real" is decontextualized, paradoxically seeking application to all contexts but not uniquely and totally specified by any.

Contextual approaches to knowledge see such "decontextualized" reality as an unrealizable fiction (Pepper, 1942). The phenomenologically real is to be found nowhere but in the ongoing, ever-changing context of the social and natural world; the real is that which is lived as it is lived (Berger & Luckmann, 1966; Sartre, 1960/1963; Strasser, 1967). The interview is a human event that yields interpretable data if approached properly. Such data reflect the participant's perspective on his/her experiences as they emerge in the context of an interview. To the objection that such reflections are not the "real" phenomena, one might respond with: "Just where else is the real to be found?"

Why Objective Interviewing Is Not Objective

Hagan (1986) provides a description of how traditional procedures for making an interview more "objective" may serve to distort the social encounter and to inhibit an understanding of the other by the interviewer. Hagan notes that the laboratory experiment serves as an idealized model for conducting an objective interview. If the interviewer is able to control all biasing factors, differences in verbal reports are assumed to reflect differences in personal attitudes and beliefs. Some of the most commonly discussed interview biases include the varying abilities of interviewees to recall events accurately, the effect of time delays between the event and its retelling, and a multitude of interviewer-induced biases, such as leading questions and demand effects. In objective interviewing, the research task is to formalize the interview into a structured, rule-governed procedure. Ideally, these rules can be consistently applied thereby minimizing inter-interview variability.

For present purposes, consider three of Hagan's concrete examples of the ways in which standard procedures cannot be mechanically applied in an interview without sometimes creating a barrier to communication.

1. *Value-free, objective questioning.* One traditional assumption is that "neutral," value-free questions are best for gaining accurate verbal data. The difficulty with this position is that any question contains underlying assumptions that may or may not fit the co-participant's world view. Hagan cites the example of interviews conducted with welfare mothers in which they were asked if they "had planned to have their children." What consistently emerged was that "family planning," in the sense of organizing a career around a family, was not relevant to these participants. The question, rather, was understood in terms of their fitness to be a mother, as implying a charge of irresponsibility. The seemingly innocuous term *planning* was not value-neutral to this group of respondents. Understanding participant perspectives is not a matter of finding a more neutral phrase but of exploring the meaning of the term for them. The dialogue revealed both the interviewer's previously unnoticed middle-class bias and the differing cultural situation in which co-participants lived. An interviewer's "neutral" is not always the interviewee's "neutral."

2. *Beginning the interview with nonthreatening impersonal questions.* This rule assumes that respondents should be eased into an interview before potentially more emotional topics are broached. Hagan notes that her "easing-in" question concerned a checklist of which home appliances each welfare mother had available to her. What emerged was that the presence

or absence of an appliance was not an impersonal fact. For example, those lacking an appliance, such as a washing machine, described how they were able to be good mothers, despite the hardships of their economic circumstances (Hagan, 1986). In retrospect, such a meaning is understandable, but it was not anticipated prior to the interview. More importantly, there was no need to anticipate the meaning of "not having a specific appliance" because it was revealed by the dialogue itself. With respect to the "easing-in" rule, participants were not hesitant to address immediately personally relevant and important issues. In the normal course of dialogue, this methodological rule is not only violated, it does not matter.

3. *Nonjudgmental responsiveness.* Interviewers are generally warned against biasing the co-participant's verbal report by giving positive or negative reactions. The standard rule is to offer affectively neutral statements, such as "I see," in response to an interviewee's statements. The problem with this form of neutral reaction is that an interview is a social encounter, and violating the social norms of conversation is not a neutral act. Hagan provides the example of a participant describing a very sad episode in her life. In such a case, an interviewer responding in a nonresponsive way may be experienced as devaluing the respondent's experience and thereby disrupt the interpersonal nature of the interview. As another example, imagine being a respondent and describing what you see as an amusing experience to which the interviewer responds with little or no reaction. Would that be an unbiased interviewer response?

The problematic nature of supposedly nonjudgmental responses has been much discussed in clinical psychology. Rogerian therapy, a clear case of nonjudgmental interviewing, has been heavily criticized by existentially oriented clinicians (May & Yalom, 1984):

When the therapist reflects only the client's words, there transpires only an amorphous kind of identity rather than two subjects acting in a world in which they both participate and in which love and hate, doubt and trust, conflicts and dependence, can come out and be understood and assimilated. . . . The [Rogerian] therapist's rigid nature closed him off to many of the patient's experiences. (p. 362)

At a minimum, this critique points to the conclusion that a phenomenological interview cannot (and should not) be conceived as a rule-driven, mechanical activity. There is no methodological guarantee that any rule applied in a specific interview encounter will have the same meaning or effect for the interviewer and the person being interviewed. For the interview to be a path or way for understanding the life-world of a co-participant, it must be allowed to emerge freely rather than to be constrained by predetermined injunctions.

Can Interview Data Be Trusted?

One major issue concerning phenomenological research is the constructed nature of interview dialogue. If experiences are constructed, at least partially, in social discourse, what guarantees do we have that different constructions (i.e., different conversations) will bear any resemblance to one another? While admitting that no guarantee exists, existential-phenomenological philosophy provides grounds for believing that reflections emerging in one dialogic context will *not* be incommensurate with, even if different from, those emerging in another context. One basis for this belief is that a person's experiential field is organized rather than chaotic. In the day-to-day flow of experience, change is experienced against the stability of one's social surroundings, activities, and self-awareness (Berger & Luckmann, 1966). The relative stability of the personal field provides one basis for expecting personal meanings to bear coherent, if not identical, intercontextual relations. While specific meanings may change across contexts, such changes are likely to bear systematic relations that can be understood within a holistic interpretive framework (Giorgi, 1989; Wittgenstein, 1951).

A second reason for believing in the intercontextual coherence of experience concerns the temporal dialectic between a person's history and the present-centered nature of remembering. In the conventional sense, a person remembers something from his/her own personal history even though the act of remembering always occurs in an ongoing, present situation. The meaning of one's past is shaped by the present context, although the past that is remembered is not totally mutable. A person's history has a certain facticity that serves as background for his or her day-to-day functioning. That is, the historical certainty of one's past is seldom questioned: We know the ways in which events of our past relate to the meanings of present dialogue. A dialogic view of remembering does not imply that reflections will necessarily be radically transformed in individual settings so as to be contextually idiosyncratic, although such a state of affairs is not precluded. Rather, the usual situation is that the act of remembering brings about a temporal fusion of the present and past in which a personal historical understanding is revised to accommodate a present perspective, and in which the present perspective is contextualized by one's history (Gadamer, 1960/1975; Sardello, 1978).

A more complex methodological issue concerns the potential for bias in the interview dialogue itself. One of the most discussed sources of such bias is the question being asked (Kvale, 1983), and much of this concern seems to arise from a failure to distinguish between open and restricted dialogues. All social science data arise from a dialogue between a researcher and a subject (using the conventional research vernacular). An example of a highly restricted dialogue may be seen in laboratory research in which an observer sets specific tasks and records only the overt behaviors and/or physiological responses of the subject. In this restricted dialogue, the privileged perspective is that of the observer; subjects are given little or no opportunity to do anything other than to react to the situation in preset ways.

Data gathered by surveys and other psychometric instruments circumscribe a more open dialogue in which respondents are given some opportunity to present unique perspectives. Psychometric instruments, however, are usually structured in terms of the researcher's preconceptions of the phenomenon. Survey methodologies typically do not allow for interactive dialogue; accordingly, there is always some indeterminacy as to how any *one* specific respondent understands the meaning of the questions and the frame of reference to be used in formulating an answer. It is for this reason that answers are presented for populations, never for individuals.

It is a mistake to assume that questions always function in the same way or serve the same purpose(s). In an open dialogue, such as typified by a phenomenological interview, questions function differently than in a psychometric instrument. The full meaning of a question emerges only from the engagement of a researcher with the participant and vice versa. Latitude exists for the participant to ascertain the researcher's frame of reference and to specify his or her own frame of reference. In a phenomenological interview, the dialogue is grounded in participant experiences of both the interview and the phenomenon; in a structured survey, the dialogue is not necessarily anchored in participant experiences – a respondent may always provide an abstract judgment concerning the researcher's understood reality.

Within the context of phenomenological interviewing, questions have a descriptive and facilitative purpose rather than one of assessing a preexisting opinion, attitude, or level of knowledge. Dialogue is an aspect of conversation rather than of a question-and-answer session, and no one question is ever critical to an understanding of the overall interview. As one illustration, imagine a situation in which the interviewee describes a particular experience but, during the description, makes no mention of her emotional state. Assume that the researcher asks a leading question such as "How angry did that make you?" when the participant's recollection is of having been pleasantly excited. In just what way will this question lead the participant to deny her own experience? Since participants in a phenomenological interview always have the privileged perspective on their experiences (a point emphasized in the interview prologue), erroneous inferences and/or occasional leading questions are likely to provide no more than a temporary distraction and will be corrected by the co-participant.

Human dialogue has a flow and coherence to it that tolerates certain breaks, as when a researcher asks a question that may not seem to follow from the participant's perspective. The point not to be overlooked is that if the researcher incessantly asks such questions, significant dialogue will not take place. Once underway, however, questions emerge from the flow of the dialogue and are to be understood within the context of the interview. The heuristic guidelines for conducting phenomenological interviews (e.g., Thompson et al., 1989) are not offered as a protection against interviewer biases or subject fallability but as ways to facilitate a descriptively rich and mutually informative dialogue.

Interpreting Qualitative Data

To deal with the volume of data produced by interviews, some interpretive framework must be applied. The researcher's choice of framework in large part specifies the methodological procedures, interpretive goals, and relevant evaluative criteria for the study. Presently available interpretive frameworks range from content-analytic procedures (Ericsson & Simon, 1984; Miles & Huberman, 1984) to "post-positivistic" hermeneutical exegetical procedures (Gadamer, 1960/1975; Ricouer, 1976; Wachterhauser, 1986). Interpretive strategies may have an explicit theoretical purpose, such as seeking to find evidence for some psychoanalytic concept, or a more atheoretical, descriptive aim, such as seeking to describe experiential patterns emerging in a given context (Thompson et al., 1989). Atheoretical interpretation does not imply that a neutral view is adopted; on the contrary, all interpretation is rendered from some perspective (Gadamer, 1960/1975; Merleau-Ponty, 1945/1962). Descriptive approaches, while atheoretical, require their own assumptions, and their goal is not to support an a priori theory nor to coerce phenomena into categories that conform to the theory (Giorgi, 1983; Polkinghorne, 1989).

For heuristic purposes, it is possible to describe interpretive frameworks in terms of the following pairs of contrasts.

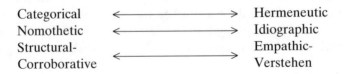

Categorical/Hermeneutic

The categorical/hermeneutic contrast refers to the form of an interpretation. At the *categorical* pole are approaches that organize qualitative data into a set of mutually exclusive categories. Such approaches employ analytic procedures that emphasize high inter-rater agreement; they also tend to present results in a quantifiable matrix and to evaluate statistically the internal consistency of the data (Kerlinger, 1986). Content analysis presents the prototypic case of a categorical interpretive approach. At the *hermeneutic* pole of this contrast are approaches that view interview data as a "text" presenting a complex network of internal relations such that no single aspect may be understood independent of reference to the text taken in its entirety. This view is exemplified by formal hermeneutic procedures (Bleicher, 1980; Gadamer, 1960/1975) in which the primary interpretive aim is to provide an overall understanding of the text; here, the focus is on meaning rather than on implementing a given set of methodological procedures.

This latter view is well expressed by Gadamer in his classic text, *Truth and Method* (1960/1975):

> The hermeneutical phenomenon is basically not a problem of method at all. It is not concerned with a method of understanding by which texts are subjected to scientific investigation like all other objects of experience. It is not concerned primarily with amassing ratified knowledge that satisfies the methodological ideal of science – yet, it is concerned, here too, with knowledge and with truth. (p. xi)

Gadamer's use of the word *truth* is meant in the sense of providing critical justification for an interpretation rendered in a particular (sociohistoric) context rather than in the sense of an atemporal, methodologically objective, certainty (Bernstein, 1986).

A more focused consideration of content analysis serves to illustrate further the categorical/hermeneutic distinction. To understand content analysis, the technique should not be considered separately from its underlying philosophy. Kassarjian (1977) describes the philosophical approach, characterizing content analysis, as follows:

> All decisions are guided by an explicit set of rules that minimize – although probably never quite eliminate – the possibility that the findings reflect the analyst's subjective predispositions rather than the content of the documents under analysis. One test of objectivity is: Can other analysts, following identical procedures with the same set of data, arrive at similar conclusions? This requirement of objectivity gives scientific standing to content analysis and differentiates it from literary criticism. (p. 10)

It is not surprising that reliability becomes a tantamount concern in content analysis:

> Since the researcher's subjectivity must be minimized to obtain a systematic, objective description of the communication's content, the issue of reliability becomes paramount. . . . The importance of reliability rests on the assurance it provides that the data obtained are independent of the measuring event, instrument, or person. Category reliability depends upon the analyst's ability to formulate categories and present to competent judges definitions of the categories so they will agree on which items of a certain population belong in a category and which do not. If this aim cannot be achieved, the understanding of the category as specified is *not yet sufficiently clear for scientific usage.* (Kassarjian, 1977, pp. 12–13)

This orientation to interpretation is motivated by a desire to remove the scientist (i.e., the interpreter) from the research enterprise. Ideally, content could be analyzed solely by recourse to definitive rules and procedures such as might be instantiated in a computer program. Since the rules for category formation will reflect the analyst's theoretical framework, it is difficult to see how such a project could even begin in a purely objective way. This critique, deriving from hermeneutic philosophy, is more encompassing than the widely noted claim that all observation is theory laden. As Otto-Apel (1985) notes:

> A scientist cannot by himself explain something for himself alone. In order to even know "what" is to be explained, he must already have come to an understanding with others on the matter. A community of interpretation always corresponds to the community of experimentation of natural scientists. Such an agreement on the intersubjective level can never be replaced by a procedure of natural science precisely because it is a condition of the possibility of objective science. (p. 331)

Otto-Apel affirms the necessity of an interpretive circle for any meaningful activity. It is precisely this necessity that content-analytic approaches attempt to circumvent by adhering to strictly specified rules. Ultimately, however, such rules are derived from, and only have meaning against, some (often implicit) interpretive background. Categorical procedures seek to deny their origin in social practice. The cost is that adherence to rules takes priority over understanding the text(s) as a total event.

With respect to content analysis, it is clear that reliability will increase as simpler categories are used. For example, with categories of "statements written in English" and "statements written in Hebrew," very high levels of inter-rater reliability will be attained among those with relevant linguistic knowledge. Such a scheme could be classed as structurally rather than semantically focused; that is, the meaning(s) of the statement is reduced to its structural features.

A concrete example of the problems brought about by such an approach is given in Kassarjian's (1977) content-analytic study on the role of African-Americans in magazine advertisements. Near perfect inter-rater agreement was attained for the categories of *all Black characters*, *all Caucasian* characters, and *integrated* characters. A more problematic category was that of *authority relationship*, which concerned whether the African-American was depicted in a position of authority vis-à-vis the Caucasian or vice versa. Sufficient levels of inter-rater agreement were not attained, and the category was discarded with the conclusion, "superior and inferior roles in interpersonal relationships between white and black could not be scientifically defined in that study."

Kassarjian's (1977) description of one such disagreement serves to clarify the differences between categorical and hermeneutic analyses of content:

For example, one ad contained white patrons in an *exclusive* restaurant sitting at a table with *expensive* linen and silver service. A black waiter with a *haughty patronizing glare* was waiting for orders. Some judges claimed the white patrons were in the superior role, giving orders to the black waiter. Other judges claimed the *intimidating* waiter was clearly in the superior role and that the patrons were pretty well at his mercy. (Italics added; p. 15)

This description reveals the importance of an interpretive background if the advertisement is to have any meaning. The underlined terms highlight the physiognomic details that set the context for the advertisement. Physiognomic perception refers to "a sensitivity to the expressive meanings of . . . people, places, and things which transcend their physical stimulus attributes" (McConville, 1978). Thus, the waiter's "haughty glare" is not an interpretation-free, objective fact. Yet given the cultural background knowledge of facial expressions, race relations, and possibly customer–service-provider roles, such a characterization may be as directly evident as describing the color of the waiter's coat. Physiognomic characterization is of a gestalt nature, emphasizing implicit relationships within the perceptual whole.

Meaning is problematic for a content-analytic approach to interpretation as a consequence of its assumption that "meaning" is evoked by the stimulus and that there is one or at least a small number of correct ways in which to characterize the meaning of an event: The waiter *really* is in a superior or inferior role. The divergent perspectives assumed by raters is seen to reflect two different interpretive "theories." For a content-analytic approach, such a situation is unacceptable because an element is or is not a member of some category. From a hermeneutic perspective, such a divergence becomes the starting point for understanding the topic or event.

Traditional estimates of inter-rater reliability place emphasis on what is seen rather than how a meaning is seen (Giorgi, 1989). For a hermeneutic approach, the emphasis is reversed. To use Kassarjian's example, an attempt could have been made to describe the background assumptions from which divergent interpretations emerged. As presently stated, it is not clear what impact "race" had on the interpretations of inferiority or superiority, paradoxically the very issue being explored. Additionally, it is not clear what meanings a restaurant setting might assume within divergent interpretations. For example, would the waiter have been seen as intimidating in a "cheap" restaurant?

More hermeneutic-like approaches may be found in some mainstream qualitative research. For example, protocol analysis seeks to represent knowledge in terms of a related set of propositional statements (Ericsson & Simon, 1984). The interpretive focus here is on developing a system of symbolic representations and precisely defined rules for their manipulation, which are assumed to reflect the essential structures of knowledge (Winograd & Flores, 1987). For present purposes, the key point is that protocol analysis itself requires the application of an interpretive framework (O'Shaugnessy, 1985). The interpretive nature of protocol analysis is particularly clear in cases where an "expert's" behavior, such as in a chess match, does not conform with propositional assumptions underlying protocol analysis; such nominally anomalous behaviors are sometimes classed as "processing errors" (Aanstoos, 1986). The concept of an expert making a "processing error" has little meaning independent of the interpretive framework of protocol analysis.

Nomothetic/Idiographic

A second distinction proposed to differentiate among interpretive frameworks is conceived as an epistemological antinomy between knowledge of a general (*nomothetic*) or particular (*idiographic*) nature. The problem of how some particular instance is recognized as an example of the more general case has occupied Western philosophers since the rise of Greek civilization (Aanstoos, 1986; Csikszentmihalyi & Rochberg-Halton, 1981; Smith & Medin, 1981). Philosophically, this antinomy manifests itself in debates of whether or not social phenomena can be subsumed under general, lawlike principles. Methodologically, it has multiple manifestations in terms of issues such as the relative value of attaining representative samples of some population or domain versus a "thick description" of specific settings and/or individuals.

To begin, even positivistic research is quite humble in offering nomothetic generalizations. A standard convention of such research is to delineate limitations on the generalizability of a particular study. If there is any point of consensus within social research, it is that all research has limitations. Indeed, McGrath and Brinberg (1983) have offered arguments that no one internally valid study should be expected to provide results externally valid for a range of contexts. The lack of general principles is sometimes used as evidence that research in social science is immature. Postempiricist philosophers, however, provide a great deal of historical evidence that, even for "mature" disciplines, atemporal general principles have not always been forthcoming (Anderson, 1983, 1986; Gergen, 1985; Kuhn, 1970). For positivistic science, it seems the development of nomothetic knowledge often exists as a valued ideal rather than as an accurate description of the current state of affairs.

A turn toward more idiographic understanding may be found in the anthropological stance of "cultural relativism." Before this position came on the scene, much of anthropology had employed a Darwinian framework in which non-Western cultures were viewed as "lower" or "earlier" stages of development. In these terms, "primitive" cultures all were evolving toward the same form – modern, Westernized culture – and could be understood from the same conceptual framework. Cultural relativists challenged the ethnocentric bias of such an evolutionary view and argued that a culture must be understood on its own terms. The paradox is that during the era of "Darwinist anthropology," researchers tended to see great differences between Western and non-Western cultures whereas in the era of cultural relativism, researchers are seeing increasing degrees of similarity between the two (Lakoff, 1987). Thus, as anthropology has come to respect idiographic differences, a groundwork seems to have been laid for more nomothetic understandings.

Proposals for radical contextualism, like those for universal generalizations, are usually offered in the abstract. Few interpretive approaches restrict themselves to idiographic statements. For example, Giorgi (1983) emphasizes that phenomenological methods, while well-suited for attaining idiographic knowledge, are equally viable for describing "general structures" of human experience. Within the specific context of consumer research, one of the more overt pronouncements of an idiographic intent is given by Holbrook, Bell, and Grayson (1989) in their study of the image of consumer products in contemporary movies:

This [interpretive] conclusion depends on the interpreter's own subjective judgment and on the critical experience he brings to the analysis of these movies. While these conclusions seem intuitively plausible, they only suggest ways in which products might be read in consumer minds within the context of these particular films. They remain idiographic with no intended claims to nomothetic generalizability. (p. 35)

In their discussion, Holbrook et al. make use of an unconventional definition of "idiographic." A more conventional usage concerns whether the interpretive conclusions derived from a specific set of films also would apply to other films (or artistic objects). For Holbrook et al., the focus is shifted away from the interpreted object to the "subjective" understanding of an interpreter. This usage reveals a perspective in which aesthetic criticism is seen as inherently "subjective." The scope of the interpreter's understanding is restricted by his/her own idiosyncratic, subjective reality.

Despite such allusions, Holbrook et al. do not choose to stay within the limitations of a "subjectivist" framework. Since conclusions have "intuitive plausibility" and suggest "ways products might be read in consumers' minds," their interpretations must somehow communicate the interpreter's idiographic understanding to other individuals, thereby providing the groundwork for a more nomothetic understanding. Holbrook et al.'s (1989) commentary on the general value of literary criticism further suggests a more nomothetic application to interpretation:

Whatever their contrasting viewpoints, all these [critical] perspectives interpret art as a microcosm of larger meanings that, together, say something important about life by commenting significantly on the human condition. (p. 35)

Even for those wishing to take a stronger stand on the side of idiographic knowledge, the social nature of communication and understanding requires them to consider more nomothetic issues. The dialectic between nomothetic and idiographic knowledge can now be stated as follows: Without particular instantiations, the general is never revealed, and without some more general conception, the particular is not recognizable. Problems arise when one side of the dialectic is pursued independent of the other. To use a clichéd example, the extreme generalist is always looking for a forest located somewhere other than in the trees, whereas the extreme particularistic denies that there is a forest to be found at all. From a dialectical view of the relationship between ideographic and nomothetic knowledge, one seeks to understand both the network of meanings connecting tree-in-relation-to-forest and the network of meanings connecting forest-as-instantiated-in-tree. Neither side of the relationship exists by itself.

Structural-Corroborative/Empathic-Verstehen

The third distinction proposed refers to the purpose of an interpretation. At the *structural-corroborative* pole, the purpose is to confirm or to apply some a priori structure to a particular human phenomenon. This structure, while bearing some relation to an individual's experiential field, does not necessarily strive for a first-person comprehensibility of human phenomena. At the *empathic-Verstehen* pole, the interpretive purpose is to understand the world as lived from the perspective of the person; thus, a first-person understanding is explicitly sought.

Interpretive approaches emphasizing structural-corroborative concerns include protocol analysis (Ericsson & Simon, 1984), structural analysis (Levi-Strauss, 1958), certain versions of psychoanalysis (Dewald, 1972), and the relatively new field of "cognitive semantics" (Johnson, 1987; Lakoff, 1987). Within protocol analysis, a logic-driven, information-processing model serves as the conceptual framework for representing the cognitive operations of human beings, with the "validity" of this model being assumed in conducting the analysis. Protocol analysis is concerned, for example, with how the decision maker perceives the problem situation but without the empathic focus of Verstehen approaches. The major goal of protocol analysis is to represent knowledge in a form akin to an implementable computer program, and this representation does not have to correspond with subjects' self-understandings or with a description of their experiences (Aanstoos, 1986).

Structural analysis is most commonly identified with the work of Levi-Strauss (1958) and is often used to understand the function of myth and mythlike elements in a given society. Within this approach, myths are viewed as closed systems (in the domain of language rather than speaking) made up of elemental units called *mythemes* (Ricouer, 1976). It is through analyzing the arrangement of mythemes that the structure of a myth is revealed. Mythemes are organized in terms of binary opposites, such as good/evil or male/female, and the myth taken as a whole functions as a logical instrument drawing together the paradoxes and contradictions of human experience. For example, Levi-Strauss analyzed Oedipal myths as dealing with the oppositional issues of: (1) undervaluing or overvaluing blood relations, and (2) determining whether men originate through autochtony (from the earth) or childbirth (from the female). Any one member of the culture may be unconscious (in the sense of being unaware) of the myth's societal function. Given this assumption, Verstehen cannot reveal the structure of the myth.

Although anthropologists generally ignore considerations of mental phenomena, Levi-Strauss contended that the structural analysis of myth reveals universal cognitive processes (Gardner, 1985; Levy, 1981); that is, the binary structure of myth reflects a basic structure of human thought. Several points of similarity can be seen between protocol analysis and structural analysis: (1) both seek to represent human cognitive capacities; (2) both seek to specify logical relations among constitutive elements; (3)

both understand relevant phenomena in terms of assumed theoretical structures; and (4) both place greater emphasis on abstracting a theoretical structure from experience than on attaining a descriptive, first-person understanding.

A transition from a structural-corroborative to a more Verstehen-based understanding may be seen in the interpretive approach utilized by psychoanalysis. Critics of conventional psychoanalytic approaches have argued that as Freud's therapeutic insights diffused throughout clinical psychology, their application became increasingly mechanistic and stereotypic (Atwood & Stolorow, 1984; May & Yalom, 1984; Spence, 1987). For these critics, structural explanations – for example, those that are captured in concepts such as repressed libidinal drives, oedipal complexes, and a variety of unconscious processes and defenses – came to predefine the experiential world of the patient. Thus, therapeutic insights became increasingly distant from the patient's everyday worldly concerns (Van den Berg, 1972).

May (1978) provides an excellent description of the tension between structural (theoretical) and Verstehen (empathic) modes of therapeutic understanding:

Can we be sure that we are seeing the patient as he really is, knowing him as he is in his own reality; or are we merely seeing projections of our own theories about him? Every psychotherapist has his knowledge of patterns and mechanisms of behavior and has at his fingertips a system of concepts developed by his school. Such a conceptual system is entirely necessary if we are to observe scientifically. But the crucial question is always more than that, namely the bridge between the system and the patient. How can we be certain that our system, admirable and beautifully wrought as it may be, has anything to do with a specific Mr. Jones, a living, immediate reality sitting opposite . . . us in the consulting room? May not this particular person require another system, another quite different frame of reference? And does not this patient slip through our fingertips, precisely to the extent that we rely on the logical consistency of our own system? (p. vii)

The movement of clinical psychology toward a more first-person understanding can be seen as a figure/ground reversal of the structural/Verstehen relation. More existentially oriented therapists place a primacy on understanding the unique situation and perceptions of a client without the structural presuppositions of psychoanalytic theory (Atwood & Stolorow, 1984; Spence, 1987). Rather than assuming that a patient's concerns and understandings are to be "explained" in terms of theoretical structures, existential analysts view the patient's experiential world as the proper focus of a therapeutic encounter (Atwood & Stolorow, 1984; May & Yalom, 1984). Whereas conventional analysts view the person as motivated by often conflicting drives, existential therapists view the person as attempting to resolve and take responsibility for the anxieties arising in his/her life. From the supposition of life-world anxieties, it can be seen that existential therapists do make assumptions in the course of the therapy although their emphasis is on Verstehen; theoretical structure is interpreted in terms of a patient's life-world rather than the life-world being interpreted in terms of theoretical structure.

Verstehen, as originally conceived by Dilthey (1883/1958), is an understanding based on *empathetic* identification in which an other's experience is relived by the interpreter (Bleicher, 1980; Wachterhauser, 1986). More contemporary versions of Verstehen place less emphasis on empathy in favor of a more conceptual understanding in which the interpreter is able to understand what the world means to another person without "reliving" a particular experience (Ricoeur, 1976). Phenomenological research methods place a primacy on Verstehen in seeking to describe phenomena from the perspective of the participants in the study (Giorgi, 1983; Myers, 1985; Thompson et al., 1989; Valle & Halling, 1989).

Under either conception of Verstehen, the problem remains as to how an interpreter is able to adopt the perspective (or to relive the experience) of another. It would seem that all interpretive understanding is, in some fashion, transposed through the perspective of the interpreter. It could even be argued that a person's reflections on his/her own experience are an abstraction from first-person understanding. Such construals render the attainment of Verstehen problematic, if not impossible. A philosophical construal, however, that casts doubt on the ability of individuals to have first-person understanding of their own experiences is most likely a pseudoproblem. The problem of Verstehen can be seen as the inverse of the problem of objectivity: Both assume that a neutral perspective is a feasible epistemological goal.

Attaining either goal, however, requires an interpreter to view phenomena from a "perspective that is no perspective at all" (Gadamer, 1960/1975). Existential interpretation argues that it is impossible to step outside of one's history to view the world from some ahistorical, transcendent perspective (Merleau-Ponty, 1945/1962). This point also has been emphasized by those supporting relativism as an epistemological doctrine (Anderson, 1983, 1986; Pepper, 1942; Peter & Olson, 1983). Thus, scientifically objective viewpoints or empathetically attuned subjective ones provide particular human perspectives rather than an a-contextual view of how things "really are" (Bernstein, 1986; Lakoff, 1987; Thompson et al., 1989). This state of affairs is not a "problem" but simply the state of human-being-in-the-world. If attaining a neutral view is taken to provide a faulty rather than an ideal picture of interpretation, the dialectic between structural-confirmative and Verstehen-empathic modes of understanding may be seen more clearly.

From a dialectical perspective, however, the antinomy becomes a matter of interpretive emphasis rather than exclusion. A theoretical structure having no contact with "lived experience" is meaningless; the structural dichotomies of Levi-Strauss are without value unless meaningful relations to human life are demonstrated (Ricoeur, 1976). Protocol analysis, although seeking abstract knowledge representations, is based on an understanding of a living human expert; similarly, "lived experience" viewed without a structural preunderstanding would be inchoate. Verstehen cannot occur without the interpreter applying some frame of reference. Understanding the world as it is for another requires both a certain perspective *and* a certain level of critical distance in which the researcher steps back to reflect on the phenomenon. The need for reflective distance is evidenced by the ethnographer's warnings about "going native" in which a researcher becomes so enmeshed in a culture that the ability to step back and critically reflect on the data is lost (Lincoln & Guba, 1987). Rollo May's call for more personalized therapeutic interpretations offers a similar acknowledgment that clinical insight still requires the use of a conceptual system. Both approaches support Gadamer's (1960/1975) contention that understanding requires the interpreter to bring to bear a preunderstanding of the world. Preunderstanding, however, does not have to be applied dogmatically or to blind an interpreter to the specific phenomenon at hand. Proponents of interpretive approaches see the hermeneutic circle as a necessary dialogue between the interpreter (and his/her preunderstanding) and the "text" (Gadamer, 1960/1975; Ricoeur, 1976). To act otherwise is to cause language to become a barrier to understanding rather than as a way to achieve it.

Phenomenological Interpretation

The goal of phenomenological research is to describe phenomena as they are lived rather than to give an abstract explanatory account. Phenomenological interpretation is premised on a set of assumptions concerning the nature of human existence. Although these assumptions serve as a basis for phenomenological understanding, they do not presuppose what meanings any specific experience will have for any specific person in some situation. If these assumptions are accepted, the resulting interpretation may aspire to more nomothetic applications. From the perspective of existential-phenomenological thought, texts such as interview transcripts are interpreted to yield descriptions of lived experience. The two primary interpretive procedures appropriate to this task are *bracketing* and the *hermeneutic circle*.

Bracketing

Bracketing is sometimes characterized as a suspension of theoretical beliefs, preconceptions, and presuppositions. Within this definition, bracketing is presented as a (subtractive) process of removing conceptual biases that may serve to distort one's interpretive vision. This conception is invariably accompanied by a caveat to the effect that complete bracketing (the *reduction*, as it is called, in phenomenological vernacular) is impossible to achieve (Merleau-Ponty, 1945/1962). An inadequacy of this negative definition is that it ignores the contextualized nature of human understanding – understanding that always requires a contextualized preunderstanding of the world (Gadamer, 1960/1975; Heidegger, 1927/1962; Merleau-Ponty, 1945/1962). To avoid conceptual inadequacy, a positive application of bracketing is needed, one that does not assume or require neutrality as an ideal or even an attainable perspective.

The original motivation for the negative conception of bracketing can be traced to Husserl (1913/1931, 1954/1970). In introducing this concept, Husserl was seeking to resolve a dilemma of great concern to philosophers historically: realism versus idealism (Strasser, 1967). Rationalist philosophers, such as Descartes and even the early Husserl himself, assumed that human beings had conscious access only to their own mental states, and, thus, the ability to distinguish the "real" from an illusion or dream was a confounding issue in the description of human experience. Husserl's solution was twofold: First, he argued that consciousness does not exist in itself but is always *of* something – the now familiar postulate of intentionality. Second, he proposed that intentionality is structured as a series of rules for constituting the objects of consciousness and that these rules are the same whether directed at real or imaginary objects. Under this reading, the phenomenological task became one of describing the structure of consciousness at any one moment, not one of making judgments concerning appearance or reality.

In its original use, bracketing involved a suspension of the "natural attitude" (i.e., preconceptions of what is real or not real) so that the phenomenologist could be open to the essential structure of consciousness. Husserl conceded that the "natural attitude" could not be completely suspended at any single point. Bracketing was an ongoing process of suspending the natural attitude until, after much effort, only the essential rules of consciousness remained. Husserl felt he never attained the reduction and described himself as a perpetual beginner at the phenomenological task (Strasser, 1967).

Husserl's use of bracketing must be understood in terms of his initial assumption that the rules of consciousness transcend situations. Once removed from this philosophical context, such a negative view is problematic. For purposes of existential-phenomenological interpretation, bracketing is better described positively, as a way of seeing. Rather than suspending worldly knowledge, the interpreter applies a world view such that a phenomenological understanding may emerge. It is a meta-theoretical assumption of existential phenomenology that this world view allows for first-person description. There is no critical test, however, which proves with absolute certainty that a phenomenological understanding is identical to a participant's lived experience.

In this use, bracketing refers to an attempt to identify and correct interpretations in which the phenomenological perspective has been coopted by incompatible suppositions. An interpretation premised on Freudian dynamics provides one such example. Other examples include an interpreter's applying his or her own standards of what constitutes an important or unimportant experience, judging a participant's reflections as illogical because they do not conform to some preestablished norm, or arguing that the "real" experience is not being described because the participant's reflections do not mesh with an imposed theoretical framework. In the present usage, there is still a process of negating incommensurate "theories," although the purpose is now to maintain consistency between an interpretation and the participant's world view.

There is still ample opportunity for bracketing to fail. Some presuppositions may simply not be recognized by the interpreter. In other cases, they may be recognized but the interpreter may be unable to give any other plausible interpretation. Three procedures are offered to overcome these limitations: The first of these requires the investigator explicitly to consider his or her reasons for conducting research on the present topic. Such interest can be acknowledged in the form of a personal statement describing the investigator's history and current concerns with the phenomenon of interest, or it can take the more focused form of what has come to be called a *bracketing interview*. In the latter case, the investigator becomes the first person interviewed about the topic of his or her investigation. This is done to provide the researcher with some feel for what it is like to be interviewed on the present topic and to provide a thematic description of his or her present understanding of the phenomenon. In both cases, the intention is not to have interviewers become objective – only to have them become more attuned to their presuppositions about the nature and meaning of the present phenomenon and thereby sensitize them to any potential demands they may impose on their co-participants either during the interview or in its subsequent interpretation.

A second procedure designed to enable the researcher to avoid imposing personal meanings onto the interpretation of research dialogues requires, whenever possible, that interpretations be rendered in terms used by participants rather than in the more abstract language common to some set of disciplines such as the social sciences. Although not an absolute criterion, interpretive terms are often most experience-near when based on body words – that is, on descriptive terms relating to the corporeality of human experience (Merleau-Ponty, 1945/1962). For example, in a phenomenological description of a modern-day homemaker's shopping experiences, a theme of restriction/freedom-from-restriction emerged (Thompson, Locander, & Pollio, 1990). Without having to implement a distinction between affect and cognition, this theme was stated in terms of a "bodily feeling" rather than in terms of an abstract idea.

A third aid to bracketing is to conduct at least some of the interpretation of an interview text in a group setting (Thompson, Locander, & Pollio, 1990). The group functions in a critical, rather than consensual, capacity. The purpose of each group member is to question the adequacy of any proposed description of interview data. Group members are in a position to notice a theoretical supposition not recognized by the primary interpreter(s); that is, group members are able to make figural what might otherwise remain a background assumption. Second, the group provides a source of alternative perspectives: Having the group discuss the relative adequacies of alternative perspectives reduces the likelihood of describing the text in a stereotyped fashion.

Finally, the group process provides a public test of whether an interpretation is directly supported by the text. In fact, members of the group regularly request the person proposing an interpretation to "show, where in the text, you got that interpretation." If the person proposing the interpretation cannot point to some specific segment of the text, or if members of the group cannot see textual support, the researcher may be reasonably sure that the interpretation is overly abstract and/or idiosyncratic. This logic bears some parallel to that of falsification (Calder & Tybout, 1987). Whereas the ability of an interpretive group to see support for an interpretation does not guarantee its adequacy, failure to see such support serves as good evidence of its lack of adequacy.

The Hermeneutic Circle

The hermeneutic circle refers to an interpretive procedure in which there is a continuous process of relating a part of the text to the whole of the text (Bleicher, 1980). The hermeneutic circle overcomes the seemingly linear character of reading by having an interpreter understand earlier portions of the text in relation to latter portions and, conversely, understand latter portions in the context of preceding ones. Thus, any given passage of the text is always understood in terms of its relation to the whole, both preceding and following, rather than as a decontextualized thing-in-itself (Kvale, 1983; Register & Henley, 1992).

It is difficult to explicate the hermeneutic circle beyond this global characterization because the process is more a matter of tacit knowledge than explicit application. The process has a fundamental ambiguity to it in that there must be an interpreter who "knows" how to interpret. A growing number of philosophers of mind are adopting the phenomenological view that much of worldly knowledge cannot be represented by a set of formally specifiable rules (Dreyfuss, 1982; Searle, 1982). For example, modeling common-sense knowledge has been notoriously elusive for researchers in artificial intelligence (Newell, 1982; Winograd & Flores, 1987). The actual practice of the hermeneutic circle also may be a nonrepresentable form of knowledge. Perhaps the best explication of the hermeneutic circle is given by the experience of reading, understanding, and describing a book.

For the present program of research, the logic of a hermeneutic approach was implemented in three ways: group interpretation, idiographic interpretation, and nomothetic interpretation. The first of these is defined by the interplay between members of an interpretive group and the interpretation offered by the primary researcher independent of the group setting. In group interpretation, a transcript is read aloud with frequent pauses to discuss potential meanings and possible interrelationships among meanings. The function of a group reading is to orient both the researcher and the interpretive group to the nature of the data, and to alleviate the difficulties of beginning to organize and interpret qualitative data. After interpreting the transcript of one interview, the majority of the remaining transcripts are interpreted by the primary researcher.

Periodically the researcher returns to the group with tentative idiographic descriptions and still more tentative nomothetic thematic descriptions. At this juncture, the group evaluates whether these descriptions are supported by the data and whether or not they provide a relatively clear description of participant experiences. This function of the group bears some resemblance to the external audit advocated by naturalistic researchers (Belk, Sherry, & Wallendorf, 1988, 1989; Hirschman, 1986; Lincoln & Guba, 1987). In an external audit, an independent judge evaluates the interpretive procedures of a study as well as the fit between the interpretation and the data to assess the trustworthiness of the study. The present group procedure incorporates some of the auditor's functions into the interpretive process itself.

A second implementation of hermeneutic principles concerns the process of idiographic interpretation. In this case, an individual transcript serves as the text that leads to a case-study description for that interview. Such idiographic descriptions resemble clinical case studies except that the focus is now on describing participant experiences of the phenomenon rather than on therapeutic insights and recommendations. Such case studies provide a summary of descriptive interpretations noting prominent meanings, relations, and patterns present in each interview. In addition, the meaning of figural domains (objects, people, events) may be discussed by the group and the investigator.

As an example, in a phenomenological investigation of shopping, the meaning of children (for some participants) in the context of their day-to-day consumer activities was "disorganization"; that is, the presence of children in a store was experienced as making the shopping experience chaotic and uncontrolled (Thompson et al., 1990). After identifying this meaning, relations were drawn to other experiential situations in which there was an awareness of order and disorder, being organized and/or disorganized, or experiencing some event as complete or incomplete. These experiential similarities were captured as aspects of the more global theme of being-in-control or being-out-of-control. Within this move to a nomothetic description, an attempt was made to capture the experience of "disorganization" in a way not restricted to any one situation but so as to retain contact with each of the contexts in which the various experiences emerged.

The third implementation of the hermeneutic circle occurs in the development of more nomothetic thematic descriptions. The whole of an interpretation is broadened to include all interviews on the same topic, and the hermeneutic circle now yields a process of interpreting each interview in the context of all other interviews. The rationale for looking across interviews is not to establish generalizability; rather, it is to improve the researcher's interpretive vision. Themes describe experiential patterns exhibited in diverse situations, and by looking across interviews, the researcher/interpreter is able to consider a more diverse set of experiences and to recognize ways in which one situation bears an experiential similarity to another. Although not a formal methodological rule, the situational diversity necessary for identifying thematic patterns is often provided by three to five interview transcripts. As such, this "rule" provides an empirical procedure comparable in intent to Husserl's use of the more reflective and personal process of imaginative variation.

With this number of interviews, give or take a few, the interpreter begins to develop a sense of descriptive patterns and relations characterizing the various interviews. This is not to imply that the interpretative process is closed. On the contrary, the researcher (and periodically the interpretive group) continually assesses how the developing thematic understanding fits each successive transcript. Since themes describe experiential commonalities, a thematic structure will be modified only when an experiential uniqueness emerges in a specific protocol. At this point, the part-to-whole procedure characteristic of hermeneutic description will be undertaken in order to yield a more inclusive thematic structure. As should be clear, a specific thematic structure, describing experiential patterns and interrelationships among themes, is the final product of an existential-phenomenological interpretation.

Existential phenomenology is not the only qualitative approach yielding thematic description. Ethnographic studies (Belk et al., 1988), semiotic analyses (Holbrook & Grayson, 1986; Sherry & Carmago, 1987), historical exegesis (McCracken, 1988), and other phenomenologically oriented methods (O'Guinn & Faber, 1989) all provide themes as their final output. Although themes are regularly presented in such studies, it seems clear that they should be viewed neither as objective entities intrinsic to the text nor as projections from an interpreter's personal world. Rather, the theme seems better construed as a perceptual entity, a pattern afforded by the data considered in arriving at the theme in the first place. Such patterns emerge in the continuing hermeneutic act of attempting to understand the interview from the point of view of the participant.

The transformation that leads from protocols to themes is not an easy one to describe. Basically it involves an insight-like process that comes from a complete immersion with both the original interview in the form of dialogue and in its subsequent written form as protocol. In achieving a thematic description, the researcher does not attempt to thematize on the basis of formal or abstract principles but, rather, to capture what the experience was like for the participant (i.e., what it meant to that person in the particular situation being discussed). Such meaning is not expressed in theoretical terms but is rendered in the words of the protocol itself. Although the theme is tied to the protocol, its task is to make the meaning of the protocol clear as to the way (or ways) in which the events described in the protocol were experienced and lived by the person. In every case, an interpretation must be supported by references to specific segments of the text. Thematic interpretation is a continuous process of going back and forth among various parts of the text in which earlier and later parts are continuously being rethematized in the light of new relations provided by an unfolding descriptive understanding of the text.

The Issue of Integrative Validity

Since phenomenological themes function interpretively, it seems clear that such themes must be required to provide a programmatically appropriate understanding of the phenomenon. Since existential phenomenology seeks a descriptive understanding of participant experiences from participant perspectives, a theme that lacks a first-person focus is not programmatically appropriate. This criterion resembles Giorgi's (1975) proposal that the key criterion of validity in qualitative research is "whether a reader, adopting the same viewpoint as articulated by the researcher, can also see what the researcher saw, whether or not he agrees with it." This criterion can be adapted to fit a specific piece of research by specifying the interpretive goals of the study. For purposes of phenomenological interpretation, the criterion of validity becomes whether a reader, adopting the world view articulated by the researcher, would be able to see textual evidence supporting the interpretation, and whether the goal of providing a first-person understanding was attained. This criteria does not preclude the existence of alternative interpretations nor does it require the reader to believe that the present interpretation is the only or even the "best" one. For example, a reader might well believe that a structural interpretation, such as one based on a psychoanalytic understanding, is superior to the one provided by a phenomenological focus on first-person description. Although important for establishing paradigmatic research values, this judgment is irrelevant to the validity of a specific piece of phenomenological research.

Some researchers have suggested that validity should be conceived in terms of a judicial paradigm rather than in terms of an idealized natural science paradigm (Polkinghorne, 1989; Spence, 1987). The utility of this stance is that validity is placed in the realm of human practice, where absolute certainty is not a requirement. From this perspective, validity is not determined by the degree of correspondence between description and reality but by whether convincing evidence has been marshalled in favor of the aptness of the description. An evaluator would not ask, "How can I be certain these themes describe the phenomenon as it *really* is for the participant?" Rather, the question would now become, "Is there convincing evidence for believing that the thematic description affords insight into the experiential world of the participants?"

Evidential support can be evaluated in two ways. The first of these is methodological: Do the investigator's procedures seem rigorous, and are they appropriate for yielding the type of understanding claimed by the study? Rigor and appropriateness both are needed for methodological credibility. For example, a researcher could conduct 1,000 mini-interviews in which a person is given 30 seconds to answer the question, "How do you feel about *X*?" and the "interpretation" would be a tabulation of the resulting "I like it"/"I don't like it" responses. In this case, the procedure of asking how people feel about something is appropriate for generating a phenomenological understanding although the interview format, the resulting verbal data, and their interpretation lack the requisite depth of systematic exploration to demonstrate methodological credibility. Conversely, behavioral observations, although based on rigorous methodology, are not usually appropriate to provide first-person descriptions of a participant's "lived" experience, although Piaget's work on infants does provide a clear case in which behavioral observation was used to provide a powerful description of the first-person world of the infant.

A second aspect to evidential support is experiential: Does the interpretation provide insight to the reader or evaluator? For purposes of clarification, insight can be assessed in terms of plausibility and illumination. Plausibility refers to whether the reader is able to see the relation between the interpretation and the data. Using the participant's own vernacular in naming and illustrating themes will facilitate establishing plausibility since statements illustrative of the theme can always be pointed out to the reader. For example, suppose that a phenomenological study of the experience of time suggested tempo as a figural aspect of the experience. This interpretation would be supported by data such as:

My experience of time is that it either goes too fast or slow. When you want it to go quickly, it drags on, and when you want it to slow down, it just flies by.

Regardless of how illuminating one may find tempo as a theme, there seems little mystery as to how it could have been derived from an excerpt of this type.

An example of implausible interpretation is given by Spence (1987), who offers the following excerpt from the transcript of a clinical interview:

Client: You [the analyst] are capable of loving me and of not caring what I look like, and for you, it wouldn't make any difference about the. . . . [60-sec pause]
Analyst: You cut something short there.
Client: The surface things.
Analyst: I think you mean the presence of a penis. (p. 55)

In commenting on this passage, Spence asks a rhetorical question: "Is that what the patient meant?" Without access to the clinical history and complete interview transcript, it is difficult to know what the client meant or the basis for the analyst's inference. There seems little way to justify the analyst's statement without reference to Freudian theory. For phenomenological purposes, then, the interpretation is implausible, although it may well have been illuminating to the patient or to another psychoanalyst reading the case.

Illumination, the second aspect of insight, has the dictionary meaning of "to clarify by shedding light upon." This definition fits quite well when used in the context of phenomenological work. Any interpretation should allow the reader to see the phenomena in a different light, to allow for a new understanding. Illumination is the most discussed aspect of insight and usually refers to the grasping of a meaningful organization or pattern (Koffka, 1935; Köhler, 1947). This "grasping of pattern" is often experienced as a sudden event. Thompson (1989) has proposed that illumination may be as limited as a change in a concept to one as broad as allowing the person to become aware of what was not previously possible. The best example of this latter type of illumination is found in Kuhn's (1970) discussion of paradigm shifts in scientific thinking and research.

Conclusion Concerning Validity

The present conception of phenomenological validity can be represented as follows:

For a phenomenological study to be judged valid, it would have to receive high marks on all four counts. It should be noted that the methodological/experiential distinction roughly maps onto the structural/Verstehen dialectic described earlier. Methodological concerns focus on the procedural structure of the research, whereas experiential concerns focus more on the meaning and significance of the interpretative results. Within the present approach, we should expect a reciprocal relation between the two: The more rigorous and appropriate the methodology, the more plausible and illuminating the results are likely to be. Conversely, if a study generates highly plausible and illuminating results, the more disposed the reader will be to judge the method as appropriate and, perhaps, rigorous. What is proposed is that both methodological and experiential concerns are relevant to phenomenolgical validity. Well-executed qualitative procedures that do not generate meaningful results are technique without soul. Brilliant interpretation may have value, but one needs to be convinced of the evidence serving to ground such findings in lived experience. Only when both criteria are met does phenomenological description attain the rigor and insight that it aspires to attain and that are likely to convince empirical researchers of its significance for psychology.

PART II

Grounding the World of Everyday Life

What existential thought supplies to phenomenology is a set of situations to be addressed by phenomenological methods. Since the present concern is with human experience it is important to understand how existential philosophy contextualizes its project. As a concrete example, consider Simone deBeauvoir's description of aging in contemporary Western society. In her book, *The Coming of Age* (1970/1973), she begins by noting that the everyday world of the old person can be captured only in terms of their own and their society's experiences of body, other people, and time.

The issue with regard to body is clear: Do I experience my body as functioning well enough for me to get around, or must I depend on others? Health is a question not only of the physical body but also one of whether the body is experienced as integrated within a meaningful personal and social world. The key experience in regard to the aging body seems to be whether the person accepts decreased possibilities and still finds some activities personally worth doing. Fortunately, bodily changes are usually gradual, and all of us learn how to deal with shortcomings if they come upon us slowly enough.

The issue with regard to others is also clear: We come to experience ourselves as old not only in terms of bodily changes but also in terms of how other people, considered singly or as representatives of society, react to us. For example, retirement is a formal social event signaling that I am no longer young. The reactions of coworkers and children (whether harsh or concerned) symbolize a change in attitude, and the meaning of retirement, and through it the meaning of aging, will emerge for me only within the context of my life with other people. The actions and opinions of other people, such as how I get along with my family and peers, may provide a measure of support. At the same time, the world of other people may provide situations that can only be lived unhappily as, for example, when I experience the death of a loved one or friend. Although the significance of all of human life depends on its interrelatedness with other people, such interrelationships are uniquely crucial in old age.

Finally, there is the issue of time. When one is old, the future shortens as the past grows. One possible consequence is a tendency to reminisce, to try to put the events of a life into a personally meaningful order. To be sure, the order is always "my order," and the fact that some biographer or historian may describe it differently at some later date is of little interest. Time in old age, however, is not of single piece; it can be experienced as exciting or mundane. As one writer put it: "Some sigh for yesterday! Some for tomorrow! But you must reach old age before you can understand the meaning – the splendid, absolute, unchallengeable, irreplaceable meaning of the word today." Another noted: "Survival is extraordinary. You are no longer attached to anything and yet you are more sensitive to all." (All excerpts from deBeauvoir, 1970/1973, p. 448.) These quotes suggest that time is not always (or necessarily) experienced as an enemy in old age, and the fact that there is so little time left may be as stimulating as it is unsettling.

Using this general description of the experience of aging in Western society as a framework, it is possible to outline an approach for systematically describing all of human experience. For existential-phenomenological thought, lived experience is always situated within the grounds of body, time, and others, and only if these grounds are described experientially will it be possible to use them in developing a first-person, descriptive psychology in which human experiences is the central focus. For this reason, the next three chapters offer thematic descriptions for the human experience of body, time, and others. To accomplish these descriptions, phenomenological interviews were conducted with adult participants concerning each of these three domains. In every interview, the co-participant was considered the expert, and the interviewer simply followed the course of the dialogue, asking questions primarily to clarify the meaning of what was said.

Following procedures described in Chapter 2, once each interview was completed, transcripts of the interview were prepared. These texts were typed with care, and only when the primary researcher was satisfied with their quality were they brought to an interpretive group for discussion. Prior to the initial interpretive session, the primary investigator was asked in a bracketing interview about his or her interest in the topic. This was done in order to help highlight specific preunderstandings that might be evoked in dealing with subsequent interviews. During the period in which any text was thematized, group members regularly asked the person offering a thematic interpretation to point out a specific aspect(s) of the text used in arriving at the theme. In general, the interpretive group took 3 to 5 hours to thematize a single interview text.

After an initial text had been thematized in a group setting, the primary researcher was responsible for thematizing most of the remaining protocols. As needed, the researcher would return to the group with a new interview, and the process of group interpretation would continue. After all texts had been thematized, initial summaries were prepared and shared with the co-participant producing that protocol. During this period, the researcher did a second interview designed to determine if the participant felt that the summary description did justice to his or her experience of the phenomenon in question. In most cases, participants were satisfied with the description; if they were not, a new summary was developed, taking relevant objections into account; upon completion, the summary was shown to the participant. At this point in the process, the participant was again asked if the summary captured his or her experience. No participant ever required a third go-round.

In all dealings with participants, an air of equality was maintained; participants were quickly given to understand that their perspective was equal to that of the researcher and that they were considered co-investigators. Almost all participants took this offer seriously both during the initial interview and during the postinterview session or sessions. Almost all noted also that they found the interview and the interpretive summary challenging and meaningful, and that they had "thought a lot between meetings about what had been discussed."

A final description of the phenomena under consideration (e.g., time, body, others) was attempted only after all individual summaries had been approved by co-participants. As the primary researcher came to provisional descriptions, they were presented to the interpretive group. When group members agreed that the description was rigorously grounded in the text and illuminating of the phenomenon, a copy of the description was sent to participants who were asked if their own experiences related to the general structure developed from protocols provided by all participants. If they had any objections, they were encouraged to report them to the primary researcher such that they could be used to clarify or reshape the final thematic description. Although it was a rare occasion when a participant responded with even moderately critical comments, such comments were taken into account in revising the description once the primary researcher had evaluated the feedback. An overall summary of the complete interview process used in the present set of studies is found in Figure II.1.

As may be seen, checks and balances were put in place at each stage of the process. The present set of results are dialogical in the most profound sense of the term: Our participants spoke, and we listened; we spoke, and they listened. Only in this way do we believe it is possible to feel some

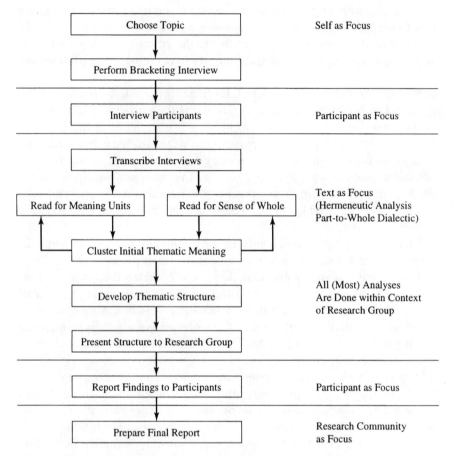

Figure II.1. Schematic summary of interview process used in the present set of studies

measure of confidence in these initial thematic mappings of topics defining some of the major grounds of human life. The following chapters have been prepared with great care; let us hope they reveal a new and interesting perspective on the human experiences of body, time, and other people.

3

The Body as Lived

Themes in the Human Experience
of the Human Body

It does not seem a matter of chance that the problem of the human body has reattracted the attention of twentieth-century philosophy. The Aristotelian synthesis forming the basis of Western thought until the time of Descartes did not admit of any role for the body other than that of object. For Aristotle, the body was separate from the soul as the matter of an object is separate from its shape. Prior to Descartes, there were two views of the body: the body as opposed to the True Self, and the body as a lesser part of the Self (Morris, 1982). These views constitute a central dynamism in classical thought that arose in reaction to what Jonas (1965) terms the *primordial monism of primitive man*. That is, the primitive knew nothing of the self; to him, all matter was suffused with life, and "death, not life, called for an explanation."

For Descartes, the body posed no special problem. Within the context of Cartesian thought, the body belonged wholly to the realm of things (*res extensa*), which was set over against the more significant realm of mind (*res cogitans*). The next step for Descartes, once he had defined thinking or mind as the essence of existence, was to describe how mind relates to body and world. The realm of flesh was "deadened" to that of object and placed at the disposal of mind, whose sole task was to think clear and distinct ideas. As a final piece, Descartes assumed that God's truthfulness guaranteed that any idea he could think clearly would express something true. The task of humanity, then, was to determine which ideas are clear and which are not. The criterion used was whether the reality named by the idea took up space; hence, the only clear idea one could have of the body, even one's own body, was that it took up space just like any other object.

This chapter is based on the unpublished doctoral dissertation *Ambiguity and Embodiment: A Phenomenological Analysis of the Lived Body* by William MacGillivray, submitted to the University of Tennessee in 1986.

In his three-volume work *Metabletica* (which has been summarized in English by Jacobs, 1968), Van den Berg has traced changes in the history of the human conception of the human body. The general trend seems to be that throughout the classical and medieval periods, the body was increasingly "deadened" and evolved to the point of being considered a mechanism no different from other physical mechanisms. One way of marking these changes is to note the progress of medical science in opening up the body to consider its inner workings and structures. It is less than 100 years from Versalius to Descartes, or from that time when medical scientists were first permitted to cut open a cadaver and peer inside. As Van den Berg notes, this action was prefigured in a number of other social changes including a growing preoccupation with themes of death and decay in art and literature. It was also prefigured by changing burial customs in which graveyards were increasingly placed outside town limits. This action excluded the dead from the realm of the living, where previously they had been buried in crypts under churches.

The transformation of living flesh into inert matter occurred about the same time as the realm of the mind was enlivened by considering it the defining characteristic of human existence. This meant that the idea of life came to be considered more important than the living of that life. This situation had, and continues to have, little power to vivify human existence, and Zaner (1966) has noted that twentieth-century philosophy has had to deal increasingly with the "radical reality" of the living human body. Indeed, philosophers who address the problem of the body are engaged in a struggle that forms a keynote of anxiety for the modern age: how to fashion a new and enlivened world of meaning in which many view matter, mind, and spirit as desiccated ideas no longer able to sustain living human commitment.

This then is the problem to be faced: How are we to restore meaning and depth to human existence so that it will recognize the human body as the core of personal existence and not as an object of detached observation or conception? Within contemporary psychology, there seem to be three major theoretical approaches to this task: psychoanalysis, Gestalt psychology, and existential phenomenology. Each view offers a different attempt to overcome the hegemony of mind by reconsidering what could be meant by body. Within psychoanalysis, this task concerns an exploration of the role of unconscious desire in expanding and limiting human knowledge and activity; within Gestalt psychology, it concerns an exploration of the body as both a figure and ground of human experience; within existential phenomenology, this task concerns an attempt to describe prereflective modes of embodied existence as fundamental to human life as it is lived. Each perspective implies a theory of the body since it is the body or, more properly, *my* body that must form the nexus of any attempt at describing human existence.

Approaches to the Body

Psychoanalysis

The central contribution of psychoanalysis had been what Merleau-Ponty called the "protean idea of the unconsciousness." Romanyshyn (1977) characterizes this idea as providing a vertical depth to intrapsychic life, with desire emerging from this core of personal existence to suffuse human activity. The unconscious retains a central ambiguity at the heart of human action, a "forgetfulness of the body and its history," which becomes a vital mystery at the core of personal existence. Repression always implicates the body since it is the body that both represses and is repressed.

It is clear that Freud relied upon the view of body-as-object, although his central insights and clinical observations carried him well beyond the limits imposed by such a conception. The intimate connection between bodily experience and ego integration, while couched in causal terminology, clearly cannot be encompassed by Cartesian concepts. The ego is haunted by a body, which it *is* at its core, and which it continually forgets and rediscovers in desire. The body ego is typically viewed as the earliest stage in the development of the mature ego, and Hoffer (1952) has characterized this early form as a "mouth ego," since the mouth is the first bodily zone by which an infant takes in the world. As a result of the infant's active use of the sucking reflex, the environment may be explored and exploited to obtain satisfaction of bodily needs.

During this phase, the infant first "finds" her hand and is able to use it to obtain substitute satisfaction by sucking. This mouth–hand schema forms a core of the early body-self, the first experience of "mineness," and the first experience of control over needs. Linn (1955) notes that this face–hand fusion forms a relatively enduring schema that reappears, for example, in neurologically impaired individuals. That is, when a child or brain-damaged adult is touched simultaneously on the hand and the face, there is a tendency for the face to predominate over the hand: The subject often reports that only the face has been touched.

In psychoanalysis, body ego is the original principle of personal organization, which forms the basis for all subsequent development and which establishes the first boundaries between self and other. Mahler and McDevitt (1982) have described the specific developmental sequences necessary for the development of a body-self. In the neonate, for example, proprioceptive-kinesthetic sensations predominate and form the "primitive core" of the ego. During the second month of life, the infant becomes more attentive to combined extero-proprioceptive sensations. At this time, the mother becomes a "beam of orientation" for the child by meeting its demands and by providing an experience of boundary in the mother–child unit.

The role of the movement in promoting this development has been studied by Kestenberg, Marcus, Robbins, Berlowe, and Buelte (1971) in their observations of child motility. Following Laban's (1947) work on movement patterns in adults, observations were made of tension and movement shapes in the actions of children during free play and in interactions with other people including their mothers. During the neonatal phase, the mother provides an experience of shape-flow for the child; moving toward ("growing") or away from ("shrinking") the child in response to the child's bodily flow of tension. During the so-called oral phase, child and mother become partners in coordinating shape-flow responses. During this phase, tension is relatively free-flowing, with the child's predominant shape-flow that of "growing" toward the mother and the world and not that of "shrinking" from the mother and the world. Movement patterns change as the child grows older, revealing an increase in the bound flow of tension and a "shrinking" flow-shape. These movement patterns are phase appropriate for the task of separation and individuation. As the child moves into succeeding stages, movement patterns shift, with an increase in both free-flowing tension and the ultilization of "growing" flow shapes.

For psychoanalysis, regression offers a general model for events that take place without cognitive (ego) control. Federn (1926, 1952), in attempting to move beyond bodiliness as an aspect of regression, introduced the concept of "ego feeling" as a way of describing experiences of personal continuity and boundedness. Such experiences also describe a basic mood, a feeling of "safety." Although body, mind, and superego feelings may be distinguished in experience, these separate feelings are part of an overall experiential structure of merging and shifting. The notion of boundary for Federn is more fluid than for Freud and refers to aspects of consciousness. Libido is the investment of feeling in the self and in the world, with the balance continually shifting even in everyday experiences such as falling asleep. Federn's views come closer than any other psychoanalyst to those of the school of Gestalt psychology and depart considerably from an emphasis upon epigenetic structure noted by other psychoanalytic theorists.

Gestalt Psychology

Gestalt psychology describes bodily experiences in terms of figure/ground principles in which much bodily experience is structured in terms of the basic polarity of Body/World. Doubtlessly influenced by developmental considerations (e.g. Koffka, 1924), the polarity that emerges does so as a result of dynamic ordering processes within the contemporary field. One way in which this process is conceptualized is in terms of the concept of "silent organization" in which the body is described as a stable ground, ordinarily not available to consciousness, that serves to structure other psychological activities.

Köhler (1947) seems to have been following the same line of analysis when he described the body image as that portion of the phenomenal field "between the front and the back." For Gestalt psychology, the body was always described as an aspect of the phenomenal field that either may become figural or remain unarticulated ground. Since the primary concern of Gestalt psychology was to establish conditions under which objects become figural within the experiential field, any object, strictly construed, is only what becomes figural within prevailing ground conditions. When applied to the body, this position attempted to describe the ground conditions within which the body would emerge as a focal aspect of experiences.

Goldstein (1939/1963) was among the first to apply Gestalt concepts to neurological impairments when he characterized an organism's "search" for good gestalts as a central organizing factor of human life and growth. The good gestalt for Goldstein was the preferred structure for an organism: "the coming to terms of the organism with the world, or that form in which the organism actualizes itself, according to its nature, in the best way" (p. 371). Goldstein argued that what was lost when a person suffered brain injury was not specific abilities but a change in his or her overall relationship to the world – a tendency to shift from an abstract orientation to a more concrete one – for example, the brain-damaged person who could not point to a specific location on his body but could swat a fly that landed on that spot. Goldstein also emphasized the danger in any attempt to view the body solely in terms of physical properties. Such an approach may be justified in describing a corpse, but the neurologist never finds other than a living, behaving person, and any attempt to reduce the body to a static thing fails to capture it as a living phenomenon (e.g., Sacks, 1985).

Using an organismic position similar to Goldstein's as their basis, Werner and Wapner (1949; Wapner & Werner, 1952) advanced a sensory-tonic theory of perception. In this theory, sensory and tonic contributions to perception are viewed as mutually interdependent. Central to their position is the assumption that an organism seeks to bring about a state of equilibrium by a variety of bodily means. The organism follows the basic path of seeking simplicity and economy of effort to establish and reestablish bodily equilibration. Sensory and tonic factors are functionally interchangeable: Vary sensory input, and tonic responses change; vary tonic input, and sensory responses change.

In one attempt to evaluate sensory-tonic theory, Shontz (1969) conducted a series of experiments on perceived arm length. In this research, results indicated that body boundaries tended to expand and contract in different contexts and tasks; for example, subjects perceived arm length to be greater when their outstretched arm approached a barrier (a wall) than when in an open space (a hallway). When asked in a different study to estimate head width, subjects overestimated width *less* when their face was touched than when it was not touched. Subjects also estimated arm length to be greater when they were instructed to point to an object. What these studies emphasize is the dependence of body perception on context: There is no bodily perception without a world in (and through) which the body moves. A change in the structure of the world brings about a change in the experiences of the body.

The primary emphasis of a Gestalt approach to body experience concerns an emphasis on context. For the most part, the body is "silent" (i.e., ground), and the person is rarely focally aware of the body per se. Although the body may not be figural, it is an aspect of the overall organization forming the ground from which any figure must emerge. Frequently the concept of figure/ground is erroneously thought to imply a bounded figure against an unstructured ground. Within the context of Gestalt psychology, both figure and ground are equally co-implicated, and it is just as appropriate to view the figure as delimited by the ground as the reverse.

Gestalt psychology, therefore, implies that there is no stable body image, no static body representation independent of its present lived context. The concept of silent organization yields the further implication that any attempt to describe the body image, to make the silent background directly available to experience, must involve a shift in the overall field of awareness. To be aware of my body is to be aware of the phenomenal field in a different way – to bring a special structure to the field of personal experience. In some sense, body image always remains "silent," and this is true even though it is possible to make aspects of such experience figural.

Existential Phenomenology

Marcel distinguished between the body as object (as subordinated to the laws of natural science) and the body as uniquely mine. In *The Mystery of Being*, (1960) Marcel wrote: "my body is mine in so far as for me my body is not an object but, rather I am my body" (p. 123). The word *mystery*, in the title, was used to suggest that the *mineness* of the body always involves me at the heart of my being. To assert that the body is mine is not to give it the status of a possession, *mon corps*, but of corporeality itself, *le corps propre*. To be in-the-world means to be in an embodied relation to that world.

The body is both familiar and unfamiliar. It is fatefully mine, vulnerable as any other object in the world, necessarily impenetrable and strange to me. As it is mine, it may be available or unavailable to me. By available, Marcel means the body may be present to self (and others) through receiving and welcoming experience. According to Marcel, modes of unavailability include: (1) encumbrance, when the person is burdened with the petty cares of life; (2) crispation, when the person closes off aspects of his/her life from others; and (3) susceptibility, when the person closes off action through anguished self-doubt.

Van den Berg (1952), following Sartre, identified three modes of embodiment. The first describes the body as landscape; the world lies spread out before me as a sphere for action and the body is pure instrumentality taking the world for its domain. A second aspect is the body as seen by others; available to a reflection that breaks up experience and objectifies the world. It is to this level that the psychologists' world of interiority belongs. Van den Berg gives the example of a traveler, arriving at the inn, impatiently awaiting his beer. For the traveler, his impatience is "over there" where the owner of the inn is talking. For someone observing the traveler, the impatience is "in" him; that is, the traveler is seen by the *other* to have an interior world of intentions and plans. The third bodily mode is found in the glance of the other, when I experience myself under his or her gaze. For Sartre, the gaze always appropriates existence; for Van den Berg, the gaze also affords the possibility of being understood. It is only in this dimension that we can speak of an interpersonal world, and it is only in this mode that there is the possibility of dialogue.

Merleau-Ponty (1945/1962) continually returned to the theme of corporeal intentionality as central to any understanding of human existence. In making the body central, Merleau-Ponty was laying the basis for a systematic psychology that would avoid the errors of both idealism and realism. For him, the body defined a fundamental category of human existence. To situate the body fully in its "landscape" is to use this perspective in investigating other human phenomena. For Merleau-Ponty, the body exists primordially – before there is thought or a reflected world – and the world exists for me only in and through the body.

Plessner considered the problem of bodiliness from the perspective that all living things form boundaries that take on specific attributes appropriate to their life situations. For example, plants are characterized by an openness of form, whereas animals are characterized by a closedness of form. By virtue of being a closed form, an animal has a *front* and is able to take a stand in the world of things. Human existence is uniquely characterized by its eccentric position: in virtue of existing, the human being *is* a body; in virtue of having a point of view on that body, the human being *has* a body. Each level of what Plessner called *positionality* defines a space, and human existence is uniquely defined by a space capable of thought and possibility.

Plessner (1961/1970) specifically described laughter and crying as revealing the ambiguity of both being a body and having a body. In laughing (and crying), the body "takes over" and answers an incomprehensible situation for the person. Despite a felt lack of control, the act reveals "the possibility of cooperation between the person and his body" (Plessner, 1961/1970, p. 33). In everyday life, the unity of the instrumental aspect of the body (being a body) and its experienced character (having a body) proceeds with little interruption. Yet this unity can be disrupted, temporally in the case of laughter and crying, more severely in the case of the psychologically or neurologically impaired individual.

The Body and Its Image: Major Research Findings

The neurologist Henry Head is generally considered to have introduced the concept of body image or body schema into contemporary scientific vocabulary. For him, body schema is a postural model of the body permitting orientation in space that enables the person to recognize and respond to changes in position (Head, 1920). Schilder (1935/1950) considered this definition of body image to capture only one aspect of a process of "perpetual inner self-construction and self-destruction." For Schilder, body image is related to the total functioning of the individual and, as such, is constantly changing and dynamic.

Developmental Considerations

One way in which the development of body image has been investigated is through young children's responses to their own images in a mirror. Infants show a lively interest in mirror reflections and by the first year are usually able to recognize themselves in the mirror. Mahler and McDevitt (1982) found that the infant between 4 and 5 months of age begins to notice his or her reflection. By 6 months, the child attends to hand movements in the mirror as well as to the reflections of other people. By the 8th month, there is a rise in excitement whenever the child notices his or her reflection. At the same time, the child's smile will be qualitatively different when gazing at mother than when looking at her own image. By 1 year, the child's expression becomes more "sober" as the reflection is "studied" by the child. Sometimes, the child will avoid mirror reflection altogether.

Dickie and Stroder (1974) also studied the young child's response to his or her image in the mirror. They found increasing interest in viewing mirror images up to age 1 and declining interest thereafter. Modaressi and Kenny (1977) view such declining interest as part of the child's overall development. In their research, Modaressi and Kenny evaluated children's reactions to both true and distorted images in the mirror. Results revealed that children, during the early phase of stranger anxiety, continued to show generally positive reactions to either image. As children moved into the stranger-anxiety phase, they showed generally negative reactions. Older children showed a more complicated pattern involving basically positive responses to the true image and negative responses to the distorted one.

Older children often have been asked to draw a human figure on the assumption that such drawings provide insight into the experiences they have of their bodies. For example, children frequently draw heads that are large relative to the rest of the figure; younger children often draw the human figure as a head only. At times, arms and legs will be drawn as radiating from the head with no representation of a trunk. Koppitz (1968) found that normal 5-year-olds regularly leave out the arms; when arms are drawn, they are just as likely be attached at the waist as at the shoulder. Indeed, proper attachment of the arms to the trunk is not expected until age 7 or 8. The conclusion often made is that children's body image is reflected in, and reflects, their relatively undifferentiated drawings. Thus, the body image of the 3- and 4-year-old is "all-head"; the latency-age child has a clear sense of the vertical axis of the body, the head-legs system, although the arms and hands are less clearly perceived and less securely attached to the image of the body.

Wallach and Bordeaux (1976) criticized these conclusions, arguing instead that figure drawings may reflect only motor skill level and be unrelated to body perception. To evaluate this possibility, they provided children with human figure puzzles and had them put these puzzles together after first having them identify specific body parts. They found that children were able to construct the human figure correctly, and that these efforts were much superior to their drawings. Children who were unable to name a body part were found not to include that part in their drawings, thereby suggesting that cognitive factors account for some of the so-called distortions in body image noted when figure drawings are evaluated.

Whereas these studies highlight the role of cognitive-linguistic factors in the articulation of body image, other studies point toward emotional and interpersonal factors. Stiles and Smith (1977), for example, found that estimations of body height by children improved when they were given an opportunity to view a film of themselves in motion. Sperry, Ulrich, and Staver (1958) found that learning-disabled children who were more active tended to improve on learning tasks: Increased bodily motility seemed to parallel an increased investment in the learning process. Quiet children made fewer improvements; their lack of bodily action seemed to reflect a withdrawal from the learning process.

Shontz (1969) asked participants to estimate personal body dimensions such as hand length, head width, arm length, waist width, and foot length. Results of these studies revealed that head width was overestimated, often by as much as 30%. Arm length, waist width, and hand length in descending order were overestimated less; for example, the hand was overestimated only by 10%. Foot length often was underestimated, usually by less than 10%. What is most significant about these findings is the invariant *ordering* of estimations provided. Although alterations in procedure could lower errors of estimation, the rank ordering of head-arm-waist-hand-foot remained invariant across tasks and procedures.

Studies involving children yield a similar rank ordering. For example, Schlater, Baker, and Wapner (1974) found a consistent underestimation of arm length relative to head width in children. Although there was a consistent improvement across age levels, the basic relation was unchanged. Koff and Kiekhofer (1978), who explicitly followed Shontz's procedures in their study of children's estimation of body size, were able to replicate the same rank orderings as found in the original studies.

The philosopher who has spent the most time in conceptualizing results of this sort is Merleau-Ponty (1945/1962). In fact, much of his discussion of the development of body can be viewed as an attempt to move past these approaches toward something more psychologically significant – what could be described best as "the psychophysical posture" structuring personal identity. For Merleau-Ponty, the structure of behavior that generates the child's personal identity has little to do with instincts or drives. Rather, it is an evolving *mode of experiencing* of both body and "other." This mode of experiencing, even in the infant, is to be understood only in the context of the specific lived-events that constitute it. For Merleau-Ponty, the infant body is one that loves, fears, hates, and longs for the external other; it is never just simply an immature object of physiology.

Neurology and the Phantom Limb

Goldstein (1939/1963) emphasized that where a neurologist often only sees symptoms, patients often experience these symptoms as answers to the demands of their present life situation. One phenomenon well known to neurologists concerns the phantom limb, which is the continued perception of a limb or other body part following loss through amputation or surgery. Although some patients report the experience of a phantom limb as painful, most report phantom sensations as not being unpleasant. The phantom limb is often reported to be more "present" to awareness than the contralateral limb (Simmel, 1958). Patients also at times try to use the phantom, and experience surprise when they fall after trying to walk on a phantom leg. At times, the phantom is reported to be in an awkward or uncomfortable position; at times, but not always, the position of the phantom corresponds to the position assumed just before amputation.

The experience of a phantom occurs across a wide range of ages; however, if amputation takes place before the age of 4, the phantom is only infrequently reported. In reviewing the relevant age data, Simmel (1966) found that if amputation took place between 6 and 8 years of age, the phantom was present in 75% of these cases. If amputation took place between 4 and 6, the phantom was presence in 60% of the cases. When amputations occurred before age 4, phantoms were found only in 20% of the cases. On the basis of these results, Simmel concluded that a phantom limb could only occur once the body image had been built up by experience.

Phantoms usually are reported only following inquiry by the doctor. Plugge (1970) asked phantom-limb patients to plunge the phantom through a wall, but his suggestion was met with looks of betrayal and incredulity, and the patients rejected the request angrily. For the amputee, the limb is experienced as both present and absent. When confronted with the inauthenticity of the phantom – the dual aspect of the missing/present limb – the patient rejects the context, thereby terminating "dialogue" with both the physician and the phantom.

Attempts have been made to account for the phantom as a type of denial (Kubie, 1975), with such denial viewed either as an automatic compensatory mechanism or as a pathological response with deep emotional roots.

Whichever interpretation is taken, the fact remains that phantoms occur and remain present for many years, long after the patient presumably has adjusted to the loss and has experienced many years of motor/postural activity that should presumably modify the body image.

In summarizing, Merleau-Ponty (1945/1962) notes that "the phantom arm is not a representation of the arm but the ambivalent presence of an arm." The amputee lives a certain attitude toward the world, and the phantom's presence is a mode of being-in-the-world that cannot be reduced to a physical or a mental event. It is a human event that has a particular structure and form: The phantom limb remains in the "circuit of existence" for the amputee partly because the continued flow of excitations from the stump help to maintain the bodily character of the phantom.

Body Image and Anorexia

A number of researchers have suggested that the anorectic's distorted body image may have a basis in perceptual distortion; that is, the anorectic, who maintains that she is fat despite having an emaciated body, may be perceiving her body as wider and heavier than it is. Such distortion partly accounts for her pursuit of thinness: She continues to diet because she perceives herself to be overweight. Slade and Russell (1972) set up a frame with movable caliperlike rods that could be moved by an examiner upon subject instruction. The task used was similar to those of Shontz (1969); the subject was to report when the distance between two rods reflected a judgment of the width of body parts and/or other objects. What they found was that anorectics consistently overestimated body width relative to control subjects, even though such subjects could accurately estimate the widths of comparison objects, their own height, and so on. Results also suggested that the magnitude of the distortion related to poor prognosis.

Crisp and Kalucy (1974) used the same method to investigate treatment outcomes, and in doing so, they found that when patients were able to shift to a more realistic appraisal of body widths, a better prognosis was indicated. Button, Fransella, and Slade (1977) repeated the experiment but failed to find differences between anorectics and control subjects: Both significantly overestimated body widths. On this basis, they concluded that there were many so-called normals who also had "distorted" body images.

Strober (1981) looked at estimation of body width scores on the Body Distortion Questionnaire (BDQ) of Fisher (1970), and on Scales 2, 7, 1, and 8 of the MMPI. Results indicated that anorectics who grossly overestimated body widths had high BDQ scores and significant elevations on Scales 1 and

8 of the MMPI. Those who did not significantly overestimate body widths showed elevations on Scales 2 and 7. Strober concluded that body image is not a unitary phenomenon and may be reflected either in enhanced interpersonal concern for the appearance of the body, or in enhanced personal concern for the integrity of the body.

Casper, Halmi, Goldberg, Eckert, and Davis (1979) have reinterpreted the results of these and other similar studies to suggest that what subjects appear to be doing in approaching these tasks is to deny their illness. The magnitude of the distortion may be taken to reflect the severity of the denial without any need to rely upon a theory of perceptual distortion. Casper et al. further note that since distortions in body image also appear in normal populations, they cannot be considered to reflect a unique distortion in anorexia. When taken in conjunction with results for other patient groups, the following generalization seems to describe all relevant data in a reasonable way: The more disturbed an individual, the more variable and inconsistent is his or her performance on tasks of body size estimation.

Body Image and Personality

Using an approach based on the Rorschach or Holzman Inkblot Tests, Fisher and his coworkers (Fisher & Cleveland, 1958; Fisher, 1970) have redefined the problem of body image in terms of an individual's ability to maintain a boundary between self and world. The personal achievement of such a boundary is viewed as an ongoing task, as each person attempts to maintain a unique, personal boundary that is consistent across time and varying tasks. The nature of the person's experience of his or her boundary can be assessed in terms of responses to the Rorschach Inkblot test. In attempting to quantify the experience of body boundaries, Fisher and Cleveland defined a so-called Barrier score, which is a summary statistic derived from all responses to Rorschach cards that articulate a boundary. They also defined a Penetration score, which is a summary value for all responses that involved penetration and/or themes of damage and destruction.

Initially, Fisher and his associates were interested in Barrier and Penetration scores for different psychosomatic disorders. They found that individuals with high Barrier scores often had psychosomatic problems involving the skin and skeleto-muscular system. High Penetration scores were associated with psychosomatic disorders affecting the interior of the body (e.g., ulcers). High-barrier subjects also were found to be more athletic and active, to see life as full of deception and mystery, and to describe definite and forceful parental figures on the Thematic Apperception Test.

The concept of the body that emerges on the basis of these investigations (and others; see Fisher, 1970) implies that body awareness enters all aspects of personal functioning. High-barrier individuals seem to experience a different phenomenal world than low-barrier individuals, and this world may be characterized as perceptually more vivid, active, and differentiated than that of the low-barrier individual.

The Present Research Program

The length and complexity of the literature concerning the human experience of the human body suggest that we are not yet at the end of the road. One method by which to open a new path would seem to be to ask people, rather directly, what they are aware of when they are aware of their body. This, in fact, was the strategy used in the present program of research in which 16 adult participants were interviewed on a one-to-one basis using phenomenological procedures. The opening question requested each person to describe the "whens" of his or her experiences of the body (i.e., "Could you please tell me some times when you are aware of your body?"). A second question concerned the "whats" of bodily experience (i.e., "Could you please tell me what you are aware of in that situation?"). Thus, all interviews dealt with two questions: one concerning the range of situations giving rise to experiences of the body, and a second concerning descriptions of the way in which the body was experienced in each of these situations.

Of the 16 individuals who participated in the study, 8 were men and 8 were women. Participants were selected in two ways. Following a brief description of its aims and purposes, 10 individuals volunteered for the study. Of these individuals, 4 were members of a local church study group, 3 were employed in a social service agency, and 3 were graduate students. The remaining 6 individuals were specifically solicited because of particular bodily skills: 2 are professional dancers, 1 is a professional actress, and 3 are skilled amateur athletes. The modal age ($N = 7$) was between 35 and 44 years; 6 participants were between 25 and 34, and 3 were between 45 and 55.

Situations in Which the Body Was Figural

Although the purpose of this study was to arrive at an overall thematic description of the way in which the lived body is experienced, it also was important to describe those situations in which bodily experiences tended to be figural. Lists of situations were produced by noting every "when" reported by participants. These situations were made more compact by combining similar events.

The following category system presents the kinds of situations reported by participants as giving rise to an awareness of the body. Eight categories were sufficient to encompass all events mentioned in the 16 interviews:

Categories

1. Using the body
2. Sensing the body
3. Presenting the body
4. Pregnancy and sexuality

5. Change over time
6. Identity
7. Awareness of others
8. Awareness of mood

Explanations

1. *Using the body*. This category refers to an awareness of the body when engaged in an activity or project. Using may be strenuous (e.g., jogging) or relatively quiet and inactive (e.g., doing paperwork). The use may be specific (e.g., walking in the woods) or general (e.g., doing everyday chores). Using refers to any action, whether directed toward the body specifically (e.g., taking a shower) or to accomplish a specific task (e.g., skiing).

2. *Sensing the body*. The body also came into awareness whenever it was felt by the person as impinging; aches and pains, illness and fatigue present typical examples. The event need not be a negative one, and sensing can be pleasurable as well as painful or neutral.

3. *Presenting the body*. This category was scored whenever the person was aware of the body as presented to other people. Appearance, dress, posture, etc., are typical examples of an awareness of the body as "on display" to others, or to oneself in the role of the other.

4. *Pregnancy and sexuality*. This category was coded separately because of its frequency and the potential significance of these events for any study of the body. Pregnancy refers to bodily experiences associated with being pregnant, including nursing. Sexuality refers to sexual intimacy and/or arousal.

5. *Change over time*. This category refers to comparisons between a present experience of the body and a past one(s). For example, a participant compared his previous feelings of discomfort with his body to his present ability to accept himself. (This example with some justification could also be coded as one of Presenting the Body.)

6. *Identity*. This category was scored when the person described an event in terms of an awareness of the meaning of the event for the self. For example, a person may be aware of his/her body "as a Christian."

7. *Awareness of others.* The presence of others may result in an awareness of the body in a number of ways. Awareness of Others was scored whenever the presence or absence of others was a major aspect of the situation.
8. *Awareness of mood.* Strong emotions were mentioned as setting events when a participant reported being aware of his/her body. Awareness of Mood was scored whenever strong feelings were noted as a major aspect of the situation.

Thematic Aspects of Bodily Experience

In reviewing the present set of interviews, experiences of the body that stood out as thematic were noted. These themes represent an attempt to capture each person's unique mode of experiencing of his/her body. Themes reflect particular aspects of participant experience, and they were compared and contrasted with one another to achieve a more general summary of themes serving to capture the human experience of the human body.

Three major themes were found to emerge from the present set of interviews. Each theme included two specific subthemes:

   I.   Experiences of Engagement
      A.   Body as vitality
      B.   Body as activity
  II.   Experiences of Corporeality
      A.   Body as instrument
      B.   Body as object
 III.   Experiences of Interpersonal Meaning
      A.   Body as appearance
      B.   Body as expression of self

Figure 3.1 presents these themes in the form of a triangle to emphasize interrelationships among the various themes and thematic pairs. It is important to keep in mind that the themes form a unity and that each emerged only in reference to all others. Although it is possible to define and delimit the domain encompassed by each of the six subthemes, each subtheme is more properly understood as providing a perspective on the overall experience. Any theme or subtheme may emerge with clarity in a particular situation and may be unexpressed in other experiences; the experience of any one theme does not preclude any other. Thus, the triangle presents the full range of possible experiences of the body, with the corners representing

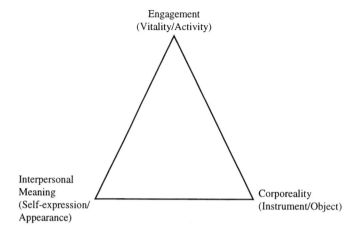

Figure 3.1. Themes in the human experience of the human body

thematic pairings that emerged with relative clarity and frequency. Any one theme, or any number of themes, however, may emerge in any given situation.

Although subthemes may be defined separately, they are best thought of as comprised of pairs forming three major thematic groupings. These pairs are close in experience, more likely to cooccur in awareness, and to be difficult to differentiate.

Experiences of Engagement. For this theme, the person experiences his or her body in terms of its full participation in some project. The focus is primarily on the world, and attention and concentration are absorbed in the project. The person may report no particular experience of the body, or a "curious absence" of any experience of the body.

1. *Body as vitality.* Vitality refers to those experiences in which the person reports feeling engaged in the world with little or no sense of the body-as-physical. Instead, there is an experience of well-being, of enlivenment, of absorption in the world. Although the experience may be enjoyable, this is not necessary; indeed, at times, feeling "caught up" in the world may be frightening, especially if the event is experienced as involving a loss of self/world boundaries.
2. *Body as activity.* Activity has as its domain the same aspects of engagement noted previously. This theme refers more directly to the concrete movements in which the person is engaged, and there is a more direct

awareness of the body as a central aspect of the experience. Although the focus is more or less directly on the body-as-physical, this category highlights the experience of being engaged in the world.

An example may serve to highlight both themes and as a point of contrast with other possible experiences. A person may experience the activity of running in many different ways. The experience is one of Vitality when she feels totally alive, bursting with energy, and fully in control. Vitality also is experienced when, as she runs, she loses a sense of her body altogether, loses all sense of time, and is wrapped up in the experience. Activity would be noted if, instead, the participant reported focusing on the act of running itself, the joy of being able to move her body after a day of inactivity, the pounding of her legs on pavement, and so on.

Specific examples derived from the various interviews are as follows:

Vitality

"And I guess [I'm aware of] the feeling of well-being; you go outside and take a deep breath and feel good all over."

Activity

"In running I enjoy the feeling of the muscles burning, the tightness of the skin with the wind on it."

"I'm ... aware of the energy level of different people and how these levels may match or contrast. . . ."

Vitality and activity

"[When walking] ... I'm aware of the good feelings of stretching the legs ... of taking in breaths ... walking in the cold rain and having it hit my face, that fits a fantasy of mine ... of Daniel Boone in the woods."

Experiences of Corporeality. The body-as-physical becomes figural at times and may be experienced as an object in a world of objects or as a means of obtaining goals: an *it* with qualities, capacities, and limits. It is described as both acting upon things and of being acted upon by them.

1. *Body as instrument.* Instrument refers to experiencing the body as a tool. This experience is described in two ways, both in terms of accomplishing certain ends and in terms of having been trained to perform skillfully. In this latter mode, the body can be experienced as composed of parts and functions that can be "broken down" and/or "built up."

2. *Body as object.* The body can be experienced as having limits just as an ordinary object has limits. It can become impaired through illness or injury. It reacts to events, is intruded upon, and intrudes into awareness. As an *it*, there may be issues of possession and ownership. At the same time, the body "owns" the person, demands attention, and calls the person back from the world and projects. While pain and illness are ordinary experiences in which the person reports becoming aware of an object quality to the body, there are other more pleasurable experiences as well, such as occur in the initial stages of sexual excitement as the body responds to the "call" of a situation not yet completely acknowledged.

Continuing with the example of the runner may clarify these additional themes. The runner experiences the instrumental quality of the body when aware of her need to coordinate aspects of pacing, breath, and speed to accomplish the run skillfully. Instrumental experiences involve running as a method for building up strength or as a way to use leisure time. The body is experienced as an object whenever pain or the need to ease, limit, or avoid pain is experienced.

Examples of these themes that were described by participants are as follows.

Instrument

"In the early stages of learning how to dance, you have to think about the process, all those pieces."

"I've come to realize that even if I gain weight I can lose it over a relatively short time period; it takes less time to get back into shape...."

Object

"I'm most aware of my body after I eat, aware and self-conscious of my belly."

"In anxiety peaks, I get a lot of body sensations I don't ordinarily get."

Instrument and object

"I'm aware of my body in the morning when I'm stiff and hungry. I will do stretching exercises for the stiffness."

"I think a lot of my awareness of my body has to do with maintenance, going to the bathroom, eating . . . my body as a car . . . making sure it is oiled and gassed up."

"When I'm aware of my body, it is generally in terms of feeling something isn't right, and I try to figure out what it is I am doing. . . ."

Experiences of Interpersonal Meaning. The body can be experienced in
terms of its social and symbolic meaning. The body partakes of the shared
meanings of the social world as well as being involved in unique and private
aspects of the self. These meanings may be open and public or closed and
private.

1. *Body as expression of self.* This theme refers to those experiences
   of value and meaning when the body-as-self is highlighted. Whenever
   the person is aware of how the situation expresses a meaning or
   a purpose for the self or others, this theme applies. Lifestyle,
   character, and interpersonal stance all are described as bodily expressions of self.
2. *Body as appearance.* This theme refers to the body as it appears to others
   or to the self in the role of an other. It applies whenever the body is
   experienced as in some way displayed before the world. While appearance applies to concrete aspects of how the person looks, it is also figural
   whenever an experience centers around how the person "appears" to
   others in the broadest sense of the word: appearing professional or
   feminine both reflect aspects of this theme.

To conclude with the example of the runner, experiencing a sense of
accomplishment and purpose through running belongs to the theme of
expression of self. Being aware of the admiring looks and gazes of others
while running expresses the theme of the body as appearance.
    Experiences of interpersonal meaning include the following statements
made by the present set of participants.

Appearance
    "I try to dress in a way that calls attention away from my body [and
    toward] . . . my face. Being fat means you have to try harder just to
    look okay."
    "I'm aware of my body just before meeting people . . . the immediate
    thing that comes to mind is . . . the face, facial features, my eyes. . . ."

Expression of self
    "I often feel I am fighting to be the way I am in a world that tries to
    dehumanize me, that tells me what to look like, what clothes to buy,
    etc."
    "For me the body reflects the tone and tenor of my experience."

Appearance and expression of self

"I started to exercise . . . a few years ago, and part of the reason for doing that had to do with [the fact that friends were also exercising] . . . to be with the group. . . . I was also aware of my age and the fact that I could be in better shape."

"I've always been hard on myself, seeing room for improvement. I guess I've fallen into the trap of the Modern American Male always trying to look like the model in *Esquire*."

Thematic Combinations. Sometimes subthemes were combined in more complicated ways. Some of these cross-theme combinations are captured in the following set of excerpts, all of which anchor on the theme of activity.

Activity/object

"When exercising, I can be very aware of my heart pumping, how rough the workout is . . . my body having a war with my mind . . . then there's an abandonment to the exercise."

Activity/instrument

"[When running] I'm often aware of my pace, the pace of my feet . . . and heartbeat and my breath. . . . When I'm feeling at my peak, that's when I'm most aware of things working together."

Activity/vitality/instrument/object

"My mind was the conductor, my body parts were the instruments. Sometimes my mind was in control; sometimes it wasn't. . . . I was attuned to the inner environment."

Some participants also presented second-order combinations of engagement and interpersonal meaning:

Vitality/expression of self

"I'm aware of my body sexually, in sexuality. I'm aware of closeness, intimacy, love, maybe some power there, too, and fun."

Activity/vitality/expression of self

"My bodily feelings will change depending on the person I'm with and the situation. Whatever emotional response the person elicits from me changes my experience. . . . In front of a group, I'm aware of how I look. . . . With my children [I'm aware] of motherly feelings. . . . With a friend I might feel "hyped up" . . . I want to move; I kind of bounce."

Activity/vitality expression of self

"I'm aware of [my body] during sex and then I'm beyond it. . . . [Sexuality] is an avenue through which something more is expressed."

A last set of thematic combinations makes situations of corporeality and interpersonal meaning most figural:

Instrument/expression of self

"Wrestling helped me to develop a better image of my body. . . . It was a way of asserting myself all alone."

Instrument/object/expression of self

"Dance is based on youth. . . . The body won't do what it will be asked to do. . . . It's a fleeting situation."

Object/appearance/expression of self

"When I'm depressed I guess I take it out on myself with a lot of name-calling. . . . I feel more 'stuck' the way I am . . . there's an immobilization."

Finally, a few participants described experiences where all three themes were salient:

Object/expression of self/vitality

"Early into a run, I'm aware of pain; later in the run, a sense of control, health, and power. There is a sense of control: that I have gotten through the pain, that I can do something that's difficult."

Object/expression of self/vitality/activity

"When I'm doing what I want to be doing, there isn't a separation [between my body and *me*]. . . . I perceive separateness when I'm critical of my body or in pain. If I'm doing something well, I'm aware of being me. . . . To be aware of my body . . . means that something isn't right."

Unique Characteristics of Particular Participants

In this section, some examples of unique participant characteristics (age, weight) are compared with the way in which the various themes were reflected in their descriptions of bodily experience.

Age and Identity. One participant was a professional dancer who discussed his struggle to maintain dancing skills as he has gotten older. A striking aspect of his interview was the focus throughout on his role as a dancer. To some extent, this may have been due to the setting for the interview; he was in dancing attire, prepared to go to class after the interview concluded. The major themes expressed by this participant emphasized instrumental and objectlike qualities of the body. This emphasis on corporeality seemed to reflect his attempt to maintain an expression of self (his dancing career) in the absence of a readily available instrument – that is, a youthful body. Corporeality emerges for him as he tries to maintain an experience of interpersonal meaning no longer easily given by the body. Within this context, experiences of engagement are relatively muted. Shifting the inter-personal meaning of his body would also likely shift experiences of corpo-reality. That is, if he decided only to teach dance, it seems likely he would come to report experiences of health and vigor that his years of disciplined work have helped to develop.

Weight and Identity. A number of participants reported comparable experiences in regard to weight. Being overweight was almost always described as an expression of the self, often as an aspect of appearance, and rarely as an aspect of the objectlike quality of the body. One participant described being fat as a "cloak" obscuring her from others. At times this experience was comforting. In the past, being overweight was an experience of being judged by others, and her life was described as dominated by the struggle to lose weight. Over the years she has gained a greater sense of control over these feelings and, in the process, stopped dieting and gained a great deal of weight. Despite this shift, her weight still remains bound up with her view of the self.

This issue of weight-as-self emerged for many participants. It certainly appears that this emphasis accurately reflects a common issue in the wider culture. That is, the pursuit of thinness, for women in this culture especially, has little to do with corporeality. Within the present study, weight was rarely an issue of health or maintenance of the body; more often it was experienced as a quest for an "ideal self," elusive and unmet.

Sexuality. Most participants noted some aspect of sexuality as giving rise to an awareness of the body. Whereas there were no striking differences between male and female participants when sexuality was context for body experience, there were differences in the quality of such experiences. Men tended to describe themes of feeling active, vital, and engaged; women tended to emphasize feelings of closeness, warmth, and vitality. When noting expressive aspects of sexuality, men tended to describe experiences of power and accomplishment; women tended to describe experiences of affection and love.

Discussion of Themes

In an attempt to describe experiences of the body as lived, three major thematic pairs emerged that adequately accounted for all of the experiences reported by participants. This structure was found to be complete, with each theme serving to provide a unique perspective on the body-as-lived. A careful examination of the various protocols revealed that the themes form systematic figure/ground relationships that emerge and recede in awareness; that is, each theme becomes figural and stands out with clarity in experience only against the overall background of all remaining themes. The ground forms the figure just as the figure forms the ground, and this relationship must be kept in mind in considering specific cases and/or examples.

In terms of prior work, the present study emphasizes the need to specify which aspect of body experience is being investigated. In this way, the appropriate "domains" of various definitions of body image used in prior studies may be clarified and subject to further critical inquiry. For purposes of clarity, the three major themes – Engagement, Corporeality, and Interpersonal Meaning – are used to develop implications of the present findings. At the same time, it should be stressed that in no sense do these themes form fixed categories or traits. Rather, they mark off figural aspects of bodily experiences as a figure/ground phenomenon. Each domain implicates all others, and none is more privileged than any other.

Experiences of Engagement

Previous studies have not specifically addressed experiences of engagement as key aspects of bodily experience. Although such experiences are implied in Schilder's (1935/1950) approach to the role of body image in all human activity, there has been little discussion of the bodiliness of human action. Despite this, experiences of engagement appear to be among the most ordinary and, for this reason, among the most difficult to articulate. The lived immediacy of the body is most clearly present when the person is absorbed in some task or project. One participant talked about engagement as an experience of "total unawareness of the body." As the interview progressed, she reconsidered, deciding that perhaps engagement was a "hyperawareness" of the body. It appears that only during extraordinary events will this most ordinary of experiences become figural.

This state of affairs may offer one reason for the relative neglect of this aspect of bodily experiencing in the literature. Indeed, some theorists explicitly deny the possibility of experiencing the body when fully involved in a task (Boss, 1979). Experiences of a devitalized world, however, have been noted by a number of researchers interested primarily in pathological disruptions in the engagement of person and world. Van den Berg (1972) has been particularly interested in clarifying a changed relationship to the world/body aspects of experience in pathological states such as depression. Other writers have addressed this theme in terms of the reconstituted world of brain-injured persons. Sacks (1984), for example, has described a number of case histories of brain-damaged individuals who demonstrate an ability to regain a lived immediacy with the world despite extraordinary impairment.

While relative neglect for experiences of engagement reflect an embeddedness in ordinary existence, this aspect of experience must be considered precisely because it is so difficult to articulate and is so often submerged in the flow of everyday life. Engagement is likely to form the "silent ground" for other experiences of the body, and any account of any experience of the lived body must take this aspect into account. For example, investigations into the experience of identity must note that when a person is fully engaged in his or her world, issues of identity are muted or even absent. When identity becomes figural, engagement is likely suppressed. Finally, experiences of engagement are relatively inaccessible to awareness and quite difficult to articulate. Precisely because of this, careful inquiry may be needed to describe how engagement forms a significant part of the underlying structure of human activity (i.e., serves as its silent organization).

Experiences of Corporeality

Many studies have investigated this aspect of the experience of the body, particularly in terms of perceptual and cognitive tasks. One of the major findings of Shontz's (1969) studies, for example, was that even when body perception was reduced to one of "pure" measurement, there were certain invariants in the perception of bodily parts that remained unchanged regardless of experimental manipulation. That is, our body is not like any other object for perception even when the task is made as objective as possible. It would appear that even for experimental subjects, heads and hands remain *my* head and *my* hand although the demands of the situation may require an evaluation of *any* head or *any* hand in neutral space.

A different locale in which this insight applies concerns anorectic and obese individuals. Although the usual assumption in both cases is that the person has a cognitive deficit – an inability to perceive "true" body proportions – Shontz's results seem to call such a premise into question. Results of the present study, however, suggest a different perspective on obesity and anorexia – namely, that when someone is pathologically fat or thin, experiences of the objectlike quality of the body are muted or absent. Indeed, it may be this "forgetting" of the objectlike quality of body that is central to weight disorders. In the present study, no participant could be considered pathologically fat or thin. Concerns about weight, however, were frequently discussed, and the experiences described were more likely to express issues of interpersonal meaning than of corporeality. One woman focused almost exclusively on her weight as an expression of self, as an issue of appearance. Only incidently was her weight seen as either instrumental or objectlike.

Moss (1982), in his discussion of obese individuals, notes that issues of ownership, responsibility, and possession are often figural for such individuals; that is, when the issue of weight becomes an aspect of self – an expression of "who-I-am" in the world – losing weight may become a struggle to gain or lose an important aspect of the self. In contrast, one participant in the present study talked about his ability to lose 50 pounds when, as a young man, he decided to shift athletic interests from football to wrestling. It would appear that dancers also have this particular ability to experience weight precisely in terms of the objectlike quality of the body. For most individuals, the gradual accretion of weight with age is only partly experienced as objectlike but, instead, "spreads out" to other aspects of experience – most notably to appearance and expression of self.

The anorectic who insists she is fatter than she appears to be is likely to be experiencing her body in terms of its interpersonal meaning, and a continuing belief in her fatness may be a communication to others of concerns about control, sexuality, or some other aspect of meaning expressed by pathological thinness. The finding that the anorectic makes a more accurate "objective" judgment about her weight following treatment may reflect the extent to which she has succeeded in separating issues of weight control from issues of interpersonal control.

One of the few differences between men and women in this study was that men tended to describe experiences of the body as instrumental and women as concerned with engagement. Such a finding seems to support the view that men are likely to break up their experience of body into parts, and to experience the body as detachable from the total field of events. This ability to detach, organize, and synthesize body image would seem to be a crucial aspect in the acquisition of skill. Women tended to report experiences of engagement, with such engagement likely to be figural when the body is experienced as coextensive with that of the world.

The phenomenon of a phantom limb seems to relate to the theme of corporeality, to be figural in terms of the objectlike and instrumental character of the phantom. It matters little whether the phantom is more or less "wired in" to the somatosensory cortex, built up through use, or a result of peripheral action of nerves at the stump. What seems to be essential for the experience is that the situation calls for an intact limb under conditions of sufficient ambiguity such that the phantom is able to complete, as Merleau-Ponty put it, "the circuit of existence." If the ambiguity is gone, as in the case where Plugge (1970) asked his patient to put the phantom through a wall, so too is the experience of the phantom.

This central ambiguity of the objectlike quality of the body may be seen in the anosagnosic's disavowal of his or her nonfunctioning "part" despite the protectiveness shown to this "alien object" in daily life (Pollio, 1982). There is a reciprocal relation between anesthetic experiences and avowal or disavowal of the body; that is, what cannot be felt-as-mine is disavowed and alien. When nerve action, or the call of activity, are experienced, the phantom becomes felt-as-mine just as surely as any other aspect of the body. In the present study, no participant reported phantomlike experiences. It does appear, however, that the ability to extend bodily experiences beyond the physical limits of the body is a normal aspect of corporeal experiencing of the body. When driving a car, for example, the body boundary expands to the contours of the automobile itself. When backing into a parking space, we feel our way into the space just as surely as we feel our hands on the steering wheel, and with more clarity than we feel our back against the car seat.

Experiences of Interpersonal Meaning

Many studies investigating body image have been concerned with the experience of the body as appearance and as an expression of self. Secord and Jourard (1953), and numerous other studies using the Body Cathexis Scale, reflect an attempt to relate experiences of the body to experiences of self. These studies benefit from a degree of consistency in aim and purpose. The scale, however, takes a highly constricted and objectified stance toward body, forcing choices about the body as an object detached from ongoing experience. The body is never just an object for the person; it is always *mine* even when it may be an object for *me*.

Throughout the interview, participants talked about body parts or bodily attributes. They referred to these parts as owned or as separate from the self, as "my leg" or "the leg." Such descriptions are inherent in English usage, and until the specific experience was clarified through the dialogue, referring to the body as an "it" did not address the experience of the person. One participant talked about her experience of running in terms of feeling the burning of the sun's rays on her skin. This was for her an experience of activity and not at all a feeling of the objectlike insistence of a body called back upon itself in pain. The Body Cathexis Scale assumes a unitary experience of the body not given by participants in this study. It would appear that this scale and others like it relate to more reflected levels of experience. Perhaps this is why it correlates with other measures of reflected awareness and little with unreflective measures such as the Barrier Scoring system developed by Fisher and Cleveland (1958).

The work of Fisher and Cleveland also appears to concern the experience of the body as an expression of self. The inkblot tasks, and the Barrier and Penetration scores derived from them, are designed to tap into a person's capacity to symbolize experiences and to integrate and synthesize perceptions under conditions of ambiguity. Fisher and Cleveland have marshalled an impressive array of evidence linking imaginative productions on inkblot tasks to a wide range of psychological and physiological phenomena. The capacity to describe boundaries for relatively amorphous inkblot forms was found to correlate with the ability to form clear and articulated experiences of the body. It was also found to correlate with the capacity to organize thoughts and to succeed on problem-solving tasks as well as with measures of blood flow to the extremities and with the production of up–down metaphors in describing personal orientation.

Experiential Themes and Theories of the Body

Merleau-Ponty (1964/1968) describes truth as a "wedge into the present," and each of the theoretical positions discussing the human experience of the human body has captured a truth about the experience of the lived body. While the explicit goal of the present program of research was to describe the human experience of the body, an implicit goal was to understand more deeply truths of human existence already glimpsed in other contexts. All truth is perspectival, and the next section discusses the deepened perspective offered by results of the present study considered in the light of previ-

Table 3.1. *Contrasting Present Findings with Other Investigations*

Major categories	Focus	Critical event(s)	Investigator	Formulations/Paradigm cases
I. Engagement	World	Using	Van den Berg	World of the Landscape
			Merleau-Ponty	The vital body
			Marcel	First Ontological Dimension
			Sartre	"I exist my body"
A. Vitality	World/Body		Becker	Vital Body
B. Activity	Body/World			
II. Corporeality	Body	Sensing/Using	Van den Berg	Third-person world
				Interiority
			Merleau-Ponty	The mechanical body
			Sartre	The body-for-others
A. Instrument	Body as available	Using	Marcel	Body as instrument
B. Object	Body as impinging	Sensing	Marcel	"Mere" flesh
			Plessner	Laughter/Crying
III. Interpersonal Meaning	Self	Presenting	Van den Berg	Intersubjective world
		Time/Identity/ Others	Merleau-Ponty	The symbolic body
			Sartre	"I am for others"; the "gaze"
			Marcel	Availability/unavailability
A. Appearance	Self as body	Presenting		
B. Expression	Self as symbol	Time/Identity/ Others	Becker	Social body

ous approaches to issues of the body. Table 3.1 presents an overview of issues to be discussed.

Experiences of Engagement

The thematic category of Engagement corresponds to Sartre's First Onto-logical Dimension (1943/1956), Van den Berg's World of the Landscape (1952), and Merleau-Ponty's Vital Order (1942/1963). Marcel (1960) refers to this dimension of bodily experience as "existing the body" or as the clearing of a space for action. Becker's (1971) concept of the Vital Body also reflects an aspect of these themes.

In many ways, this experience of the body is most ordinary. It refers to the experience of being absorbed in tasks presented by the world. A num-ber of participants talked about this "nonexperience" of the body: "In physical activity . . . I'm sort of out of it." The landscape is where I dwell, as Grene (1982) noted, and there is often no clear experience of a body separate from activity. Most of the situations described concerned events that were relatively out of the ordinary, especially of strenuous physical activity and exercise. Participants tended to describe this aspect of body experience either in terms of a heightened awareness of the body or in terms of a curious absence of the body as the world unfolded. As one participant put it: "I am completely aware of my body, not in a video sense, but of my body moving in space."

Experiences of Corporeality

The categories of Instrument and Object correspond to Sartre's Second Ontological Dimension (1943/1956), Van den Berg's World of Interiority (1952), and Merleau-Ponty's Physical Order (1942/1963). Marcel (1960) refers to this dimension of the body as instrument, as "mere" flesh. The experiences of the body captured by the theme of corporeality refer to experiences when the body itself is the focus. The body can be experienced as instrumental in terms of its utility; I "use" it to accomplish goals. As an instrument, "it" develops and acquires skills through training and use. The body also may be experienced as an object in terms of a need to maintain and care for it, and I experience its mutable character through pain and illness.

Theorists concerned with redefining dualistic thinking frequently note that the body in its corporeality is haunted by a duality, a duality that is inherent in bodiliness and not epiphenomenal. Being and having a body are irreducible aspects of existence. Although none of the participants referred to the "uncanniness" of body in the dramatic style adopted by Zaner (1981), there certainly was an awareness of the unavailability of the body: a "feeling of resentment at being limited by illness," a feeling that the body was "copping out on the deal" by aging. A number of participants also talked about being "surprised" at finding that they were "out of shape."

Experiences of Interpersonal Meaning

The categories of Appearance and Expression of Self correspond to Sartre's Third Ontological Dimension (1943/1956), Van den Berg's Intersubjective World (1952), and Merleau-Ponty's Human Order (1942/1963). Marcel (1960) refers to this dimension in terms of participation and human presence. The experiences of body referred to by this theme concern experiences of the self as figural against the ground of my body and my activity. Whereas Sartre described this dimension primarily as falling under the "gaze" of the other, themes of interpersonal meaning that emerged in the present study tended to concern a range of experiences in which the self becomes figural in awareness.

A number of theorists describe this category of bodily experience as emerging against a ground of will and desire. Becker (1971) contrasts the Vital Body with the Social Body constrained by norms and rules. Experiences noted by participants are less unitary than those in Becker's category and seem to conform more with Brandt's (1968) description, with different qualities experienced as relatively "close" or "distant" from a sense of self that was both fluid and emergent. Participants provided a number of differing experiences of value, meaning, and identity that articulated a range of self-experiences including a social self (e.g., being a professional), an ego self (of values, attitudes, etc.), an ideal self, and so on. These "selves" could be described further as close or distant from a core sense of self, and as relatively fixed or rigid.

Although the themes of engagement, corporeality, and interpersonal meaning refer to personal experience, the social and intersubjective aspects of bodily experience also are important to note. That is, issues of aging, weight, physical fitness, and health emerged with clarity throughout the interviews. One participant talked about how he became more aware of the need to exercise when colleagues began to take more interest in sports and physical fitness. As such, he viewed it as a way of being sociable, which also appealed to his competitive spirit. To place any of these experiences in a position of privilege over any of the others seems an error.

Marcel (1960) distinguishes between a problem and a mystery. A problem is a situation that demands a solution or points to a resolution. Marcel describes the body as a mystery since embodiment is necessarily an incomplete process. The body is a mystery since all possible experiences are available to it. That is, since my body is *me*, I may assume any number of perspectives on it. At the same time, each perspective constitutes a stance, a unique and irreversible position, that imposes limits and establishes the horizon of my experience. I am able to assume any particular perspective, but, to use Sartre's phase, I am always condemned to a perspective that is both incomplete and mysterious. Such is, and must be, the lot of a being who both *is* a body and *has* a body.

4

Time in Human Life

Marilyn Dapkus Chapman

Time is among the most stubbornly abstract and concretely relevant aspects of human life. Our everyday awareness is permeated with thoughts of time, and this awareness is reflected in such ordinary objects as clocks and calendars as well as in such ordinary expressions as "time flies," "spending/wasting/losing time," "time heals all wounds," and so on. Even if we had neither clocks nor maxims, there would still be the human experience of birth and death, daily and seasonal change, and the linguistic markings of a now, a before, and an after. Human beings regularly experience changes in tempo where they, or the events to which they are present, speed up or slow down and/or change from being maddeningly predictable to maddeningly unpredictable. If this were not enough, our reflections on time range all the way from the incomprehensible – eternity – to the more mundane – seconds, minutes, days, weeks. Time has been characterized as a "structural coordinate" of reality (Keen, 1970), as the "currency of life" (Hale, 1993), and as a major existential ground to human existence (Pollio, 1982). Perhaps some unknown graffiti artist put it best: "Time is nature's way of keeping everything from happening at once."

Each discipline has its own collection of temporal units and concepts: circadian rhythms in zoology, solar and lunar cycles in astronomy, and the theories of relativity and evolution in physics and biology, respectively. In terms of human science, history often divides time into periods ranging from a few weeks – the Cuban Missile Crisis – to a decade – the Roaring Twenties – to a few hundred years – the Middle Ages. Religious groups partition their respective versions of human history into B.C. and A.D. and

This chapter is based on the unpublished doctoral dissertation *A Phenomenological Analysis of the Experience of Time* by Marilyn Dapkus, submitted to the University of Tennessee in 1984. An initial description of these results can be found in Dapkus, 1985.

93

their year into culturally determined events as familiar as Easter or as exotic as the Cattle Festival of the Neur (Evans-Pritchard, 1940). Our world is a temporal one, and this is as true of personal experience as of the conceptual worlds spun by scientific, historical, and religious thought.

Psychological Research on Time

The study of time in psychology encompasses a broad range of topics and methods. An experimental psychologist studying the effect of walking rate on judgments of 40-sec intervals (Newman, 1972) is said to be studying time as is the clinical psychologist experimenting with a timer in the therapeutic hour (Ingram, 1979) or describing the development of object constancy in acutely ill patients (Seeman, 1976). The social psychologist studying the ability of adolescent boys to delay gratification (Levine & Spivek, 1957) is said to be studying time as is the researcher evaluating the ability of laboratory subjects to estimate 5-, 10-, or 20-sec intervals (Getsinger, 1976). A number of excellent reviews of this literature exist (Doob, 1971; Fraisse, 1963; Gorman & Wessman, 1977; Hortocollis, 1983; Shallis, 1982; Zelkind & Sprug, 1974), and there is little need to review this research except to arrange it along lines more conceptually useful for the present study of the human experience of time.

To help in this task, this section of the chapter organizes relevant prior research in terms of three major subsections. In the first subsection, "Temporal Dimensions of Behavior," topics such as tempo or consistency are the object of study; in the second subsection, "Cognitive Functions Associated with Time," the major focus is the ability of individuals to estimate temporal intervals and to differentiate between past, present, and future. The third subsection, "Subjective Representations of Time," describes various human representations of time as well as our very human reactions to these symbolic creations.

Temporal Dimensions of Behavior

There seems to be a consensus among psychoanalytic theorists that our most rudimentary sense of time originates in the periodicity of physiological processes such as hunger and sleep (Colarusso, 1979; Erikson, 1956; Fenichel, 1945; Gifford, 1960; Hortocollis, 1974; Morris, 1983; Yates, 1945). Of these processes, hunger has received the greatest attention. Stated simply by Yates: "The first kind of time that is recognized is that my body feels it is time for food." In his early writings on the origins of neuroses, Fenichel (1945) postulated that basic diurnal and physiological rhythms such as heartbeat, breathing, and pulse convey kinesthetic sensations that are basic to the differentiation of temporal intervals and thus to a sense of time.

The existence of individual variations in biological rhythm or tempo has been found in such diverse behaviors as talking (Chapple, 1940; Goldman-Eisler, 1952), walking (Newman, 1972), tapping (Denner, Wapner, McFarland, & Werner, 1963), and solving arithmetic problems (Burnam, Pennebaker, & Glass, 1975). Attempts to correlate personal rhythm with estimates of temporal interval have discovered that when personal rhythm is disturbed – for example, by altering the preferred rate of walking (Newman, 1972) – disturbances in one's sense of the passage of time also ensue. The existence of an individual "temporal comfort range" has been suggested by Kir-Stimon (1977) such that "when this tempo and rhythm are encroached on by others, environmental factors, psychological or physical problems, one's lifestyle is distorted and, with it, one's sense of well-being."

Variations in tempo have been found among different personality types. The impatient, rushed tempo of the so-called Type A personality has been well documented. These individuals have been found to work at near maximum capacity in the absence of any external deadline (Burnam et al., 1975) and to be at a disadvantage in tasks requiring a slower rate of responding (Glass Snyder, & Hollis, 1974). Psychomotor retardation is a hallmark of depression, and a rapid flight of speech and thought is diagnostic of mania. The rate and periodicity of events in time are perhaps most disturbed in acute psychotic states: Thoughts race or come to a standstill – "like a gramophone running down" (Freedman, 1974) – and biological periodicities such as hunger, the menses, and elimination are dissociated from their physical bases and appear to occur "out of the blue" (Seeman, 1976).

Although the existence of individual tempo as a characteristic of personal temperament has been well documented, there is equally compelling evidence for a convergence of tempos between individuals (Goldman-Eisler, 1952; Welkowitz, Cariffe, & Feldstein, 1976). In their study of speech patterns, for example, Welkowitz et al. found a marked convergence between individuals after only three 30-min conversations. A similar convergence of "conversations" – this time, between mother and infant – has been studied by Beebe, Stern, and Jaffe (1979), who found that minute adaptations to patterns of voice, face, and hands led to a dance of interaction in which mothers and infants become so attuned to one another as to appear to move in unison.

The time constraints and temporal rhythms of psychotherapy have been conceptualized as attempts at repairing childhood experiences of interpersonal relationships that were either chaotic or asynchronous. Within this context, the fixed time sessions of psychoanalytic therapy have been thought to allow controlled regression to take place; thus, the therapeutic process is both "timeless" and "timebound" (Namnum, 1972). The rhythms of therapist behavior, similarly, are thought to provide a structure that allows healing and growth to take place: "The analyst who is generally silent reassures the patient by continuing his silence; the verbally active analyst reassures by his continued talking" (Ingram, 1979).

Cognitive Functions Associated with Time

Out of our earliest sense of time as cycles of wakefulness and hunger, we come to understand time as an abstract system. Thus, we learn to use words describing the flow of time (Ames, 1946), to differentiate past, present, and future and, finally, to grasp duration and to estimate temporal intervals. Whether we "construct time" as a defense against need (Ingram, 1979) or as part of a cognitive maturational process (Piaget, 1927/1969) is a matter of interpretation. What does not seem to be a matter of interpretation is that the operationalization of time begins with the child's earliest interactions with the environment but does not emerge in abstract form until the period of formal operations in adolescence (Piaget). Prior to this stage of development, time and space seem to be undifferentiated in the child's mind; indeed, the calendar is believed by many children to "make time," and tearing off calendar sheets is thought by some children to bring about an actual advance in time (Werner, 1957). The operationalization of time, as Piaget (1927/1969) noted, is "tantamount to freeing oneself from the present, to transcending space by a mobile effort, i.e., by reversible operations. To follow time along the simple and irreversible course of events is simply to live it without taking cognizance of it. To know it, on the other hand, is to retrace it in either direction" (p. 259).

One of the earliest indicators of the child's knowledge of time concerns the use of words related to time. "Now," the first time word, appears at 18 months and is followed by "sometime" at 24 months, "tomorrow" at 30 months, and "yesterday" at 36 months (Ames, 1946). The development of this vocabulary seems to trace the emergence of a rudimentary sense of time that begins in the present. What is present is next differentiated from what is nonpresent, and the child refers to an absent situation ("sometime") rather than to one that is definitely past or future (Lewis, 1937). In general, references to the future develop before references to the past, and linguistic knowledge of larger divisions of time comes later in childhood: for example, the days of the week at 5 years of age, the months at 7 years of age, and the years at 8 years of age (Ames, 1946).

A more sophisticated appreciation of past, present, and future seems to take place in adolescence (Colarusso, 1988). The occurrence of physiological changes associated with puberty are believed to foster this change: "Puberty is actually a major demarcator of time sense, an indicator of significant psychological change which brings with it the sense of the passage of time, of movement from one development phase to another, and more specifically a sharp division of life into the physically/sexually immature past and the physically/sexually mature present." Further shifts also occur in young adulthood and at midlife, when there will be a "gradual shift from time left to live to time lived" (Colarusso, 1991).

The first expressions indicating a grasp of duration appear at about 3 years of age (Ames, 1946). The meaning of longer intervals – "How long will it be until you're grown up?" – takes place at around age 7 and precedes the child's ability to estimate short intervals – "How long have we been talking?" – at around age 12 (Bradley, 1947). Duration of intervals relative to the total life span also change as we grow older. William James (1890) was among the first to note that the same duration of clock time is experienced as much shorter for an older person than for a younger one. Janet (1877) explained this phenomenon in terms of a ratio effect: For a 12-year-old and a 20-year-old estimating the length of a 6-year period, it is clear that 6 is a larger proportion of 12 than of 20. James, however, preferred to explain this effect not in terms of ratios but in terms of vividness and habit: In youth, events are more vivid and exciting and not tied to habitual action; hence, everything has more detail, and the young person tends to linger over events thereby lengthening their perceived duration. Lecomte du Nouy (1936), drawing on the observation that wounds heal more rapidly in infancy and childhood than in adult life, suggested that human beings need greater "quantities" of time when older to do the same work as when younger: hence, 6 years for the child amounts to more time, biologically and psychologically, than for the adult.

Results concerning the effects of both depression and anxiety on time estimation have been mixed, depending on the methodologies and definitions used. Depressive individuals, for example, may underestimate prospective time intervals but overestimate retrospective ones (Kuhs 1991). Other studies have found depressive individuals to demonstrate impaired judgment for short but not for long intervals, or not at all (Tysk, 1984); in both cases, such results were obtained despite the subjective experience of time as slowed (Wyrick & Wyrick, 1977). Anxiety and fear seem to lengthen time estimates according to Watts and Sharrock (1984), who found that spider-phobic subjects instructed to "just look at a spider" placed nearby overestimated the elapsed time interval. Gross distortions in the estimation of a day also have been reported for psychotic individuals (Freedman, 1974) as have telescoping and interpenetrations of events from the past, present, and future (Seeman, 1976; Melges & Freeman, 1977).

More enduring personality characteristics also seem to affect a person's ability to estimate temporal intervals. Buchwald and Blatt (1974), for example, differentiated between action-oriented and ideationally oriented individuals in the following terms:

> The action oriented individual has less capacity to delay and postpone, his needs are more immediate, he has less of a sense of the future, he feels impatient and more compelled to act, and he underestimates the passage of time. . . . The ideationally oriented individual tends to think rather than act. He ruminates about decisions and is always engaged in some kind of mental activity, so a time period is filled and its length is overestimated (p. 643).

Finally, the estimation of temporal intervals has been found to depend on the situation; for example, anecdotal accounts of automobile accidents suggest that during an accident one's experience of time may either speed up or slow down, usually the latter. As one observer put it: "I had the impression that the car turned over in slow motion" (McKellar, 1968). In this situation, the most frequent description is that the person comes to experience him- or herself as a spectator to the event rather than an active agent or participant (also see supporting work by Fraisse, 1963, indicating that spectators to an accident involving someone else also experience a "lengthening" of time.) In contrast to such experiences of temporal expansion, time intervals are described as shorter when one is an active agent. In this connection, Fraisse (1963) describes two incidents, one in which individuals were trapped underground in a mining accident and a second in which different individuals were trapped in the rubble of an earthquake. In both cases, individuals underestimated the length of time they were underground; for example, the miners, on emerging from 3 weeks of attempting to free themselves from a mine shaft spontaneously volunteered that they were glad to have been rescued after "only 4 or 5 days."

Subjective Representations of Time

Not content to estimate time, we endow it with properties that often seem to transform it into a living being. So, for example, we create Father or Mother Time (Colarusso, 1987) as well as a collection of other figurative renditions (e.g., see Hales' 1993 nine temporal dimensions invoking such images as "Faustian" or "Gaian" time). Generally speaking, subjective representations of time are obtained from individual subjects on the basis of interviews and questionnaires or from other more figurative sources such as literature or poetry. In Knapp and Garbutt's (1958) Metaphor Test, for example, subjects are asked to rank order 25 quasi-literary metaphors of time ("a speeding train," "a burning candle," etc.) according to how well they "evoke for you a satisfying image of time." Using these ratings, it was possible to identify three different clusters of time imagery: Dynamic-Historical, Naturalistic-Passive, and Humanistic. Factor analyses of subject responses to a different set of time items led Calabresi and Cohen (1968) to identify four factors: Time Anxiety, Time Submissiveness, Time Possessiveness, and Time Flexibility.

A number of methods and questionnaires also have been developed to characterized a person's representation of, and feelings about, relationships among past, present, and future events and actions. Cottle's (1967) Circles Test, for example, attempts to measure the perception of relationships between time zones by having subjects draw circles according to the following instructions: "Think of the past, present, and future as being in the shape of circles. Now arrange these circle in any way you want to show how you feel about the relationship of the past, present, and future. . . . Label each circle to show which one is the past, which one is the present, and which one is the future" (p. 63).

Further attempts to characterize the human experiences of past, present, and future have employed a variety of techniques including sentence completion (Kastenbaum, 1965) and story telling (LeShan, 1952) in addition to the construction of time lines (Cottle, 1968). The precise meaning of these tests is somewhat in doubt, since it is unclear whether they all measure the same or different constructs (Ruiz & Krauss, 1967). The major conclusion to emerge from this work, however, seems to be that having an orderly temporal perspective is a "good thing," since being able to order events in time has been shown to correlate both with higher levels of achievement (Cottle, 1969) and with self-actualization (Getsinger, 1976). A less well-developed sense of temporal perspective, on the other hand, seems to be associated with occupying a social position out of the social mainstream as, for example, would be the case for alcoholics (Roos & Albers, 1965), sociopaths (Getsinger, 1976), character disorders (Miller, 1964), and individuals in lower socioeconomic classes (LeShan, 1952). The development of a less than cohesive sense of past, present, and future is not surprising, notes LeShan, if one grows up in an environment where food, shelter, heat, and personal safety are unpredictable. Erikson (1968) writes of a personal "mistrust" of time, which seems to arise out of early experiences of emotional and physical hardship:

Our most malignantly regressed young people are in fact clearly possessed by general attitudes which represent something of a mistrust of time as such and every delay appears to be a deceit, every wait an experience of impotence, every hope a danger, every plan a catastrophe, every possible provider a potential traitor. Therefore, time must be made to stand still (p. 187).

In general, the more disturbed the individual, the greater his or her need to control time. Calabresi and Cohen (1968) found in their factor analytic study of time attitudes among patient and nonpatient populations that more severely disturbed individuals scored highest on the "Time Anxiety" factor.

Anxiety about the flow of time and need to control time are striking characteristics of . . . this factor. . . . The future is threatening because it cannot be controlled; the past, because it is not mastered through the chronological sequence of memories. . . . Rigidity in planning, fear of commitments, etc., . . . are objective measures of time and expressions of the need to control time. (p. 435)

Variations in temporal experience also have been found in anxious individuals (Nelson & Groman, 1978), depressed individuals (Dilling & Rabin, 1967), obsessive-compulsive individuals (Fenichel, 1945; Spiegel, 1981), and in narcissistic personality disorders (Kurtz, 1988), as well as in schizophrenic patients (Seeman, 1976).

Philosophical Analyses of Time

The most enlightening descriptions of the human experience of time do not derive from individuals participating in clinical or laboratory studies but from more theoretical analyses of time having their origins in philosophy. Although there are many starting points, reaching back to Kant and before, contemporary analysis must begin with Bergson and James, both of whose specific views concerning time form a background to their more general reflections on other aspects of human existence.

For Bergson (1896/1991), there is no more crucial distinction than between scientific and lived time. Scientific time always assumes a spatial representation, such as a line from past through present to future or the movement of a pointer on a clock or other chronometer. The view of time that emerges from such a representation is an abstract one in which time is conceptualized as an extended homogeneous medium capable of decomposition into standard units. Human or lived time is neither so fixed nor so regular and is better described as "flowing" in an episodic and inhomogeneous way. Human time, what Bergson called *duration*, is lively and irregular and experientially distinct from metric time. Although the scientist's time can be equated with duration, it frequently yields the paradox of human time being out of synchrony with measured time.

James's (1890) analysis begins by noting the universal experience of a now, which he terms the *sensible* or *specious present*. The latter term is used to suggest that we are unable to grasp the present in itself and only are able to do so once it has passed. Just as resting places in consciousness are more easily noted than transitions, so too the ends of an interval are more noticeable than the "passage of time" itself. For this reason, James argued, the psychological present could not be a fixed amount of clock time; rather, it is better described as an interval just long enough for a meaningful part of the task in progress to be noticed.

The interval that James described is empty of content. Yet the truth of the matter is that the present teems with activity and the end of one "present" is defined by a change in what captures our attention. Since we are focally aware of what we are doing, and not of time, "what we are doing" always appears as a figure against the ground of time – a background silent until summoned for consideration. As should be clear, the present we talk about is not the present we talk in. Since for James all action take place in the present, it is the past and the future that have to be constructed. Since past and future are experienced only in the present, our ideas of time must grow in two directions from the present. Here there are two possibilities: remembering for the past and anticipating or planning for the future. Although we may think of time as a line running from past to future through present, a better description is that past and future are past and future only in the present. The idea of time, the abstract system, has to be derived from reflections in an unreflected present.

From a small interval of the directly experienced present, James builds the abstract human concept of time. Husserl (1913/1931) took a somewhat similar route in describing temporal experience. The *inner consciousness of time*, to use Husserl's phrase, is experienced as a constantly moving pattern, and events emerge only against the complete world of the person and his or her mode(s) of dealing with it. No event is without its portent of what is to come, which takes the experiential form of waiting for, longing for, expecting, and so on. Husserl termed the pattern of these modes the *protentions* of an event. Similarly, no event is without its relationship to what has gone before – what Husserl termed its *retentions*. Strictly speaking, for Husserl, there is no present because time is continuously arriving and leaving, and personal experience does not pass through a series of nows, as James suggested; with the arrival of every moment, the experience of all other moments is changed.

For Heidegger (1927/1962), the situation is different: There is (are) no present(s), and time is not a succession of moments or events. The future is not ahead of the past, nor the past before the present. Temporality temporalizes itself as future-which-lapses-into-past-by-coming-into-present. A major starting point to Heidegger's analysis concerns his description of *Dasein*, or personal existence. Although *Dasein* is always in-the-world, one of its most significant aspects is that it is always *Geworfen* (thrown or cast, from the German *zu warfen*, to throw) beyond its own willing into the world. Despite such situatedness, a second aspect of *Dasein* is that of striving toward a new mode of being. Here Heidegger makes use of one of many wordplays that occur in his writing when he notes that *Dasein*, in addition to "being thrown," only becomes truly human when it "throws" itself forward as project (*Entwurf* in German). Hence, one of the essential aspects of human existence is its "projected throwness." Such "throwness' is neither an intellectual act nor one of self-projection; human existence is such that it only comes upon itself in the midst of some situation (i.e., *Geworfen*) and has to assume its own future on the basis of some forward project (*Entwurf*).

Unfortunately, the forward thrust of human existence is beset by a world that prevents authentic becoming while encouraging stagnation and fallenness (*Verfallenheit*). For Heidegger, the conditions of technology and of our dependence on the reactions of others in the daily marketplaces of social interaction alienate *Dasein* from continuous projection, thereby leading to an inauthentic mode of existence. Such existence is concerned with chatter rather than speaking, tinkering rather than creating, impressing rather than being, "they" (*das Man*) rather than personal existence (*Dasein*). In short, the "projected throwness" of human life is impeded, and all there is, is an alienated "throwness" that separates human existence from itself and from authentic relationships to time, the world, and other people.

Only one experience has the possibility of calling *Dasein* back from alienation to authentic projection, and that experience is dread (*Angst*) or, more precisely, the dread of possible nothingness (i.e., death). The Angst that accompanies a confrontation with the loss of all being-in-the-world has two consequences for the human experience of time: (1) It makes a view of life in its entirety a possibility and, in so doing, frees the person for an authentic mode of being that Heidegger termed being-to-death; and (2) it makes the future – the not-yet-here – that aspect of time which organizes personal experience, including what others would call one's present being-in-time. The first of these consequences suggests that time is not the world's time but my time, that time is a personal and not an abstract experience. From this view flow the additional consequences that personal time is finite, not only in terms of a being-toward-death but also in terms of its origins. Looking back from the possibility of nonbeing, Dasein is able to face its origin, or throwness, which recognizes that the world I was thrown into is the world that I must accept and be responsible for as uniquely mine (*eigne*); it also suggests that I must attempt to live the project that is my life authentically (*eigentlich*; as mine).

A second consequence that derives from recognizing time as personal is that the most significant domain of time is what is usually called the future. Time is never experienced as arriving; it is always experienced as passing, and to grasp time at any level, we do not grasp a series of nows, as James and to a lesser extent Husserl suggested, but in the order future-to-past-to-present. The future orientation of *Dasein* makes each event of what is ordinarily called the past assume its relationship to a future which then becomes my present mode of experiencing it. The events of a life flow from a consideration of nonbeing – its future – and it is this confrontation that organizes *Dasein* into a sensible form. Time emerges episodically, with the most significant changes occurring from the future to the past, both of which situate me in a present.

But how does all of this occur, psychologically speaking? Here we need turn to Merleau-Ponty's (1945/1962) analysis of time, an analysis that has a decidedly present-centered orientation. Like all of Merleau-Ponty's work, it is concerned not only with philosophical implications but also with the way in which time is, or becomes, present to human experience. The key concept here is what he calls the "bursting forth" of time, by analogy with a flowering plant bursting forth from its pod. In using this metaphor of dehiscence, or bursting forth, Merleau-Ponty indicates an affinity with Bergson, who described our experiences of time as inhomogeneous, as well as with James and Husserl, who rooted their descriptions of time in the present. But Merleau-Ponty's present is different from the more conceptual present of Husserl or the more specious present of James in that it emerges from personal bodily rootedness in the present situation.

For Merleau-Ponty, it is in the present that being and consciousness coincide. Merleau-Ponty uses this co-incidence to remind us that (the stream of) consciousness and (the stream of) time are intimately related, and that both are situated in the world. Whereas it is true that we, as subjects, can only grasp ourselves through reflection on the past or in some interpretation of the future, it is also true that we are always situated in some present. Unlike Heidegger, death does not assume a critical role for Merleau-Ponty's analysis of time. In fact, at one point Merleau-Ponty says: "I live then, not in order to die, but forever," meaning by "forever" a continuing rootedness in and to my present situation.

Just as the experience of an object always depends upon the perspective from which it is grasped, so too the experience of time requires a continuously varying perspective between the perceiver and the specific aspect of time experienced. Since we are always rooted in some present situation, events experienced as relating to time "explode," thereby changing our relationship to what went before and what is to come. The present is that point on which past, future, and present turn; time is not a line running from left to right but a network of changing meanings. The present moment is neither some abstract unit nor a derived thought but some specific event that stands out to provide a glimpse, as T. S. Eliot says, of "time past and time future" as these are "given in time present."

For Merleau-Ponty, the experience of time depends upon the experience of moments that burst forward as uniquely revealing of time to the person. If this is the case, it should be possible to come to an empirical description of the human experience of time by asking people in one way or another to describe moments that stand out for them in their personal awareness of time. This is precisely the way in which the present project unfolds – by asking individuals initially to describe their experiences of time and of then being sensitive to the specific moments that they chose to present as these unique experiences.

The Present Research Program

To develop a thematic description of the human experience of time, a single basic request – "Tell me about your experience of time" – was posed initially to 20 adult participants. Most participants sought additional clarification and, once given such direction, were able to comply with the request quite easily. For example, one interview began with the following exchange:

Investigator: Tell me about your experience of time.
Participant: What do you mean? Does it go fast or slow for me? I mean, when you ask about the experience of time, I think of so many different things. Maybe you can ask me something more specific.
Investigator: OK – think about an experience, an event, or a period in your life when you were particularly aware of time, and tell me about it.
Participant: OK, that gives me a little more to go on: Um . . . let's see. Well, when I think about time in my life, . . .

All participants were volunteers from a local church study group. Of the total group, 10 participants were male and 10 were female; their average age was approximately 43 years old. The majority were college educated, married with one or more children, and could be described as falling into a middle-class socioeconomic category; that is, they were employed as teachers, engineers, accountants, and so forth.

Each person participated in a lengthy dialogue that began with the request just described. Following this, the ensuing dialogue was thematized and next shared with the participant who (at that time) was then engaged in a second, briefer, conversation concerning his or her reactions to the initial description. After all individuals had an opportunity to participate in the second dialogue, resulting summaries were used as the basis on which to develop an overall thematic description of the human experience of time for all participants. Once this description was prepared, it was again presented to individual participants, who were then asked to comment on how it did or did not fit their specific experiences of time.

Themes in the Experience of Time

On the basis of these procedures, four major themes emerged that all participants agreed captured the essential aspects of their experience of time:

1. *Change/Continuity:* This theme was experienced in terms of the way things change and yet have continuity over time.
2. *Limits/Choices:* This theme was experienced in terms of the choices we make and limits we must accept in regard to what we do with our time.
3. *Now/Never:* This theme was experienced in terms of getting the things we want or feel we need in time.
4. *Fast/Slow:* This theme was experienced in terms of the rate (fast or slow) and/or pattern (consistent, inconsistent, cyclic, etc.) of our experiences in and of time.

The four themes bear a relationship to one another that can be presented best in the form of a pyramid, as in Figure 4.1. The four themes define the complete experience of time, although at any one moment, an individual may be aware of only one aspect of the experience – that is, of any given point on the figure. Experientially, it is as difficult to differentiate one theme from another as it is to say where one corner of the figure begins and another ends. We are more likely to describe our experience of time in terms of a combination of themes rather than in terms of single, isolated themes.

A further elaboration of the meaning of each of the four themes follows.

Change/Continuity ("becoming in time"). This theme captures the experience of things changing yet staying the same. Notions of us having a past, present, and future are based on an awareness of the fact that things outside us have a past, present, and future and continue to change or to stay the same. On a personal level, this theme concerns an awareness of personal

Figure 4.1. Themes in the human experience of time

development or of our "becoming" in time. Participants who were particularly attuned to this aspect of the experience of time were apt to discuss changes in themselves, their children, and their parents over time.

> Since I've had children, I've been more aware of time because you see them grow up; you see them change from year to year. My daughter – who I can look at eyeball to eyeball now – it seemed like yesterday I was cradling her in my arms.

> I've always thought about the life span because I was raised with old people – there was a daily reminder of age and how me and my mother fit into the total continuum of ages. . . . I loved it; it gave me an understanding and appreciation of old people, the stories about the good old days. . . .

Experiences associated with this theme enable us to create a sensible framework for our existence as it unfolds across the life span. Awareness of the limited nature of our life is a pivotal one, and one that gives new meaning to the time we have and what we do with that time:

> I'm most aware of time when I'm with my parents . . . because of their age. You realize that they won't be around for too many more years. It makes me aware that you don't have unlimited time, and that we don't always do the things we should, the little things for people.

Our lives unfold as change within a stream of continuity. Too much of either change or continuity can be experienced as detrimental to feelings of well-being. Continuity provides stability, yet too much can be boring or, at worst, stagnating to growth. Change is exciting, yet an excess of change, particularly during times of great personal growth as in childhood, can be unsettling. One participant reflects on her experience of change growing up in a family that was constantly moving:

It seemed like everything we did was temporary. I knew when I entered a school that I wouldn't be there next year, and chances were that I wouldn't be there for the rest of the year. There wasn't any feeling of permanence; I just expected things to be over quickly.

The same participant reported the experience of having "itchy feet" as an adult, becoming bored when staying in one place too long. This feeling persisted until her dawning realization of the importance of continuity in establishing relationships and a sense of connection to a place:

It wasn't until recently that I turned the corner on this. I realized that "home is home," and time plays a big function in that. You don't develop good friendships overnight – it's a matter of interacting for years and years because you can't have all these experiences compressed in a short amount of time.

Limits/Choices ("doing in time"). This theme captures the experience of doing things in time – the choices we make and the limits we accept in order to do the things we choose to do. Almost all participants experienced themselves as not having enough time to do everything they wanted to do. Such limits, however, were experienced as forcing them to make choices, which then served to give meaning to their lives:

I'm most aware of time at work – not having enough time to do everything, and to do everything well, and that's a real frustration. I make lists of things I need to do . . . and if I get interrupted . . . , I get tense and frustrated, 'cause I feel I'm not doing as good a job as I should.

It drives some people crazy not to be busy all the time. I think it's nice to be at peace with yourself . . . and not feel like you have to be completely producing something every second in order to be a productive member of society.

Our experiences of "doing in time" concern how we cope with what we experience as limited amounts of time. Time thus becomes a commodity, like money, either to be wasted or well spent. Everyone has a different definition of what it means to "waste" time:

"Wasting time" is when you kill time. You have an hour to spare and you kill it by doing nothing. . . . It's very passive. . . . You can't be productive all the time, but you can get into the habit of wasting time.

For some, "doing nothing" is a waste of time; for others, it is the height of relaxation, a time of rejuvenation. One participant observed, "I think it's almost an art to be able to be with yourself and not be busy and be happy."

Although most participants bemoaned the fact that they did not have "enough time to do everything," there also was a recognition that limits force us to make choices that provide definition and meaning in our lives: We choose to spend time on the things we value most, whether it is a career, a clean house, or time with our children. The ability to make choices, and to accept the limits they impose, increases as we mature and contributes to our feelings of competence and self-esteem. Denying that there are limits, or believing that there are so many limits that we have no choices, denies both the reality and meaning of life:

You put yourself in different levels of bondage with the choices you make – having a family, a mortgage, etc. It's exhilarating, but it's also a commitment, an obligation. Only in old age do you get free of the bondage. . . . I don't know if I'll even be able to handle that kind of relief.

The vitality of life for this participant consists of making choices and of assuming the "bondage" in life that she experiences as both exhilarating and burdensome.

Now/Never ("having in time"). This theme captures our most basic experience of time, the temporal dimension of going after the things that we want and/or feel we need in life. Developmentally, this theme seems to capture our earliest experiences of time and, without other experiences or modes of thought to temper it, describes an urgency to experiences defining Now and Never: We want something *now*, or we feel we will *never* get it. The following excerpts provide examples of this theme:

I've been very aware of time – time has gone very, very slowly – on diets, in the past. When you're waiting from meal to meal, living for the moment you eat the next time, time seems to drag.

I really experienced time in the military, overseas. Every hour and second that ticked by was closer to leaving. The 7 months seemed like an eternity at the time, but looking back, it went very quickly. . . . Time was the thing that kept me from going home, because I had to experience a certain amount of it before I could do what I really wanted.

Time is experienced as an obstacle, a "useless transition" to borrow one participant's phrase, to getting the things we want. The experience of "having in time" is thus often more focused on the thing we want than on time itself. Participants frequently reported a lack of awareness of time when fully immersed in the enjoyment of having the things they wanted. Childhood, for many participants, was described as a time of satisfaction and, as such, a relatively "timeless" period of life. One participant related:

As a child, it seemed like there was lots of time. I had time to do something by myself everyday. . . . Everything was as it ought to be. I think that when a child is happy, they don't think about time or worry about time.

As one matures, the focus shifts from having "things" in time to an experience of "having" time itself. The balance shifts from childhood to adulthood in the amount of time we *have* left, from "more of it is ahead of us" to "more of it is behind us," so that the time remaining becomes increasingly valuable.

Time is extremely valuable to me. I probably regard it as an unredeemable commodity. I'm more thrifty with how I spend the minutes of my day than how I spend the dollars in my pocket.

Fast/Slow ("tempo"). This theme emerged as a thread that ran through each of the other major themes and described experiences of having, doing, and becoming in time in terms of the rate and pattern at which life events took place. Experiences of rate (i.e., fast or slow) can alternately be expressed in terms of whether it takes a "long time" or a "short time" to have, do, or become what we want. Patterns may emerge over time, so that we may experience things taking place in a consistent or inconsistent manner or, perhaps, in a regular pattern – for example, in the form of a repeating cycle. The following excerpts exemplify this theme:

I've probably been still longer during this period of time than I've ever been, except when I'm asleep. I'm constantly on the move.

I'm afraid that as I get older time will seem like it's running away, going faster, getting away from me faster than I want it to.

Descriptions of this experience often began with the statement, "Time goes . . . (quickly or slowly)", as if to imply that in contrast to time, something else is moving at a different rate. For example, if "time is going too quickly," there is the implication that the person is not keeping up (i.e., is not going fast enough). For each of the other three major themes, time can be experienced as going too quickly or too slowly, depending on whether we are having, doing, or becoming at a rate that is experienced as consistent or inconsistent with our present desires and needs.

1. *Tempo and having in time*. Perhaps the most poignant descriptions of an awareness of the rate at which time passed occurred in the context of "having in time." Time can go painfully slow when waiting to have the things we want, whether it be the next meal for a dieter, the end of a tour

of duty for a serviceman, or presents on Christmas morning for a child. Time spent waiting to escape a painful situation can be very long:

When I grieved over my mother, I felt that time would never come between me and that grief. It did, but it took a very long time.

Whereas time spent waiting seems to go too slowly, time spent having the things we want seems to go too quickly. Here, the focus seems to shift from getting the things we want or wanted to holding on to them. Rather than time now being our enemy, or an obstacle that keeps us from what we want, it has become a force that is experienced as taking away what we now have.

2. *Tempo and doing in time.* The experience of the rate at which time passes is influenced by the things we choose to do during that time. The rate of doing seems to affect our perception of the passage of time (e.g., participants report that time spent in a slow, relaxed manner often seems to go slowly, whereas time spent in a more focused activity, usually working, goes more quickly). In addition, time spent in an enjoyable manner is experienced as going quickly, whereas time spent doing things we do not enjoy is experienced as going more slowly.

There are things we can do to affect our perception of the rate of the passage of time when waiting to have something we want. Thus, participants described an interaction between the themes of Now/Never and Limits/Choices. An example cited by several participants was the use of certain "techniques" to deal with painful waiting – for example, the period of waiting that preceded coming home from a tour of duty in Vietnam. One individual reported that he coped with the pain of not being with his family by filling his hours with doing:

To deal with [this experience], I tried to find things to do. Instead of looking forward to 5:00 as being the end of the day, as I do now, the hour of the day made very little difference. I took any task that ran to late at night; work used up the time faster. Or read – it used up the space. It was a distraction, it distracted me from thinking about the bigger time.

3. *Tempo and becoming in time.* Participants reported that their perception of the rate at which things change seems to vary according to their perception of the number of changes occurring as well as with the novelty of these changes. Participants universally expressed the feeling that time goes slowly in childhood, a time of many changes and new experiences. One participant observed:

When I was a child, time and the whole world was experienced more vividly. You could stop on the way to school and observe a budding dandelion and encompass the whole spectrum of spring in that one flower . . . colors are more vivid when you're experiencing them for the first time.

Our perception of the rate at which time passes also seems to change over the life span as a consequence of our changing perspectives on the amount of time that has passed relative to the total lifespan we expect to have. Participants often noted that the rate at which time passed speeded up after the age of 40. As the value of the remaining time increased, participants reported experiencing time more in terms of "having"; that is, time itself becomes the precious commodity, and the more we attempt to hold on to it, the faster we experience it as going.

Reminders of the changing, yet continuous, nature of things in life were described as soothing the discomfort and pain of not having the things we want or need . . . now. The same servicemen who "kept busy" while on a tour of duty eased the pain of their wait with daily reminders that time was passing, and things would change, by marking time off on a calendar:

In the military, you count the time until you get out. You have a calendar above the bunk, counting the days, hours, minutes, seconds . . . until you get out.

Individual and Group Differences in Themes

The percentage of interview items, what Colaizzi (1978) calls *significant statements*, containing reference to each of the four themes, both singly and in combination, was scored for each participant, and average values were computed for the group as a whole. Of the four major themes, the greatest percentage of items (83%) contained references to Limits/Choices, followed by Change/Continuity (63%), Tempo (54%), and, finally, Now/Never (18%). For 15 of the 20 participants, Limits/Choices was the most widely discussed aspect of their experience; this theme appeared in an average of 94% of their interview items. For the remaining 5 participants, Change/Continuity was the more figural experience, appearing in an average of 87% of their statements. For no participant was the theme Now/Never or Tempo the most extensively discussed aspect of their experience of time.

Participants were most likely to discuss their experiences of time in terms of a combination of themes rather than in terms of a single theme. This was particularly true for the themes of Fast/Slow and Now/Never, which rarely were described on their own. The greatest percentage of statements for all participants contained reference to two themes (41%), followed by items referring to three themes (31%) and then to one theme (21%). Responses referring to three themes appeared to be at the upper limits of complexity to discuss, as the number of statements referring to all four themes comprised only 6% of the total number of items.

Given these results, it is possible to speculate that the demographics of the present group may have affected the frequency with which each of the various themes was described. For example, would the same pattern have emerged if participants had been different in terms of age, educational, occupational, or socioeconomic level? The present group was chosen to define a relatively mature and articulate group of individuals who had sufficient experience with time to discuss the topic easily and well. Perhaps a younger, less reflective, or less "mainstream" group might have presented a different pattern of significant statements.

The low percentage of responses containing references to the theme of Now/Never, and the preponderance of references to the themes of Limits/Choices and Change/Continuity suggest that individuals in this group have moved beyond a preoccupation with "having it *now*" to one of actively "making it happen." Members of the present group of participants represent a highly productive and creative collection of people. Their reflections on having in time (Now/Never) typically concerned memories of childhood, when their urgency of "having it now" was greatest. Having in time also tended to be figural for these participants when they reported experiencing present stress – for example, during illness or grief or during those events where the need for immediate relief was experienced as greatest. Dieting, for several participants, also seemed to bring about a concern with this theme, increasing the urgency of having the next meal *now*. Perhaps a less privileged group of individuals – for example, those who are in a perpetual state of financial, physical, or emotional difficulty – might be less focused on limits and choices and more keenly focused on issues of "now or never."

The preponderance of statements concerning the theme of Limits/Choices reinforces the notion that this group of individuals is quite aware of setting goals and achieving a certain level of success both in their careers and in their personal lives. Their orientation toward life is an active rather than a passive one, and their specific awareness of time would seem to reflect this. The most common lament was "there is never enough time to do everything . . . (perfectly)." Working mothers reported juggling career and home responsibilities, often making painful choices as to how their priorities, and their time, would be managed. The interview itself was described as a "time pressure" by several participants and seemed to heighten an awareness of the limits on their time and of all of the specific things they had yet to do that day. A less goal- and achievement-oriented group of participants might not have felt as constrained by limits on their time nor that personal choices were quite so important.

In terms of age, participants were largely in what would seem best characterized as their "middle years." Mentioned by several participants were notions of "midlife crises" – that moment of awareness of passing the midpoint in one's life and of beginning to evaluate one's total life in terms of goals that had or had not been met. Being at this juncture seemed to heighten participants' awareness of becoming in time, particularly in terms of noticing and describing changes in themselves, their children, and their parents. The cyclic nature of life was mentioned by several participants as they watched themselves assume roles with their children that they once saw only in their parents. A younger group of participants may not have had this set of life experiences on which to draw and, thus, may have been less aware of the interplay of change and continuity in the unfolding of their lives.

General Discussion of Themes

The four themes described – Now/Never, Limits/Choices, Change/Continuity, and Fast/Slow – were found adequate to thematize participant responses to the request, "Tell me about your experience of time." Each theme seems to capture an essential element of the experience of time as well as of something significant about life in general. Putting the matter somewhat schematically, "having in time" (Now/Never) seems concerned with getting the things we want and need in life, "doing in time" (Limits/Choices) seems concerned with our role in making things happen, and "becoming in time" (Change/Continuity) seems concerned with the unfolding nature of ourselves and the world around us. Finally, "tempo" (Fast/Slow) seems to characterize our experience of how quickly or slowly our doings, havings, and becomings take place.

Participants tended to describe their experiences of time in terms of a constant interplay of themes. The interview method did not constrain participants to discuss isolated aspects of their experiences of time (e.g., how fast or slowly time passed) but rather allowed – even invited – them to discuss the experience of time in all of its complexity. Discussion of the "experience of time" was often interwoven with discussion of such personally meaningful subjects as births, deaths, critical illnesses, and triumphs and disappointments in life.

Discussion of their experiences of time seemed to lead some participants to a greater awareness of the moment, even to the extent that they were able to stop and examine whether giving this interview, or engaging in some other activity, was what they now wanted to be doing with their time. The interview also seemed to invite a reassessment of their use of time in terms of the larger perspective of their life – in other words, to locate their doing in the context of their becoming:

My dream is that at some point I'll slow down and learn to relax, spend my time on more important things. Much of what I do, I think it's important at the time, but probably isn't, in the long run of life. It would be more important to sit down and talk to the children when they want to tell me something, rather than say, "Wait until I get dinner ready. . . ." The things you're preoccupied with, like having a clean house, are not that important, but it's a value, so you can't throw it out completely. But you can change it a little.

Most participants reported a sense of being carried away by too much activity in their lives and somehow losing sight of something important in life. Periods of quiet reflection – often described (guiltily) by participants as "doing nothing" – were experienced as interludes necessary to maintain a perspective on the important things in life. One participant thoroughly enjoys her periods of quiet reflection, and "doing nothing" appears to her to define an experience of enjoying time as a time to become, to unfold, to create.

One can't hear time and one can't see time, but when I'm absolutely alone and I can hear the clock buzzing, it's just me and that clock sitting there. It's totally relaxing – doing absolutely nothing – and I always hear the clock in the room, grinding its wheels. . . . I think, "This moment's passing . . . what does this mean to me?" It's free association – I look at a nail on the wall and think, "Oh, I remember when I put that nail in." – it's like being in an eggshell, and the only thing that reminds me that the world is going on is the sound of the clock in the room.

It may be noted in this excerpt that there is an integration of three of the major themes characterizing the experience of time. "Having in time" is expressed in terms of *having* an abundance of time itself, which for this participant provides the opportunity for an emotionally nourishing, rejuvenating, and creative experience. "Doing in time" is expressed in terms of a choice to "do nothing," which for this participant is a productive use of her time, in terms of maintaining her emotional well-being. "Becoming in time" is expressed in terms of the experience of having time to reflect on the moment as it unfolds in the stream of past, present, and future.

Discussion of their experiences of time seemed to lead nearly every participant to touch on the larger role of time in their lives, and of the role of death in providing a structure, and forcing some sense of meaning, to their lives. As one participant observed:

Since my father's death, I'm more aware that time has a limit. . . . I still tend to think that I have many more years, which is probably why I'm not motivated to make some changes now. A person diagnosed as having a terminal disease will immediately set some new priorities, make some changes. If you're not hit over the head, it's easy to keep doing it the old way.

Once again, the issue of death seemed to bring about an integration of the three major themes characterizing the adult experience of time. Time, later in life, becomes our most precious possession as we become increasingly aware of a dwindling supply. As such, the object of our experience of "having in time" becomes time itself. Milestones such as midlife crises, retirement, and deaths of parents, among others, promote a greater awareness of our lives and what is to come. Awareness of death often was described as a catalyst for a reexamination of the choices we have made in life and for what we choose to do with the time we have left:

I'd be very disappointed if I died before I'd relaxed, before I'd done what I really wanted to do, before I felt more free.

Relationship to Philosophical Analyses of Time

While these highly specific and concrete descriptions may seem a bit removed from philosophical reflection, it is clear that existential and phenomenological philosophy not only emerge from but also must return (and be relevant) to everyday concerns. What this means is that each of the major themes described by the present group of participants should make a significant appearance in more philosophical descriptions of the experience of time. From James to Bergson, and from Husserl to Heidegger and Merleau-Ponty, it seems clear that concerns about change and continuity, limits and choices, now and never, and, to a lesser extent, tempo make a significant appearance in each of their analyses. That this occurs is not surprising; however abstract the philosopher may be as a philosopher, the selfsame philosopher is destined to live unreflectedly in the world of everyday reality from which his or her more abstract descriptions emerge. If the real is to be described, as existential phenomenology requires, philosophy and psychology must begin and end in the unremarkable world of direct experience.

James usually followed this maxim, and his analysis of time is no exception. In terms of the present set of themes, James was most concerned with change and continuity, more precisely with how experiences of change yield a continuous conception of time. James built up the continuous aspect of time in terms of an initial awareness of change, the specious present, that was experienced only in retrospect and was later extended in two directions on the basis of memory and anticipation. Despite the significance of these processes, the core event is the experience of an interval long enough for a psychologically meaningful event to occur. For James, change yields continuity, with the concept of time-as-system emerging only later from reflections on these initial experiences and events.

For Bergson, the crucial issue concerns a return to the primary intuition of time as a heterogenous medium composed of episodic events and their interrelationships. Once time has been spatialized, as in scientific and practical thought, it loses its spontaneous upsurge and becomes a passive background to the worlds of science and society. The way we are able to get back to more primary experiences of temporal duration is in terms of episodes of memory that spontaneously break in on us. In terms of the present structure, the most perceptual of the themes concerns tempo, and if Bergson's theory specifies time as a ground to existence, its perceptual qualities (primarily tempo) must be considered in conjunction with those of change. Although duration is continuous (if episodic), it is the perceptual encountering of such episodes that separates them into events and lived time into a heterogeneous collection of events. For Bergson, change and tempo are crucial, and it is a corruption of experience to carve time into units of equal size and represent it as a line.

Husserl, as usual, worried about the various ways in which time was to be described phenomenologically. The essential insight here concerns a focus on the perceptual form of a specific moment as experienced from a number of different vantage points. In this, Husserl's view is similar to James's; the perception of a single moment is progressively profiled as it approaches and recedes from an experience of maximum presence. Thus, it is my continuous rootedness in the present, combined with perspectival changes in my experiences of meaningful events, that yield the sensibly continuous aspect of the experience we call time.

Since the perception of time is an intentional event, similar to other perceptual events, the specific nature of the unreflected linking of perceiver to time is crucial. It is not so much that I construct "past" and "future" from an uninvolved perspective in the "present"; rather, the whole of my existence is involved with the future in terms of my continuing projects – initially as a *now* in relationship to a *never*, later as a *now* sensibly related to experiences of change and continuity. Time is neither a line nor a collection of "*nows*" strung out one before/after the other; rather, it is always experienced in terms of my intentional relatedness to the world. Although the abstract continuity of time is achieved on the basis of reflection, it is only an unreflected intentional relatedness to the world that guarantees the continuity of time in the first place.

If Husserl, along with James, roots us in the present and works to derive other aspects of our experience of time from this perspective, Heidegger describes the human experience of time not only in terms of the themes of continuity and change but more powerfully in terms of limits and choices. For Heidegger, the world of everyday reality is an inauthentic one, which leaves human existence at the mercy of its categories, time included. It is only when a human being faces the ambiguous limit defining the situation of death that life reorganizes itself and is able to move from inauthentic to chosen. Only if I confront the limit of nonbeing (i.e., noncontinuity) is it possible for me to make choices that will allow me to change from a life governed by "them" to one in which "throwness" is transformed into projection.

Although issues of continuity and change concern the human experience of time, such experiences only become human time when limits are faced and choices made. The experience of authentic time is not concerned with the present but with limits to continuity in the form of death. To be sure, human beings, prior to a genuine confrontation with nonbeing, make choices and accept limits, although such limits and the choices they entail are determined by others. It is during this period of fallenness that clock and calendar time dominate existence, and lived time is obscured by concerns with inauthentic doing and being. It is also here that we are concerned with wanting what others want us to want and, therefore, with experiences of *now* and *never*.

The anxiety of an inauthentic life, if faced squarely, has the possibility of freeing *Dasein* from its inauthentic constraints. The dread brought about by facing nonbeing allows the person to confront the patterns of life, with both its changes and its continuities, and in this way to come to a personal experience of time capable of grounding an authentic human existence. Heidegger's analysis suggests that time "flows" not from past through present to future but from future to past and then to present. In this approach, we are required to appropriate our life as our own including both its ending and its beginning. The present emerges not as the first stage in an appreciation of time but as the last – that moment at which I choose my destiny and accept the terms of its perceived constraints and possibilities.

Although Merleau-Ponty does not disagree with much of Heidegger's analysis, he is more concerned with the intentional relatedness that each person has to the present situation; in this way, he is as close to James and Husserl as to Heidegger. For Merleau-Ponty, each moment bursts upon the person as different from the last, thereby revealing the heterogeneity of our intentional relatedness to what is yet to come and what has already been.

Since human existence is always in-the-world, Merleau-Ponty views the experience of time in terms of the perception of time which, like all perceptions, is sensitive to change and continuity – *change* in which aspects are figural, *continuity* in which aspects relate to the situations of one's life. Although Merleau-Ponty recognizes the transformative power of an authentic confrontation with the possibility of death, his interest in the embodied nature of human existence seems to define the present as the primary domain of temporal experience.

These views suggest that there is an intrinsic relationship between subjectivity and time, as James, Heidegger, and Merleau-Ponty have all noted. It seems no accident that both time and consciousness have been metaphorically rendered in terms of a stream, or just that image conveying change and continuity together with an intuition of tempo. The limiting nature of death is viewed not as an absolute existential event in need of confrontation but as an abstract possibility never to be fully realized. Whereas limits imposed by nonbeing play some role in Merleau-Ponty's view of lived time, it is much less significant than in Heidegger's. Human beings choose, and thereby accept limits, and such choices (and their limits) always take place in terms of their personal rootedness to, and in, some present situation. For Merleau-Ponty, such rootedness provides an experience of continuity and change as lived by the person, not as hovered over in a more reflective mode such as described by James.

Relationship to Psychological Research on Time

Psychological research on time was discussed in terms of three major topics: The first concerned the temporal dimensions of behavior; the second, various cognitive functions associated with an understanding of clock and calendar time; and the third, with subjective representations of time. Results of the present thematic analysis contribute to this body of research by providing a potential framework for organizing existing theoretical and empirical notions about time deriving from psychological analyses of human development.

The theme of Now/Never, or "having in time," emerges most strongly in the psychological literature as a concern with gratification (or deprivation) of what usually are termed basic needs, particularly in regard to early parent–child relationships. "Having in time" is thus the temporal component of a more general theme of having, which is a cornerstone to every major psychological theory of development. Freud's oral stage, Erikson's (1956) stage of trust vs. mistrust, and the object relations (Mahler, Pine, & Bergman, 1975) stage of symbolic union with the mother, all describe variations on the theme of "having." The timely gratification of a need – whether food, security, or other people – is essential to the development of the infant, including its ability to delay gratification later in life. Asynchrony between the child's need and the mother's willingness and ability to deal with that need – that is, when the "child's time and the mother's time do not tally" (Yates, 1935) – is thought to lead to disruptions in the child's sense of personal cohesion, safety, and, ultimately, time. The literature on deprivation of need – for example, that by Goldberg (1971) on "waiting" – suggests that it is the infantile person who is unable to wait, who is unable to tolerate frustration or pain, and who, like an "addict without drugs," is unable to endure the *never* of not-*now*.

The theme of Limits/Choices emerges in the psychological literature concerning issues of control, whether of others, ourselves, or of time itself. The theme of "doing" typically appears as a major component in various psychological theories of development – for example, in Freud's anal stage or in Erikson's (1956) stage of autonomy vs. shame and doubt. The temporal aspect of this theme concerns making choices and accepting limits as to how one's time is spent. Disruptions in the normal development of autonomy and self-control may lead either to exaggerated attempts to control time (e.g., to the so-called obsessive character who has to "watch, check, count, measure, and plan") or to a renunciation of all control (e.g., the so-called hysteric who notes "I'm a blob, helpless" and is unable to control anything). Competency in managing time is a theme identified in several of the time-experience questionnaires – for example, in Calabresi and Cohen's (1968) temporal factors of Time Submissiveness ("It is important to make good use of your time") and Time Possessiveness ("Time spent sleeping is wasted time").

The theme of Change/Continuity, or "becoming in time," emerges in all of the various stages of human development, from the child's first establishment of object permanence to his or her coming to terms with mortality in midlife. The child's notion of object permanence (Piaget, 1927/1969) and its interpersonal counterpart, object constancy (Mahler et al., 1975), emerge out of repeated, reliable experiences of change within a context of reassuring continuity. The concept of "trust in time" (Erikson, 1956) speaks to a faith that time will continue to unfold in a reliable and life-sustaining manner. An individual's "temporal perspective" (Getsinger, 1976) evolves over the life span, with certain events serving to highlight the changing or continuous nature of existence – for example, puberty, which highlights the end of the beginning, and midlife, which highlights the beginning of the end (Colarusso, 1991). The ultimate appreciation of the changing yet continuous nature of life seems to concern an appreciation for life as a cycle of birth, death, and rebirth. Rituals celebrating the cyclic regeneration of time are common across cultures, including our own image of the new year as a baby and the preceding year as an old man cut down by the scythe of time (Pollock, 1971).

Finally, the theme of Fast/Slow, or tempo, appears throughout the psychological research literature as the single most salient aspect to the human experience of time. Our most rudimentary sense of time originates in the tempo of bodily processes: feeding and sleep cycles, breathing, pulse, elimination (Fenichel, 1945). The tempo of time itself – the sense of whether time "goes" fast or slow – varies by emotional state, personality trait, and/ or situational location. Since the theme of tempo most often was described by present participants in conjunction with one or more of the remaining themes, the question may arise as to which of these themes is focal when time is reported as "going" too fast or too slow. The literature on the asynchrony of feeding cycles between mother and infant seems to concern the tempo of "having in time" (Yates, 1935), and the literature describing the urgent, time-rushed tempos of the Type A personality seems to focus on "doing in time" (Yarnold & Grimm, 1982), whereas the literature concerning depressed patients, who describe experiences of time as slowed down and a future devoid of personal meaning (Kuhs, 1991), seems to involve disruptions in an individual's ongoing sense of becoming in time.

Relevance for Clinical Issues

If time is a major ground to human existence, we would expect certain diagnostic categories used by clinical practitioners to exhibit identifying characteristics with regard to the patient's experience of time. Throughout the psychological literature, there have been frequent references to differences in the temporal experiences of different personality types and of individuals in different affective states, and the present collection of themes should prove useful in organizing existing theoretical notions about the psychopathology of temporal experiences into a more extended conceptual framework.

The temporal theme of Now/Never would seem, most accurately, to describe those individuals who cannot wait: addicts, sociopaths, and other individuals for whom "having it now" is a (or the) driving force in their lives. Fenichel (1945) long ago noted that people having specific substance addictions tend to view other people not as individuals but, more globally, as "deliverers of needed supplies". For such individuals, the exigencies of the moment were described as transcending concern for what had gone before, or what was yet to come.

A different view of the Now/Never theme has been offered by LeShan (1952), who notes that the child who grows up on the streets experiences quick sequences of tension and relief: "One does not frustrate oneself for long periods or plan action with goals far in the future. The future generally is an indefinite, vague, diffuse region, and its rewards and punishments are too uncertain to have much motivating value." Getsinger's (1976) study of the temporal perspective of the sociopath confirms the notion that such individuals live in a fleeting present that is only weakly related either to past behavior or to future possibilities.

The temporal theme of Limits/Choices captures the experience of those individuals for whom control is a significant personal issue. The individual diagnosed as obsessive, or as obsessive-compulsive, is probably the one most often identified with this issue. Again, Fenichel (1945) was among the first clinical practitioners to note that psychological maneuvers such as are defining of the so-called obsessive-compulsive individual seem to originate in a mistrust of the natural flow of things, particularly those aspects of the world that cannot be controlled, such as time or emotion. A later theorist (Ingram, 1979) noted that the obsessive-compulsive individual is "mystified by time as a constant flow of reality that refuses to be pinned down" and, thus, "uses time to organize his life and help save him from sinking into what may seem to him a morass of memories, fantasies, and fleeting thoughts."

The theme of Change/Continuity seems to capture the experience of individuals whose primary clinical issues concern the sensible unfolding of past, present, and future. Such individuals may be given over to excessive introspection, thereby suggesting that they continuously ruminate on the meaning of life and, if something is found to be lacking, become depressed. When such an individual becomes depressed, the future is experienced as losing its meaning, and the person comes to characterize such a loss as a loss in his or her sense of a sensible unfolding in time. In pathological mourning, to take one further and more specific example, the person attempts to "stop the clock" by mulling over what he or she might have done to prevent the loss; under these conditions, present and future are both robbed of their vitality and meaning (Spiegel, 1981).

Issues of change and continuity also emerge in regard to the psychotherapist, who may be considered as both a "condenser and dilator" (Kafka, 1972) of time, since it is he or she who allows the patient to venture through past, present, and future in order to enable a reintegration of temporal experiences and, concomitantly, to help in the development of a more cohesive sense of personal organization. The most profound difficulty with coming to terms with the natural unfolding of life concerns an acceptance of our own death:

Death is the epitome of narcissistic mortification. For each individual, death is the end of his time, the moment of death the extinction of the self, the final experience of self-awareness. To confound this inevitable vicissitude of time, man has created art, science and religion; nonetheless, he remains impotent against the inexorable passage of time. (Arlow, 1986, p. 525)

One final way in which to relate the present thematic structure to an understanding of clinical praxis concerns the diagnostic category known as the *character disorder*. According to Miller (1964), a person diagnosed as a character disorder may be characterized somewhat fancifully as attempting to "walk through snow without leaving footprints" – that is, by behaving as if potentialities are never lost or left behind. Consider the following quote from one such individual:

About a career, I hope you won't laugh, but I have given serious thought to medicine. Being in the hospital all these times does teach you something. . . . You want to know how much schooling I've had? Well, I almost finished. I was going to take the GED test in the Army, but I never got to it. I imagine if I went back and talked to the principal of that high school that. . . . (Miller, 1964, p. 535)

Why does this individual demonstrate such disregard for the realities of his life? How can he overlook the fact that what he has done will shape what he has and will become? In Miller's terms, this individual has become an "ahistoric" person, one for whom the "meaningful relationship between the moment at hand and those which are past and future does not exist." How does an awareness of the relationship between past, present, and future, an awareness of change within a context of continuity, develop for most of us, and what has gone wrong in the case of an individual diagnosed as a "character disorder?"

According to Miller, rudimentary experiences of change and continuity begin with an awareness that "the loved one returns," a situation that provides the basis for a variety of experiences such as "I am the kind of person who lives in the kind of world where people do return," or "I'm worth returning to." Thus, the cohesiveness of time for both the character-disorder individual and the rest of us depends on the repeated and reliable gratification of needs early in life. Without the experience of a loved other person who returns, the child and, later, the adult will not have an opportunity to learn to wait, with the consequences that his or her experience of time will always remain that of Now or Never. Writes Miller (1964): "Unable to tie together moments in time, [the character disorder] never develops a sense of future and history but lives instead a mode of existence which is marked by its impulsiveness and discontinuity" (p. 537).

Without the context of a meaningful sense of personal continuity – or of the potential for becoming in time – the character disorder is unable to make authentic meaningful choices or to accept the limits implied by those choices that would give significance to his life. For the person living this type of existence, everything must always seem possible; unfortunately, the price for such a stance is that nothing can ever be experienced as real, and Miller (1964) is led to conclude, somewhat more generally, that "the vitality of life resides in an awareness of the necessity of choosing and surrendering. By accepting one potentiality, we surrender another. By surrendering no potentiality, we lose them all" (p. 539). In this, the paradox of the individual diagnosed as a "character disorder" yields a more general conclusion about human life: Each of us must always choose, and every choice we make necessarily involves a limit and a renunciation. Although this fact of existence shows up in a number of different contexts, it probably appears nowhere more poignantly than in our relationship to and with time.

5

The Human Experience of Other People

For psychology, few questions are as fundamental as those of how we stand in relation to others of our kind. Independent of the type of psychology in which we engage, or the theoretical tradition we reflect, an account of how we experience other people needs to be given. The primacy of our experiences with other people was well noted by William James (1890) when he wrote:

We are not only gregarious animals, liking to be in sight of our fellows, but we have an innate propensity to get ourselves noticed, and noticed favorably, by our kind. No more fiendish punishment could be devised, were such a thing physically possible, than that one should be turned loose in a society and remain absolutely unnoticed by all the members thereof. If no one turned round when we entered, answered when we spoke, or minded what we did, but if every person we met "cut us dead", and acted as if we were nonexisting things, a kind of rage and impotent despair would ere long well up in us, from which the cruellest bodily tortures would be relief. (p. 201)

From Allport to Zimbardo, each of social psychology's major practitioners may be viewed as attempting to deal with some aspect of other people and their effects on the individual. Attribution, attraction, and person perception are but a few of the subtopics emerging from social psychology to focus attention on specific aspects of this question.

The attempt to understand the experience and effects of the other on the self is not a question unique to social psychology. From the early writings of Aristotle, Hegel, and Nietzsche to the somewhat later writings of Freud and McDougall, to the more recent writings of Goffman and Schutz, the question of the other has been, and continues to be, of great importance to psychology. What is clear in all of these writings is that any proper apprecia-

This chapter is based in part on the unpublished research conducted by Bethany Nowell and presented in part at the 1991 Meetings of the Southeastern Psychological Association in New Orleans, LA.

tion for what it means to be human must consider the sociopersonal world into which human existence is thrown. Along with the major grounds of time and body, a phenomenology of the other is necessary to contextualize any attempt at describing human experience. Since traditional psychology also considered this topic of importance, it turns out that there is much to be said from a number of different perspectives, the most significant of which are provided by psychoanalytic psychology, phenomenological sociology, and existential philosophy.

The Psychoanalytic Perspective

The hallmark of early Freudian psychology was its insistence on biological determinism. The whole of personality development was viewed in terms of the epigenetic significance of specific bodily zones such as the mouth, anus, and genitals. Because society does not tolerate the open satisfaction of urges associated with these zones, the infant, and later the child and adult, are forced to renounce erotic satisfactions associated with them. This is accomplished by finding a substitute form of gratification, as in the case of sublimation, or by repressing the pleasure deriving from one or more of these zones. Sometimes repression would lead to fixation on a particular bodily zone, such that the person could give up neither the object nor the aim of a particular developmental stage. Under this theory, all adult tendencies are capable of being traced back to their relevant developmental period, and Freud offered a typology of neuroses based on the vicissitudes of libido.

Within this view, other people serve one of two possible roles: They satisfy or they frustrate the developing infant. Thus, Freud (1914/1957) linked early experiences with the mother to a type of sexually satisfying, auto-eroticism that was related to nourishment. The first love, however, was a love of self, a feeling based on pleasurable body sensations. The mother was an object of love but only insofar as she provided body pleasure. A similar line of analysis was applied to later experiences of satisfaction and frustration: The other was significant to the degree that his or her actions affected the self in a relatively direct biological way.

The biological orientation of the theory also emerges in Freud's emphasis on instinctual desires grappling with external frustrations. All significant instinctual processes originate in the id, whose primary purpose is to attain pleasure through the release of tension. The world does not always cooperate with these desires, so the ego arises to serve as an interface between the id and the world of people and objects. A final aspect of the person, the superego, derives from the child's attempts to satisfy, or please, the parents as they seek to incorporate social mores and values into the child. Although the superego is the bearer of social morality, it remains a part of the interior world and, together with the id, places a number of constraints on the successful functioning of the ego largely by making the person feel anxious over certain real or projected actions.

From his clinical work, Freud (e.g., 1895/1966) also introduced the world of others in terms of the concepts of transference and countertransference. As is well known, transference is the tendency of a patient to repeat, in therapy, prior ways of relating to significant figures in his or her (usually past) life. Countertransference is a therapeutic mistake should the therapist respond in a manner appropriate to the past figure but not appropriate to the present situation (i.e., by scolding the patient as if he or she were the parent and the patient were the child). What both phenomena attest to is the very human tendency to structure present relationships in terms of past ones, and to lose sight of present possibilities in the confusing jumble of interactions. The significance of these phenomena was not lost on Freud, who eventually came to see transference and its interpretation as among the most significant aspects of psychoanalytic psychotherapy.

Despite the success of early psychoanalysis in describing the development of personality in both its normal and neurotic modes, the theory remained one in which the biological world took precedence over the interpersonal world of the child and later the adult. By giving precedence to instincts over relationships, Freud set in motion a line of reasoning that emphasized internal conflict as a basic component of what it means to be a person. A more recent version of psychoanalytic theory known as *object relations theory* (e.g., Mitchell, 1988) assumes that the baby is born not only with biological instincts but with a tendency to relate to other people. Unfortunately, this relational tendency is structured not only in terms of pleasure-seeking instincts but in terms of destructive ones as well. Since the destructive instincts are initially more salient, the infant strives to distance itself from the tension created by these instincts by externalizing them as "not mine." This is done to make the "internal" world safer, although the price of such "projection" is that the world is experienced in a paranoid way (i.e., as potentially damaging to me).

Using Freudian theory as her base, Klein (1928) suggested that the superego serves to arouse anxiety over the infant's destructive tendencies toward others and their (expected) retaliation. In explaining this cycle of aggression toward and from the other, the infant becomes aware of its differentiation from the world setting in motion its earliest intimations of a me and a you. Two consequences of the projected aggression-retribution cycle also are of importance. (1) Reactions to the infant's "aggression," as in the case where it bites the mother's breast, are transformed by the mother into one in which no retaliation is experienced. On this basis, the infant comes to realize that there is a "me" who is doing the projecting and some other person who is doing the responding. (2) Since the infant has little or no capacity to integrate "good" and "bad" feelings, the image of the satisfying mother is experienced as separate from that of the frustrating mother. Although the child eventually does come to recognize the needed person as a totality with good and bad features, such integration will only take place on the basis of repeated dealings with the mother in which she provides a good-enough (and not a perfect) environment for such learning to take place.

What these theories suggest (see Fairbairn, 1952) is that it is in the nature of babies to relate to others and to have others relate to them. Although the significant world is still an "inner" one, it is now of a fully personal nature. In this world, all of the infant's early relationships are symbolized, some of which are realistic and some of which are not. It is the job of continuing experience with other people to emphasize the realistic ones and to keep in check those that promise too much in the way of excitement or rejection. The process of growth is to bring these so-called splits together into a cohesive unit that will come to define the world of the person in his or her relationships to other people.

This emphasis on a cohesive sense of self finds further development in the psychoanalytic theories of Kohut (1984), whose main concern is to chronicle the development of what he calls a "healthy and cohesive self." In contrast to earlier psychoanalytic notions of how such development progresses, Kohut believes it is based both on empathic attunement of the caregiver with the child as well as on "optimal frustrations" of the child by the caregiver. Optimal frustrations are those experiences of the child in which failures of empathy on the part of the caregiver allow the child to develop a capacity to manage anxiety and to experience a self different from the caregiver. Optimal frustrations do not facilitate healthy development unless they occur in the context of a healthy relationship.

Empirical Research on Attachment Behaviors in Children

Much of this theoretical emphasis on interpersonal aspects of development finds an empirical counterpart in the work of Bowlby and Ainsworth (e.g., Bowlby, 1958; Ainsworth, 1985, 1989). In his earliest work, Bowlby observed infants who had been removed from their parents and placed in the care of strangers. Using the ethological concept of instinctive action patterns, Bowlby postulated "primary drives of clinging and/or following which are capable potentially of tying infant to mother." This shift from an emphasis on physiological drives to interpersonal ones represented a break with classical psychoanalytic theory. In attempting to place his views in relation to more classical ones, Bowlby (1958) noted that "Whereas Freud's later theories conceive of the organism as starting with a quantum of unstructured psychic energy which during development becomes progressively more structured, ethology conceives of it as starting with a number of highly structured responses which in the course of development become so elaborated, through processes of integration and learning . . . that the resulting behavior is of amazing variety and plasticity" (pp. 364–365).

Significant additions to attachment theory and research have been made by Ainsworth. Using a number of standard laboratory procedures, in combination with relevant fieldwork, Ainsworth assessed individual differences in infant attachment behaviors that could be related to later behavioral patterns as well as to personal functioning as a whole. Sometimes specific findings were presented that were contrary to popular beliefs concerning child rearing; thus, Ainsworth found that a mother's prompt responsiveness to an infant's crying led the infant to less crying and fussiness later on rather than to more crying and fussing. A second example revealed that picking up a child when he or she initiated bodily contact fostered self-reliance and tended to eliminate clingy behavior (Ainsworth, 1985).

Other researchers have also turned their attention to patterns of attachment in the years beyond infancy (e.g., Ainsworth, 1989; Main, Kaplan, & Cassidy, 1985; Sroufe, 1979). In general, these results suggest that throughout "the first year, the infant gradually builds up expectations of regularities of what happens to him or her. At first these are primitive, as the infant's sleep–wake and other cycles become adapted to caregiving rhythms, but at some stage . . . the infant begins to organize these expectations internally into 'working models' of the physical environment, attachment figures, and himself or herself" (Ainsworth, 1989, p. 710). As the child continues to develop, the capacity to influence others through language, coupled with a confidence in the stability of "mutual understanding" between family members, enables the child to tolerate increasingly longer periods of separation. Increased locomotor abilities also allow the child to wander from the side of the mother and to establish relationships with playmates.

In both theory and research, the psychoanalytic tradition sets in motion an organism other people respond to primarily in terms of satisfying or frustrating it. For this tradition, the organism is a biological entity that develops into an effective self only if conditions are right. In this system, the other person functions primarily with respect to the needs, wishes, and desires of the infant. As a consequence of its experiences with other people, images of past interactions are "taken into," and represented in, the self as beneficent or malevolent. Every present interaction takes its initial form from prior interactions, with the total process called *transference*. If the other person resists transferential categorization, a more contemporaneous patterning emerges that is distinct from prior ones based on the transferred template. Society is internalized in the form of a superego, whose essential function is to restrain and, later, modulate satisfaction. Often, the superego is instituted in the form of specific "internal objects" (i.e., people) who speak to the self in a form usually referred to as *conscience*.

The Phenomenological Perspective

If psychoanalysis views everything important about other people as within the self, the phenomenological tradition places major emphasis on the person in the present situation. From a phenomenological perspective, such as that described by Schutz in 1932, other people are experienced in terms of four temporally organized worlds including the immediate world of others (called *Umwelt*), the world of contemporaries (*Mitwelt*), the world of predecessors (*Vorwelt*), and the world of successors (*Folgewelt*). Of these worlds, only individuals in my *Umwelt* are directly experienced, and only members of my *Mitwelt* may become directly present to me.

How I experience and relate to other people depends upon the specific world in which they are "located" for me. The most characteristic and, therefore, most significant human realm is that of face-to-face interaction. Within this domain, I may either assume an impersonal (or They) orientation toward the other or a more personal (or You) orientation; only the second circumstance defines the basis of a true face-to-face situation. Within the context of a You orientation, all interactions are defined by the experience of a simultaneous You orientation by the other and by the self, and only in the context of such a relationship is it possible to attain a genuine understanding of the other person. Such understanding is a directly embodied perception, not an intuition or a judgment. Although many psychologists might prefer to use words like "infer" or "read" to describe how we understand other people in face-to-face interactions, the social phenomenologist suggests that the process is direct and unreflected and, therefore, very much like ordinary perceptual "seeing" (e.g., Gibson, 1979).

Although it is quite true that as we become more socially sophisticated we may try to "hide" the meaning of our actions – for example, stage fright by actors or lecturers – it is also true that the specific form a behavior takes will sometimes reveal its meaning. In his analysis of laughing, for example, Pollio (1983) noted that the behavior of laughter, as a perceptual form for someone other than the laugher, presents the physiognomy of an "explosion." For the laugher, the experience is similar – a release from the ordinary constraints of the social world which, for the moment, leaves the person "lighter" and "freer." Within the context of this dual experience by the perceiver and the laugher, the conclusion must be that the behavioral form presents the experience of the laugher, and that interpersonal "understanding" of this experience is direct, especially if the other person joins in with laughter of his/her own.

But not all behaviors are as directly comprehensible as laughter. In fact, many of the actions that we engage in as adults are designed to cover too clear an expression of our feelings, and it is at this point that inference is required to "read" the meaning of someone else's behavior. In its most pernicious form, such actions transform face-to-face interactions from We situations into situations of impression-management or even deception, and it is at this point that Goffman's (1959) analysis of the self–other dialectic as analogous to a staged performance is most revealing. In this approach, social interaction is viewed as an attempt to manage the impression that one makes by treating the other as an audience to be convinced and, perhaps, even conned. To this end, all sorts of rituals are performed, including the development of a personally useful "line" (termed face) designed to promote the interests of the actor. The metaphors of to "gain face" and to "lose face" provide testimony to Goffman's somewhat estranged views of how self and other experience one another in the prototypical situation of face-to-face interaction.

Goffman's analysis of contemporary society offers a relatively manipulative view of relationships. Even if the aim were not to manipulate the other, but simply to get along, the cumulative effect of self-presentation would be to promote distance between people. Under these conditions of modern life, it is not surprising to find that much of contemporary social psychology concerns such topics as forming impressions or attributing reasons for the actions of others. These interests suggest that we experience others as events to understand rather than as people to be experienced. There is a peculiar distance involved when the meaning of the other, either to himself or to us, requires a reflective rather than a perceptual act. Although it may be too strong to say that the drama of communal life requires distance, deception, discretion, and deliberation, it does not seem wrong to say that we frequently experience the other as an event to be understood rather than one to be encountered.

One of the more useful descriptions of the multiple relations possible in the face-to-face situation is provided by Luft and Ingram (e.g., Luft, 1969) in their playful matrix of human interaction known as the *Johari Window*. This analytic device begins with the explication of a two-by-two matrix in which one dimension is labeled "known to other" and "not known to other" and in which the second dimension is labeled "known to self" and "not known to self." This arrangement yields four cells: Open (known to self/ known to other), Blind (not known to self/known to other), Hidden (Not known to other/known to self) and Unknown (Not known to self/not known to other). The words used to characterize each cell indicate Luft and Ingram's attitude toward that cell, with the Open cell being the most desirable for face-to-face interactions and with the Hidden and Blind cells indicating less desirable aspects of such interaction. If we take Goffman's analysis seriously, these two cells represent ways of gaining and losing face. As should be obvious, every face-to-face interaction partakes of these three possible sets of relationship between the self and the other.

But what about the Unknown cell? Is it just a logical extension of the structure of the diagram? Luft (1969), in discussing this quadrant, notes that although we and the other may fear the unknown in our interaction, it is an area of possibility for both of us. This assertion suggests that the self and the other frequently do unexpected things in relation that could not be done in isolation. Quadrant 4 is the emergent region in any interpersonal relationship, and it contains "untapped resources" for the person and the other. Only when something "Unknown" comes into the "Open" does a relationship develop in new and meaningful ways.

Face-to-face interaction takes place not only between pairs of people – what social psychology calls a *dyad* – but in larger collectivities described as groups ranging from three to a hundred thousand or more. The specific numbers are unimportant; what *is* important is our experience of groups and our place in them, and this insight forms the core of a phenomenological (or a Gestalt) analysis of social behavior. Without going into any of the specific details of work by such early pioneers as Lewin, Heider, and Asch, the core assumption is easily derived from more general Gestalt perceptual theory – namely, that society as both an objective fact and a perceptual experience serves as a continuing ground for any and all experience. Within this context, the group is transformed into an experiential Gestalt and may be described in terms of such familiar principles of perceptual organization as cohesiveness or, more generally, structure.

Group influences are not usually experienced in a reflected mode of awareness. Asch's (1951) classic studies (as well as others; e.g., by Sherif, 1936) describe the effect of group influence on such perceptual judgments as the estimation of the length of a line or the amount by which an erratic light was seen to move. For this approach, the mere presence of other people does not necessarily imply that I will experience myself as "in a group." Although the presence of other people does lead me not to perform behaviors that are essentially solitary, such as injecting myself with insulin, the mere presence of other people is sometimes of little more significance than any other object – for example, when I walk around someone to get to the door.

Probably one of the more interesting experiences we have of being in a group concerns the difference between crowds and mobs. Within the context of historically significant crowds, such as civil rights demonstrations in the late 1960s, the crucial experience both for members of the crowd as well as for nonmembers was the sheer number of individuals. For purposeful crowds such as these, each person, although not identifiable by his or her uniqueness, still assumes responsibility for both him- or herself and his or her peers. Such crowds usually disperse peacefully unless engaged by some outside force attempting to disrupt the sense of purpose and we-ness represented by the crowd.

Not all crowds are orderly or brought together within a setting in which each individual takes responsibility for personal actions. Sometimes crowds congeal around highly charged social or personal issues, run amok, and perform antisocial acts such as vandalism or lynching; when this occurs, the crowd has become a mob, and no individual is or wants to be responsible for what goes on. Although mobs sometimes provide rallying points for historical change – as in the storming of the Bastille or in the opening moments of the Russian Revolution – they are usually much more local in cause and consequence. A historically significant mob is one that is able to transcend itself and become something other than a mob – a "something" that comes to embody and carry forward the ideas that historians will later give to it.

These ideas are central to Sartre's grand thesis concerning social behavior, politics, and history – his so-called Critique of Dialectical Reason. In the introduction to *Search for A Method* (1960/1963), Sartre uses the pair of terms signified/signifying and signifying/signified in an attempt to describe the role of mob action in historical change. He notes that the historically significant mob – say the one storming the Bastille – is traditionally viewed as a collection of anonymous individuals who are *signified* by their act. The act, of course, is *signifying* of social change, political revolution, and a change in the course of history. Sartre admonishes us, however, to recognize that any *signifying* event can only be *signified* when the individual chooses to act with significance. What this analysis is meant to suggest is that an individual in either a crowd or a mob experiences him- or herself differently than in other situations. In perceptual terms, the individual in a mob seems for the duration of the event to experience a loss of personal boundedness and, with it, any clear articulation of what is and is not permissible. Although it may be going too far to describe the person in a mob as having no individual configuration, it does seem that personal organization is experienced as less well formed and more defined by the ever-changing currents of the mob. The mob, rather than the person, is the better-defined figure, and the person may not even recognize him- or herself after the event is over.

These descriptions all concern aspects of the social world present to me in the here-and-now – what Schutz (and before him, von Uexkull) termed the *Umwelt*. The world of others is a complex one composed not only by those with whom I am presently interacting but also by those I can know only indirectly: my contemporaries, my ancestors (more broadly, my predecessors), and my successors. Although it is difficult to describe how Schutz means for these classes of relationships to affect the self, it is possible to consider them as ground conditions against which all present interactions emerge as figural. My contemporary experience of other people is, thus, consistently grounded by my taught, imagined, recalled, or projected experience with others who lived before me, who will live after me, or who only lived as heroes and heroines in the book I read or have read.

In a famous passage, Schutz (1932/1967) presents his description of the world of contemporaries, and we could do no better than to quote it in full:

Entering the world of contemporaries itself, we pass through one region after another: (1) the region of those whom I once encountered face to face and could encounter again (for instance, my absent friend); then (2) comes the region of those once encountered by the person I am now talking to (for instance, your friend, whom you are promising to introduce to me); next (3) the region of those who are as yet *pure* contemporaries but whom I will soon meet (such as the colleague whose books I have read and whom I am now on my way to visit); then (4) those contemporaries of whose existence I know, not as concrete individuals, but as points in social space as defined by a certain function (for instance, the postal employee who will process my letter); then (5) those collective entities whose function and organization I know while not being able to name any of their members, such as the Canadian Parliament; then (6) collective entities which are by their very nature anonymous and of which I could never in principle have direct experience, such as "state" and "nation"; then (7) objective configurations of meaning which have been instituted in the world of my contemporaries and which live a kind of anonymous life of their own, such as the interstate commerce clause and the rules of French grammar; and finally (8) artifacts of any kind which bear witness to . . . some unknown person. (pp. 180–81)

The further the I moves into the world of its contemporaries, the more likely it is to encounter a world generated by others and populated by social realities similar to those enumerated in items (5) through (8). For this reason, it is important to describe how we experience the world of others as it is transformed into law, rule, symbol, or artifact – in short, into the world of other people not having a direct presence. To attempt this task, Berger and Luckmann (1966) suggest that we follow two seemingly contradictory maxims: one from Durkheim – "Consider social facts as things" – and a second from Weber – "For sociology, the object of cognition is the subjective meaning-complex of action."

The significance of these quotes is made clear by the titles of the second and third major sections of Berger and Luckmann's text: "Society as Objective Reality" and "Society as Subjective Reality." The first, or Durkheimian, aspect of social reality is given by an experience of the immutability (i.e., "thingness") of certain aspects of the social world such as its institutions, laws, and social rules. For every person born into, or living in, a specific culture, the institutions of that culture are experienced as fixed aspects of the personal world, and the individual's life is experienced as an episode located in an objective history of heroes and villains, rules and roles. The society is experienced as external to the person, and the person's mode of being takes place in regard to a persistent reality defined by society experienced as an objective thing.

The actions and meanings of the individual also depend upon subjective meanings, to come now to Weber's maxim, on the basis of "external" enforcements such as laws and by personal "oughts" internalized from the social order as conscience. It is here that other people, such as parents or teachers, in their role as primary socializing agents, attain the role assigned them by psychoanalysis – namely, as satisfiers and frustrators. It is also here (and in other situations termed secondary socializations) that conscience and identity develop, with crucial experiences relating to the punitive and rewarding role played by significant others as well as to experiences of the other as a mirror for the self. The first of these roles is described in terms close to those used by psychoanalysis and, to some degree, it is Berger and Luckmann's purpose to effect a rapprochement between Freudian psychology and phenomenological theory. Viewing the other as mirror, likewise, is concerned with theoretical rapprochement, this time between the Meadian concept of the looking-glass self and those of psychoanalysis and sociological theory. It is only in the second case that the other is rendered as a complex perceptual event, and it is the experience of the other-as-mirror that is most emphasized by Berger and Luckmann.

If we combine Mead's description of the other-as-mirror with the obvious fact that some people are more significant than others, we come to the concept of significant other – or to those specific others responsible for primary socialization. As should be obvious, the most long-lasting and significant mirroring that takes place concerns significant others, and if there is any incongruity between the person and the mirroring provided, the person will experience the situation as distressing. Although some distress will result if personal feelings and mirroring by nonsignificant others are in conflict, the distress will be much less powerful in this case, and the person may seek significant other(s) for help. In field terms, the mirroring provided by significant others is more articulated and compelling than by nonsignificant others. Here, as elsewhere, other people are construed as complex perceptual events having greater or lesser degrees of differentiation and/or significance for the self.

Whether the other is experienced as a mirror (Mead) or audience (Goffman), the important point is that the other's significance is given in terms of a synchrony between its actions and my actions. In the case of an audience metaphor, the effect of the self on the other seems more designed to impress than to gain direct support. In the case of a mirror, the synchrony between self and other is more direct and provides feedback concerning my actions. In addition to their role as mirror or audience, there are two other ways in which the self may experience the other and vice versa – as an object or as a dialogical partner – and these two possibilities form the basis of an existential approach to our experiences of, and with, other people.

The Existential Perspective

The existential analysis of the role that other people play in human life is frequently couched in terms of the specific situation of dialogue or, more simply, conversation. This situation is an extremely useful one for describing experiences of other people since conversation, considered as a social act, partakes of the many roles possible between two people.

One aspect of language that makes it a unique interactional domain concerns the structured nature of the system taken up and used by partners in the dialogue. Every culture contrives to have its members speak its own specific tongue, and each tongue has both silent constraints and public possibilities. Although it may be going too far to view different languages as fundamentally untranslatable, it is true, nonetheless, that what is easily sayable in one language is not so easily sayable in a different one. One does not have to go as far as Whorf (1956) did to realize that a language expresses both a culture and a style of life.

This insight has been strongly emphasized and developed in the social constructivist literature, where already established linguistic usage is afforded a significant role in the way we structure our experience of any and all topics. Within Berger and Luckmann's (1966) version of the theory, language is characterized as one of the major "objectifiers" of social and personal experience. Even though it originates in the face-to-face situation, language also is useful for experiencing the not-here and not-now, not only in terms of writing but in terms of hypothetical events and ideas that need never have been experienced directly. Just as language frees me from my here-and-now, so too it forces me to observe its rules and patterns and to notice those aspects of my world made figural by having a name – my self, my group, my country, and so on. These "typifications," as Berger and Luckmann term them, have a sense of anonymity to them since any specific experience labeled (and categorized) by language can be replaced by any other falling in the same category.

Language offers a bridge to different areas of everyday reality as well as a way to integrate my experience with those of my contemporaries. Within language, the influence of other people extends beyond the here-and-now. Through language, they not only are able to help or hinder me; they also are present to me in terms of their ideas and values. Language provides an unnoticed influence on all aspects of my life, including situations I have never been present to nor am likely to experience directly. If we add the influence that language makes possible in terms of knowledge, the massive role that other people and their ideas play in my life reaches significant proportions. Even if language-based influences are construed as ground rather than figure, we can always reflect on them as linguistics does, or make them into artistic objects as poetry and literature do. Aside from face-to-face interactions – which usually also involve speaking – there is no other aspect of the interpersonal world that influences social life as significantly as the sedimented speakings that we know as language.

The existential approach to speaking does not focus on language, however, but on the face-to-face situation of speaking. This emphasis suggests that conversation provides a paradigmatic case for discerning how we experience other people across the gulf created by technology, rational philosophy, and popular culture. For Heidegger (1927/1962), language is the magical route by which human beings achieve connectedness to one another and, more significantly, to Being itself. The language of Being is neither the "idle chatter" or gossip of everyday life nor is it the hyperprecise and asceptic language of science and technology; rather, the language of Being is poetry, metaphor, and wordplay, all of which abound in

Heidegger's own writings and provide the way for human beings to dwell meaningfully in the world.

Unfortunately, contemporary humankind does not dwell poetically and seems determined to alienate itself from others of its kind and, even, from existence itself. Such Fallenness takes many different forms; in regard to others, it concerns my feelings about people as "Them" (*Das Man*) and their feelings about me as a "them." The impersonality of *Das Man*, when referring to You and I, serves to alienate us from what Heidegger sees as the essential task of personal existence: to recontact the authentic nature of human existence from within the midst of a situation into which we have been thrown (i.e., contemporary culture). Within the context of this analysis, other people are, or may become, the distractors of each self from the pursuit of authentic being.

Although Heidegger's answer, as to how we are to reappropriate personal meaning, is in terms of an honest confrontation with nonbeing, we should not miss two implications of this view: (1) each person achieves authentic existence – being-to-death – alone; and (2) an authentic confrontation with death involves facing the possibility that all which is significant for meaningful life will be lost, including my relatedness to others. Although the first implication suggests that our life with others may sometimes be a barrier to authentic existence, the second implication suggests that one of the reasons death is so difficult is that it specifies other people as one aspect of what it is that will be lost. As Rollo May (1983) noted, we share the experience of being-to-death only with other people, and such commonality lends a difference to relationships between Me and You and between Me and some object or theory. What differentiates the two is the experience the I has of a shared destiny with You.

If Heidegger is not optimistic about the role that others play in our quest for authenticity, Sartre is even less sanguine. One aspect of the Sartrean view is to be found in the oft-quoted line from the play *No Exit*: "Hell is other people." Within the context of the play, which concerns a triangle of relationships involving a weak man, a strong lesbian, and a third woman desired by both, the quote suggests that others are unable to fulfill the desires of the self and serve only to lead the self to no exit from an essentially bleak and alienating existence.

Two additional situations fill out the Sartrean view of the self–other dialectic; one concerns love, and the second, being looked at by another. Sartre's analysis of the first situation involves a complex dialectic between master and slave and between being-for-itself and being-in-itself. The core aspect to his analysis is that the lover seeks, as free agent, the possession of the other person as object while requiring the beloved to remain as much a free agent as possible. The same set of relationships also holds from the side of the other; namely, I am to be possessed as an object while still retaining as many aspects of being free as possible. Neither I, nor the one I desire, can ever get what we want, and all sorts of complex relationships are possible, including that of a masochistic relationship in which the other gives up his or her freedom so as to live as my "unfree" object.

Sartre's analysis of love derives from a contrast between being-for-itself and being-in-itself. In his analysis of this relationship, Sartre describes the vain attempt of consciousness to turn itself into a thing at the same time as it recognizes its own freedom. Within social science, the hypothesis that human behavior is determined derives from this exercise of bad faith in regard to personal freedom. Sartre's analysis of love arises from a similar matrix of interrelationships; namely, it is impossible for being-for-itself to reduce itself or any other human being to only a single form of being. Like all human projects, love is incomplete, and no matter how "perfect" the love between two people, there is no possibility of perfect harmony – love, like all other human projects, exists in an essential and unresolvable tension.

Sartre's analysis of human relationships also applies to his approach to being-for-others. The major aspect of this analysis concerns his discussion of the Look, a situation in which someone is looking at me and I feel vulnerable under his or her gaze. Consider the famous example of a person looking through a keyhole to catch someone in a compromising situation; at that moment, I control the situation, and the other is totally dominated by my gaze. Now suppose, to continue the example, that someone catches me in this situation; I now become the object and feel captured by the look of the other. In neither case has there been any contact between two human beings; only two people objectified by each other's stare. Although the stare of another makes my body an object for him or her, my personal experience is that of shame; being looked at by someone else who finds me wanting or, in Sartre's case, as simply an unfree object.

Sartre's analysis of the gaze partakes of the same unflattering social dialectic of being-for-itself reduced to the impossible situation of being-in-itself. In terms of my experience of other people, it seems clear that I have only two possibilities: I can attempt to turn him or her into an object (i.e., rob the person of freedom), or I can accept domination by the other and accept being an object for him or her. In both cases, as is the case of loving, I can neither make the other or myself into an object because I cannot give up my freedom. The generalization of this experience is that the existence of even one other person always yields the possibility of my (or the other's) reduction to a thing. We are both always at risk, and this risk is not accidental; it is an essential aspect of social existence.

Standing in contrast to these views of Sartre and, to a lesser extent, Heidegger are those of Martin Buber (1923/1970). Buber is no Pollyanna; he does see the inauthentic and the stultifying in the contemporary social world. At the same time, however, he sees the chance of unexpected possibilities in his description of the I–Thou experience. Buber's analysis begins with the declaration that the world is twofold in accordance with the words we speak: I–It and I–Thou. What this means is that every I – every person – takes some relational stand in regard to the social and natural world, and it is in this stand that the specific nature of the I appears. Because the pattern of this relationship defines what sort of person the I is, the I of an I–Thou relationship is different from the I of an I–It relationship. In the case of I–It, the person relates to everything in his or her world as an object the I can use or manipulate. The world of I–It is set in time and space: It involves order, categories, laws, and regulations. It is a world of things that can be sensed, understood, used, and categorized.

The world that Buber calls "Thou" is not set in the world of time and space as we usually understand them. It does not offer logic, use, or order as its consequence: I–Thou is a domain of "pure relation" where all there is, is relating – what Buber calls "meeting." To meet another human being as Thou, the I has to stop being a particular He or She, Person, or Thing. If and when this happens, the other person truly becomes Thou, the I truly becomes I, and both I and Thou live in the light of the pure relationship of I and Thou.

The idea of pure relation is difficult to understand, and Buber suggests that one way to think about it is in terms of a "true" conversation between people – that is, where the participants do not know how it will progress and in which they find themselves saying and experiencing things they had no idea they were going to do or say. Such conversations are always charged with "presentness." To understand what might be meant by presentness, Buber suggests we try to experience the difference between the English phrase "far away" and the Zulu phrase: "There where someone cries out 'Mother, I am lost.' "

The world of I–It is more familiar. Although Buber's analysis of this world is nowhere near as uncompromising or harsh as the one portrayed by Sartre and Heidegger, it is nonetheless clear in recognizing the thinglike qualities of both the I and the You when they relate as I to It. An I–It relationship between people involves treating, and being treated as, a countable object in a world of countable objects. It also involves attempting to use or manipulate others for the advantage of the self.

Whereas Buber's phenomenology of the self–other dialectic has a number of implications for psychotherapy, theology, and our relationship to God and Nature, probably the most important implication in the present context is that it suggests human beings are always defined by the actions they take in regard to other people. Sometimes we fail to take into account the humanness of the Other. In that moment, we treat him or her as an It, a thing no different from other things. Sometimes, if we are lucky, we enter into relationship with another person that grants to him or her a humanness equal to what we would hope for ourselves. In that moment, we are changed, for the I that exists in humanness with another is different and more human than the one who does not. Although we may want to experience such meeting, it is not something that can be coaxed or taken from the world. Although the world of Thou is a difficult one in which to feel comfortable, it provides a necessary moment in our history. Without Thou, we could never be fully human.

Buber's reasonable optimism regarding the social conditions of human existence stands in contrast to those of other existentialists, not only because Buber is not an atheist but also because he sees a new and different role for dialogue in human life. Speaking, in his view, is not the idle chatter helping to pass the meaningless moments of a life but rather the "surplus of our existence over natural being (Merleau-Ponty, 1945/1962)." As such, it makes its appearance "like the boiling point of a liquid, when in the density of being, volumes of empty space are built up and move outwards. . . . [Speaking] is not an instrument, it is a manifestation, a revelation of intimate being and of the psychic link which unites us to the world and our fellow human being" (Merleau-Ponty, 1945/1962, p. 196). In concluding his discussion of our awareness of other people, Merleau-Ponty echos Buber in describing the experience of dialogue as "consummate reciprocity."

I am freed from myself, for the other person's thoughts are certainly his; they are not of my making, though I do grasp them the moment they come into being. . . . And indeed, the objection which my interlocutor raises to what I say draws from me thoughts which I had no idea I possessed, so that at the same time that I lend him thoughts, he reciprocates by making me think. It is only retrospectively, when I have withdrawn from the dialogue and am recalling it that I am able to reintegrate it into my life and make of it an episode in my private history, and that the other recedes into his absence, or, in so far as he remains present for me, is felt as a threat. (p. 354)

What these analyses suggest is that the situation of dialogue reveals an unproblematic aspect of our experience with other people. Speaking is that situation in which the limits of personal expression are guided by a need to communicate, and the conversation reveals the degree to which these two intentions merge with one another. In this situation, the other and the self are in a relation that requires neither fusion nor separation. The situation of dialogue – authentic dialogue – reveals the so-called problem of other minds as a pseudoproblem, since it is in the essence of human nature not to be alienated from but to be prereflectively related to the other. Although all sorts of posturing and artifice may transform I–Thou into I–It, the possibility of I–Thou is always present.

Buber and Merleau-Ponty, thus, present an alternative to the more dour pronouncements of Sartre and Heidegger. While recognizing that we have and do become alienated from one another, both stress that the other is sometimes experienced as that aspect of the world which fulfills, enhances, and completes the lonely existence of a solitary individual. Although we may have to appropriate an experience of impending death to be fully human, both Buber and Merleau-Ponty do not see others as impeding us but rather as fellow travelers who may (or may not) choose to take the same or a similar journey. The realization of a journey toward nonbeing is awesome, but it does not have to be taken alone.

The Present Research Program

To attempt an empirical description of the ways in which contemporary individuals experience other people, 20 adult participants were interviewed on a one-to-one basis and were asked to respond to the following two requests. (1) "Can you tell me of some times when you are aware of other people?" (2) "Please tell me what you are aware of in that situation." All co-participants were recruited from a number of night-school classes in social and humanistic psychology. Participants in both groups were older than the majority of undergraduate students, with the range varying from 22 to 45 years of age. Eleven of the participants were women; 9 were men. Fourteen were married, 10 had children, and only 2 lived with their parents.

Participants reported finding the opening two requests interesting to answer and described a wide variety of situations during which they were aware of other people. The ubiquitous nature of the experience of other people seemed to require a special stance since some participants had a bit of initial difficulty in selecting relevant experiences. As one participant stated, "It is like turning off a light switch when you leave a room; you know that you did, because you always do, but you couldn't say for sure that you did it." Despite this, all participants described at least five, and usually more, situations in which they were aware of other people. Some examples referred to particular events; others referred to more general conditions.

Situations in Which Other People Are Figural

Present participants described experiences that occurred in a variety of places, although work and school provided the majority of situations. Many participants spoke of relationships with family members, friends, or lovers. Public places, such as shopping malls, movie theaters, and sporting events also were described by participants. Some mentioned sports and exercise, such as basketball, football, or aerobics class, as well as various social occasions, such as parties, weddings, and dances. Driving an automobile also was a frequent occasion for an awareness of other people.

The following nine categories describe the situations that typically formed the ground of specific experiences described in the various interviews. Although the categories comprise all of the situations mentioned, they are not designed to be mutually exclusive. Wherever possible, the specific wording of the participant was retained in naming a category. The final list of situations involved the following categories:

Categories

1. Unusual behavior or appearance
2. Having a good relationship with someone
3. Feeling judged by (and judging) others
4. Feeling concern for others
5. Threatening situations
6. When people are irritating
7. When people are pulling for me
8. When someone reminds me of someone else
9. Being bored

Explanations

1. *Unusual behavior or appearance.* The examples defining this category point to the fact that people who are unusual stand out. It includes such situations as "when someone is offbeat," "when people dress in strange or odd ways," and "when people do unexpected things."
2. *Having a good relationship with someone.* Many people spoke about being sensitive to persons with whom they have (or want to have) a close relationship. This category includes times of feeling especially related, such as "when someone is very important to me" and "when I feel close to someone." Also included were instances where participants felt shut off from friends, lovers, or family members. Some participants reported

being aware of other people in the context of wanting to develop a relationship.

3. *Feeling judged by (and judging) others.* Almost all participants mentioned being particularly aware of other people when embarrassed, ashamed, or feeling in some way inadequate. Some examples are "when I am wondering if I look the way I should" and "when I feel threatened that I might be judged by others." Almost all participants also spoke about times when they categorized or judged other people, such as during the first meeting of two people, and at the workplace, where part of a person's job is to judge others.

4. *Feeling concern for others.* Situations in which a sense of responsibility and concern for others was a significant aspect were reported by participants. Participants also become aware of others when concerned about their well-being; two people talked about being especially worried about a friend.

5. *Threatening situations.* Several people spoke of being aware of people when a sense of threat was an aspect of the situation. Sometimes the threat was of violence, as "when I am trying to avoid an altercation" and "when someone is physically hurting someone."

6. *When people are irritating.* For some participants, "irritating behavior" gave rise to an awareness of others. One participant spoke of people who are distracting in class because they are noisy. Sometimes participants were aware of annoying other people. One man became aware of other people studying at the campus library when he disturbed their "barrier of silence" by coming near their study carrel to look for books.

7. *When people are pulling for me.* At times, participants reported becoming aware of other people when they felt supported, assisted, or encouraged by them. Participants also were aware of others when they felt that they were performing, or "on stage." One person reported becoming especially aware of a person who made a special effort to help him when he was having a bad day. Another noted that he was aware of others when he was feeling "witty and funny"; he had a sense of entertaining them.

8. *When someone reminds me of someone.* Some participants became aware of others when they noticed something familiar about the other person. Often, this familiarity is associated with a good memory from the past. One man said that he became aware of women who dressed in a certain manner or wore their hair a certain way.

9. *Being bored.* For many participants, boredom was a situation giving rise to an awareness of other people. Participants reported "people-watching" when faced with little to do or think about. This phenomenon

occurred in many different places, such as in shopping malls, on public transportation, or while driving an automobile.

Themes in the Experience of Other People

The analysis of all 20 protocols produced a set of three themes describing the experience of others as reported by participants. These themes include all of the experiences reported by all participants:

1. *Relationship* (Proximity/Connection/Synchrony). This theme refers to our awareness of relationships in day-to-day interactions with other people. Included are feelings of relatedness and synchrony, as well as those of alienation or being out of synchrony.
2. *Comparison* (Similarity/Difference). This theme refers to our tendency to be aware of and to categorize other people as similar to and different from ourselves, each other, and/or some social norm.
3. *Benefit* (Utility/Satisfaction/Annoyance). This theme refers to the fact that we experience people in terms of their meeting of our needs and desires and those of other people. Sometimes people are experienced as hindrances or even as threats. The theme also includes experience of other people in which they are judged as being good or bad for the self and/or for others.

These three themes were found to form the essential structure of participant experiences of other people. The themes, however, are not mutually exclusive; each theme should be thought of as a figural aspect of the experience of other people at different times and in different situations. Which aspect is prominent depends on the situation as well as upon the individual describing the experience. The structure of the participant's experience of others can be presented in the form of a triangle (see Figure 5.1), with each theme forming only part of a whole that includes all three themes. Each theme (or combination of themes) may become more figural as other aspects temporarily recede into the background, as in the figure/ground relationship of a reversible figure. Specific examples of each theme follow.

Theme 1. Experiences of Relationship (Proximity/Connection/Synchrony). Connection refers to an awareness of feelings of relationship and to those of feeling disconnected, or alienated, from others. Feelings of relatedness with a fellow football team member were figural in an experience recalled by one young man after scoring an exciting touchdown.

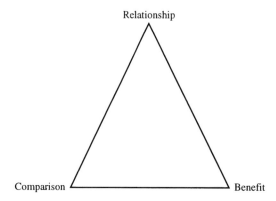

Figure 5.1. Thematic structure of the experience of others by the self

At that moment, it was like he didn't care who I was, and I didn't care who he was; we were just friends because of what happened. It was just, you know, I guess, "amigos on the field."

One woman sometimes feels alienated by others when she tries to meet new people at parties or other social gatherings.

I'm real aware of people if I try to reach out verbally, or try to get to know someone, and I'm rebuffed. I don't know why.

Within the context of close relationships, experiences reported by participants sometimes had more to do with alienation than connection. One woman spoke about experiences during an argument.

I am more aware of someone, of that feeling [when I've hurt someone], than of a love feeling. In going through a difficulty in a personal relationship, I am more aware of that person than when we are happily in love.

Sometimes an awareness of connections that other people make with one another is the focal aspect of an experience of other people.

I went to class, and I didn't know anyone in there, and I was really interested in how they would pair off and how they would meet. It seemed that most people in the class didn't know each other, so I think I was aware of who was talking to who, and who was sitting near who. And maybe I was sensitive to that for the first 2 or 3 weeks.

Theme 2: Experiences of Comparison (Similarity/Difference). Comparison is a key aspect to the experience of other people. Often the experience of similarity and difference occurs in the context of work, where one participant's job was to make discriminations among people (i.e., to categorize them).

We have a lot of different types of patients who come in, and it's necessary that I be aware of their moods and how ill they are and that sort of thing. Because we have a lot of people and frequently they have to wait for a good while. And so it's important that I know something about them, so that I can pick out anyone who needs a little faster service or that has a real problem.

While performing activities that do not require concentrated attention, participants reported that they often become aware of the people who are around them; they "people-watch."

Aerobics class, now there's a good one. I'm very aware of other people in aerobics class. Mostly, that's because I've got that huge mirror in front of me. And I can see everyone bouncing around. Sometimes when I'm in the back of the room, I have to look around because I can't see the instructor and I need to see what the other people are doing. And of course while we're bouncing around, I'm thinking am I looking stupid and should I look more like that person?

One participant reported being aware of how others were acting different from himself. Often, just the fact that people are different from one another is a salient aspect of the experience, especially when participants talked about "people-watching."

Well, I'm sort of a people-watcher at times, so I tend to notice groups of people – what people are together, what they look like, try to make judgments about them, separate them into classes. Basically what type of people are they. Sometimes I'm just out there looking at the differences and the different types of people that there are out there. Just for the sake of looking. Not for any particular reason – just to be looking, it's interesting.

Consider the following examples. The first two reflect the common case of attending to a difference; the third shows how the behavior of someone may become figural when it is experienced as different:

Somebody might come in dressed nice essentially like everybody else – a pair of blue jeans, some shirt . . . but they may have just a little more "style" about them.

One obvious time when people stand out is if you go to see them perform. Mary and I went to see Elton John – I knew about him . . . the clothes and all that. I came to watch him, there was no interaction – Just a spectator, I was not doing anything but watching. . . . He definitely stood out.

I've been at times . . . you know . . . where somebody was drunk or disorderly, you know, and they *stand out*. They get out of the realm of having a good time and get carried away, due to the fact that they are drunk – they have become louder and, you know, . . . they are definitely different from other people there . . . because, you know, . . . maybe there are one or two of them that are drunk and acting that way, and everybody else is well in control of themselves.

Theme 3: Experiences of Benefit (Utility/Satisfaction/Annoyance). This theme has to do with experiences of other people that show them to be useful, satisfying, or beneficial to the self and/or to others. People are experienced as providing emotional support, encouragement, or physical assistance. Alternatively, people are experienced as annoying, frustrating, or hindering.

A guy . . . stopped and helped me. [We] weren't good friends, and it shocked me and surprised me that he pulled over and helped me.

I started watching this guy who was holding things up – I don't really know what his problem was; he kinda seemed unprepared or something. But as time went by, people standing in line started talking about him – about how long he was taking, about the hurry they were in. He had turned a simple "running into the bank" into a chore.

Sometimes people are experienced as a hindrance to well-being or even as a threat to personal safety. Several participants mentioned that sometimes they are aware that a sense of potential danger or harm is an important aspect of the experience when in the presence of certain people or situations.

An awareness of being the center of attention also may serve to make other people salient to the self in a somewhat unpleasant way. One woman remembered arriving late to a wedding ceremony and suddenly finding herself as a disruption.

It was startling to have all eyes turn on me, and I was a little embarrassed that the focus was taken off the bride and groom and put onto myself and my companions. . . .

While driving an automobile, many people become aware of other drivers. Most often, participants spoke about trying to second-guess the actions of other drivers, to be able to react if necessary.

I'm always trying to figure out what that guy next to me or in front of me is going to do – not only his vehicle but his psyche as well. Is he going to cut in front of me because there's a truck in front of him? I need to second-guess that.

Experiences in Which More Than One Aspect Is Figural

Most of the experiences reported in the various interviews did not exemplify only one of the three themes. In fact, all three usually were present;

one or two aspects, however, were more figural in capturing the meaning and significance of the experience for the person.

Experiences of Relation and Comparison. The potential for meaningful relationship with another person often brings forth an awareness of differences between people. The ways in which a particular person stands out from a crowd sometimes becomes figural along with a hope for connection. The process involves selection: Are they like me? different from the last guy? (etc.)

I think I am subconsciously or consciously looking for people that are like me – to talk to, to meet, and get to know. I have a great interest in people and like to make friends, so I think I'm looking for interesting people that I would like to get to know. And generally I flock toward people that I assume are more like me.

One participant spoke of an experience with two close friends in which she was aware of the possibility that she might become alienated from them as a result of changes she is making in her life.

But I remember at that moment being particularly aware of them. And I didn't want to feel alienated, I wanted their understanding, knowing how different it was from the lifestyle they were choosing. . . . We've all been afraid as our lives changed . . . we could lose touch, because our values changed.

Sometimes the experience of another person is bound up in feelings of connectedness but at the same time with feelings of being different.

I'm sort of a logical and reasonable person, and he plays more on his emotions. So I don't really know how to deal with somebody who doesn't do things in what seems to be a perfectly logical manner. . . . So I don't think I understand the way he is, and so that's probably why I worry more about him . . . and really just try to have a good relationship with him,

Experiences of Relation and Benefit. Experiencing relatedness with people as promoting a sense of well-being was a situation described by participants. Conversely, people also spoke of the experience of alienation from others as hurtful and uncomfortable.

One man, a pole-vaulter, described an experience of being connected to and energized by a crowd.

It was almost like I had everyone else inside my body watching me and wanting me to do it, and I could just feel like – the energy coming from everybody else. It really helped.

The situation of missing one's wife served as the occasion for experiencing themes of connection and benefit.

I guess when I am alone I miss Bev more than anything else. We're together about most of the time, and then when I'm alone, that's the first person I miss – I miss having her around to comfort me, and the satisfaction of having her with me.

One woman sometimes is aware of being uncomfortable when she feels close to others. At times, she believes that she is overly sensitive to people who are close to her.

You know, I think in a lot of ways I'm too sensitive as far as that I let people's own problems – as far as their everyday life – just the way they get caught up in things.... And you know sometimes I can't cope with that because it's just too much, going along with what I have to do. Because I want to be sensitive to her needs, but yet it is hard to do that without being overly sensitive and taking on her burden for myself.

Experiences of Benefit and Comparison. The experience of being compared to others has an evaluative component. Participants reported feeling embarrassed or ashamed, as if devalued by the other person. Sometimes this was a very painful experience.

I went to a play, and I'd never been to a play before. I was even conscious of when to clap – I didn't – this was a new situation I've never been in. I was into checking out the others, you know, what's going on here? I didn't know how to be.

When participants felt that they were in some way not conforming to an external standard, or felt unusual in some way, they reported becoming aware of what the other person was thinking about them, and whether such thoughts were complimentary or otherwise.

You know, in the military, you're in the fishbowl, and everybody's watching you.... There are strict guidelines, how you cut your hair, what color T-shirts to wear.... I watch people more if I'm in uniform than I do in civilian clothes because I wonder what they think.... You wonder if you get a good response or a negative one.

Some people feel that at times it is important to look for changes in another person, either because that person may be having some particular difficulty or out of a sense of responsibility.

I am thinking about having lunch with a friend recently, whom I've been concerned about, because I thought she was drinking too heavily. I had not seen her for a month, so I invited her to lunch. And I think at that time I was really very aware of her appearance and what she was saying, how she looked, ... and casual conversation about what she was doing ... because I was concerned, and I was looking for signs of a problem.

Competition is an experience in which the aspects of comparison and evaluation are figural.

We are sort of competitive, me and a couple of friends. . . . I am aware of how much they study compared to how much I study. . . . Later on, I'll ask myself, "Did I not do as well because I just didn't study as hard?"

Another man described competition in the following way.

A lot of time in competition you try to analyze your opponent. If I played basketball one-on-one against somebody, I look for leaning right or leaning left – or back on the heels. You analyze somebody. If you play to win, you have to be aware of your opponent.

Experiences in Which all Three Themes Are Figural

Some experiences described by participants are clearly encompassed by all three themes. For example, the excitement of becoming attracted to someone special in the hope of a relationship is an experience that expresses all three themes. In the following excerpt, the woman is excited about the possibilities of relating to someone who is very different from other people she knows.

There wasn't anyone exciting, or really compatible, that I knew. And then all of a sudden, there was somebody from abroad. . . . He had been other places. He could speak more than one language. So there was the thrill of the challenge. . . . [It is] just so different to know somebody who doesn't care what other people think, who has more to talk about than the weather, who has met different people, had different relationships.

The threat of alienation from soneone important can bring about fears of being negatively judged. The man reporting the following experience becomes especially aware of subtle differences in the behavior of his supervisor at work whenever called into the supervisor's office.

His tone of voice, his eye contact, his body language, where he is at in his office when he calls me in. If he's sitting down with his desk as a barrier . . . it's not okay because I know I'm in trouble. But if he stands up and says come on in, I know everything is alright.

One young man described changes in his sense of connectedness to family members after the death of his grandfather. He described the experience of becoming aware of how much he values relationships among family members as a result of the loss.

Just like, everyone was together . . . that changed my awareness of people to this day about that group of people, my aunts and uncles . . . like we all have something in common now. . . . It might be about death, and it might be about family, I guess, or life maybe. About how we are all, like, still living and are all together, maybe, and we all realize that life has a high quality. It's like precious to all of us, maybe, and when we're together, it's like we live pretty good, I guess, like everyone's together.

As noted, most every event has each of the themes within it. Consider these examples where all these themes can be seen in a single event.

I guess I know what they are going through. A very difficult time in their life, like maybe a death in the family or something. And you can see the hurt, and the disappointment, and the loss in their faces – and the way they act. . . . It just stirs emotions within me; I feel for those people. I don't know, the loss I guess, . . . or the tragedy, just magnifies those people in my mind.

[In the context of a grown-up child] Well, I think you miss slapping them on the butt, giving them a kiss, just making small talk. Asking them about their day, just asking them what they want to do. When they are gone all the time, I think you're going to realize, at least I do, you miss that. You haven't seen them in a while, and you wish they were around. Not for any terribly, at least on the outside, meaningful reason, something but . . . something within you, maybe getting him to laugh, sitting there in the rocking chair together; we just enjoy being with each other, you know, very nonverbal type of stuff. I think those are the kinds of things you miss in absence.

Relationship to Prior Theories of People

Three different approaches to how we experience other people are presented by psychoanalytic, phenomenological, and existential theories of human life. If the present set of interviews describes significant aspects of this experience, it should be possible to note the major concerns of each approach in terms of one or more of the themes of relation, benefit, and comparison. As an overview, it seems appropriate to identify the major concerns of psychoanalysis with the theme of benefit and to a lesser degree with that of connection. It likewise seems possible to identify the major concern of phenomenology with the theme of comparison and to a lesser extent with that of connection. Even in overview, the existential group has to be partitioned into those having an essential concern for the fate and experience of the individual (e.g., Heidegger and Sartre) and those having more significant concerns for issues transpiring between people (e.g., Buber and to a lesser extent Merleau-Ponty). Under this division, it is possible to identify the major concerns of Sartre and Heidegger as those of benefit (usually hindrance) and to a lesser degree connection. Buber and Merleau-Ponty, while recognizing similar themes in I–It relationships, provide a more inclusive scheme in which all three themes are considered but in which the theme of correlation is most strongly emphasized.

From a classic psychoanalytic perspective, the theme of benefit is best rendered in terms of satisfaction and frustration; that is, the other person is experienced as a source of either or both of these possibilities. Since the individual is viewed as a relatively well-defined unit (a self or ego), re-membered or significant others are described as "internal objects," or, more simply, as representations who still satisfy and/or frustrate the person. Whereas classic psychoanalysis was structured primarily in terms of biologi-cal satisfactions and frustrations, the new themes of object relations also include a "need" for relating. Despite the addition of this more relational need, other people are still experienced in regard to satisfying or distorting the relational need for attachment. What seems to have happened is that while clinical practice and empirical observation have extended the list of issues to include attachment, the experience of other people is still struc-tured in terms of their benefit to the individual in meeting or frustrating biological and/or interpersonal needs. Such is the case even in the phenom-enon of transference, in which present relationships are experienced in terms of prior satisfying or frustrating ones.

Turning now to phenomenology, the major theme is that of perceiving (and thinking about) other people as complex field events in which social action is not distinct from social perception. For this perspective, the other person is experienced in many different modes: sometimes as a mirror, sometimes as an audience, sometimes as simple, sometimes as complex, and sometimes in terms of a desire to influence or control. One situation is described as uniquely significant, that of face-to-face interaction in which the self and other are co-present to one another. Such presence does not mean that other events (e.g., social roles or language) do not serve to contextualize or ground the interactions, only that the present face-to-face situation is crucial.

Given this orientation, the theme of comparison – at both a perceptual and cognitive level – seems to capture a major aspect of our experiences of other people from a phenomenological perspective on social interaction. The fact that others mirror us both in behavior and in dialogue gives a depth to face-to-face interactions and suggests that the theme of connections is also of significance to phenomenological approaches. The nature of such connection is captured both in terms of spatial metaphors – near, far, and close – as well as in terms of temporal ones – synchrony, anticipating what the other says and does, and so on. Since much of what ends up being our concept of self is given in the mirroring reactions of others, the issues of connection and relationship become, for some phenomenological analyses, at least as important as they are for object relations theorists of the psycho-analytic school.

Finally we come to existential theory. Both Sartre and Heidegger view the other as a hindrance to an authentic confrontation with Being. At its best, *Das Man* distracts the person from the task of confronting personal being-toward-death. At its worst, *Das Man* creates a master–slave dialectic that appears in both the most and least intimate of situations: loving and staring at someone else. Both Heidegger and Sartre see the task of human interaction as an essentially unresolvable one which, at the extreme, is described by the phrase: "Hell is others." While we cannot live without relationships, we can never be fulfilled within them. It is the combination of this emphasis on the theme of hindrance with the subsidiary theme of being-for-others that defines this class of existential theory.

It is worth noting a similarity between this position and that of classic psychoanalysis. Relatedness is the condition that we require to exist as people although such relatedness is often experienced as hindering or frustrating. Perhaps it is enough to classify Freud as an early existentialist; perhaps what also is required is to seek a deeper similarity between the psychoanalytic and existential positions. Such similarity is to be found in the fact that both psychoanalysis and existentialism originated as a reaction to the values of Western Europe (and the United States) in the midst of a mechanistic age. This similarity of historical context seems to make sensible the specific ways in which the themes of connection and frustration have been combined by both perspectives, in which the human being is viewed as alone and in confrontation with a repudiating and dehumanizing world. Although psychoanalysis may be part of the problem for existential thinkers, both existentialism and psychoanalysis tend to describe the human experience of other human beings as essentially a barrier to individual agency and independence.

Despite a generally pessimistic tone to Freud, Sartre, and, to a lesser extent, Heidegger, Buber describes our experience of other people and the human world in terms that describe both the dehumanization of contemporary life by technology and the possibility for previously unknown relatedness and freedom in dialogic encounter. For Buber (and Merleau-Ponty), the individual always has the possibility of an unexpected encounter that can restore his or her rootedness in the worlds of other people, God, and nature. As such, Buber simultaneously recognizes themes of relatedness (and alienation), benefit (and hindrance), and the great significance of a special situation of meeting in which a new, dual-faced, experience takes place where the self and the other stay "self and other" at the same time as they experience a "between" more powerful and significant than either the I or Thou alone. Such uncanny experiences, when compared to more ordinary ones, provide the wherewithal for a return to the world of I–It relationship and make that world bearable and possible. In Buber's approach, all three themes are significant, although any single theme may be especially significant in some specific situation. If one aspect to this view is most significant, it must be that of authentic relationship in which both comparison and benefit have their origin and from which they ultimately derive their human meaning.

PART III

Selected Topics from Everyday Life

The next five chapters explore topics meant to be of interest to the research psychologist and the clinical practitioner. They deal with events and phenomena concerning our interactions with other people, our experiences of a self that falls apart, and our provisional understandings of mortality and death. Although only one of these topics uniquely emphasizes pathological concerns, all are potentially significant for such concerns. For this reason, the topics explored in Part III have been contextualized not only in terms of their locations within philosophy, religion, and psychology but also in terms of clinical theory and practice. Each topic, however, derives from the world of everyday life, and it is this location that ultimately will determine whether present descriptions are capable of providing a useful experiential basis on which to develop relevant clinical interventions.

Each of the following chapters, therefore, is based on the assumption of a comprehensible relationship between everyday human experience and the technique and practice of psychotherapy. In its own way, each chapter seeks to fulfill Merleau-Ponty's suggestion that the world of abstract thought and technique must be contextualized in terms of everyday life so as to recapture the living meaning of our techniques and our concepts. Each chapter describes thematic meanings for such human events as feeling alone, making amends, being in love, falling apart, and developing a personal meaning for the idea and reality of death. Although some of these phenomena occur frequently, and others only once, all have their place in the unfolding narrative that characterizes what we mean by the term *human life*. And all are implicated in the task of helping to reorient a life that temporarily may have lost its direction or sense.

155

6

Feeling Alone

James Edward Barrell

The term *aloneness* may be understood in many different ways. In the simplest case, other people are physically absent. Despite this state of affairs, not everyone will experience a sense of aloneness, especially if other people are imagined or if the person has no desire to be with them at that moment. Similarly, a person may be surrounded by other people and still experience an uncomfortable sense of being alone, particularly if he or she feels excluded from participating with them in a meaningful way. Aloneness does not refer to an objective circumstance but to a psychological mode of being, and whether it is experienced as pleasurable or painful, problematic or liberating, always depends upon the meaning that each specific situation has for the person undergoing it.

Being alone is not only a common human condition but one so close to what human existence is about as to be inevitable and unavoidable. As Paul Tillich (1963) noted:

[Man] is not only alone; he also knows that he is alone. Aware of what he is, he therefore asks the question of his aloneness. He asks why he is alone and how he can overcome his being alone. He cannot stand it either. It is his destiny to be alone and to be aware of it. Not even God can take away this destiny from him. (p. 15)

In examining prior work on aloneness, four major perspectives can be discerned: psychodynamic, sociological, existential, and phenomenological. From a psychodynamic perspective, aloneness is frequently characterized as a condition of the person, and sources of aloneness are sought both in the intrapsychic world and in the developmental history of the individual. The sociological perspective views aloneness as having its origin in societal and

This chapter is based on the unpublished doctoral dissertation *A Phenomenological Analysis of the Experience of Being Alone*, submitted to the University of Tennessee in 1988.

157

cultural conditions and processes. From an existential perspective, aloneness is characterized as an essential aspect of being human. Finally, the phenomenological perspective concerns itself with describing what the experience of aloneness is like for the person undergoing it. By focusing on the world of experience, this perspective ultimately would seem to have the possibility of recovering the unreflected matrix from which the intrapsychic, societal, and existential perspectives derive.

Psychodynamic Perspectives on Aloneness

From a psychodynamic point of view, aloneness is a psychological state influenced by characterological and developmental factors, and this litera- ture focuses almost exclusively on painful experiences of aloneness – spe- cifically loneliness – to the exclusion of more positive forms such as solitude. Peplau and Perlman (1982) mention three points of agreement concerning the way in which loneliness has been viewed: "First, loneliness results from deficiencies in a person's relationships. . . . Second, loneliness is a subjective experience. . . . Third, the experience of loneliness is unpleasant and dis- tressing" (p. 3).

Loneliness seems so intrinsic to the nature of mental illness that Van den Berg (1972) has characterized psychopathology as the science of loneliness. Fromm-Reichmann also (1959) stressed the importance of loneliness in understanding mental disorder. Although the relationship between loneli- ness and mental illness has been recognized by many different theorists, there has been little agreement as to the exact nature of this relationship. For Zilboorg (1938), it is necessary to differentiate between normal lone- someness, which has a temporary quality to it, and pathological loneliness, which is apt to be chronic and is thought to be characterized by the psycho- logical triad of narcissism, megalomania, and hostility. Pathological loneli- ness is viewed as involving both narcissism and megalomania because it is assumed to include an intense need for other people to mirror one's own grandiose love of self – a need that has its developmental roots in an upbringing that served to perpetuate the infant's, and later, the child's illusions of omnipotence. In meeting the outside world, the child with this type of orientation necessarily will be rejected, thereby producing hostility toward others and subsequent episodes of loneliness.

More than 60 years ago, Horney (1937) viewed loneliness as symptom- atic of a more general neurotic adjustment to life. In fact, the experience of loneliness may be a major characteristic of the neurotic person since such a person is simultaneously incapable of loving and of having a great need for love. Horney argued that chronic loneliness may reflect a basic underlying anxiety that was fostered by a rejecting parental attitude, which left the child with an "all pervading feeling of being lonely and helpless in a hostile world" (1937, p. 89).

Rubins (1964), while sharing many of Horney's views of the development of neurosis, claims that loneliness originates in a neurotic conflict between the person's glorified need for love and affection and an underlying feeling of low self-esteem. The experience of loneliness is composed of two forces: a centrifugal one, which drives the person toward others and away from inner experience, and a centripetal one, which drives the person to fill an inner emptiness with the experience of another person. These forces are active whenever there is a disruption in either the outer pole of interpersonal relationships or in the inner pole of unconscious needs, and loneliness emerges as a consequence of such temporary disruptions in personal equilibrium.

Given these views, a number of empirical studies have attempted to relate loneliness to specific forms of psychopathology. In research employing undergraduate students, Stokes (1985) reported a correlation of .51 between loneliness as measured by the UCLA Loneliness Scale and neuroticism as measured by the Eysenck Personality Questionnaire. Hojat (1983), using the same two measures, reported a correlation of .50. Schill, Toves, and Ramaniah (1981) administered the UCLA Loneliness Scale and the Cornell Medical Index to college sophomores to investigate possible correlations between loneliness and other psychiatric categories. Results revealed correlations of .47 with feelings of fear and inadequacy; .38 with hypochondriasis; .38 with excessive sensitivity and suspiciousness; .44 with anger, acting out, and blaming; .32 with nervousness and anxiety; .38 with neurocirculatory psychosomatic symptoms; .32 with pathological startle reaction; and .28 with gastrointestinal psychosomatic symptoms.

Research revealing greater problems in self-concept and personality development in lonely individuals provides indirect support for a relationship between loneliness and psychopathology. Nerviano and Gross (1976) administered a variety of personality tests and the Bradley Loneliness Scale to chronic alcoholics and discovered that alcoholics who were also lonely produced scores indicating a more immature personality, poorer impulse control, and greater emotional instability. Jones, Freeman, and Goswick (1981) found a correlation of $-.45$ between loneliness and self-esteem. Using a measure of interpersonal behavior, Eddy (1961) discovered that loneliness was correlated positively with discrepancies between one's actual and ideal self (.71) and between one's rating of oneself and ratings of how one believes others perceive him (.63). Finally, Loucks (1980) examined the relationship between self-concept and loneliness by administering the

Bradley Loneliness Scale and the Tennessee Self-Concept Scale to under-graduates. She found that greater loneliness was related both to a negative self-concept and to an uncertainty in one's self-concept.

Loneliness and Depression

Loneliness also has consistently been linked to depression, although theorists have had difficulty in distinguishing between the two as well as in disentangling their respective dynamics. It is commonly held that if any emotional state is to be found together with the experience of loneliness, it would most likely be depression (Peplau & Perlman, 1982). Despite such common cooccurrence, there is some evidence to suggest that loneliness and depression are distinguishable psychological states.

One of the more interesting differentiations between the two was offered by Leiderman (1980), who pointed out that depression is experienced more as a sense of loss and loneliness more as a sense of incompleteness. Loneliness occurs both with and without depression, and when loneliness and depression occur together, anger is also likely to be present. Although depression may be related to aggressive feelings toward another person, loneliness also is related to yearning for someone to provide a sense of completeness. Leiderman (1980) notes that "the frequent association of loneliness with depressive affect can be explained developmentally in terms of the fact that inadequate mothering, along with separation, frequently accompanies situations in which self–other differentiation is also pathological, a pattern leading to a confusion of depression with loneliness."

The correlation between loneliness and depression, however, is a well-established research finding. For example, Peplau and Perlman (1982) report that most correlations obtained between loneliness and depression have been found to vary between +.50 and +.60. In this regard, Hojat (1983) found a positive correlation of .54 between loneliness and depression, and Bragg (1979) obtained one of .49 with the same two measures. Moore and Schultz (1983) found a correlation of .66 between scores on the UCLA Loneliness Scale and the Zung Depression Scale, and Loucks (1974) found a correlation of .61 between loneliness and the depression dimension of the Profile of Mood States Scale. Weeks, Michela, Peplau, and Bragg (1980) and Anderson et al. (1983) also found correlations between loneliness and depression of .52 and .58, respectively. In general, results suggest that people who are lonely also tend to report experiencing more depression than nonlonely individuals.

Eisemann (1984) compared clinically depressed psychiatric patients with normal controls and found that patients diagnosed with brief reactive depression scored highest on a self-report measure of loneliness. Chronically depressed patients, such as those suffering from unipolar or bipolar depression, complained less of loneliness although still reporting greater loneliness than the relevant control group. These results suggest that the experience of loneliness is associated more typically with temporary rather than chronic forms of depression.

Rubenstein and Shaver (1982) employed factor analysis to determine the feelings most commonly reported to be associated with loneliness. Results of their analysis revealed four factors: desperation, depression, impatient boredom, and self-deprecation, with the first of these reported most frequently. Rubenstein and Shaver conceptualized the depression and self-deprecation factors as representing reactions to loneliness and not as aspects of loneliness per se.

Although loneliness has been strongly linked to depression, empirical research suggests that people who tend to be lonely also tend to experience anxiety (Hojat, 1983; Jones et al., 1981; Loucks, 1974; Moore & Schultz, 1983; Peplau & Perlman, 1982). Fromm-Reichmann (1959) points to a conceptual confusion between loneliness and anxiety, since terms such as loneliness, fear of loneliness, and anxiety are sometimes used interchangeably in psychiatric parlance. The role of anxiety as crucial to mental disturbance has been a traditional focus of psychiatry, and Fromm-Reichmann recommends that such a one-sided stance be corrected by increased attention to the significant role of loneliness. She notes that the experience of real loneliness is so horrible that it "is beyond anxiety and tension . . . [and that] . . . only as its all engulfing intensity decreases can the person utilize anxiety-provoking defenses against it" (in Hartog, Audy, & Cohen, 1980, p. 348). For this view, anxiety constitutes a last defense against real loneliness, with the two states most closely linked during periods of acute difficulty.

In contrast to other psychodynamic theorists, Winnicott (1958) focused on the positive aspects of a capacity to be alone, which he believes to be an important sign of emotional maturity. The developmental origins of the capacity to be alone arise from experiences of being alone in the presence of someone; specifically, the infant's experiences of being alone in the presence of its mother. An experience of relatedness between mother and infant in these early experiences is necessary for the development of an infant's ability to tolerate subsequent periods of being alone. The reliable and caring presence of the mother makes it possible for the infant to be alone and to enjoy being alone for limited periods of time. Good-enough mothering allows the infant to internalize relationship to the mothering one and, thereby, to construct a belief in a benign environment.

Winnicott (1958) sums up his views on the development of the capacity to be alone as follows:

Gradually, the ego supportive environment is introjected and built into the individual's personality, so that there comes about a capacity to be alone. Even so, theoretically, there is always someone present, someone who is equated ultimately and unconsciously with the mother, the person who, in the early days and weeks, was temporarily identified with her infant, and for the time being was interested in nothing else but the care of her own infant. (p. 36)

Sociological Perspectives on Aloneness

From a sociological perspective, aloneness usually means being isolated within the context of the social world. Rather than focusing on characterological aspects of aloneness, the person's detachment or separation from social situations is emphasized. Weiss (1973) differentiates between the experiences of social and emotional isolation: Emotional isolation refers to the absence of an attachment figure, whereas social isolation refers to the absence of an accessible social network. Although these forms of isolation are not mutually exclusive, their delineation suggests the importance of considering aloneness as a social and an intrapsychic phenomenon.

Many researchers have identified trends in American society that they deem responsible for an increasing prevalence of aloneness (Bernikow, 1982; Gordon, 1976). One of the more significant of these is the loss of community, which refers to a generalized breakdown in the social structures needed to provide an individual with stable and meaningful relationships. Such a breakdown is likely to lead to a deficit in social relationships and to potentially severe isolation for the individual. The loss of community would seem to be the byproduct of numerous social forces, the most significant of which concerns geographic mobility, the isolation of the nuclear family, and the characteristic American emphasis on individualism.

Geographic Mobility

In 1976, Gordon reported that 40 million Americans change residence each year and that Americans average 14 moves over the course of a lifetime. Three important consequences of geographic mobility, relevant to aloneness, concern a disruption in family ties, a lack of a sense of belonging, and an alteration in one's typical style of relating to others. In terms of the first of these consequences, a disruption in family ties means that the extended family is often left behind and visited only on special occasions (Bowman, 1995). In addition to losing touch with one's family, the person also often loses touch with significant friends (Gordon, 1976), and these losses pressure the dislocated family to be self-sufficient in providing for interpersonal needs. As one example, Gordon describes increasing marital demands that arise due to geographic mobility:

In the past, husband and wife were to be "the one" for each other, the perfect companion. Now a woman or man must be not only confidant and lover, but family, community, friends – all things to one another. (p. 19)

A second consequence to geographic mobility is the loss of a "sense of belonging" to some community. Unfamiliarity breeds an anonymity that serves to undermine the process of integration into a new community: The incidence of friendly spontaneity is diminished in a nation of strangers (Bowman, 1955). There also are changes in community structure that increasingly take on an impersonal air, with the structures of modern urban and suburban communities strongly antagonistic to a sense of belonging. Finally, with geographic mobility, the kaleidoscope of faces that makes up one's community changes so often that one feels there is nothing substantial or permanent to which to belong (Packard, 1972).

A final implication to geographic mobility is that styles of interpersonal relating change. Packard (1972) pointed out an increase in hyperactive sociability to cope with the loss of community – a sociability that is a facade behind which lie chronic feelings of loneliness. There also may be a marked decrease in involvement, and "people who keep moving from place to place tend to develop a sense of detachment that is isolating" (Bowman, 1955). Lacking a sense of belonging, the person may withdraw from social life, and one of the most striking manifestations of a highly mobile lifestyle is the movement away from making interpersonal commitments. Thus, there also seems to be a trend toward transient relationships, well-suited to people apt to be here today and gone tomorrow.

In discussing early empirical research concerning the social roots of aloneness, Rubenstein and Shaver (1982) interviewed 50 Americans in different parts of the country to determine self-reported reasons for being lonely. They found no relationship between the number of previous moves and current loneliness; on this basis, they concluded that geographic mobility may be unrelated to adult loneliness. An alternative possibility is that geographic mobility yields experiences of both leaving and of being left. Being left behind may in some cases be an even more powerful precipitant of loneliness since the separation is less likely to be experienced as a choice by the person left behind (i.e., they may feel abandoned). Rapid changes in

the membership of communities also may create a form of relative movement in which an individual may experience living in a different place
without any change in location.

On the basis of interviewing, 1,050 adults in northern California, Fischer
and Phillips (1982) found that although individuals tended to be more
socially isolated immediately following a move, they seemed able to reconstruct social networks within a year. On this basis, they concluded that
geographic mobility was not an important factor in producing chronic social
isolation. As these authors themselves recognized, however, there is some
problem in equating the quantity of interpersonal relationships with the
experience of isolation. Maximizing social contacts does not necessarily
allay aloneness, and Packard's (1972) characterization of hyperactive sociability may be relevant to making sense of the "quick recovery" reported by
subjects in this study.

Isolation of the Nuclear Family

Geographic mobility places unique strains on the nuclear family. Conger
(1981) noted that in the past two to three decades the nuclear family has
become increasingly isolated and estranged from other social institutions.
He views this as due to a sense of powerlessness in response to overwhelming social forces from which the nuclear family withdraws. Under this state
of affairs, the family is then expected to meet almost all of the interpersonal
needs of its members.

The modern nuclear family is the "community" for the child and, increasingly, but to a lesser extent, for the adult. For this reason, internal
strife and breakdown are felt most acutely by children. Changes in family
composition and structure occasioned by an increase in divorce, working
mothers, and single-parent homes disrupt affectional bonds, and the television or the babysitter frequently becomes the maternal substitute. In modern American society, the child more than losing a sense of community may
be prevented from ever gaining one.

Individualism

As early as 1830, de Tocqueville commented that with democratic individualism, "each man is forever thrown back on himself alone, and there is
danger that he may be shut up in the solitude of his own heart" (1830/1969,
p. 508). In his book *The Pursuit of Loneliness* (1970), Slater proposes that
our commitment to individualism is at the root of loneliness in contemporary American society. He notes three fundamental desires that are neces-

sarily frustrated by an individualistic orientation: the desire for community, the desire for engagement, and the desire for dependency. Slater (1970) further notes that the trouble with individualism is that it represents an "attempt to deny the reality and importance of human interdependence" (p. 26).

Bellah, Madsen, Sullivan, Swidler, and Tipton (1985) also emphasize the continued impact of individualism on American life. Since "individualism lies at the very core of American culture," such emphasis is viewed as undermining the capacity for commitment. Bellah et al. further note that it is hard to commit oneself to others when the attitude is that, in the end, one is really alone and only has oneself to answer to. Americans are seen as struggling to maintain a balance between private attachments and public involvements. Since we are more dependent on others than ever before, an individualistic orientation is viewed as even more destructive.

Among the many manifestations of individualism analyzed by social theorists and researchers, three seem to bear most strongly on the experience of aloneness: technology, competition, and instrumentality. In terms of technology, Slater (1970) contends that the boom of technology in America has engendered widespread aloneness:

One of the major goals of technology . . . is to "free" us from the necessity of relating to, depending upon, or controlling other people . . . [and] the more we have succeeded in doing this, the more we have felt disconnected, lonely, unprotected, and unsafe. (p. 26)

The resulting emphasis on convenience as opposed to contact serves to separate us from one another and to make us all the more dependent on impersonal technological mechanisms; for example, we are more apt to turn on a television set than to visit a friend. Slater (1970) notes that "our economy depends upon our willingness to turn to things rather than people for gratification" (p. 93). In fact, our interactions with people become increasingly dissatisfying since technology produces an impersonal manner of relating, and we may relate to one another in a mechanical way rather than as people in relationships.

Fromm (1941, 1955) also has addressed the issue of how relationships in a capitalistic society become competitive and alienating. Capitalism represents an obvious outgrowth of an individualistic philosophy of life, with human relationships governed by the competition for goods. In contemporary American society, beneath the surface of superficial friendliness and cooperation, is an intense self-seeking competitiveness. Through competition we become alienated from one another, and given this state of affairs,

only instrumental relationships bring people together in a society dominated by an ideology of individualism.

What is modern man's relationship to his fellow men? It is one between two
abstractions, two living machines, who use each other. The employer uses the one
whom he employs; the salesman uses his customers. Everybody is to everybody else
a commodity, always to be treated with a certain friendliness, because even if he is
not of use now, he may be later. (Fromm, 1955, p. 139)

It may be argued that Fromm's characterization of the capitalistic tendency toward instrumentalization is dated in light of recent developments.
Lasch (1979), in a somewhat more recent book, however, assures us that
individualism and instrumentality are still alive and well:

Americans have not really become more sociable and cooperative, as the theorists
of other-direction and conformity would like us to believe; they have merely become more adept at exploiting the conventions of interpersonal relations for their
own benefit. (p. 66)

Lasch (1979) further describes the exploitation of others for personal
benefit as a manifestation of narcissism in American culture. With narcissism, the other is seen as a vehicle for the gratification of the self. An
orientation such as this certainly runs the risk of losing sight of the other's
needs and, therefore, of leaving the other unfulfilled. A person with this
orientation is also easily dissatisfied by the imperfect empathy of the other
and, therefore, is prone to narcissistic injury. Under this state of affairs,
disruptions in interpersonal relationships are likely thereby increasing the
probability of feeling painfully alone.

Existential Perspectives on Aloneness

From an existential perspective, aloneness is a fact of human existence, and
separateness is a fundamental condition. Rather than attempting to prevent
or relieve loneliness, such experiences are accepted as inevitable, and the
problem becomes one of how we are to learn to live with loneliness. Although an awareness of isolation is painful, it also may be a productive
condition if faced honestly.

Aloneness and the Human Condition

Tillich (1963) claims that the experience of aloneness is a central aspect to
the human condition, although he does note that there are two sides to each
person's aloneness: (1) loneliness, which represents "the pain of being
alone," and (2) solitude, which represents "the glory of being alone" (p. 18).

Loneliness may be experienced when others who help us forget ultimate aloneness leave us or when we realize our ultimate isolation in the midst of others. Tillich describes two forms of ultimate loneliness: the loneliness of guilt and the loneliness of death. The loneliness of guilt refers to realizing the total responsibility that we have for our own lives; the loneliness of death refers to the fate of having to anticipate our death and to die alone.

Tillich (1963) assures us that "loneliness can be conquered only by those who can bear solitude" (p. 21). Since solitude is a source of creativity and religious experience, Tillich believes that it is only during such experiences that human beings become more aware of themselves and of their connection to God and other people. Sartre (1957), like Tillich, viewed human aloneness as inevitable, although he also characterized it in terms of a radical freedom in which we are nothing but what we make of ourselves. Sartre further claimed that each person is responsible for all people, and when an individual chooses for him- or herself through action, he or she also chooses for all of humankind. Such pervasive responsibility produces an experience of aloneness similar to the loneliness of guilt discussed by Tillich (1963), although the Sartrean loneliness may be even more profound since one is responsible both for one's own life and for that of others.

Although the majority of existential theorists believe that the basic condition of the person is aloneness, Buber (1923/1970) argues for the primacy of relationship. I and Thou are interconnected, interdependent beings, and "the relation to Thou is unmediated" (p. 62). Buber's views are a far cry from other existentialists, who tend to characterize relatedness as a way of coping with existential isolation. Buber's ideas, thus, suggest that experiences of both relatedness and aloneness are inextricable from what it means to be human. It may be that the person is both alone and at one with the world. Whereas Tillich and Sartre have emphasized the fundamental condition of isolation, Buber has insisted on the importance of the relational aspects of human existence.

Buber makes the further point that the I–Thou and I–It attitudes are interrelated aspects of existence, noting that I–Thou and I–It are an "intricately entangled series of events." If It represents the fundamental separation of person and world, it would seem that although the experience of aloneness may be avoided temporarily, we ultimately must return to such a state. As Buber (1923/1970) notes: "Every You (Thou) in the world is doomed by its nature to become a thing or at least to enter into thinghood again and again" (p. 69). Thus, even in relationships with a predominantly I–Thou orientation, existential aloneness cannot be avoided.

As with Buber, Fromm (1956) believes in the importance of overcoming our painful awareness of separateness through relating. An awareness of our essential aloneness "makes [our] separate disunited existence an unbearable prison," and "we would become insane [if we] could not [be] liberated from this prison and reach out [and] unite in some form or other with [people]; with the world outside" (p. 8). Fromm (1956) discusses several historical attempts to overcome the experience of separateness but claims that "the full answer lies in the achievement of interpersonal union, of fusion with another person, in love" (p. 18).

Fromm differentiates between mature love and symbiotic union. Although it is possible to escape from the unbearable feeling of isolation and separateness in symbiotic union, such relationships fail to affirm an independent individual. By contrast:

Mature love is union under the condition of preserving one's integrity, one's individuality. Love is an active power in man; a power which breaks through the walls which separate man from his fellow men, which unites him with others; love makes him overcome the sense of isolation and separateness, yet it permits him to be himself, to retain his integrity. In love the paradox occurs that two beings become one and yet remain two. (p. 21)

As is clear, Fromm's notion of mature love is similar to I–Thou relationships described by Buber.

Jaspers (1932/1969) comments that "I cannot come to myself without entering into communication, and I cannot enter communication without being lonely" (p. 56). The capacity for loneliness and the capacity for what Jaspers terms *existential communication* are inseparable. Existential communication refers to a way of relating that is quite similar to that described by Buber as I–Thou and by Fromm as mature love. Loneliness and solitude (terms that Jaspers appears to use interchangeably) are the result of an experience of not yet being able to become one's self with the other, along with a readiness to enter into existential communication. Even when existential communication occurs, loneliness is still possible, since it is always a "coming to" rather than an "arrival at" self-being; thus, communication is always incomplete. According to Jaspers, existential communication demands willingness to experience loneliness and solitude. The communication of loneliness and solitude is essential since they are ultimate truths, and only truth is able to unite individuals.

In *Being and Time* (1927/1962), Heidegger distinguishes between two modes of being that relate to facing or fleeing one's fundamental aloneness. In what he labels the *authentic* mode of existence, the person chooses and acts with full awareness of ultimate responsibility, inevitable death, and aloneness. In what Heidegger labels the *inauthentic* mode of existence, the individual flees from an awareness of the human condition by allowing his or her existence to be shaped totally by others. Such a person denies the experience of existential aloneness by becoming absorbed into the group and living according to their dictates and values.

Moustakas (1961, 1972), adopting a Heideggerian viewpoint, distinguishes between existential loneliness and loneliness anxiety, thereby suggesting that loneliness defines an authentic mode of existence and that loneliness anxiety defines an inauthentic mode of existence. The experience of loneliness is viewed as normal and essential for human growth; loneliness anxiety is viewed as an unhealthy defense "that attempts to eliminate [loneliness] by constantly seeking activity with others or by continually keeping busy to avoid facing the crucial questions of life and death" (1972, p. 20). Loneliness anxiety warns us of impending loneliness, however, and incites us to take measures to avoid it. By not allowing oneself to experience loneliness, the person may leave a significant aspect of being underdeveloped.

To the extent that aloneness is a basic condition of human life, existentialist thought considers the confirmation of this condition to produce a more authentic mode of being. Any attempt to flee the condition of aloneness, however, suggests an attitude of bad faith. When loneliness refers to an awareness of one's existential condition, it means that one is facing one's aloneness; when loneliness refers to a preoccupation with needing to relate to others, it means that one is fleeing one's aloneness: both aspects usually are present in any concrete episode of loneliness.

Phenomenological Perspectives on Aloneness

From a phenomenological point of view, the experience of being alone, rather than its causes or consequences, is primary. Sadler (1978) notes that many authors have confused "the experience itself with something that precedes or flows from it" (p. 160). Psychodynamic perspectives, for example, focus on the developmental roots of loneliness as well as upon problems associated with it. Sociological perspectives attend primarily to social factors considered to increase isolation, alienation, and loneliness. Existential views concern the meaning of aloneness as well as the ways in which individuals attempt to cope with its inevitability.

A phenomenological perspective takes human experience as its concern and attempts to describe experience as it presents itself in life. For this reason, phenomenologically oriented approaches to aloneness have focused on two major topics: (1) the nature of experiences of alienation from self and others, and (2) a phenomenological description of the experience of aloneness.

In terms of the first topic, Van den Berg (1972) has discussed relationships between mental illness and the experience of alienation from others. Of the mental patient, he asserts that "loneliness is the central core of his illness, no matter what his illness . . . loneliness is the nucleus of psychiatry" (p. 105). He also claims that the essential difference between a healthy person and one who is mentally ill is that whereas the former shares the same phenomenological world with others, the latter does not. The schizophrenic's delusions and hallucinations are not shared by others and serve to isolate the schizophrenic from the social world. Van den Berg notes that the schizophrenic is so alienated that he or she is not aware of a distinction between personal reality and the reality of others and, although extremely isolated, does not necessarily feel lonely.

Rogers (1961) identified two elements in the experience of loneliness: estrangement from self and estrangement from others. Self-estrangement involves both distrust and disregard for one's own experience. Rogers points out that because we are conditioned to suppress feelings, a discrepancy develops between what we think we should feel and what we feel. Alienation from one's own experience takes away one basis of relating and serves to isolate the person from other people. Loneliness begins with self-alienation that has estrangement from others as its consequence. As with Laing (1965), loneliness for Rogers involves a division between a real and a false self and invariably is a sign of a psychopathological condition.

In terms of the second major topic, Sadler (1978) investigated the experience of solitude, which he notes "reverberates with pleasure and a sense of fulfillment rather than pain and deprivation." Although Sadler does not clearly describe the specific procedures used to obtain his results, he does note an interest in portraying the universal features of the experience of loneliness as well as in discovering the various experiential ways in which people report feeling lonely. In characterizing the experiential aspects of loneliness, Sadler describes a reflexive component in which the person's focus is turned on the self. In this mode, the person comes to feel that there is something wrong in the personal world, and loneliness is experienced as a form of self-perception and self-definition. It also may be experienced as a frustrated expectation where the person is lacking others. Loneliness is, thus, a painful form of self-awareness that communicates to the person that a basic relationship to the world is deficient.

Sadler (1978) differentiates five types of loneliness: interpersonal, social, cultural, cosmic, and psychological, with each representing a specific source of distress. In the interpersonal domain, one perceives oneself as separated from a significant other: "The experience may be a general form of longing for companionship or love; or it can be a very specific longing for a particular individual, as in the experience of separation of grief" (p. 162). The social domain involves perceiving oneself as separate from a highly regarded group. In the cultural domain of loneliness, one suffers a self-recognition of estrangement from a cultural home; the experience is often described as *alienation* or *anomie*. The cosmic dimension of loneliness concerns an experience of emptiness that entails a suffering self-recognition of separateness from some ultimate source of meaning and life, such as God or nature. Finally, the psychological domain of loneliness is a type of loneliness in which one feels separated from what one regards to be the self. In this case, the person experiences feeling divided and being out of touch with him- or herself.

The types of loneliness described by Sadler are similar to those noted by Gaev (1976), who also distinguished five types: loneliness of the inner self, physical loneliness, emotional loneliness, social loneliness, and spiritual loneliness. The loneliness of the inner self is described as a feeling of estrangement from one's feelings and desires. This experience of self-alienation is similar to that discussed by Rogers as intrinsic to mental illness. Although inner loneliness is experienced as a sense of alienation from self, it seems to focus on wanting to be in touch with oneself, a situation fundamentally different from wanting to create a link between oneself and others. Self-alienation may be more accurately described as an experience of being lost rather than one of being lonely; referring to it as a type of loneliness may cloud this distinction.

A second category is physical loneliness: "the feeling of frustration and longing for physical closeness, contact, and touch of significant others" (Gaev, 1976, p. 9). Closely related is the category of emotional loneliness, which is characterized as "the feeling of sadness when our need for closeness of significant others is frustrated." In this way of feeling lonely, the need for emotional closeness and intimacy through communication is emphasized. With both physical and emotional closeness, there is a longing for a significant other similar to the interpersonal type of loneliness described by Sadler.

Social loneliness is described as the experience of not being able to find a place, or a way of being, in the social context. This state of affairs can take several forms, such as peer loneliness, lack of acceptance in a friendship group or with colleagues, the loneliness of those who cannot identify with a meaningful role in society, the loneliness of the prejudiced or outcast, and cultural loneliness as with those who migrate from one country or from one region to another. This form of loneliness appears to blend together the social and cultural dimensions discussed by Sadler.

The last form of loneliness is spiritual loneliness. By this, Gaev means the isolation or alienation that occurs when one is unable to find meaning in one's life. Spiritual loneliness is clearly the equivalent to what Sadler termed the *cosmic dimension of loneliness*. This form of loneliness also appears similar to the existential loneliness discussed by Tillich and others.

In a study employing the method of conceptual encounter developed by de Rivera (1981), Nisenbaum (1984) defined what he termed nine *structures of aloneness*. Each of these structures was defined by a unique pattern of four elements: situation, transformation, instruction, and function.

Structure 1

Situation: You realize you lack connectedness with important others.

Transformation: You experience yourself sinking inward and away from others.

Instruction: Don't merge.

Function: To prevent despair at the total loss of the possibility of meaning.

This structure describes an extreme and overwhelming form of painful aloneness, where the person feels far away from and invisible to others.

Structure 2

Situation: You realize that closeness is warranted here with these others, but that would make you vulnerable and exposed as rejectable.

Transformation: You experience a shell forming around you.

Instruction: Don't come out – stay in the shell.

Function: To preserve safety.

Here, the person feels cut off from others and hides from them out of a fear of being rejected.

Structure 3

Situation: You realize no one shares the difficult choice of conduct you face.

Transformation: You experience a steely core of resolve as the task looms large.

Instruction: Isolate yourself – don't be distracted.

Function: To preserve determination in facing the challenge and taking responsibility.

In this type of aloneness, one experiences having to face life's choices on one's own.

Structure 4

> *Situation:* You feel something is happening that calls for a particular other to be there.
>
> *Transformation:* You experience being held back from fully participating.
>
> *Instruction:* Wish they were here.
>
> *Function:* To not give up, to prevent separation and confirm yourself as a social being.

Here, one experiences the potential to enjoy a situation and wishes that a particular other was there to share it.

Structure 5

> *Situation:* You feel stranded and know that you ought to be in a familiar setting or with people who would make you feel secure.
>
> *Transformation:* You experience the restlessness of trying but being unable to reunite with the part of you that is still in its former surrounds.
>
> *Instruction:* Wish you were there, where they still are.
>
> *Function:* To replenish and renew yourself through a sense of belonging.

In this way of being alone, the person experiences a sense of homesickness or longing to be in a familiar setting where others care about him or her.

Structure 6

> *Situation:* You are without the presence of a special other person, and you feel the need for his/her proximity.
>
> *Transformation:* You experience the craving for closeness and intimacy.
>
> *Instruction:* Reach out, draw him/her, convince him/her to be here.
>
> *Function:* To love and feel loved.

Here, the person misses the physical presence of a special other person and feels the need for physical proximity.

Structure 7

> *Situation:* You feel that the other does not acknowledge or confirm you and your intense neediness of him/her.
>
> *Transformation:* You experience a welling up of neediness.
>
> *Instruction:* Show the world how desperately you need the other. Idealize and possess the other.

Function: To feel righteous, superior, and threatened by nothing else in the world save the other's rejection.

In Structure 7, the person experiences an intense neediness toward another person that is not acknowledged in return.

Structure 8

Situation: You feel comfort, serenity, and equanimity in your privacy.
Transformation: You experience the peace, totality, and unity.
Instruction: Be one with the world.
Function: To feel complete, secure, a part of everything.

With this type of aloneness, the person feels unique, self-contained, and complete regardless of the presence or absence of others in his or her surroundings.

Structure 9

Situation: You feel the absence of a human presence, a void of humanity out there where a person (or people) should be.
Transformation: You experience the emptiness inside yourself and become incomplete.
Instruction: Fill the void by wishing for him/her/them to be here.
Function: To prevent despair at a total loss of the possibility of meaning that would come if you accepted that they were truly gone.

In experiencing the absence of a person wished to be present, the person becomes preoccupied with the void that surrounds as well as with a sense of emptiness and incompleteness within.

Although each structural description is meant to be complete in itself, it seems clear that some are opposite to one another; for example, Structure 9 is the converse of Structure 7. Although Nisenbaum suggests that specific relationships among types are possible, as the foregoing example suggests, it is clear that others are precluded by their very nature. In general, however, each structure is viewed as an experiential alternative, and it is possible, as Nisenbaum proposes, to think of "each structure as an available option ... [where] ... each person may exercise a particular series of 'choices' about how his or her experience (will be) organized." As should be clear, Nisenbaum's analysis suggests that loneliness not only describes an existential situation concerned with real human problems but also one in which a wide range of emotions is possible.

The Present Research Program

Despite the number and variety of studies concerned with the topic of loneliness, few have described what it feels like to experience being lonely. In looking over this literature, it seems that most theoretical discussions of loneliness have focused on its possible antecedents. In this regard, developmental "causes" have been suggested that serve to increase the likelihood of loneliness in adult life (Bowlby, 1977; Guntrip, 1969; Sullivan, 1953). Social factors also have been suggested that seem to contribute to an increased prevalence of loneliness in contemporary American society. Aspects of the American social character, such as individualism and other-directedness (Bellah et al., 1985; Riesman, Glazer, & Denny, 1961; Slater, 1970), combined with external changes in the nature of social living, such as geographic mobility, also have been viewed as contributing to loneliness. Thus, a great deal of theorizing has attempted to deduce the "causes" of loneliness, few of which, unfortunately, have been empirically validated or lend themselves to such validation.

In addition to speculation about possible antecedents, theorists also have attempted to relate loneliness to various forms of psychopathology (Fromm-Reichmann, 1959; Horney, 1937; Zilboorg, 1938), despite scant empirical evidence to substantiate such claims (Peplau & Perlman, 1982). In empirical research, more "normal" incidents of loneliness have been correlated with a diverse range of phenomena including heightened levels of different emotions (Peplau & Perlman, 1982; Loucks, 1974, 1980; Weeks et al., 1980) as well as with a variety of personal characteristics (Anderson et al., 1983; Hojat, 1983; Jones et al., 1981; Peplau & Perlman, 1982). Despite all of this work, there is still relatively little information as to what an individual's experience of loneliness is like. The goal of the present research, therefore, is to describe the ways in which people experience the situation of loneliness by going back to the phenomenon as it is lived and experienced by individuals, and to offer a thematic description encompassing the fundamental meanings that it holds for them.

To accomplish this goal, 10 male and 10 female adults served as participants in a series of phenomenological interviews. Participants were volunteers from a local university, a church study group, and a community singles group. Across all 20 participants, the average age was 36.6 years; the majority were college-educated, unmarried, and had one or no children. Of the unmarried participants, the majority were divorced, a possible consequence of several participants having been solicited from a local singles group. Participants were either employed outside of the home, in graduate school, or homemakers caring for children. All participants described themselves as from a middle-class socioeconomic bracket.

Each participant took part in an audiotaped phenomenological interview that lasted from 60 to 90 minutes. Each participant selected the specific experiences that he or she chose to talk about during the interview. The opening question for each interview was the same: "When are you most aware of feeling alone?" The person would then talk about several situations in which he or she felt alone; each of these situations was then followed up by asking the participant what he or she was aware of in that situation.

Once themes were derived from individual protocols, all participants were mailed a thematic summary of their interview and were asked for feedback. When this step was complete, the list of themes was revised until all protocols could be evaluated on the basis of comparable thematic meanings. Following this, a final structural description was written that was found to be both comprehensible (that is, written in language close to the original words of the participant) and comprehensive (that is, able to account for all specific examples described by participants).

Results of this procedure revealed that there were a number of ways of feeling alone, each of which was taken to define a theme. The structure of the experience of feeling alone was found to consist of the following four major themes, each comprised of two minor subthemes.

I. Missing
   A. Yearning
   B. Emptiness
II. Barrier
   A. Different
   B. Indifferent
III. Vulnerability
   A. Unsupported
   B. Exposed
IV. Freedom
   A. Freedom to
   B. Freedom from

Thematic categories are related to one another in ways that are best illustrated in the form of Figure 6.1; in this figure, each major theme serves to define one of the four corners. The two subthemes of each major theme also are located at each corner, as is the emotion most often found in connection with that theme. Lines interconnecting the various themes are

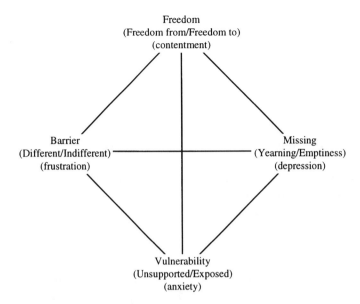

Figure 6.1. The thematic structure of the experience of feeling alone

meant to suggest that each theme may be (and was) combined with any other theme in the description of a specific experience of feeling alone. Following is a brief rendering of each theme, together with its respective subthemes.

The Theme of Missing

In this theme, the person experiences wanting but does not now have a relationship that offers positive possibilities. In this context, the person focuses both on the absence of a relationship with someone else as well as on the experience of missing such a relationship. The following description by one participant provides a good example:

When I see families that look happy and are interacting with each other like my husband and I did before he died, particularly with mothers and fathers around my age, I feel alone. I feel like a part of me is missing. It's like an amputation, like I'm not a whole person. I feel like my husband and I were one, and now half of that is gone, which makes a void there. I miss the companionship, laughter, and intimacy that I had with my husband, and I would like to have it again. I do not want to take anything away from the happy couples I see. I just wish I also had what they have.

In the Missing theme, it may be a particular other, more general others, or a type of relationship that is missed. Other people are usually, but not necessarily, physically absent. The Missing theme often involves grief or other situations of loss; sometimes it concerns missed opportunities for relating. This type of aloneness was typically labeled "feeling alone" by participants and was most strongly associated with feelings of depression. The Missing theme consisted of two subthemes: Yearning and Emptiness.

Yearning. For the Yearning subtheme, the focus is on some other person, or on a type of relationship, that is absent rather than on the emptiness experienced as present. Sometimes there is also a yearning for some other person or for some type of relationship that is not there. Memories or fantasies of the person missed may sometimes be triggered by specific surroundings, objects, or places. Yearning also may be evoked by seeing the other person in a relationship that one desires but does not now have.

Emptiness. For the Emptiness subtheme, the person focuses on the presence of an absence rather than on someone who is missing. The person who feels stuck in the emptiness of the present may experience emptiness in a variety of ways. One may feel lost, without a sense of purpose, and incomplete, like a part of the self is missing. There also may be the experience of a void within the body as well as a loss of interest in activities. The stillness, quietness, and inactivity of the person's surroundings frequently are described as standing out.

The Theme of Barrier

In the Barrier theme, the person reports wanting to relate to another person(s) and experiences a block or obstacle to such relating. Here, the focus is on what stands in the way of relating, on a barrier to connection or relatedness, rather than on the absence of the other. The following description provides a good example of this theme:

When I went to the mountains with a woman I was dating and I was photographing, she did not complain, and I felt close to her until we had a conversation and I found that she neither understood nor cared to try to understand what photography meant to me. I had a desire to be close and share that part of me with her, and with her reaction, I felt less close and more alone, like I am the only one who really understands what I am doing, and this person has disappointed me because they don't even care to try to understand.

The Barrier theme expresses a situation in which the person feels separate, disconnected, and cut off from others, as if there were a wall between the self and other people. The person may feel like an outsider and, therefore, outside the activities in which others are engaged. One also may feel caught on the inside where others have no access to the person's unique experiences. Other people are usually, but not necessarily, physically present in this way of feeling alone. Common situations in which participants experienced barriers include attempts to communicate with someone else, trying to belong to a group, and being in a crowd of strangers. Some of the labels used for this type of experience were "feeling isolated," "alienated," or "estranged." The Barrier them was associated with a feeling of frustration. This theme also consisted of two subthemes: Different and Indifferent.

Different. For the Different subtheme, the focus is on the difference or discrepancy between oneself and others, this difference being experienced as creating a barrier to relating. The person may feel that he or she does not "fit in"; he or she may also feel out of place in relation to a group of others. The person also may feel like he or she is on a different "wavelength" or in a different place in not being understood by, or in not understanding, others.

Indifferent. For this subtheme, the focus is on an attitude of indifference between the self and other people that is experienced as creating a barrier to relating. Other people may be experienced as indifferent toward the person, such as when one is ignored or more actively excluded; alternately, the person may feel indifferent toward others, such as when making no attempt to engage with others or when more actively withdrawing.

The Theme of Vulnerability

In the Vulnerability theme, the person experiences a desire to avoid threats to his or her personal well-being, such as physical injury or a loss of self-esteem, and becomes aware of the heightened possibility of threat either by being without support or by being exposed to danger. The individual focuses on vulnerability in being on his or her own. The following description provides an example:

I felt alone when I took the wrong airplane to the wrong place and was by myself with no money in the middle of the airport. I had all this baggage that was just ripping, and all these things were falling all over the place. It was in the middle of the night, and my boyfriend was supposed to be picking me up in an airport 10 hours from where I was. I stood in the middle of the airport and I cried, hoping that somebody would feel sorry for me and wondering what am I going to do now.

Being on one's own, without either support or protection, is seen as both limiting one's ability to do something and as exposing oneself to possible negative consequences. The person may feel overwhelmed, helpless, or out of control. The focus is neither on missing others nor on barriers to relating; rather, it is on the self, one's own limitations, and the vulnerability of one's projects in the world. Other people may be physically present or absent when this theme is experienced as figural. The experience is typically described as feeling alone, rather than feeling lonely, and was associated with the emotions of fear and anxiety. The Vulnerability theme was also found to consist of two subthemes: Unsupported and Exposed.

Unsupported. For this subtheme, the focus is on a lack of support from others. The person worries about being able to realize projects without help and reports feeling overwhelmed by burdens and responsibilities. Supportive others may be unavailable, or the person may conceal burdens and responsibilities from them.

Exposed. For this subtheme, the focus is on feeling unprotected and exposed to danger or threat. Other people, in addition to being unsupportive, also may be experienced as a source of threat. For this subtheme, the person feels vulnerable, unprotected, and defenseless in relation to another person's possible negative appraisal. The person also may feel exposed and visible to others, as reflected in phrases such as feeling "on display," "on the spot," "all eyes were on me," and so forth. Typical situations include social gatherings, such as parties, and performance situations, such as work and school.

The Theme of Freedom

For the Freedom theme, there is a desire to be and do what one wants to be and do without interference by other people. There is also an awareness of the ways in which being disengaged allows one to realize such goals. The person focuses on his or her freedom in being by him- or herself. The following description provides a good example:

When I go for a walk alone in the evening just to relax and not to deal with worries, I enjoy feeling alone. When I enjoy feeling alone, I am conscious of being alone, and I feel good just to be away for awhile. I am free from having anything to worry about, anyone pressuring me, and responsibilities. I am able to relax and do what I want to, and I am able to heal from whatever is happening, such as resting because of my disease, or letting go of or becoming and expressing negative feelings I am having about stressful events.

In contrast to the other three themes, the theme of Freedom expresses positive possibilities and consequences to being alone. Others are usually, but not necessarily, physically absent when this theme is experienced. In being alone in this way, the person reports experiencing a wholeness and an open field of possibilities rather than a limited or closed field of possibilities combined with a feeling of personal emptiness or vulnerability. In being disengaged from other people who are present, the barrier or separation is experienced as a protection or sanctuary within which the person reports a feeling of freedom. Common situations include being alone at home or in nature, or when engaging in activities made difficult by the presence of others such as writing. Solitude is an appropriate label for this experience, which is generally termed being alone rather than feeling alone. The Freedom theme was associated with positive emotions such as contentment and relief and consisted of two subthemes: Freedom to and Freedom from.

Freedom to. For this subtheme, the person reported focusing on choices and possibilities in being alone. He or she experiences the freedom to do and be what is wanted, and there may be a sense of wholeness and connection with the self.

Freedom from. For this subtheme, the person focuses on the absence of limits and constraints in being alone. Other people are viewed as a limit to one's freedom, and not relating to them is experienced as being free of such limits. The person reports experiencing a freedom from the distractions, demands, interferences, and intrusions of other people.

Interrelationships of Themes and Situations

Situations of feeling alone described by participants were of two general types: (1) being alone, and (2) being with others. Both general situations could be further divided into six different types of settings. Two settings were found for each category of being alone: (a) at home and (b) outdoors; and four settings were found for being with others: (c) one-to-one interactions, (d) social gatherings, (e) work and school, and (f) crowds. The relative frequency with which each of the various themes occurred in the two types of situations as well as in the six types of settings is presented in Table 6.1.

Overall, participants reported more examples of feeling alone in the presence of others than when physically alone. Different themes were found to occur more frequently in different situations; for example, the Missing and Freedom themes occurred predominantly when one was

Table 6.1. *Frequency of Themes for Situations and Settings*[a]

	Theme				
	Missing	Barrier	Vulnerability	Freedom	Total
Situations					
Being alone	43	0	9	26	78
Being with others	15	72	32	7	126
Settings					
Being alone					
At home	34	0	7	9	50
Outdoors	5	0	0	12	17
Being with others					
One-to-one interactions	0	28	12	0	40
Social gatherings	9	20	6	3	38
Work and school	0	13	8	0	21
Crowds	5	8	5	3	21

[a] *Note*: Values in the lower part of the table do not add to those in the top part of the table since not all examples could be coded into these categories.

physically alone, whereas the Barrier and Vulnerability themes occurred primarily when one was in the presence of other people. Despite these trends, all themes, with the exception of Barrier, were found in situations when the person was alone as well as when the person was with others. Such results suggest a relationship between themes and situations, although there is also a certain flexibility to these pairings since the same situation may have different meanings, and different situations may have the same meaning.

Interrelationships among Thematic Structures

Often participants described more than one meaning of feeling alone in a given context. Different themes and subthemes were sometimes experienced together in the same situation or at different time during the unfolding of an event(s). Participants sometimes compared and contrasted different themes and subthemes by discussing together different situations of feeling alone. The most commonly occurring thematic combination was Barrier and Vulnerability (which occurred in 20 different descriptions); the least common thematic combination was Vulnerability and Freedom (which occurred only twice). The Missing and Vulnerability themes

Table 6.2. *Frequency of Theme Scores for Participants*

| Participant | Themes | | | | |
	Missing	Barrier	Vulnerability	Freedom	Total
1	7	3	0	0	10
2	4	9	5	4	22
3	1	2	4	3	10
4	2	4	1	3	10
5	4	1	0	1	6
6	6	4	0	1	11
7	2	3	5	1	11
8	6	2	2	3	13
9	5	3	7	1	16
10	4	3	2	1	10
11	0	9	1	2	12
12	2	9	3	1	15
13	9	7	2	0	18
14	3	10	4	2	19
15	4	8	6	1	19
16	2	6	3	0	11
17	3	5	4	0	12
18	3	2	4	4	13
19	1	7	1	1	11
20	6	1	1	7	15
Total	74	99	55	36	264
Percent	28.0	37.5	20.9	13.6	100

cooccurred six times with the Barrier theme, whereas the Barrier theme coocurred most often with the Vulnerability theme. The Freedom theme occurred most often in connection with the Missing theme (seven cases). The fact that almost every possible combination of theme and subtheme was found suggests both the interrelatedness as well as relative independence of the various themes; it also reflects the variety of ways in which individuals experience the meanings of feeling alone.

The Distribution of Themes Across Participants

An examination also was made of the number of times each participant described each theme; Table 6.2 presents relevant values for all 20 participants. All themes were reported by the majority of participants, and 13 of the 20 participants gave at least one example of all four themes. In terms of specific themes, all participants produced at least one example of the Barrier theme; only one participant failed to produce an example of the Missing theme; three did not produce an example of the Vulnerability theme; and four did not report examples of the Freedom theme. Overall, however, results indicate the generality of themes across participants and suggest that most individuals reported experiences in which each of the various ways of feeling alone was figural.

Despite obvious differences in the total number of times one or another theme was mentioned, individual participants did tend to discuss a particular way of feeling alone in their interview suggesting that certain themes or meanings of feeling alone are more figural for different individuals. The assumption here is that themes more frequently mentioned by a participant in the course of an interview serve to indicate that this particular theme was more significant. Given this assumption, results suggest that different ways of feeling alone are dominant for different individuals, although it also seems clear that the theme of freedom was least frequently expressed and that of barrier was most frequently expressed.

During the interviews, participants talked about experiences of feeling alone at many different times during the life span. Age, marital status, occupation, and other demographic characteristics at the time of the experience of feeling alone often were different from the participant's present life situation. Relating a participant's current demographic characteristics to experiences in the past might lead to erroneous conclusions. For this reason, only the sex of the participant could be validly related to the frequency with which the various themes were expressed in any given participant's interview. When such results were examined, it was found that, overall, male participants tended to provide more examples of the Missing theme and that female participants tended to emphasize Vulnerability more frequently. The number of Barrier and Freedom themes in the interview protocols of males and females was approximately equal.

Implications of Present Findings

Previous research and theorizing, although sometimes differentiating among various forms of loneliness, has not based such differentiations on empirical descriptions of the experience. The discovery of four major meaning themes, each with two variations, suggests that there are many different ways of feeling alone and that various theoretical perspectives may be seen as illuminating or emphasizing one or another particular aspect(s) of the overall experience.

The psychodynamic perspective, for example, tends to focus on painful experiences of aloneness and, therefore, to equate loneliness with painful aloneness. Results of the present interviews suggest that loneliness and painful aloneness are not synonymous. In fact, there are several distinct forms of painful aloneness that individuals may not even label "feeling lonely." In terms of both the Barrier and Vulnerability themes some participants stated that they felt painfully alone but not lonely. In contrast, experiences involving the Missing theme almost always were described as "feeling lonely." By concentrating primarily on the experience of loneliness, psychodynamically oriented theorists seem to have emphasized the theme of Missing to the exclusion of all others.

As an exception to the almost total neglect of positive forms of aloneness in the psychodynamic literature, Winnicott (1958) described the capacity to be alone. This capacity may be viewed as relating to the Freedom theme, and experiences of freedom and contentment in being alone would be conceptualized by Winnicott in terms of developmental factors. It is interesting to note that several participants commented on having an increased capacity to experience a sense of freedom and enjoyment in being alone when aware of having an ongoing supportive or intimate relationship in their lives. Times of aloneness are well tolerated and even enjoyed when experienced as temporary. Furthermore, a background sense of relatedness sustains the experience of well-being in such periods of being alone.

The sociological perspective focuses on societal forces that serve to increase the prevalence and severity of painful aloneness; so, for example, social isolation and alienation usually are emphasized in this literature. For present participants, experiences of "feeling isolated" or "feeling alienated" tended to be used in connection with examples expressing the theme of Barrier. The discussion of isolation and alienation from a sociological perspective suggests that the Barrier theme may receive greater attention from social scientists than is the case for any of the remaining themes.

The existential perspective considers the experience of aloneness as intrinsic to what it means to be human. Both painful and pleasurable experiences of feeling alone are discussed in this literature. Although most of the themes described by the present set of participants are represented in the existential approach, they are rarely distinguished from one another. Terms like loneliness, loneliness anxiety, solitude, aloneness, and fear of aloneness are used impressionistically – and differently – by different authors. Although the use of these terms is meant to suggest that aloneness is considered in broad perspective, the lack of a phenomenological description of the ways in which various forms of aloneness are experienced leads to a confusing mixture of ideas on this topic.

In terms of phenomenological work, Sadler (1978) differentiated five different categories of loneliness: interpersonal, social, cultural, cosmic, and psychological; similar categories were described by Gaev (1976). Relationships between these findings and those of the present study are unclear, since Sadler and Gaev differentiated forms of loneliness on the basis of what the person was alone in relation to, rather than in terms of what the separateness from or lack of another person meant to the participant as in the present study.

Results of present description are consistent with, but more comprehensive than, those reported by Nisenbaum (1984). Nisenbaum, as may be recalled, described nine varieties of aloneness, each with a distinct experiential structure. Although all major themes in the current study are reflected to some extent in the structures described by Nisenbaum, several subthemes were not captured in any of his specific structures. Differences between Nisenbaum's results and those of the current study may have been contributed to by methodological differences. In contrast to the present study, Nisenbaum brought an "a priori" categorization of experience to the research topic rather than letting significant meanings emerge from the dialogue as done in the present set of interviews.

One important aspect of the present results is that different emotions were associated by participants with different thematic meanings. Whereas the Missing theme was most commonly accompanied by feelings of depression, the Barrier theme was most related to feelings of frustration and anger. Similarly, whereas the Vulnerability theme was associated with feelings of anxiety, the Freedom theme was related to more positive emotions, such as contentment.

These specific pairings make sense not only in terms of present results but also in terms of earlier phenomenological descriptions of various emotions as these are experienced in a wide variety of situations (see Price, Barrell, & Barrell, 1985). Within the context of present work, the theme of Missing was described as involving wanting but not having a positive relationship with some other person(s). Since there is often a desire for the immediate presence of someone who is absent, the person may experience a sense of the impossibility of getting what is wanted. The desire for a positive goal along with low expectations of achieving it has been shown to be a necessary and sufficient condition for the experience of depression (Price et al., 1985).

Turning now to the theme of Barrier, it may be recalled that it was characterized as involving an attempt to relate to other people that was blocked by one or another impediment. Attempts at action that are experienced as yielding experiences of "feeling blocked" have been described as providing the necessary and sufficient conditions for the experience of anger and frustration (Price et al., 1985). Similarly, the theme of Vulnerability involves wanting to avoid threats to oneself but feeling uncertain about being able to do so. The desire to avoid negative outcomes accompanied by an uncertain expectation of being able to do so has been found a necessary and sufficient condition for the experience of anxiety (Price et al., 1985).

Finally, the theme of Freedom was described as involving both wanting and having the freedom to do what one wants to do and to be free from the constraints of interacting with others. Unlike each of the remaining themes, this meaning of loneliness describes a situation in which the person is able to achieve goals or desires. Positive outcomes, or high expectations of positive outcomes, that are experienced as significant have been described a both necessary and sufficient conditions for positive emotions, such as contentment, satisfaction, and excitement (Price et al., 1985). In addition to representing different meaning structures of feeling alone, each of the four themes also describes a different structure of emotional experience.

The prior empirical and theoretical literature relating loneliness to emotional experience has strongly suggested that loneliness is most consistently and strongly associated with depression (Bragg, 1979; Leiderman, 1980; Peplau & Perlman, 1982). Within the context of the present study, the theme of Missing was most frequently associated with depression. Experiences of loss, traditionally recognized as central to many forms of depression, were frequently reported in conjunction with this theme. It appears that depression is most prominent in experiences of feeling lonely and missing others. Nevertheless, the theme of Missing refers only to one particular way of feeling alone, and depression is only one emotion associated with aloneness.

Although loneliness has been most strongly linked to depression, other emotional correlates also have been described, such as anxiety, tension, anger, and frustration (Loucks, 1974; Peplau & Perlman, 1982). Different ways of feeling lonely and/or alone may be correlated with different emotions; specifically, anger and frustration may reflect aloneness involving an experience of Barrier, whereas anxiety and tension may reflect an experience of aloneness involving themes of Vulnerability. Positive emotions were probably not found in previous studies primarily because the focus was on painful forms of aloneness and not on those usually termed *solitude*.

Relationships Between Psychopathology and Themes of Aloneness

Many different clinical theorists have associated loneliness with a wide variety of psychopathology, including schizophrenia (Fromm-Reichmann, 1959), depression (von Witzleben, 1958), narcissism (Ziboorg, 1938), and neurosis (Horney, 1937). There has been much disagreement regarding the psychological disorder most clearly associated with loneliness, and several theories have proposed that different forms of loneliness may relate to different disorders. Some theorists have even suggested that loneliness is central to all forms of psychopathology since the person with mental illness, by definition, is psychologically separate from others (Laing, 1965; Van den Berg, 1972). Overall, there is a confusing array of ideas regarding the relationship of loneliness to psychopathology.

The experience of feeling alone in psychological disorders may represent an extreme manifestation of ways of feeling alone found in less pathological individuals. The theme of Missing, which is linked to depression and to the experience of loss, may represent that way of feeling alone most related to clinical depression. The theme of Barrier, which involves an inability to relate to others and is intensified by withdrawal, may in extreme cases represent a schizoid problem or potential schizophrenia. The theme of Vulnerability, which involves feeling anxious and threatened, may be more evident in anxiety disorders or in paranoid states than in other psychopathological conditions. Although these ideas are speculative, they may help to explain why the topic of loneliness has been found to relate to so many different types of psychological disorder.

Another potential relationship between psychopathology and the present thematic structure concerns the possibility that mental illness may reflect the presence of some complex combination of the various themes defining the experience of feeling alone. The psychologically destructive consequences of complex forms of loneliness have been commented on by Sadler (1978), who noted that separation and loss often yield a situation of extreme personal distress. Several examples were described in the present set of interviews in which a participant simultaneously described experiencing each of the various themes characterizing painful aloneness. Many participants also commented on the overwhelming and psychologically incapacitating quality of such an experience in comparison to more single-valued incidents, suggesting that extremely disturbed psychological states involve a complex combination of the different meanings of aloneness. The presence of complex forms of feeling alone in psychopathology may help to explain the difficulty that theorists have had in distinguishing among the various ways of feeling lonely that are frequently described in the psychodynamic literature.

Implications for Psychological Treatment

Within the past few decades, a number of therapeutic strategies have been proposed for dealing with loneliness (Natale, 1986; Rook, 1984). Most of these tend to focus on promoting the social bonding of people suffering from loneliness. Various means of promoting social bonding have been offered, including improving social skills, modifying dysfunctional beliefs, improving self-esteem, and providing opportunities for social contacts and enjoyable activities. Cognitive-behavioral strategies also have been utilized (Young, 1982) as have approaches focusing on "working through" difficulties in the relationship between therapist and client (Gerardi, 1986). Therapy approaches that attempt to resolve the client's religious issues (Paloutzian & Janigan, 1986; Parsons & Wicks, 1986) and develop a tolerance for time alone (Rook & Peplau, 1982; Young, 1982) also have been proposed.

The variety of forms of aloneness described in this research suggest different treatment strategies for different types of aloneness. For example, when the theme of Missing is figural, the person may need to be in contact with people to fill an interpersonal void. With the theme of Barrier, however, being around other people might only heighten one's sense of alienation or aloneness; thus, the person would need to be taught how to relate more effectively to others and, thereby, to bridge the gap that isolates. With the theme of Vulnerability, the person might be offered support or, alternatively, be taught to function with more effective autonomy. Since each of the various forms of aloneness involves a distinct personal meaning, different changes in attitude and behavior may be required for dealing effectively with each of its different meanings.

Treatment strategies for loneliness proposed in the literature may be effective for certain forms of aloneness but not for others. For example, providing opportunities for social contact and enjoyable activities may be most effective for treating aloneness related to the theme of Missing; teaching social skills may be most appropriate for treating aloneness related to the theme of Barrier; improving self-esteem may be most useful for alleviating distress brought about by experiences of vulnerability. Applying treatment techniques "across the board," without distinguishing among different forms of painful aloneness, is likely to reduce the effectiveness of the intervention. It would seem more desirable, not to mention effective, to design treatment approaches consistent with the type or types of aloneness experienced by the client.

Essential to designing an effective treatment approach is a careful interviewing of the client regarding the meaning of aloneness for him or her. The therapist's questions should be aimed at eliciting descriptions of what the client's feeling alone is like: It is not enough to know that someone feels alone; one must also know "how" he or she feels alone and what it means. Only by considering the experience and meanings of feeling alone of a particular individual will it be possible to understand what that person's aloneness means, so that a treatment strategy can be developed to accommodate the specifics of the situation.

A thematically oriented approach to the treatment of painful aloneness must focus, therefore, not on the external situation of an individual but on the meanings of aloneness for the individual. Results of the present set of dialogues suggest certain ways in which painful experiences of aloneness may be transformed into more meaningful ones. For example, one may transform an experience of Missing by focusing on the presence of the self instead of on the absence of the other. In a similar way, it may be possible to transform the experience of Barrier by treating separation from others as a sanctuary rather than as an obstacle to relating. Finally, experiences of Vulnerability may be transformed by focusing on what the person can do instead of on what the person is unable to do when alone. Although such transformations may be difficult, exploring other ways of making a situation meaningful is intrinsic to the process of psychological growth considered from an existential-phenomenological point of view.

7

Making Amends
The Psychology of Reparation

At first glance, reparation might seem an unusual topic for psychology to consider since the verb *to repair* occurs most often not in the world of interpersonal relations but in the realm of things that break or no longer work. But people also break; they have broken hearts and broken lives, and they, too, seek ways to put the pieces of their lives and hearts back together again. To be human is to have difficulties in interpersonal relationships and, sometimes, to have relationships that break apart. We all know what it is to go about the work of "making up"; if the stakes are high enough or the rupture severe enough, we may even seek professional help to assist us in repairing a broken relationship or marriage.

Despite an initial impression to the contrary, we do talk about fixing interpersonal relationships in somewhat the same way as we talk about fixing broken vases and automobiles. Images of wholeness and perfection are among the most elementary prototypes of human consciousness, and a family of metaphors has grown up to describe experiences of this type. Consider, for example, how we speak of some event or object as *complete* or *incomplete*: A chef may taste a sauce and determine that "it *needs* something"; an individual grieving the death of a loved one may describe his or her experience as "*feeling incomplete.*" In both cases, the present state of lack or incompleteness is experienced against a ground of wholeness or perfection.

A different metaphor for perfection refers to a concern with *balance*. When we admire the beauty of a painting or the elegance of a fine athlete, we respond to their qualities of proportion and fluidity. The Gestalt Law of Prägnanz suggests that we naturally seek to create a sense of balance in

This chapter is based on the unpublished doctoral dissertation *A Phenomenological Study of The Experience of Reparation* by Michael Hawthorne, submitted to the University of Tennessee in 1989.

191

figures initially experienced as unbalanced. A related metaphor concerns the contrast between *clean* and *dirty*. New garments with stains are sold with a warning marking them as "imperfect." The Old Testament instructed people to offer unblemished animals for sacrifices, and sin was often referred to as a "stain." To be perfect is to be pure, without blemish.

Perhaps because perfection is so fragile an experience, the creation and/ or restoration of a sense of perfection is a powerful motif in our culture. Although many different prototypes are relevant to experiences of repairing an interpersonal relationship, those stressing brokenness seem especially revealing – that is, as involving a process of putting pieces together again or of restoring wholeness to a broken relationship. Broken things can be mended and restored to wholeness, and the child who takes a damaged toy to mother is amazed by her ability to repair the toy with loving care and a little glue. The world is a safer place when mistakes can be amended.

Yet there are aspects of our lives that seem irreparable. The more we move from vases and toys to interpersonal phenomena, the less sure we are that damage can be repaired. A reputation is a difficult thing to save; hurt feelings are slow to heal, and tensions between individuals sometimes continue for a lifetime. Even if we want to make amends, it is not always possible to do so. The world is a much more complicated place when we recognize that not all mistakes can be repaired.

Contexts for Studying Reparation

The concept of reparation derives from a variety of contexts: religious, legal, and psychological. Foremost among these is the religious context in which experiences of atonement and repentance are critical. Both the Jewish and Christian faiths teach that sin *separates* us from God and from each other and that repentance and atonement effect a restoration of these relationships.

The Religious Context

The Jewish Tradition. Within the Jewish tradition, two fundamental principles characterize the cultural experience of reparation: restitution and repentance. The Jewish law of the *Pentateuch* seemed to demand a punishment equal to a crime. The talion principle ("an eye for an eye") existed in other cultures before Israel, although the concept of "measure for measure" became a fundamental basis of Jewish civil law. The question of motive was often a decisive factor in determining guilt punishable by the measure-for-measure rule. "If it could be proven that a person intended to do injury to another, . . . then what he intended to do to his fellow man was done to him" (Priest, 1980, p. 148).

To many rabbis, the administration of literal punishment was not only impractical but inhumane. Some scholars insist that *lex talionis* was already obsolete in Biblical times and that "the only unquestionable law of retaliation in the Mosaic code refers to *intentional* murder for which there is no other retribution but *life-for-life* in the literal sense" (Miklisanski, 1947, p. 300). Compensation for damages by exchanging money and/or property became an alternative to vengeful retribution. The concept of positive compensation was implied within the measure-for-measure principle (i.e., the victim was to get some *satisfaction* from the perpetrator for whatever suffering was endured).

If restitution took care of a victim's experience of loss, repentance was the way for a guilty party to address the experience vis à vis God. As the law was written, the mere presentation of a sacrifice without repentance did not relieve the debt incurred by committing a crime or breaking a commandment. The role of repentance (*teshuvah*) in Jewish tradition is dialectically bound with that of sin; to understand repentance, one must understand sin (Soloveitchik, 1984). By definition, sin has two fundamental aspects: binding and defiling. Sin *binds* the person in a juridical sense with an obligation to repay, much like a commercial debt. Knowledge of this kind of sin comes through the intellect, and the rabbis stated that a nominal level of repentance was effective to remove the need for punishment.

Soloveitchik (1984) suggested that people who experience sin only in the juridical sense and who offer the minimal confession to indemnify themselves typically do so out of fear of punishment. Such repentance, however, is significant because it limits the experience of sin and punishment to the human order only. The public, communal confession brings acquittal but stops short of a more self-revealing confession capable of leading to a personal transformation.

Sin also *defiles*, and this, clearly, is the more profound sense of sin. If one is open to the existential consequences of defiling sin, it brings a self-effacement, a lessening of one's own worth, a revulsion in the soul. Sin as impurity necessitates purification through *taharah*, repentance (literally, cleanliness). The rabbis believed that the "personality" of the sinner remained defiled after communal confession (*Kapparah*), whereas *taharah* repentance achieved a complete cleansing of the soul.

The most important aspect to the experience of sin is feeling alienated from God. According to Soloveitchik, this experience is comparable to mourning the loss of a loved one for, in sin, the person has lost God. In the same way as mourning inevitably contains an element of self-torture and torment, so too does the sinner begin to feel "contempt and disgust toward himself," and only pain pushes him or her to "knock on the locked gates" that separate the penitent from God. The role of suffering in repentance is central in Jewish tradition and serves as the way in which the sinner reclaims the self and removes the sin. In this way, reparation and repentance move from the domain of economics and law to a more symbolic and spiritual realm.

The Christian Tradition. Christian theologians also viewed the primary consequences of sin as estrangement from God and alienation from other human beings. Many New Testament scriptures suggest that sin made us "enemies" of and "hostile" to God. In addition, certain aspects of Christian theology suggest that Jesus defined sin as including the realm of intention as well as that of action.

The major difference, however, between the Judaic and Christian traditions concerning the proposed remedy for sin is that Christians believe that Jesus established a new covenant with the world that was based not on law but on grace. Christians believe that Jesus' death reconciled them to God; that is, an atonement (formerly "at-onement") was effected because Christ, through His death, propitiated the anger of God. The grace of God also is shown in that He allowed His son to be payment for human debt. This view is in line with the earlier Judaic understanding of "satisfaction" as involving juridical and commercial claims.

Some Christian theologians have emphasized that a new covenant was founded in grace and, therefore, supersedes forensic satisfaction. God's fundamental character was defined not in terms of justice but in terms of love and mercy. "A God who forgives because His justice has been satisfied does not really forgive" (Wolf, 1957, p. 113). They point to New Testament scripture, which suggests that, through Jesus, God reconciled Himself to human beings – not that Jesus reconciled human beings to God.

This view presents a different conception of grace and forgiveness, and it represents a broad understanding in Christian experience. Grace is the unsolicited giving of unmerited favor; forgiveness is offered to those who accept it. Since the suspension of a retributive attitude is opposed to a "natural" or rational perspective, the Christian ideal of forgiving even the person who does not deserve it is a "logical paradox" (Kolnai, 1977). For many, Christ's last words on the cross ("Forgive them Father, for they know not what they do") is the perfect expression of Christian forgiveness.

Christians believe that Jesus understood law in terms of reconciliation and restoration of relationship and, for this reason, believed that the entire law could be summed up in the commandment to love God and one's neighbor. The disciples of Jesus were encouraged to look upon God as a father who loved His children and who cared for them individually. The imagery of the New Testament covenant personalizes God's relationship with His people. The parable of the prodigal son teaches that there is joy in heaven upon the return of even just one repentant sinner.

In the Book of Luke, Jesus commanded His followers to "turn the other cheek," a teaching that corresponded to His forgiveness of those who crucified Him. Not only were His followers to forgive the unrepentant, they were to forgive the outwardly hostile. Jesus' commandment to forgive others was anchored in the sense that God's forgiveness was an unspeakably generous gift. His interpretation of the law also suggested that no person could ever deserve salvation through good deeds, piety, or scrupulous obedience of the law. Christians were never to forget that they are saved by grace, and that they merit God's forgiveness as little as the worst sinner. God freely exchanges forgiveness of sin for an attitude of repentance, and the experience of divine grace must alter the Christian's demand for rational justice from others in the interhuman world.

Retribution and Restitution in the Legal Context

Violations of relationships also have legal implications. Western legal tradition is the distillation of centuries of religious, social, cultural, and moral influences. Our implicit understanding of fair and reasonable dispositions of interpersonal problems often are anchored in conceptions of civil and criminal justice, and what we expect in the way of a reparation is shaped by our traditions of jurisprudence.

Retribution. The legal code, similar to religious doctrine, also affirms a universal tendency toward reciprocity and balance in interpersonal exchange (Eckhoff, 1974). The contemporary legal term for balance in western civil and criminal justice is *proportionality*. Even a cursory survey of legal history teaches that proportionality has always been defined within the context of society, and the amount of pain that a society deems is deserved by a criminal for a particular offense depends upon how heinous the crime is in its eyes at the time. In early America, for example, criminals were hung for stealing horses. The death penalty is now reserved in this country for the punishment of first-degree murder; one era's misdemeanor is another's felony.

Our need for retribution has been civilized to the extent that we leave it to the state to capture, prosecute, and punish violators. Nevertheless, the personal urge to "get even" remains strong. One criminal justice expert has gone so far as to speculate that revenge in the form of just retribution is the "glue that holds the social fabric together" (McAnany, 1977, p. 210). Without it, offenders would be compelled to "take the law into their own hands," thereby creating the possibility of anarchy.

Restitution. Legal scholars note that the gradual tempering of *lex talionis* was an historical process reflecting a general decrease in the use of violence as a means of solving disputes. Schafer (1970) points out that toward the end of the Middle Ages, legal violations in which one party hurt another party became subject to private promise of proper restitution. Practice of the civil law of "torts" became distinct from criminal law, and compensating the injured party for loss took the place of punishment.

The intent of "paying damages" is to restore the person to a "pre-event status" or to "wholeness." Consider the settlement of a minor car accident: To the cost of car repair and medical treatments, a jury might add an extra sum to compensate for "pain and suffering." The legal notion of wholeness is based on the idea that a monetary award restores the person and his or her property to the way they were before the offense.

But there are limitations to a legal application of the reparative concept. Responsibility of offenders often goes beyond the loss of property. If the car accident led to a fatality, how is the payment of money an effective restitution for the death of a child or spouse? Compensating the family in the amount of the potential life's earnings of a single mother, for example, may provide for food and shelter but fail to restore a sense of wholeness. Seeing an offender punished may reduce anger, but vicarious vengeance does even less than compensation to address the lasting experience of incompleteness.

The role of remorse is often important in the victim's experience of satisfaction in legal reparations. If an offender shows regret that is "proportional" to the extent of the crime, it may be easier for the victim to deal with his or her lack of wholeness. That the offender must live with a "life sentence" of guilt matches the pain and disruption of the victim's own life. When an offender expresses remorse, a sense of balance between the parties is restored in a way that is probably more important than simple financial considerations.

The Law and Reparation. When negotiation of conflict and damage is viewed from a legal standpoint, the focus is decidedly on punishment, although punishment often comes up short in our experience of justice in civil matters. The legal system may constrain a person to pay compensation, but it often cannot make the victim whole again. Neither can it compel an offender to feel bad for the crime or to empathize with the victim. One can only be partially satisfied by vicarious vengeance.

The end result of most civil proceedings is minimally satisfying at best; reconciliation and improved understanding are rarely outcomes of a legal trial. We typically go to court when efforts to negotiate have failed, when differences are "irreconcilable." Courtrooms are not a place for dialogue. Lawyers stand in our place to argue our position; judges and juries unravel stories of disagreement and damage. Guilt and responsibility are not dynamic, human concepts in a courtroom; instead, they become concrete realities written in the judgment. As important as the law is to society, it is limited in its ability to restore balance, wholeness, and community.

Guilt, Forgiveness, and Reparation in the Psychological Context

Psychological perspectives offer additional insight into the dynamics of resolving conflict. As one example, consider results of a study performed at Seattle University in which participants were asked to discuss specific times in their lives when forgiving an important person was an issue for them (Rowe, Halling, Davies, Leifer, Powers, & van Bronkhorst, 1989). Results of this study revealed that the situation of injury was experienced as a "disruption to the wholeness or integrity of one's life" and that following such an injury, participants felt angry, off-center, and distant from the damaging person. The experience of injury also was self-referential; that is, participants reported believing themselves to be the target of intentional malice by the other person.

Across all participants, an initial preoccupation with the event of injury was common, frequently involving fantasies of revenge. Participants acknowledged that they felt an apology was required for any change to occur in the relationship, and at that point, they were still "clinging" to hurt and anger, refusing to "let go." If the relationship was an important one, thoughts of revenge were interspered with wishes for reconciliation. An important aspect to this development was letting go of the self-referential perspective. At this point, questioning the self became common: "Did I do something to bring about his or her actions?" It was such letting go that allowed participants to feel "freed from hanging onto the injury."

Participants also reported being "surprised" by their openness to forgive. The willingness to allow resolution was seen as the single most critical component in forgiving and was always recognized after it had occurred. The conditions for resolution previously thought to be necessary rarely matched the actual trajectory and experience of the forgiving event. Forgiveness could not be manufactured, forced, or predicted. It happened as a quiet, unforeseen resolution to change participants' relationships both to themselves and to the other person. The situation of injury was experienced in a new light that allowed both parties to connect in ways other than as "victim and victimizer." In gradually opening themselves to the other, participants reported reclaiming a world that was familiar yet transformed by the present moment of forgiving.

The Psychodynamics of Forgiveness. Pattison, a psychoanalyst, addressed the psychodynamics of forgiving and failing to forgive (Pattison, 1965). In this approach, the need for forgiveness is referred back to the ambivalence felt in early child–parent relationships. Since the child is often frustrated by parental restrictions, he/she first learns to obey rules strictly out of a fear of retaliation. Pattison believed that at this level of morality, punishment is the only resolution for guilt. As long as the child relates to the parent (in Buber's terms) as an It, there can be no experience of forgiving because only the self exists. Only when both parties are capable of intimate relationship is the process of forgiveness likely to yield reconciliation of the loving union. Although punishment may be anticipated as requisite for forgiveness, sacrifice alone does not bring about forgiveness nor a restoration of relationship.

Pattison identified four steps in any act of reconciliation: confession, remorse, restitution, and mutual acceptance. Each step can be distorted by the influence of a punitive view of forgiveness. Confession is the recognition of the part that one has played in the estrangement of the other. Remorse is more than punitive self-flagellation; it is a "recognition of the hostility expressed toward the Thou and the desire to be reconciled in love" (Pattison, 1965, p. 110). If a person provides restitution to avoid retaliation, the punitive model of the I–It relationship is still operative. Properly conceived, restitution reestablishes the conditions of an I–Thou relationship. It is not given as a response to demands or the threat of punishment; it is given because love compels a restoration of the other. When we are guilty, according to Pattison, we are loathe to give up our need for punishment and for giving restitution to expiate our wrong.

Forgiveness requires the willing participation of a forgiver. Both parties must accept dependence on the love of the other and meet to work out a reunion. Forgiving is the extension of one's love to a person who has violated it. Pattison quoted Ferenczi as saying that the forgiver must share the experience of "guilt, anguish, and estrangement" with the offender. The willingness to reconcile is shown by the forgiver in choosing to forego retaliation and to receive the reparative efforts.

The psychological experience of forgiveness seems to have little to do with the adequacy of expiatory gifts. It seems better described as a deliberate act to turn away from the urge to retaliate in order to embrace the opportunity to reestablish relationship. It is serendipitous and unpredictable; forgiveness sometimes happens when it should not. In this way, reconciliation recalls the religious concept of grace – unmerited favor – and suggests that both theology and psychology share a reconciliatory understanding of forgiveness.

The Psychology of Guilt. Nearly all who study the topic of guilt view it as fundamental reality of the human condition (Amato, 1982). One of the most extensive analyses of this topic has been provided by Buber, whose views are founded on the belief that an individual's primary responsibility is to enter into dialogue with God. Buber spoke of conscience as God's voice calling to the individual "to fulfill the personal intention of being for which he was created" (Schlipp, 1967, p. 175). Guilt is the experiential consequence of a failure to answer the call "to become."

When we are guilty, it is not because we have failed to realize our potentialities, which we cannot know in the abstract, but because we have failed to bring the resources we find available to us at a given moment into our response to a particular situation that calls us out. This means that we cannot be guilty a priori to any ideal conception of the self, but only in relation to those moment-by-moment choices to authenticate ourselves that come to us in the concrete situation. (Friedman, 1965, pp. 49–50)

In his essay, "Guilt and Guilt Feelings," Buber addressed the experience of guilt and its ontic character. Buber charged that (psychoanalytic) psychology tended to view guilt only as feeling derived from fear of violating parental rules and values; therefore, guilt was not a "real" situation of existence.

As a result of this basic attitude, guilt was simply not allowed to acquire an ontic character; it had to be derived from the transgression against ancient and modern taboos, against parental and social tribunals. The feeling of guilt was now to be understood as essentially only the consequence of dread of punishment and censure by this tribunal, as a consequence of the child's fear of "loss of love" or, at times, when it was a question of imaginary guilt, or as a "need for punishment" of a libidinal nature, as "moral masochism" which is complemented by the sadism of the "superego." (Buber, 1957, p. 115)

Buber also was troubled by the psychoanalytic "solution" for guilt (i.e., the practice of seeking to trace back the elements of "unconscious guilt" and to unmask the neurosis evoking specific feelings of guilt).

Buber did not deny that neuroses exist or that a person could feel guilty over a neurotic fear or taboo. But he was more concerned that psychoanalysis seemed to obscure the fundamental situation of guilt – when an individual knows that he or she *is* guilty. Buber further suggested that guilt does not exist because there are taboos but rather that the invention of taboos proves the primal fact that "man can become guilty and know it" (Buber, 1957, p. 117).

Buber defined "existential guilt" as that which has existential importance. Each person stands in an objective relationship to other human beings and is responsible for injuries to the human order that he or she causes. Real guilt is dialogical in the sense that responsibility to authenticate one's own existence cannot be separated from one's responsibility to others. Human beings are never guilty toward themselves alone, and Buber suggested that the function of guilt is to push an individual to make reparation for the injuries caused by action or lack of action.

The action demanded by conscience to fulfill reparation for existential guilt is found in three events: illumination, perseverance, and reconciliation. The event of illumination corresponds to the confession of guilt and sin in the spheres of law and faith, respectively. Buber describes self-illumination as an intense examination of the depths of guilt: as a light illuminating the "abyss of I-with-me." It is only in this light that an individual can come to know his/her guilty condition. Unless one overcomes a resistance to illumination, confession is meaningless.

The second event – perseverance – is best interpreted as an ongoing process rather than as a discrete event. Buber suggests that this process is a matter of actively seeking to remain in the illumination. "Persevering" connotes a continuous and steady desire to understand and acknowledge how one is truly guilty, with such acknowledgment leading to a humble, responsible, and conscientious participation in the interhuman world.

If people were guilty only toward themselves, they would have only to take the road of self-illumination and perseverance. Because one is always guilty in relation to another person, reparative action to the one injured is required. For this reason, reconciliation is incomplete without a direct encounter with the injured person that communicates the assumption of responsibility and a sincere effort to make reparation. Buber's perspective is that these acts are authentic only if they emerge from a person transformed by the experience of illuminated existential guilt. Premeditated, strategic restitutions reveal an attempt to escape the recognition of one's guilty state.

Psychoanalytic Views on Reparation. The major proponent of the role played by reparation in human development derives from the theoretical school founded by Klein and carried forward by Winnicott. Although Klein's theory is controversial, perhaps the most uncontroversial thing to be said is that she focused attention on the infant's earliest relationships and attempted to describe the infant's experiences of aggressive feelings. So, for example, in sessions of child analysis, Klein (1933/1975) reported seeing young patients dramatically expressing an intense "fear of being devoured, or cut up or torn to pieces, or . . . [their] . . . terror of being surrounded and pursued by menacing figures" (p. 249). Since these children had not been subjected to such situations in life, Klein believed that the source of this anxiety was instinctual.

Klein believed that children come into the world with a powerful urge to destroy and to consume. She called this early phase of life the period of "maximal sadism" because she felt that the death instinct was experienced as immediate and intense during this period of development. Given this primordial state of affairs, the developing ego's vital first function is to project the experiential source of this sadism outward, thereby making the "internal" world safe from destructive power.

One consequence of such early projection is that the external world comes to be experienced as malevolent, devouring, and menacing:

The child . . . is therefore prepared from the outset to view the real, external world as more or less hostile to itself, and peopled with objects ready to make attacks on it. (Klein, 1933/1975, p. 254)

According to Klein, the resulting anxiety is "paranoid" in the sense that the child fears persecution in the form of sadistic attacks by objects, even though the danger is projected from the infant. Since Klein felt that the child comes into the world in a "paranoid position," all interactions are charged by an awareness of vulnerability and the fear of retaliatory attack.

Klein further suggested that the primitive superego evokes anxiety about aggressive impulses that impel the child to destroy objects. This, in turn, leads to an increase of anxiety about the consequences of destruction. As long as the child remains in the developmental situation of the so-called paranoid position, the superego only arouses anxiety and the "most violent of defense mechanisms." When the child's sadism diminishes and love comes to the fore, the superego is modified and, instead of evoking anxiety, comes to generate feelings of guilt. At many points in her writings, Klein brings up such themes as "constructive tendencies" and "restitutive phantasies." These reparative fantasies are to mature superego guilt what destructive fantasies were to primitive superego anxiety.

For Klein, reparation is the only effective resolution of an infant's tendency to hurt mother together with its need to identify with her in fact and function: "If the baby has, in his aggressive phantasies, injured his mother by hurting and tearing her up, he may soon build up phantasies that he is putting the bits together and repairing her." Klein further theorized that the infant's experience of reparative functioning (and, later, reparative activities) facilitates the development and integration of the ego. Normal experiences of frustration then serve to mobilize reparative drives; rather than leading to disintegration and increased anxiety, such experiences allow the child to discover that people are more resilient than imagined and that fantasies and impulses do not lead to a loss of the person.

Winnicott (1963) elaborated Klein's concept of a "benign cycle" of using-and-replacing, destroying-and-recreating, and damaging-and-repairing. Insofar as the baby continues to find relief from anxiety by means of reparative activity, Winnicott felt that the baby was freed to become more bold in her experiencing the world and her own body. All instinctual drives are less frightening because of the infant's confidence that something can be done to restore things. A mature love, for this view, involves concern about the result of one's loving and a willingness to be responsible both for damages imagined and for depletion of the person receiving "voracious" loving.

A further component to mature love is the capacity for identification, and it is only when a person can put aside his/her own interests and impulses that he or she can truly identify with and love another. Because of a relaxation of the fear that mother, or any other loved person, will retaliate for aggressiveness, the child is increasingly able to focus on the feelings of others. Indeed, Klein felt that a capacity to consider the situation of another and to sacrifice one's own gratification is developed in this period. Thus, Klein considers both depression (over the possible loss of a loved one) and guilt to be significant developmental achievements. In this theory, pangs of guilt are healthy proof of maturity, when not overwhelming, and are at the heart of those social motives demonstrating a capacity for identification and love. Ultimately, it is the sense of guilt relevant to one's fantasies and actions that yields the steady operation of conscience.

Winnicott (1963) preferred to call this feeling "concern" rather than guilt because he felt it connoted a much more positive quality:

The word "concern" is used to cover in a positive way a [phenomenon] that is covered in a negative way by the word "guilt." A sense of guilt is anxiety linked with the concept of ambivalence, and implies a degree of integration in the individual ego that allows for the retention of good object-image along with the idea of the destruction of it. Concern implies further integration and further growth and relates in a positive way to the individual's sense of responsibility especially in respect of relationships into which the instinctual drives have entered. Concern refers to the fact that the individual *cares* or *minds*, and both feels and accepts responsibility. (p. 112)

Summary. In this review of psychological perspectives on guilt, forgiveness, and reparation, many themes emerged that also occur in religious and legal contexts. The fundamental experience of guilt appears to be alienation and mourning. When one violates a relationship, one loses the presence of the other and a future with him/her. This loss can be experienced as catastrophic. Although we can develop a neurotic relationship to guilt, the more important human situation is when we accept responsibility for behavior that tears relational bonds apart.

The balancing of interpersonal accounts and the desire for getting even appear to be universal: If injured, we retaliate; if we have done the injuring, we fear retaliation. Human beings are well equipped with psychological defenses to avoid full consciousness of responsibility, and may even deny culpability. Relating to other people in a self-absorbed, I–It fashion keeps us bound to a punitive, and paranoid, position in which *lex talionis* seems a reasonable mode of negotiating conflict. Appeasement gifts and sacrifices can be offered to expiate sin and satisfy anger; they also can be seen as hollow if intended merely to escape punishment.

Reconciliation takes place only when the offender examines the situation and willingly acknowledges his or her guilt. The person's desire for restoring the wholeness of his or her world and that of others compels him or her to pay the debt and "put back" what has been "taken." This is more than a coerced penance to gain acquittal: By apology, compensation, and even reparative fantasy, an image of wholeness is recreated.

This set of activities still does not guarantee reconciliation. The literature on forgiveness indicates that mutual acceptance of the opportunity to restore is required. Courts are not commonly known for mercy, but the expression "I'm throwing myself at the mercy of the court" represents an awareness that sometimes we ask for a release of anger not merited by anything we are or have done. Forgiveness involves a decision to suspend a rightful retaliatory response, choosing instead to extend grace: At-onement takes two.

The Present Program of Research

In order to describe the thematic structure of the experience of reparation, participants were selected who were willing and able to discuss this issue.

To secure participants, solicitations were made at adult church study groups and in graduate classes in psychology and education. The selection process began with a brief description of reparation, and individuals were asked if they felt they would like to discuss this topic. The final group of participants consisted of 14 individuals – 7 males and 7 females – between the ages of 21 and 61 (the median age was 38 years). Before the interview began, each participant was presented with a brief, dictionary-like, definition of reparation and asked to respond to the following questions: "Can you think of a specific situation in which you were involved in an experience like this . . . a time when you were aware of the process happening? Please tell me about it."

Following each interview, protocols were prepared from audiotapes of the interviews. These protocols were then used as the basic texts from which thematic results were derived. Interpretive analysis of the various interviews revealed that two salient phenomena characterized every interview: One concerned an experience of breach, and the second concerned an experience of coming to terms with that breach. Reparation was described as only one of three ways that people described coming to terms with their experiences of breach. These results suggest that coming to terms with a breach can be understood only when cast against the grounds that it routinely and naturally selects. For this reason, it is necessary to describe many different types of experiences before describing the focal experience of reparation.

Grounds for Experiencing Breach

Within the various protocols, the experience of a breach invariably was described as taking place within the contexts of time and relationships with other people. Both grounds were described at some point in all narratives, and both were interwoven in all experiences or reparation. The experience of time was described as the most general ground, and an awareness of the passage of time was implied even when not referred to explicitly. Statements concerning time set the following general themes for participant stories: time passes; some things change; some things stay the same. Time emerged as a fundamental ground because all aspects of the reparative process were described as influenced by experiences of change and continuity: For example, the stinging experience of being assaulted by a group of bullies in high school was described as painful even 30 years after the event.

In the present set of protocols, time also was introduced to establish a context for the unfolding of a specific story. All narratives were set with respect to a particular age (e.g., "when I was only fourteen") and/or a life era (e.g., "around the time of my divorce"). Participants pointed out that the passage of time led to a *change* in them, the other person, and/or the situation, which in turn altered their relationship to, and experience of, breach.

It's a tragic thing that it took so many years for me to realize the importance of communication and of saying thank you. Now that I've grown older, I realize that there are things you can't take for granted.

Participants also conveyed the continuity of their experience of breach despite the passage of time.

It's not cool to come back and want to fight somebody two years later about something when you were a kid. You're supposed to forget about it. I think I was a little different in that I really did remember the situation. . . .

Time also was described in terms of the limitations it imposes. Participants were aware that opportunities to act in response to breach are limited by time.

He knew he was going to die two years ago, and I'm sure that was another reason that he was making amends.

A second major ground concerned experiences of relationships that were breached. The most general delimitation concerned the specific kind of relationship involved in the reparative incident; these included friends, lovers, spouses, ex-spouses, business partners, strangers, parents and children, employees, employers, and God.

The qualities of relationship also were made figural by introducing themes of closeness, power, and former status.

My mother and I are constantly at an uneasy truce. Even though I have grown children, she still thinks I'm her child and tries to tell me everything I should do.

My father and I are not that close emotionally. We have a kind of distant relationship. . . .

Further cases specifically related to the personal characteristics of both parties.

He used to get his feelings hurt very easily. He felt like he was neglected.

She'd rather not think about unpleasant things.

I am a person who very much needs to be needed, and he was a person who needs to have somebody take care of him. He needs a mother, and so we fit very well.

Comments regarding personal values were used to establish the basis upon which decisions in interpersonal matters were made. These statements ranged from a discussion of religious heritage to comments about beliefs that have emerged from experience.

I'm a recovering alcoholic. One of the steps in the A.A. program is making amends by identifying people you have harmed over your period of alcoholism and being willing to repair those relationships. . . .

Another way participants described experiencing relational boundaries was in terms of family heritage. Such statements made it clear that interpersonal styles were influenced by what was experienced as "correct" in the family setting.

Maybe my family is where I picked up my style because I can't think of many times when I saw people apologizing.

A final group of statements revealed the general interpersonal style of the characters in the various narratives.

People can bring problems and angers or whatever in my office, and we can sit down and hash them out. No matter what it is, we can work it out.

She is likely to carry a grudge, whereas I'm not likely to hang onto or remember them.

Experiencing the Breach

Specific incidents of breach concerned a wide spectrum of events ranging from mild verbal insults to killing enemies in war. Stories centered on such events as a fiance breaking her engagement, a clerk stealing money from a customer, a person expressing anger at God, and a mother losing control of her temper when dealing with her child. When participants described breaks in relationship, they were aware of three interdependent aspects of the experience: locus of responsibility, changes in self/other/relational boundaries, and degree of urgency.

One fundamental aspect to the experience of breach was a concern with who was responsible. In most narratives, participants clearly experienced one person as injurer and the other as victim. Awareness of this theme was expressed in several ways; many focused on who was at fault.

I did feel that I had something to apologize for with her. That was definitely my wrong.

It was clear to *me* we are *both* at fault. She is clear that I was at fault, and she is just now becoming clear that she was at fault.

Acceptance or avoidance of blame also appeared in participant narratives. Some participants clarified the difference between the experience of "owning up to" a breach and one of "excusing" it. They also described situational and personal factors influencing the perception of who was to blame:

The offended person can make reparation. But for me to do that now, I would have to sell myself and lie. The reparation with him would be possible if I said "I was wrong, you were right. I take full responsibility for it."

You have to remember that you're also at fault. Somehow, in some way, you have contributed – even if it's only a minuscule amount.

A final way in which participants described responsibility was in terms of intention, and this was described as a critically important aspect of many participant experiences of breach. The degree of blame typically related to the perception of whether the person had acted with a conscious intention to hurt.

I felt like a rat because I deliberately created a very hurtful situation.

I didn't realize at the time that she needed me to support her *more* than she needed me working. I sort of ignored that or wasn't aware of it. I was kind of blind to it.

A related issue concerned the perception of how both parties were affected. Perceptions of the level of impact varied across narratives; in most cases, participants spoke of lasting and profound (generally negative) changes. Many statements concerned changes in the self. Comments focused on the disruptive experience of dealing with the break at the time as well as with uncomfortable memories that still linger. For some, the experience of breach was felt to have little impact; others described it as one of personal devastation. Most participants experienced a significant loss of the sense of wholeness; the continuity of their experience had been interrupted by breach.

I didn't eat, study, or go to class. I lost twenty ponds. I was very hurt and very angry and very confused.

You have something in your mind, and it was left unfinished. It's not how you are or how you feel.

Another aspect of participant experience concerned how the other was changed by the breach. The content of these changes matched those described as occurring in the self. For example, participants worried if the breach had disrupted them or caused irreparable harm or if it had even been noticed; most times, they did have some basis on which to judge its impact on the other. Participants often spoke of their assessment of how the other now felt about them (i.e., angry, disappointed, waiting to get revenge, etc.).

Participants also described an awareness of changes in relationship. In general, they reported feeling cut off and alienated from the other. The relationship that existed before was interrupted or shattered in some respect, leading the person to describe his or her experience in terms such as "distance" and "barrier." People who felt they could trust each other now felt distrust at a most basic level. Where there once was closeness, there now was a "rift"; where there was openness, there was now a sense of "closed."

A third facet to the experience of breach concerned the perceived urgency to do something about it. When participants were aware of a breach, they made an estimate of the extent to which they and/or the other experienced a need to act in response to the breach.

The importance to me of making reparation at a given time runs on a continuum, depending upon which burner these things are on. I notice different degrees of gnawing or discomfort depending upon how inevitable or how urgent pulling out and dispatching things are.

Applying this participant's metaphor, it is possible to see a continuum of perceived urgency. Statements indicating least urgency reflected a simple awareness of breach, where the breach was neither agitating nor troublesome. Other comments indicated that the awareness of breach was uncomfortable and led to a feeling of uneasiness. Such statements reflected a tolerance for discomfort, and although a response was sometimes seen as inevitable, the individual was content to postpone action.

The next level described an awareness experienced as an urgent need to act properly:

They do not feel urgent, but they're on the back burner as something I will take care of in due time. . . . It's still something that *bugs* me. It's there, but it's not *that* urgent. It's something I'm going to do.

The perceived severity of the violation often influenced the degree of urgency felt with regard to responding to the breach.

I guess the degree of violation is what makes it stick and what lets it go.

Experiences of breach cut across more than one subcategory. The themes of responsibility, changes, and urgency were interwoven in the description of a breach experience. The following passage is an example of how one participant experienced the interrelatedness of these aspects.

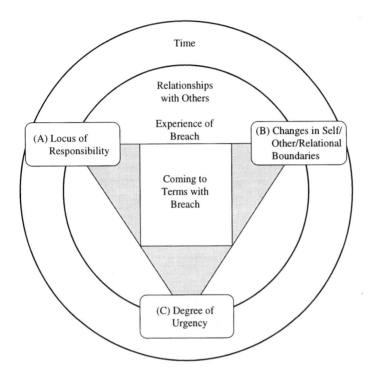

Figure 7.1. Structural relationships among the grounds of the experience of breach

I start feeling all this guilt. "How could I do that to her, it's not her fault." All this really makes me feel *guilty*, like I'm a monster or a horrible person. Scum of the earth. I don't know how I could say that to someone that I'm supposed to love. I don't know who said "I hate you" first, but it really doesn't matter, because I'm the adult supposedly.

Relationship of Grounds to the Experiences of Breach

The grounds of Time and Relationships with Others related to the experience of breach in the stable, yet dynamic, pattern presented by Figure 7.1. The position of the grounds symbolizes their relative proximity to each other and to the person's figural experience of breach. Themes located nearer the center of the figure are grounded by more peripheral ones; outer grounds set a context for the pattern of inner grounds. Complex experiences such as breach – and coming to terms with it – can neither be represented nor discussed as linear phenomena. As with all figure–ground phenomena, changes in one aspect of the pattern affect all others.

Each account of breach was uniquely situated in terms of experiences of time and relationships with others. Relationship boundaries always were set within a temporal context and relative to the individual's experience of the passage of time. Relationship boundaries became the ground out of which a violation of boundary (i.e., a breach) stood out as figural. The particulars of each experience of breach were always co-constituted by temporal and interpersonal contexts.

Coming to Terms with Breach

Emerging from the context set by the experience of breach were three distinct modes of coming to terms with it: Retaliating, Retaining, and Repairing. These reactions addressed the relational status quo in different ways, and each allowed for different modes of resolution.

Retaliating. Participants told narratives in which characters came to terms with their experience of breach by retaliating. By reengaging the other in a hostile manner, they responded to the breach by escalating the conflict. When people were injured – and, consequently, hurt and/or angry – their first response was retaliatory. Participants described hasty, unthinking actions intended to change the status quo by "getting even" with the other, whom they saw as responsible for the breach. Often they were outraged at the action (or inaction) of the other and were left with a powerful sense that something had to be done to restore a sense of balance.

In most situations, the participant's focus was on the other, moving against and attacking him or her to exact "revenge." The goal of many retaliations was neither to reconcile nor to establish closure in the relationship; rather, it was to express hostility and to escalate the conflict. The experience of time for a person seeking retaliation was generally limited to the present; concerns about the welfare of the other and the future of their relationship were pushed aside.

Retaliatory feelings also were present in lingering fantasies and premeditated responses concocted long after the breach event was over. The intensity of fantasy and the desire to act were related to the severity and importance of the breach to the injured party. The passage of time did little to dull the piercing anger that some participants reported feeling.

The prospect of forgiving (or of accepting the reparative efforts of) the other was quite remote for some participants. Other comments concerning retaliation involved situations where people were distant from the breach event and yet still quite conflicted:

When I'm angry at somebody, I *want* to be angry, and I don't want to know about them. . . . I know that the moment I start trying to understand them, I'll start forgiving them, and I want to be mad.

Some retaliatory statements concerned hostility expressed about a failed attempt at reparation. Within this context, participants spoke of their experiences when aspects of retaliation were noted in what was initially designed to be a reparative encounter. Participants distinguished these "getting-even" resolutions from true reparations. Such comments were helpful for defining the difference between reparation and retaliation.

You really hurt me. I want to get my wounds bandaged. I want you to do penance. I want you to hurt 'cause I'm hurt.

In most cases, the result of retaliating was an increase in the experience of interpersonal tension and distance. Few participants saw resolution of the breach resulting from an expression of hostility. One participant spoke about the value of an open communication style that allows for the quick expression and resolution of anger.

Retaining. Other experiences of breach were related to holding on to a status quo. There were many ways in which this experience was described; a common thread concerned the theme of moving away from the other. Instead of moving against the other to retaliate or toward the other to repair, the person who held on to the breach typically focused on the self. Participants frequently experienced being entrenched in positions from which compromise – or even discussion – was impossible.

Analysis of narratives told from the perspective of injurers suggested that guilt was the primary feeling held onto or retained. These individuals were painfully aware that they had not been forgiven and were unable to initiate a successful reparative encounter.

I have always felt really guilty because I had made that decision. . . . His hurt has always stayed with me. I've always felt guilty about it. . . . There is something I remember and carry along unresolved.

Not surprisingly, those who experienced themselves as injured carried feelings of hurt and anger. They felt that they had been mistreated and had not found an opportunity to have their grievance addressed in a way that relieved them of their sense of injustice and violation.

The bulk of descriptions concerning the retaining mode dealt with reasons why coming to terms "was impossible." Sometimes the death of the other person prevented the completion of a reparative exchange.

If I had my father back today, those are things I would say I was sorry for. I didn't take advantage of the opportunity then, and now it's not there. It sits with me badly.

My father is dead. . . . (T)here was no going back and getting an apology from him. I made myself remember the good things because Lord knows I could remember the bad ones. The bones in both my wrists are cracked or chipped at one point or another because of him.

Pride and inhibition also were mentioned as obstacles to repairing. It was extremely difficult for individuals to muster the courage to approach the other to ask forgiveness. Another reason given for retaining the breach was the feeling that a status quo was better than the disruption that a reparative attempt was projected to cause. Although some participants expressed dissatisfaction with the present situation, they believed that more harm than good would come from efforts to reconcile.

If I could find her, I would apologize to her. I think she's probably married now and wouldn't want to hear it. She might want to hear it but wouldn't want me to interfere.

Participants spoke of various ways that the passage of time influenced the resolution of a retained experience of breach. "Time heals all wounds" is a maxim that described how some people experienced releasing the experience of breach. Although problems in a relationship were quite figural at one point, participants recognized years later that they were not now as aware of such feelings – even though they took no action to resolve the problem.

I never really even mentioned it to her or that I was hurt. She was there, and she knew I was there, and it was just never spoken of. It took me a week or so until I got over it.

Although the passage of time attenuated the experience of breach for some participants, many reported being aware that hurt feelings accumulated over time. The following passage captures the experience of participants who feel that a remnant of the breach is always retained when a conflict is left unresolved.

She eventually forgets and forgives even though he never says, "I'm sorry" unless something really drastic happens. He'll eventually come back and say he really didn't mean to hit her or whatever. But usually it just sort of gets tucked away somewhere.

Repairing. Participants also described situations in which they moved toward another person with the intention of repairing a breached relationship. These individuals not only described offering and accepting apologies but also tried to work through the forgiveness process by contemplation and imagination. The word "apology" was used often by participants to denote a broad range of reparative actions beyond the stereotyped "I'm sorry."

In contrast to many retaliatory actions, reparation was never described as an impulsive act fueled by intense emotion; rather, repairing was presented as the result of reflection and "cooling off." Unlike retaining, reparation was not described as coming from brooding self-absorption. Instead, participants described repairing as an active, other-oriented response to breach requiring an open, and potentially, vulnerable posture. While not every reparative attempt led to resolution, consensual closure on the breach experience only occurred as the result of an effective exchange between people.

It is important to point out that participants were aware of an underlying assessment of the intentions of both the person giving an apology and the person receiving it. Part of reparative process is to judge the sincerity and trustworthiness of the other. Participants made distinctions between reparation and other actions by describing the difference between "good-faith" and "bad-faith" efforts. Many actions described in the interviews failed to elicit closure for one person and/or the other, and participants described their present understandings for such failed attempts. On the other hand, many reparative actions were experienced as effective, and participants described how and why that was so.

The interpersonal stance of the reparative mode is experienced as significantly different from those of retaliating and retaining. The words and metaphors used to describe repairing connote a posture of opening, bridging, receiving. In fact, the word *openness* occurred frequently throughout the interviews. Breaches were experienced as rifts or barriers that separated people and closed off communication; reparation was experienced as an effort to "clear the channel" of what formerly obstructed it. Openness was frequently associated with bringing problems "up," "on to the front burner," and "out in the open"; this was usually described in contrast to keeping them "down," "buried," "out of sight."

Another metaphor frequently used to describe the experience of coming to terms by repairing was "bridging the gap." This imagery suggests that one faces and confronts a rift, reaching across to reestablish connection:

I'm big on going back and trying to make amends, doing whatever it takes short of selling myself. I have spent a lot of time in the last seven years going back to people trying to bridge a gap that I thought was there. . . . I believe that there is always something that can bridge a gap, and I have lots of energy, and I sense that I can figure out a way to pull it off.

Related to an experience of openness and bridging was that of receptiveness. Instead of withdrawing from the other, a person who participates in a reparation experience moves toward the other receptively. The experience of breach is released, and there is openness to a fresh start. Another critical aspect of the experience of reparation concerns vulnerability. Participants described their experience of the humility that reparation requires in bodily terms. They felt that the act of asking for forgiveness opened them up to risk.

1. *The object of repairing.* A new-start reparation required at least one of the parties to recognize a desire for change as well as to demonstrate a willingness to let go of the breach. Repairs did not happen without some instigation toward change by one party or the other. The typical pattern was for one person to initiate an encounter by inviting the other to consider a change. In a successful reparation, the temporal perspective shifted from a troubled past to possibilities in the present and future.

Depending on the particular experience of breach, participants reported hoping that their actions would restore a sense of wholeness to the self, the other, and/or the relationship. In some situations, participants experienced the urgency of the breach situation as relating to their own feelings of incompleteness. They focused on how they would be changed. Other participants described the reparative action as for the other person; their experience centered on what a change in the status quo would allow for the other. Finally, some participants experienced their urgency to act as related to restoring the relationship.

In the following quote, a young man asks his father to let go of his disappointment in him and to meet him on new terms. Unless the father releases his disappointment, both are stuck in the experience of breach. It is clear that the young man wants to feel better himself; however, he is primarily concerned with his father's hurt feelings.

Like most children, I'm sensitive to my parent's attitudes about me. One of the things I said I was sorry about is that I had to be involved in an unhappy view that my father had of me. I was sorry that I had disappointed him. I *hate* to do that because I admire him and respect his position. I said, "I'm sorry. We have a relationship and certain attitudes toward each other which are uncomfortable. I want to repair these. I'm doing it this way because I care about and respect you."

In certain circumstances, the experience of the participant was that both the self and the other were restored by the reparative action taken. The following quote is an example of a dual focus on the self and the other:

I was consciously *looking* for ways to make atonement. Rather than do things to destroy their marriage – which I could have done – I did things to enhance their marriage. . . . But my motivation was twofold. Consciously, I wanted to atone for the problems I had caused. Less consciously, I wanted to change myself, to *be* the person I wanted to be. It's sort of an identification with my own ideal self.

2. *The action of repairing.* Three aspects of the reparative process stood out as defining characteristics. First, people experienced reestablishing relational boundaries by directly addressing the issue of responsibility for the breach. Most of the time this was described as occurring in the context of a confession, an explicit admission of fault. This action speaks to one critically important aspect of the experience of breach: locus of responsibility. The person who takes the first step generally assumes a greater responsibility for the breach than he/she did before the apology. The fact that the locus of responsibility for breach shifts, allows for a feeling of relief from the experience of breach. This is particularly true for participants whose primary experience of breach was of being victimized by another person.

Second, participants describe a changing of perspective that characterizes an effective reparative process. In breach situations, participants reported being emotionally invested in maintaining their view of the breach. Participants felt that they lost the capacity to judge history clearly; sometimes they reported being completely blind to the outlook of the other. A primary component of a good-faith reparation is the willingness to consider the other's view of things. The empathy described in many narratives related to a willingness to experience the extent of the other's experience of injury. The sincerity of a person's empathy was often felt if it "*cost*" to make the apology. When participants experienced the other as attempting to placate them or to put them off, they felt that the other was trying to "get off cheap." This perception of bad faith frequently interrupted the reparative action.

Third, the action of reparation provides the injurer an opportunity to do something to earn relief. Apologies and other reparative gestures were experienced as "taking care of" a wrong done and, thus, worked as an expiation. Participants expected such actions to erase their experience of breach. For many participants, it was difficult to imagine a reconciliation being possible without action. Several compared this experience to the giving of penance.

What I did seemed to take care of the feeling that I had inside that provoked me to do something. . . . I had tried to be honest and to get to the point where I could resolve in my own mind, "I messed up. I made a mistake. I have done all that I can right now to repair it. I'm sorry it happened, and this is what I've tried to do." At that point, I felt pretty good about what I'd done. I felt like I'd tried to make amends in that way.

3. *The mutuality of repairing.* Coming to terms with the breach in a reparative mode requires the participation of the other. Situations in which participants experienced a satisfying bridging of the rift were described as *reciprocal encounters.* Once an initial invitation was made, the distinction between injured and injurer faded as both took the opportunity to discover the means by which to restore the relationship. The willing offer of forgiveness was experienced as flowing from the meeting of two people resolved to release their experiences of breach. Reparation was experienced as a "we" and not an "I" event.

It goes two ways. *I'm* forgiven, and *he's* forgiven me for screwing up.

We found a better way to live. I guess it's a form of reparation. Understanding that the way we were heading was destructive and unhappy and not fulfilling for one of us. We saw how we had each been *self*-destructive. Reparations were really made most meaningfully to ourselves. As that worked out, it spilled over into each other.

4. *Reparations that fail.* Participants drew distinctions between sincere reparative attempts and those that were experienced as insensitive and off-putting. Although some explanations were judged as trustworthy efforts to settle a dispute, many were experienced as attempts at self-justification. Such explanatory maneuvers did not work because they did not convince the injured party that his/her perspective was understood, and the experience of breach could not be released unless that occurred. Gestures experienced as perfunctory, hollow, or impersonal also were poorly received. In the following case, a reparative attempt failed because the participant did not discern the other assuming responsibility for breach, adopting her perspective, and/or being personally concerned for her welfare.

I guess he apologized for not telling me or lying in the first place about breaking up with his girlfriend. But it seemed to me that it was still very perfunctory. "I'm doing this because I know I have to and it's going to make me feel better, not because I really want to."

Presenting material gifts to the injured without apologizing was experienced as adding insult to injury and often created a more difficult situation. Similarly, the perception that the gesture was manipulative or strategic led to failed reparations. A final disqualifying feature was the repetitive nature of the affront: Participants were not inclined to accept an apology from someone who had hurt them before in the same way.

5. *The experience of reparation.* Reparation was experienced by participants as restoring a lost sense of wholeness. Each participant described relationships that were experienced as broken in some respect. They felt interrupted by the relational breach such that experiences of themselves,

the other, and their world were changed. They experienced the loss of a sense of closeness, communion, or trust – all of which had been taken for granted at an earlier time. They were now aware of a sense of distance, barrier, and alienation. They felt compelled to relive painful events, carrying uncomfortable feelings of guilt, anger, and disappointment. They lost the vital, present-focused experience of the other.

As a mode of coming to terms with these events and experiences, reparation was described as an effort to address and change the sense of distance and loss. Participants who described the repairing mode wanted to fix what felt broken, and they were able to imagine a way to accomplish the restoration; not only did they experience a hope for reconciliation, they experienced it as possible. The actions they took were sensibly related both to their experience of breach and to their expectations of the future.

In contrast to the closed, protective posture of retaining and the more aggressive, attacking posture of retaliating, the posture of reparation was described as open, vulnerable, humble, receptive. Reparation was risk. When met by another person who appreciated their initiative, participants were aware of a relaxation in the tight grasp on their perspective of the breach event; they felt understood and were willing to consider the other's experience as distinct from their own.

Repairing gestures initiated by those perceived as injurers helped both parties to sense relief from the oppressive experience of breach. Instead of seeing a barrier between them, people were able to reestablish communication that allowed them to look together for a solution. A sense of balance returned to the relationship when responsibility for the breach was addressed and relational boundaries were either reaffirmed or redefined. Participants thus experienced a closure in the open breach.

The intention of the other also must be considered in describing how participants reported coming to terms with breach, since it was never experienced as a solitary event. Three modes of coming to terms were experienced as directed toward someone who, in turn, was coming to terms in some way. Even when the other was not physically present, because of separation or death, participants spoke in transactional terms; that is, they imagined what the other would do.

Over time people reported changing their relationship to breach and, hence, to their mode of resolving it. Maturity, intervening events, and reflection on the situation of breach that occur with the passage of time, all affect the way a breach is experienced and dealt with. The quality of an interpersonal exchange can be dramatically transformed in a moment.

Perspective of INJURED

	Retaliating	Retaining	Repairing
Retaliating	1 *War*	2	3
Retaining	4	5 *Stalemate*	6
Repairing	7	8	9 *Dialogue*

Perspective of INJURER

Figure 7.2. Structural dynamics of coming to terms with the experience of breach

Moreover, a change in one person's way of dealing with breach frequently allowed change for the other – for better or worse.

The emergent structure of coming to terms with breach thus demands consideration of both the interpersonal and temporal aspects of the experience. Since participant perspectives were cast in terms of an injured and an injurer, a description was developed to incorporate both points of view. The three-by-three matrix shown in Figure 7.2 represents an attempt to describe various ways of experiencing the interpersonal complexity of coming to terms with breach.

The top row of the figure presents the perspective of the injured, who can adopt a retaliating, retaining, or repairing mode vis à vis the injurer. The left side refers to the injurer's perspective of coming to terms. The nine interior cells of the matrix correspond to distinct interpersonal situations in which the participant's mode of coming to terms met with that of the other. Different narratives described experiences of all nine situations. The three situations corresponding to symmetrical experiences of retaliating, retaining, and repairing (Cells 1, 3, and 9) seem best characterized as War, Stalemate, and Dialogue, respectively. The experience of these situations was sufficiently uniform to warrant a common descriptive label. The other six situations lacked uniformity and are left unlabeled.

- *Retaliation as provocation: Cells 1, 2, and 4.* The major characteristic of a retaliatory mode of coming to terms with breach was the experience of altering relational boundaries by moving against the other person. Retaliatory actions were immediately experienced as a provocation to reciprocate in kind. As a consequence of this provocation, the relationship was almost always experienced as modified in some way. The triad of Situations depicted in Cells 1, 2, and 4 frequently occurred together in various narratives. Exchanges characterizing Situations 1, 2, and 4 were described as the most unstable since they tended to be experienced as blending into one another. Typically, exchanges experienced as unfolding in these situations were seen as distinct moments – in action or fantasy – within the same heated, angry exchange. Although these transactions could be replayed repetitively without resolution, retaliatory situations tended to be brief because they were experienced as intense and distancing. Anger was experienced as occurring in bursts rather than in sustained interactions.
- *Cell 5: Stalemate.* The descriptive label for Situation 5 was chosen to connote an experience of impasse. In these situations, the status quo is preserved because both parties experience themselves as not wanting to move or are unable to move either toward reconciliation or retaliation. The basic structure of these situations involves an injurer who holds onto an experience of guilt and an injured party who holds onto a sense of grievance. The experience of breach was described as active to a greater or lesser degree for both parties, even when both individuals focused on – or were resigned to – maintaining the status quo. People described this situation as an extremely frustrating experience of waiting for the other to change.
- *Asymmetrical reparations: Cells 3, 6, 7, and 8.* The situations described so far do not concern the process of reparation per se. They are helpful, however, in providing a framework for experiences described as involving reparations. Asymmetrical reparation encounters were among the most complex and painful for participants: All involved situations in which one individual moved toward the other with a reparative intent but felt rebuffed in his or her attempt. Participants described situations in which they experienced putting themselves at risk only to be cast down or ignored. When a relationship was torn by conflict in this way, its resolution was unpredictable. These situations were experienced as failed reparative attempts, with the most frequent resolution that of Stalemate. It was possible for one person to experience letting go of a breach despite the other's refusal to participate; this was the exception

rather than the rule and tended to occur on the basis of religious beliefs and/or personal values.

- *Situation 3.* The Biblical injunction "turn the other cheek" enjoins the believer to forgive in all circumstances, even if the enemy continues to antagonize and injure. One of the relational possibilities described in the narratives concerned the situation in which a person offers reparative gestures to the person who had hurt him/her once – only to be hurt again. The injured offers an invitation to dialogue and forgiveness while the injurer adds insult to injury.
- *Situation 6.* All narratives defining this situation were told from the perspective of the injured. Participants spoke of failed reparative efforts in which they experienced the other person as unwilling to respond by acknowledging his or her role in the breach. Because participant perceptions of breach did not match, the resulting situation could not allow a consensual resolution. Participants experienced the relational status quo changing in this situation only if the injured was willing to release the breach and forgive unconditionally. If that was not experienced as possible, no change occurred.
- *Situation 7.* The next asymmetrical situation is one in which the injurer experiences a retaliatory rejection to his or her efforts to repair (i.e., as a transaction of revenge). Instead of accepting the reparation, participants described an unwillingness to relinquish their anger and proceeded to get even with expressions of bitterness, thereby blocking a restoration of relationship. Descriptive information about this situation was provided from the perspective of both the injured and the injurer, although participants only told such narratives in which they were injurers. These stories focused on feelings of pained helplessness because the participant's best efforts were thrown back without appreciation.
- *Situation 8.* The final asymmetrical situation concerned exchanges in which the experience of breach held by the injured person was unchanged by a repairing gesture offered by the injurer. Despite efforts to establish dialogue, the other person was experienced as making it clear that he or she was unwilling to relinquish his or her anger. Again, the conflict in what both wanted to happen prevented a reciprocal effort. When participants who experienced being injured by a breach told their stories, they focused on an apology that they had deemed inadequate, in bad faith, or tied to terms that felt unacceptable. Although individuals often were willing to reconcile, the apologies they heard did not convince them that their perspective had been understood. They perceived a "slickness" to the effort that made it feel easy and cheap;

they reported feeling that they had no choice but to reject the demeaning apology.

- *Cell 9: Dialogue.* The situation of dialogue is possible only when two people meet in joint effort. Such exchanges are initiated by one person whose words and/or actions are experienced as expressing a sincere apology or offer of forgiveness. The other person is then experienced as responding in a way that communicates a similar openness to dialogue in the present – both to work out problems of the past and to open possibilities for a new future. People reported feeling relief when dialogue was reestablished after the frustrating experience of alienation. The single most important characteristic of reparative dialogue is that both parties release the experience of breach and both reach a satisfying resolution. The following comments highlight the central features that distinguish such transactions.

I've often made an apology for something that I didn't think was necessary to apologize for. I would continue to think about it and try to understand what was wrong with what I did. I guess it's just as frustrating to try to apologize for something for which you're guilty and not have it accepted. Maybe the key thing here is some degree of honesty is missing from that process. If an apology is sincerely offered and accepted, then it's a very healthy outcome. If apology is offered and you can't understand why, and it is accepted, it's not quite as good an outcome – because there is some dishonesty there. Or if an apology is sincerely offered and not accepted, again there's a lack of trust or perhaps enough miscommunication to at least call honesty into question. Maybe the only positive outcome of apology is when it's freely given and freely accepted.

Participants made it clear that they could not force dialogue, no matter how desperately they wanted it. They described a mysterious, intangible moment when both parties to the estrangement no longer experienced breach but rather relationship. One woman, who described her experience of forgiving her mother, felt surprised when her openness to dialogue was reciprocated:

One day out of the blue she said, "I wish I had known. I wish I had it in me to stop it." That cleared up a lot of bad feelings. It was a big relief. It's a burden to feel as if your mother doesn't care. And even though you can forgive, *emotionally* it's such a relief to know "I care. I just can't allow myself to admit it." That's a *whole* different statement than, "Tough luck. Too bad?" ... As a result of her being able to say that to me and me saying, "I needed to hear that, and I'm trying to get over the anger," she started telling me about her sexual abuse as a child. My mother *never* shared things like that. These were things she hadn't even shared with herself. They would not have happened if I had not been able to forgive her, if she had not been able to tell me she was sorry, if I had not been able to tell her, "I forgive you anyway, whether you're sorry or not."

Implications of Present Findings

There are many ways in which we represent our experience of feeling whole, and at least as many of expressing our sense of incompleteness or loss. Participants in the present study described experiences of breach in terms of feeling separated from another person as well as in terms of losing a sense of trust and connectedness. In a variety of ways, they felt at odds with and distanced from someone with whom they once enjoyed closeness and intimacy. Instead of experiencing communication, they were aware of tension and barriers to dialogue. Participants felt stuck with unpleasant feelings and memories; their present-oriented experiences of the world were interrupted, and they felt compelled to relive the past to find answers for questions of responsibility for the breach. In certain circumstances, they had an ill-defined sense that something was owed to them or to the other. In other circumstances, participants felt very clear about what was wrong and what would have to be done.

The pain of breach was often most – and most meaningfully – felt as a loss of the presence of the other. Participants mourned the ending of the relationship, especially if the person was important to them. They often sensed great urgency to change the situation and found it uncomfortable to leave the breach unresolved. The breach was experienced as unfinished business creating a sense of personal disequilibrium. Something was "wrong" that continued to draw their attention. In certain situations, people resolved this tension by moving toward the other person to repair the imbalance. They initiated reparation or received reparations and, thereby, experienced a closing of the breach combined with a returned sense of wholeness.

Participants made it clear that coming to terms is experienced as a dynamic, interpersonal event. The intentions and actions of a person are never comprehensible in a vacuum; making sense of and responding to breach always involves the (real or imagined) presence of someone else. The experience of coming to terms with breach could be characterized only by describing the experience of both parties. The nine distinct interpersonal situations described by participants represent all possible interactions of the various modes of retaliating, retaining, and repairing. Coming to terms with breach was not described as an event but as a lived process. A person's experience of breach is constantly updated, particularly as a result of new encounters with the other person that now feel different. Experiences of breach also may be transformed by third-party intervention, by imagining the possibility of change in the other, and by value-directed initiatives – as well as by the simple passage of time.

Reparation as Dialogue

Dialogue was chosen to label the situation of two people meeting with reparative intent because it captures both the process and the result of meeting to address jointly the experience of breach. One useful way to describe the fragility of the reparative process is in terms of Buber's (1923/ 1970) notions of dialogue. Dialogue is a lived event that is neither coerced nor scheduled; true meetings happen only when there is mutual openness. For Buber, human beings cannot create dialogue with another human being; they can only set a context for it by providing an opportunity for two people to step toward each other. It is by grace that dialogue occurs in any moment, but grace is not attained because it is sought. It is ours only to move toward meeting, hoping for reciprocity.

Participants made it plain that for many breach situations, there was no way to imagine a restoration of relationship. One way to describe this situation phenomenologically is to point out that dialogue requires mutual meeting; meeting in which the joint experience of otherness is transformed into presentness. Participants were sensitive to the quality and sincerity of the other's interpersonal presence. Most of the stories regarding the retaining mode involved an assessment of the other and/or of the situation as not encouraging mutuality. For example, when an individual sensed that his or her hurt feelings were being disregarded or belittled, it was clear to the person that the other had not done his or her part in the meeting; instead of feeling drawn toward the other person for the possibility of repairing, the repairing person experienced a need to protect him- or herself by remaining an It for the other. Those who were able to see only retaliatory modes were even more entrenched in an I–It relation, and their sense of alienation was more intense.

Reparation restores dialogue and presence. It is mutual meeting that sometimes transforms It to Thou. It happens only when interpersonal conditions allow but does not always happen because conditions are right. In our culture, there are gestures and attitudes that demonstrate empathic presentness and signify the authenticity of our intentions. Confession, repentance, and apology are ways that we go about taking our step toward the other. But these measures do not guarantee that the other will experience them as genuine or as "enough." When a person experiences a situation as one in which he or she is made to feel like an It, dialogue simply will not happen. Sadly, this is the most common situation; genuine reparation is rare.

Relationship of Present Themes to Religious Contexts. The concept of repentance was introduced as one way in which to deal with estrangement from God. The prayer of repentance was characterized by Soloveitchik (1984) as a "knocking on the locked gates" separating the person from God. Certainly participants felt separated from other people in circumstances of breach, and apology, confession, and repentance were important motifs in their experience of reparation. Although a person may falsely represent him- or herself as guilty and remorseful, repentance sets conditions for dialogue and, thus, for the restoration of relationships. Saying "sorry" is how we acknowledge our responsibility for breach and communicate our empathy for the perspective of the other. Gestures alone are experienced as hollow without the personal encounter that changes the experience of breach for the one felt to be injured.

That many participants referred to Christian themes of forgiveness is not surprising since all were raised in a Christian faith. Among the most interesting narratives told were those involving the counterintuitive measure of initiating forgiveness when the person experienced him- or herself as the injured party. In none of these stories was there a suggestion that this was a masochistic or self-defeating action; instead, participants described these situations as discovering a freedom to recast their experience of breach in new terms. The agony of these narratives was not in the release of a grudge but in the moments and years of experiencing self-confinement. The decision to continue holding another accountable for a breach kept both as prisoners of their shared past.

Relationship to Legal Contexts. The religious point of grace finds its counterpoint in the realm of law where some individuals described a dogged insistence on holding out for "justice" – an insistence that prevented a reparative moment. When we interact with each other on a legalistic basis, we are compelled to hold the experience of breach steady until there is a feeling of "satisfaction." Many participants reported that the achievement of, or fantasies about, retribution often ended up feeling unsatisfying because the relationship was still severed. Their experience of breach had not yet been appreciated by the other.

The theme of *restitution* per se did not often come up in the interviews, perhaps because the term implies a positive relationship to the concept of payment of debt. When material possessions were exchanged, typically they were experienced as gestures of appeasement rather than of good faith. One participant did speak, however, of his plan to repay money that he had embezzled from a customer. Curiously, he planned this act as an anonymous gesture; this seemed to be in contrast to other stories he told of very personal and public reparative encounters. In this particular circumstance, he felt that an impersonal compensation was sufficient to absolve him from his guilt. Although it is true that he anticipated a great change in his experience of the breach, it was not as a result of establishing dialogue.

Relationship to Psychological Contexts. Hannah Arendt (1958) observed that human beings require two dialectical faculties for interpersonal relationships in the world: the capacity to promise and the capacity to forgive. The former is the remedy for "unpredictability" and provides the possibility of a secure future; the latter is the remedy for "irreversibility" and represents the possibility of redemption from one's past. Although Arendt recognized that vengeance was very much a part of the human condition, she noted that unless people were able to "release" trespasses, they were "bound" to the process of action and reaction, offense and retribution.

Participants who described the experience of forgiving and being forgiven spoke of "being freed from the past." In seeing a new way to cast their experience of breach against the grounds of time and relationship, they experienced release from an oppressive burden. People who had been anticipating a retaliatory response were surprised by the willingness of the other to forgive and to focus on the present. Forgiveness, like dialogue, cannot be predicted, and it is difficult to understand how we arrive at the moment of forgiveness. Arendt believed that the only reasonable justification for the decision to forgive is the primacy and significance of the relationship; one forgives the offense to recover the presence of the other.

Klein's (1933/1975) theory of the infant's "paranoid" stance is an interesting and evocative rendering of a way in which the world can be experienced. If one is continually aware of danger and can only attribute malevolence to others, the world is an anxious place. We know what it is to feel incomplete without a Thou. Such anxiety takes on a different and sadder character if one is painfully aware that the presence of Thou has been lost. We know what it is to mourn and desperately to seek a remedy that will bring the other back.

Klein confirmed what Buber called "our melancholy fate": that we inevitably lose our Thou, sometimes due to our own actions and wishes and sometimes due to no obvious reason at all. In our loving and in our hating, we turn and are turned away from Thou. We have no choice but to bear the pain of acknowledging that the damage is irreparable, that a sense of wholeness may not be restored. We must also recognize that nothing we do can guarantee us secure present possession of Thou. No amount of effort or agony makes Thou return or the depression of separateness depart. One can merely do what is appropriate: to stand next to the other, thereby creating an opportunity for the spontaneity of relatedness to emerge again in dialogue, if we are fortunate enough for it to occur.

8

Love and Loving

Randall Lang

Despite all of the attention devoted to it, there are few aspects of human experience more puzzling, paradoxical, or problematic than that of love. It is a topic that generates endless words and strong and confusing emotions: We often express a desire for love yet are afraid of being consumed by it; we often assume that we know what it means to love or to be loved, yet we have profound difficulties in describing what it is or how we experience it. We also often seem to wonder whether the love we now feel is "real" or "genuine," as though a counterfeit variety could masquerade as true love and not be readily recognized for what it is.

What the word *love* means varies a great deal depending upon who uses it and how it is used. What seems to be agreed upon, however, is that there are many different kinds of love. Some years ago, Rollo May (1969) noted that Western culture tends to think about love in terms of four different categories: (1) sex, lust, and libido; (2) eros, construed as an urge toward higher forms of relationship and creativity; (3) philia, or brotherly love; and (4) agape, or divine, selfless love. Any authentic love between people is, in May's view, "a blending, in varying proportions of these four."

Another distinction often made in regard to love is that between being moved and moving. Is love something one experiences as overcoming – something we fall into, either in spite of or against our will – or is it something we choose and willingly cultivate (Fromm, 1956)? As with Fromm, May (1969) has noted that an inability to love often relates to a paralysis of the will. This element of loving entails a distinction between giving and receiving, between being active and being passive, and between the experience of "entering into" versus "falling for." A related issue con-

This chapter is based on the unpublished doctoral dissertation *A Phenomenological Description of the Experience of Being in Love*, presented to the University of Tennessee in 1988.

227

cerns whether men and women love differently, and whether love is experienced as self-surrender or self-fulfillment (de Beauvoir, 1952).

Regardless of how it is defined, the manner in which one loves, or fails to love, is a form of self-expression inseparable from what is usually termed *character*, *identity*, or *personality*. The manner in which one loves may be seen as an expression of pathology and immaturity or, alternatively, as one of integration and maturity. To understand what love means in the life of an individual is to understand something about who he/she is as well as to have some sense for the significant events, experiences, and relationships characterizing his or her life.

Our understanding of love is directly related to our understanding of larger issues of psychological development – what psychoanalysists might call the finding and becoming of a "self," including the nature and extent of human attachments (Pine, 1978/1980). It is here that the problem of love intersects with that of narcissism, which, from one point of view, would seem to define an inability to love and, from another point of view, would seem to define a failure to consolidate a secure sense of identity. In either case, such considerations suggest that psychoanalytic theory should have something significant to say about love as, indeed, turns out to be the case.

Psychoanalytic Perspectives on Love

According to Menninger (1942), the central principle in Freud's thought regarding love is "that one does not 'fall' in love; one 'grows' into love and love grows in him; and this starts not in adolescence nor in maturity but in infancy" (p. 224). In fact, Freud's theory of infant development addresses the maturational course of sexuality, which forms an obvious biological ground to the individual's capacity to love. In a 1912 paper, for example, Freud made a distinction between a "sensual trend" and an "affectionate trend" in human development.

Of these two currents, affection is the older. It springs from the very earliest years of childhood, and was formed on the foundation provided by the interests of the self preservative instinct. . . . This tender feeling represents the earliest childish choice of object. (1912/1963, pp. 59–60)

Failure to combine the sensual and affectionate trends yields an inability to love the same person in both an erotic and a tender way. In fact, "the depth to which anyone is in love, as contrasted with his purely sensual desire, may be measured by the size of the share taken by . . . instincts of affection" (Freud, 1921/1955, p. 112). Freud construed an inability to love as the consequence of a failure to resolve Oedipal conflicts. For the most part, the postpubertal choice of love object "bears the stamp both of the object cathexes and identifications which are inherent in the Oedipus complex, and of the prohibition against incest" (Laplanche & Pontalis, 1973, p. 285).

Love and Gender

Psychoanalytic theory, no less than certain forms of common wisdom, have it that love is different for men and women. Traditionally, women were thought to be more romantic than their male counterparts (Chodorow, 1978). As Chodorow noted, however, a number of studies suggest that the conventional wisdom is at best misleading, if not altogether wrong. Such a mass of conflicting research data has been collected that virtually any position can be supported or refuted by a selective choice of references ranging from one asserting no gender differences to one asserting no similarities (Chodorow, 1978; Maccoby & Jacklin, 1974). Although Simone de Beauvoir's early views on love poignantly expressed a familiar view regarding differences between the sexes in their experiences of love, it remains unclear how accurate her view is at present. Is it, in fact, the case that women surrender themselves more fully, in essence, "losing" themselves, so that for women "to love is to relinquish everything for the benefit of a master" (de Beauvoir, 1952, p. 604)?

Such a view of romantic surrender does not seem to accord with later research findings that seem to suggest that: (1) females tend to be more pragmatic and less quick to fall in love than males (Baum, 1971; Dion & Dion, 1973; Kephart, 1967; Rubin, 1973); (2) as financial parity between the sexes approaches, females tend to initiate and survive terminations in relationships with less depression and turmoil than males (Goethals, 1973; Rubin, 1973); and (3) females evidence fewer symptoms of psychological distress than males, including suicide, subsequent to divorce or the death of a spouse (Bernard, 1972).

It is also possible that the nature of love, and differences in the experience of love for men and women, are changing as conceptions of masculinity and femininity change. Traditional attitudes toward love, as a complementary relationship between men and women who define themselves as masculine and feminine in relation to one another, are now being challenged, and it seems as if both sexes are conforming less to traditionally understood sex roles. Consequently, love, once defined in terms of an opposition between the sexes, appears to be giving way to a perspective in which loving relationships require the development of what has been termed an "androgynous" self (Schwartz, 1979). According to this view, mature intimacy involves an ability to identify with and value those aspects of self culturally labeled as *masculine* or *feminine* in order to enable a more complete connection with one's partner. Thus, in the continuing evolution of female sexuality, the category of passivity so crucial to de Beauvoir's analysis seems largely to have been left behind.

Freud (1905/1938) considered the early mother–infant relation, modified by Oedipal conflict, to be the source of later adult erotic strivings. For the male child, this involved repressing Oedipal longings for the mother and identifying with the father. Freud (1925/1963) considered the female Oedipal phase to be symmetrical with that of the male, resulting in the female child's recognition of her "castrated" state. Thus, for the male child, the narcissistic wound of castration was only a threat; for the female, it was an already accomplished fact.

The Freudian account also came to define femininity as a renunciation of a desired but inaccessible masculine orientation as well as an acceptance of a passive orientation, with its corresponding dependence on, and need for, men. From this point of view, the feminine character was defined by passivity and masochism while simultaneously equating masculinity with strength and virtue. If these contrasting attitudes are related back to de Beauvoir (1952), it follows that in love a woman's "surrender" to a man entails a kind of envious admiration for that which she can never be and yet needs as a source of confirmation for her as female. The male attitude toward love, from this perspective, would involve a kind of narcissistic condescension, magnanimously bestowed to allow the female to partake of masculine superiority as long as she does not exceed the bounds of a subordinate station in life.

Beginning some 20 years ago, a number of theorists within psychoanalysis itself have come to refute this position. In one such revision, Gilligan (1982) presented her perspective on gender differences in the following words: "In their portrayal of relationships, women replace the bias of men toward separation with a representation of the interdependence of self and other, both in love and in work" (p. 170). This description recognizes a widespread outcome of the different developmental and emotional tasks facing male and female children in the process of growing up. Both male and female children must inevitably renounce their intense feelings for the mother, and children of both sexes must contend with attachment to and dependence upon a maternal figure who represents omnipotence to them (Chodorow, 1978, 1980).

In differentiating from the overwhelming maternal figure, the male has the advantage of a different anatomy, thereby facilitating a fledgling identity. Although this state of affairs leaves the male child to contend with a longing for – and fear of – remerging with the maternal figure, it also establishes the source of masculine identity. Because of obvious anatomical differences, the male defines himself in terms of the attitude: "This is not-me." Relative to women, men are thought to exhibit greater defensive guarding of autonomous boundaries, and passionate love is represented by the mythic image of a seductive siren who lures the male to destruction. The experience of falling in love, therefore, is likely for some men to yield an experience of defensively proving his adequacy or, more correctly, his superiority. The successful meeting of this challenge brings with it the possibility of being admired, as well as a temporary release from the dread of not being good enough.

Unlike the male, however, the female child has no anatomical distinctions to enable her to define an identity in contrast to mother. In this situation, the mother is not the rival of the daughter for the affections of the father, but, conversely, the father is the rival for the exclusive affections of the mother. For the female child, a turn to the father is a means of initiating the development of a sense of separateness in response to her attachment to an omnipotent maternal figure (Chodorow, 1978). Fathers, thus, have a different significance to daughters than mothers to sons. The father, often idealized as someone special, nevertheless remains a secondary figure in the female's world, and attachment to the father is unlikely to result in a complete change of love object:

This libidinal turning to her father does not substitute for her attachment to her mother. Instead, a girl retains her preoedipal tie to her mother (an intense tie involved with issues of primary identification, primary love, dependence, and separation) and builds oedipal attachments to both her mother and her father upon it. (Chodorow, 1978, pp. 192–193)

A number of differences evolve out of these Oedipal asymmetries.

These differences include varying forms of superego operation; differences in what identification with the parent of the same gender means; differences in what doubt about femininity and doubt about masculinity consist [of]; the particular ways in which each does and does not give up the mother as a love object; and implications for asymmetries in modes of libidinal relationship and heterosexual love. (Chodorow, 1978, pp. 165–166)

This last asymmetry, heterosexual love, is for females not firmly established. "Men tend to remain emotionally secondary, though this varies according to the mother–daughter relationship, the quality of the father's interaction with his daughter, and the mother–father relationship" (Chodorow, 1978, p. 167). Despite this, the female's developmental preoccupation with interpersonal relationships produces an orientation to value being in a relationship over that of being separate. Within contemporary psychoanalytic theory, a woman's sense of self depends upon being connected to the world and others; for a man, it involves a separation from the world and others. The relational abilities and sense of connection paradoxically make females less dependent on any one particular relationship yet more likely to be able to offer love and confirmation. From this point of view, women seem to idealize love yet are better prepared to do without it than men. Men, on the other hand, seem to require love and confirmation yet disparage it.

Adult Development and Human Love

Within psychoanalysis, Erikson (1963) is best known for his detailed theoretical descriptions of the human life cycle. In contrast to Freud, Erikson noted that human development does not stop at adolescence. Rather, human beings always have the possibility for change in relation to life events and transitions taking place at later points in the life cycle. As is well known, Erikson identified eight psychological crises that must be negotiated across the life cycle, with the nature of the resolution at each stage profoundly influenced by those of earlier stages. The experience of love, therefore, will be influenced by the style and nature of resolutions made at previous stages, combined with the person's present mode of dealing with relevant issues and concerns.

For example, an individual who had never come to terms with the early life conflict between trust and mistrust will have difficulties in intimate relationships entailing either an unwillingness (or an inability) to allow vulnerability or dependency on another. Poor resolution of another early crisis, that of autonomy, should yield difficulties in relating to another person in a balanced coordination of self and other love (Bach, 1980). As one becomes older, however, newly arising crises are superimposed over earlier ones resulting in the potential for pathological layering of interacting issues, any one of which could exert a distorting influence on current relationships.

Although an Eriksonian view of human development is complex, it offers a more reasonable view of adult life than the more simplistic one of adult interactions simply mirroring earlier ones. The interaction between issues of life development and love would seem to concern the manner in which partners are likely to fit together more or less harmoniously, or to clash with one another more or less violently (Sager & Hunt, 1979). In Erikson's view, the most fulfilling love relationships are those between individuals who have developed a quality that Erikson termed "ego identity."

In discussing relationships between adult identity and love, Swidler (1980) noted that what is usually termed "human nature" is historically something contingent. In regard to love, for example, the "self" in Protestant tradition was considered as established once and for all in adulthood and would stand or fall on the basis of committing to a single love relationship: "Identity was symbolized through choosing whom to love and remaining true to one's choice against all opposition. The love relationship that defies convention, family, or class barriers asserts the autonomy of the individual" (p. 124). Although love initially expressed a rebellion against parental and social authority, it nevertheless was the way by which one reentered the social order and assumed new obligations as wife and mother or husband and father.

With social and cultural changes characterized as the "new narcissism" by Lasch (1979), Swidler notes that more recent conceptions of self and, concomitantly, of love are changing. If we view adult life as involving continuing developmental crises, combined with a commitment to continual growth and change, the new moral imperative becomes fidelity to one's own developmental needs. Here, the obligation of love is not synonymous with a concern for one's partner but rather as a vehicle for self-development. One may no longer depend upon one's love to provide meaning to one's life; rather, the person must now bring an independent sense of meaning to the relationship as a foundation upon which dialogue, love, and growth are to be built.

Humanistic-Existential Views of Love

Building on both a psychoanalytic ancestry and later humanistic leanings, Fromm (1956) approached the issue of love as requiring a distinction between the need to be loved and the capacity to love. As a starting point, Fromm challenged Freud's view that love is a manifestation of libido, and that self-love is identical with selfishness. By contrast, Fromm posited that selfishness and the inability to love others both stem from a corresponding lack of self-regard:

> The attitudes toward others and toward ourselves, far from being contradictory, are basically conjunctive. . . . Genuine love is an expression of productiveness and implies care, respect, responsibility, and knowledge. It is . . . an active striving for the growth and happiness of the loved person, rooted in one's own capacity to love. (Fromm, 1956, p. 59)

The manner in which one loves, or fails to love, is an expression of how well an individual has come to terms with one of the essential conditions of human existence – that of needing "to overcome a sense of separateness" and to "leave the prison of ... aloneness" (pp. 8–9). One may attempt to cope with separateness in a variety of ways, each of which entails the cultivation of illusions that deny or avoid an acknowledgment of separateness.

Fromm categorized such illusions into one of four different, and nonproductive, orientations toward the social world: (1) receptive, (2) exploitative, (3) hoarding, and (4) marketing. All four orientations share the conviction that love is something one "gets" from the outside world through various machinations and manipulations, and that love serves to meet a fundamental insufficiency in oneself. As such, love involves a desire to possess another as a means of protecting oneself from the reality and pain of separateness. For Fromm (1956), erotic love is stimulated by the anxiety of aloneness and easily misleads people "to conclude that they love each other when they want each other physically" (p. 54).

Fromm (1956) also distinguishes between the passive receipt of love, which he relates to a kind of symbiotic union (and the related submission, whereby one obliterates "unbearable feelings of isolation and separateness by making himself part and parcel of another person" [p. 19], and the paradoxical conditions of mature love in which one actively unites with another, thereby overcoming separation and isolation while still retaining individuality and integrity. In this sense, love is an active expression of a productive orientation toward life that embodies the accomplishment of choosing responsibly. The capacity to love is inseparable from one's capacity to will – which is not to say that one wills love – but rather that the capacity to love is inseparable from the capacity to take a stand. When active self-expression is combined with care, knowledge, and respect for another, it becomes love. For Fromm, love is not a "falling for" but a "standing in."

Fromm's perspective on the role of love in human life is shared by a number of other theorists often identified as expressing a humanistic-existential point of view. From this perspective, the mutually determining relations between will, choice, and meaning are focal points of concern. It is in coming to terms with the specific nature of human existence (its "thrownness") that the burden of freedom and responsibility for choosing become manifest. The existential situation in which love must take place concerns both the interpersonal separateness described by Fromm and the bodily nature of love alluded to by Freud. The body serves, at once, as the medium through which authentic being, relationship, and love are expressed and, simultaneously, as both a source of alienation and a constant reminder of frailty and death.

Within this context, Becker (1973), and before him Rank (1931, 1936), described passionate love as a solution to the problem of creatureliness – that is, to the problem of attempting to create meaning in the face of one's bodily nature and the inevitability of death. To the degree that loving relationships are thought to transcend the limitations of bodily reality, they express both a creative and a religious impulse. In this regard, they attempt to defeat the passage of time and to establish a metaphoric resemblance between being in love and being in heaven. From this perspective, the Oedipus complex for the male is reconceptualized as the individual's attempt to cheat death by becoming father to himself. One may also attempt to cheat death by merging with another person: "The self-glorification that [one] needed in his innermost nature he now looked for in the love partner. . . . We could call this 'transference beatification' " (Becker, 1973, pp. 160–161).

Laing (1961) describes romanticized interactions of this sort as a collusive relationship and points out that those for whom love means redemption from death are assured of disillusionment. May (1969) also has noted that the task of a human being is to unite love and will, and that will always begins in the capacity to say "no." Although will initiates a fall from paradise, it also is central to the psychological task "of achieving new relationships . . . characterized by the choice of which [person] to love, which groups to devote [oneself] to, and by the conscious building of those affections" (May, 1969, p. 283). May's analysis implies that the capacity to choose love necessitates a willingness to accept the inevitability of death. The value of another as loved is founded not on the illusory power to preserve the self against decay and death but as a choice to care and appreciate that which is transitory, not in spite of death, but precisely because of it. Such a choice implies qualities of "courage, maturity, integration, and wholeness [which] become touchstones and criteria of our response to life's possibilities" (May, 1969, p. 283).

In one of the few empirical studies dealing with the topic of love from an existential point of view, Prasinos and Tittler (1984) began by accepting the existence of six different styles of human love: Eros (passionate), Ludus (game playing), Storge (friendship), Mania (possessive), Agape (selfless), and Pragma (logical). In addition to determining the specific type of love preferred by an individual, Prasinos and Tittler also asked participants to complete a questionnaire concerning such issues as fear of death and the experience of meaning in life as well as more standard psychological questionnaires concerning issues such as self-esteem and ego strength. As one example of their findings, canonical correlations computed among all variables revealed that Agape and Mania were maximally dissimilar from one another, with those participants preferring love styles related to Agape scoring higher on measures termed *life regard, spirituality, self-esteem,* and *ego strength.* Participants who indicated a preference for love styles related to Mania scored lowest on these dimensions. On the basis of results for each of the other love styles, Prasinos and Tittler concluded that:

Lovestyle grows out of and is reflective of the larger existential matrix of the individual. Thus, an individual's characteristic approach to intimacy is seen to relate to the other major dimensions of his or her . . . life circumstances. How one loves is part of the larger picture of how one relates to life and to the fact of one's existence. (p. 108)

The Social Psychology of Love and Attraction

The social-psychological literature dealing with love runs the gamut from a concern with the sexual aspects of passionate love (e.g., Buss, 1988; Hatfield & Sprecher, 1986) to one concerned with the elements of a "successful" marriage (e.g., Lauer & Lauer, 1985) all by way of a concern with interpersonal attraction and mate selection (e.g., Walster, Walster, & Berscheid, 1978). In addition to the sociologist's, biologist's, and social psychologist's interest in the demographics of courtship and sexual behavior, there is also the earlier and continuing work concerning the question of how terms such as *loving* and *liking* are to be understood and conceptualized. An examination of this research, for example, suggests that not all authors differentiate between loving and liking, with some authors treating them as involving only a difference in degree (Veerhusen, 1979; Steck, Levitan, McLane, & Kelley, 1992) and with others treating them as qualitatively different phenomena (Rubin, 1973; Smith, 1981).

Perhaps the most clear-cut attempt to define the complex nature of human love has been presented in a series of factor analytic studies by Sternberg (1986, 1987). Results of these studies suggest not only that love is defined by factors such as intimacy, passion, and commitment (which are taken to represent the emotional, motivational, and cognitive aspects of love) but that any given experience of loving may be characterized by a specific balance among factors. Sternberg's results also allow for a reasoned basis by which to specify many of the varieties of love described by other investigators (i.e., romantic love, friendship, companionate love, etc.). For example, full consummate love involves the presence of intimacy, passion, and commitment; infatuation involves passion in the absence of intimacy and commitment; and liking involves the presence of intimacy combined with an absence of passion and commitment.

Although definition has been the focus of some studies, the majority have been concerned with interpersonal attraction and mate selection. Literally hundreds of studies have been concerned with one or another of these topics in which an attempt was made to identify sociopersonal variables influencing relatively early forms of interpersonal preferences such as attraction between first-time acquaintances. One of the earliest, and most obvious, sociological variables considered concerned the factor of proximity in determining who falls in love with whom (Clarke, 1952; Katz & Hill, 1958; Kephart, 1961). The overriding conclusion to all of this early work seems best captured in the following quote: "Cherished notions about romantic love notwithstanding, it appears that when all is said and done, the 'one and only' may have a better than 50–50 chance of living within walking distance!" (Kephart, 1961, p. 269).

Turning now to more personal factors affecting interpersonal attraction, early investigators (Dittes, 1959; Jacobs, Berscheid, & Walster, 1971; Walster, 1965) suggested that people tend to be more receptive and needful of affection, as well as more sensitive to rejection, when personal esteem is low. In a correlational study of individual differences in self-esteem and various aspects of love, Dion and Dion (1975) found that subjects with low self-esteem, relative to those with high self-esteem, expressed attitudes of greater love, greater liking, and more trust with respect to current romantic partners. Subjects with high self-esteem, who also were low in defensiveness, reported more frequent instances of romantic love, presumably as a consequence of having high self-esteem.

Later results concerning the relationship between self-esteem and receptivity to friendly overtures did not hold up (Sprecher & Hatfeld, 1982), suggesting that the best summary of the relationship between self-esteem and the pursuit of romantic activity is that high self-esteem allows individuals to follow goals, such as pursuing a romantic relationship, despite the probability of failure. Because individuals with high self-esteem have attained these, and other, goals in the past, they do not have a strong need to approach everyone to whom they are attracted. Individuals with low self-esteem, on the other hand, have a greater need for positive regard from other people but are more concerned about looking foolish if they fail to receive such regard. Thus, individuals with high self-esteem have less need for positive regard but have greater assurance in going after it, whereas individuals with low self-esteem have greater need and lower assurance. Because need and self-assurance cancel each other out, the overall outcome is that self-esteem has little direct effect on the need for affection (Dion & Dion, 1988).

A second factor that has been assumed to affect the need for, and pursuit of, romantic activity is that of personal dependency. In this research, a number of investigators (Bardis, 1971, 1979; Hinkle & Sporakowski, 1975; O'Grady, 1981; Rubin, 1970, 1973; Shostrom & Kavanaugh, 1971; Swenson, 1961, 1972, 1973; Swenson & Gilner, 1964) have developed and used a variety of scales designed to measure romantic love. On the Rubin Scale, three components defined on the basis of correlational analysis were labeled as *attachment, caring,* and *intimacy.* An additional attitude defined by the Rubin Scale is assumed to represent a need for "dependent affiliation," and research by Berscheid and Fei (1977) found that the higher that both men and women scored on dependency within a particular relationship, the more likely they were to state that they were in love with their partners.

In a more elaborate attempt to evaluate the role of dependency in love relationships, Hattis (1965) had people rate their current partners on six different dimensions: (1) respect, (2) outgoing feelings, (3) erotic feelings, (4) desire for outgoing feelings from the partner, (5) feelings of closeness and intimacy, and (6) feelings of hostility. In comparison to ratings of dependency, Hattis found that subjects rated all other factors more highly, suggesting that dependency was not an overly significant factor in either the need for, or pursuit of, romantic relationships.

Perhaps the most systematic work concerning the effects of personality factors on love has been provided by Dion and Dion (1988). In this research, measures of both experiences of romantic involvement and attitudes toward love were correlated with four different sets of personality variables including self-esteem, defensiveness, locus of control, and self-actualization. Since results involving the complex effects of high and low self-esteem on romantic relationships have already been described, we need now to consider results involving the remaining variables. In general, individuals with an internal locus of control were more cautious in their approach to love relationships than those with an external locus of control. No difference, however, was found between the intensity of involvement in love affairs for individuals with an internal or an external locus of control. Defensiveness was complexly intertwined with self-esteem, such that individuals who were high on self-esteem and low in defensiveness reported being in love most frequently, and those who were high on both measures reported being in love least frequently. Finally, Dion and Dion found that both high and low self-actualizers were able to engage in loving relationships, with those high in self-actualization more open to romantic love than those low in self-actualization. On the other hand, low self-actualizers reported greater esteem and appreciation for their partners than did high self-actualizers.

Although this is not the place to engage in an extended critique of correlational studies involving so-called personality measures, it is necessary to point out that such research is relatively unconcerned with either the moderating effect that different social or historical contexts may have on "personality traits" or with the personal meaning of either love or of one's psychometrically determined personality characteristics. If we combine these problems with the fact that there are many different types of love and loving – which are situationally, culturally, and historically contingent – it comes as little surprise that correlational patterns linking personal dispositions and love are complex and sometimes contradictory. Although it may be true that love and personality are themselves also complex and contradictory, removing both partners to the correlation from their sociohistorical and situational contexts can only add to the confusion.

Perhaps a more obvious omission, and one that has been noted by social psychologist researchers, is that relationships between members of a loving pair must be taken into account in describing the nature of the relationship. Research in this area has tended to be concerned with issues of similarities and differences in the attitudes, personal qualities, and appearance of individuals in loving relationships. In terms of personality, research findings (Barry, 1970; Boyden, Carroll, & Maier, 1984) report relatively consistent, but weak, relationships between interpersonal attraction and similarity in personal attributes. In terms of more long-lasting relationships, Cespi and Horbener (1990) report that husbands and wives who have similar personalities as measured by standard psychological tests report greater marital happiness than those who have less similar patterns. In terms of attitude, early and more recent research by Byrne and his collaborators (Byrne, Ervin, & Lambert, 1970; Byrne, 1971; Byrne, Clore, & Smeaton, 1986) suggests that individuals are more attracted to someone who they believe has or reports having similar attitudes to their own. In speculating on why this should be the case, Byrne et al. (1986) propose that in initial contacts with others, we first make a judgment of dissimilar/similar. If the other is judged as dissimilar, he or she is avoided; if the other is judged as similar, we are likely to continue the present interaction, with even further contact as the outcome of strong degrees of similarity between the two individuals.

By far and away the major focus of research concerning similarity as a factor in romantic relationships has dealt with the issue of physical attractiveness, where the usual assumption is that people prefer intimate relationships with someone of comparable physical attractiveness. Although laboratory research concerning such preferences has been mixed – with some studies supporting similarity as a factor (e.g., Dion & Dion, 1973) and others not supporting it as a factor (e.g., Huston, 1973) – extralaboratory research (e.g., Feingold, 1988) has tended to support what has come to be called the *matching hypothesis*. The only bit of contrary evidence to this pattern concerns the finding (by Murstein & Christy, 1976) of little or no correlation between long-term partners in physical attractiveness – more will be said of this later.

Not all psychologists, however, agree with a strict interpretation of the matching hypothesis. On conceptual grounds, Izard (1963), Maslow (1950, 1970), and Hoffman (1958) have suggested that mature, psychologically secure individuals have little need to have their personal characteristics – attractiveness included – mirrored in lovers and companions. Despite this general stance, Maslow also has suggested that some traits do exhibit a tendency toward consistency – for example, honesty and sincerity. Dymond (1954), using the MMPI, and Cattell and Nesselroade (1967), using the Cattell 16 PF, did find support for the effects of similarity. In both of these studies, results indicated that self-reported happily married spouses were more similar in response than spouses in marriages that were less secure and/or happy. An extension of this view by Winch, Ktsanes, and Ktsanes (1954), Winch (1958), and Kerchoff and Davis (1962) suggests that complementarity rather than strict similarity is fundamental to successful marital relations – that is, where the personal traits of both partners complement, rather than replicate, each other.

The idea that "opposites attract" has also led to much research concerning the relationship between interpersonal attraction and a possible fit between individuals of opposite temperament or personality. Although early research tended to support this view (e.g., Winch, 1958; Kerchoff & Davis, 1962), the bulk of later evidence seems to suggest that opposites neither attract nor repel when the focus is on continuing relationships (O'Leary & Smith, 1991). Although a simple version of this hypothesis no longer seems plausible, a new version known as *complementary of resources* does seem more plausible, and the major research domain in which it has been evaluated concerns the trade-off between financial resources and beauty. Here, the relevant early study is by Elder (1969), who found that attractive women had an advantage in obtaining financially successful mates.

Although this pattern may seem unreasonable, given the social changes that have occurred and continue to occur, more recent research has continued to suggest a trade-off between beauty and money. For example, an examination of personal advertisements in newspapers as well as in commercial material supplied by dating services indicates, as one research put it, that "men are presented as success objects and women as sex objects" (Davis, 1990). In a cross-cultural study of ratings by men and women in 33 different countries, Buss (1989) found that men rated "good looks" more important in a mate than women did, and that women rated "ambition" and "financial prospects" as more important in a mate than men did. In addition, both men and women reported a preference for the man to be older than the woman.

Although Buss (1989) interpreted these results in terms of the sociobiological criteria of survival – that is, these patterns serve to promote the survival of infants born to rich (old) husbands and attractive (young) wives – such an account is not the only one possible. For example, the hindsight of sociobiological theory scarcely even qualifies as proving a casual relationship. Also, a more socially sensitive hypothesis could deal with the same result by assuming that women, who have been historically denied the possibility of obtaining financial resources, have either been forced or have chosen to obtain access to such resources in this way (Caporeal, 1989). Finally, there are conflicting data – even within Buss's own work – where it also was found that both women and men rated attributes such as "kind" and "intelligent" as more important than "physical attractiveness" and "earning power." Additional research by Buss (1988), using undergraduate students as subjects, revealed that both young women and young men valued many of the same acts and/or attributes; these included such things as sense of humor, offering help, being sympathetic, and spending a lot of time with the other person.

What seems to be missing in many of these reports is a sensitivity to age and stage of life; that is, what is likely to be important to undergraduate students in love relationships is not likely to be quite as relevant to individuals in midlife or older. In an attempt to locate many of the factors relating to romantic relations within the cycle of courtship and love, Murstein (1972, 1986, 1987) has attempted to describe changes over time in the significance of various factors such as physical attractiveness, shared values, and role fulfillment. According to this analysis, during the early stages of a relationship, "stimulus" factors such as physical attractiveness dominate, although there is also some small emphasis on shared values and an even smaller emphasis on predicting how well the other person will fulfill the role of husband or wife. During a second stage of courtship, similarity of value becomes a more salient factor, although physical attractiveness still remains quite significant. Finally, in more long-term relationships, the ability of either the husband or wife (or significant other) to fulfill the relevant intimate role becomes most significant, with shared values still significant, and "stimulus" factors now less significant.

Although Murstein's discussion relates primarily to courtship, this approach also seems applicable to more long-lasting relationships. In fact, partial support for a developmental analysis of this type is to be found in early work by Tharp (1963), who observed that satisfied marital partners tend to report that their role expectations have been met, whereas dissatisfied couples tend to report having their role expectations disappointed. Additional studies have explored the relation between marital satisfaction and marital roles; for example, Fiore and Swenson (1977), using the Swenson love scale (1973), found that 35 couples in functional marriages expressed significantly more affection, moral support, and encouragement than did 35 couples in dysfunctional marriages. No differences were found between groups in terms of expectations of expressions of love in these marriages. Laurence (1980), in a more qualitative study, found that the establishment and maintenance of a shared sense of couple identity – which he termed *couple constancy* – was central to marital happiness and longevity.

What seems most clear from this selective review of social-psychological research on the topic of love is that early forms of love such as attraction have been studied more frequently than later forms of love such as would seem to be involved in successful marriages. Within the context of these analyses, support can be found for the role of similarity – both in personality and in physical appearance – between potential partners as promoting a continuing relationship. When the appropriate distinctions are made between liking and loving, as well as among the various factors contributing to the nature of a love relationship, the conclusion seems to be that two types of love may be described as prototypical: passionate love and companionate love. Although it seems a bit facile to see passionate love as more important early in a relationship, and companionate love as more significant in later aspects of the relationship, such a relative emphasis is in accord with the more philosophical position proposed by Fromm (1956) – namely, that enduring love relationships tend to involve care, knowledge of the other, respect, and responsibility. It also appears that passionate love has as a fundamental requirement a high degree of arousal, which is often experienced and described as "being infatuated." Whether or not arousal leads to more enduring types of love seems related to factors other than arousal. A number of years ago, Kephart (1961) and Bell (1971) observed somewhat wryly that few people describe themselves as currently "infatuated"; such a characterization is usually reserved for past love affairs, viewed from a current perspective of loss and/or disillusionment (Ellis & Harper, 1961).

The Present Research Program

Overall, the varied perspectives addressed by prior theoretical and empirical research lead to a view of love as a complex and multifaceted event.
These characteristics would seem to make the topic of love an ideal candi-
date for phenomenological investigation: Not only do perspectives vary; so,
too, does the meaning of love as it changes and evolves over time. To
capture experiences of love (and loving) as these unfold, rather than at a
single point in time, it is necessary to obtain first-person descriptions from
individuals older than those usually studied in standard social science research. For this reason, the present study involved participants who ranged
from 26 to 65 years of age and who, by self-selection, agreed to discuss their
experiences of "long-term love relationships." Each interview began by
asking participants to discuss the following question: "Can you tell me
about some time or times in your life that you loved someone?" Two
further questions, if not spontaneously raised by participants, also served to
organize the dialogue:

1. Has your experience of loving changed over time?
2. Is there a difference for you between "loving" and "being in love"?

Eighteen participants were interviewed about their personal experiences
of loving. Interviews ranged in length from 45 to 90 minutes, with most
lasting about an hour. As is typical in phenomenological research, the
interviewer attempted to follow the natural flow of the conversation rather
than to introduce new questions unrelated to what the participant had been
discussing. Some participants tended to respond with full, rich descriptions;
others offered brief, more truncated responses. In all cases, however, the
goal of the interview was to obtain a clear and comprehensive description of
participant experiences and to check back with each participant during the
interview to determine if the interviewer had understood the specifics of
what they said.

Of the 18 persons interviewed, 9 were male and 9 were female. Fourteen
participants were affiliated with an area church, and a number regularly
attended a marriage enrichment and communication program. Fifteen
participants were married, two were divorced, and one was single. In
terms of educational level, all participants had at least some college
education, with eight having a master's degree and two a doctorate. All
participants fell within the definition of a middle-class socioeconomic
bracket.

In Love Versus Loving

At one time or another during the interview, all participants described a difference between "loving" and being "in love." For some participants, being "in love" was described as the opposite of "loving," as in the sense of feeling "viscerally excited when in love" and as "peaceful and calm in loving." Being "in love" often was described as based on sexual attraction and as being extremely intense and instantaneous. Some participants related experiences of "love at first sight" in the following terms:

> Oh, that was a fun time! A shining time, just a euphoric time! Passionate! Sexual! I knew I was in love almost immediately. Real damn close to love at first sight. I fell in love with her physicality, sensuality, the looks in her eyes, her smile. It felt electric! It was like a comet!

> There was something about her smile. She was extremely attractive. Within two weeks, I found myself absolutely in love. Whenever I saw her, I became extremely excited. Ecstatic! I never understood what intoxicating meant in terms of relationship, but it felt very much like a drug. I felt intoxicated!

Relationships described as "loving," on the other hand, were universally characterized as active and reciprocal, entailing "real relationship," interaction, and knowledge of the partner. "In-love" experiences were described as "infatuation," "fantasy," "idealized," and were experienced passively, as in "falling for" or being "overwhelmed." *Loving* was described as entailing a sense of security and stability, whereas *in love* was described as a "roller coaster of feelings" with a fundamental feeling of insecurity and uncertainty pervading the relationship.

Such uncertainty was related by participants to recognizing a barrier or obstacle that prevented or disrupted reciprocity in ongoing erotic relationships. Participants described a preoccupation with the object of their passion, especially when there was uncertainty. Participants also reported a sense of frustration, confusion, and discomfort regarding such preoccupation, both longing for the other to "respond to" their feelings and yet anxious and hesitant to engage him or her. Depending on the degree of responsiveness, participants described emotions ranging from "horribly depressed" to "extremely excited," "elated," "euphoric."

Although participants varied considerably in regard to their reported susceptibility to falling in love, it is clear that a transition occurs in "loving" whether or not a passionate "in-love" experience initiated the relationship. All participants indicated *loving* and *in love* as different experiences, although not mutually exclusive. They may, but do not necessarily, occur together. When they do, the relationship was described as enriched. Much of what appears to influence whether infatuation leads to ongoing loving, or to the dissolution of a relationship, was related by participants to what they discovered about each other during the period of early involvement.

Situations. A wide variety of events and situations was found to trigger an awareness of loving. Some participants reported that they "don't think much about love" and tend to "take it for granted." For some participants, the present interview was the first opportunity that they had taken to reflect on the experience of loving and attempt to put it into words. The nature of a loving experience seemed to be something that emerged as participants talked about how loving had changed over the course of their lives.

A total of 23 different situations were identified as times during which participants reported becoming aware of loving. The two most frequently reported situations were described as: (1) when alone with partner, and (2) when separated or away from partner. A list containing all 23 specific situations reported by participants is presented in Table 8.1.

Not all situations were categorizable without referring back to the relevant transcript, and sometimes not even then, since participants tended to speak with different degrees of specificity and vagueness. For example, for one participant, a loving situation was described when his wife was pregnant. This situation spans 9 months and, unless the participant tells us, it is not clear as to whether his awareness tended to occur when they were together, when they were apart and he was remembering her, or, perhaps, at other times as well. Without more information, it is unclear whether this is an awareness of the other as one's object or whether mutuality characterizes the situation. In the case of the participant who described this situation, he spoke in a general sense and did not specify whether his awareness occurred when he was with his mate or apart from her and reflecting on their relationship. In other cases, participants stated that they were aware of loving in a variety of situations that take place when together with one's mate or when apart from him or her. For example, some individuals reported experiencing loving feelings when passing a nostalgic location alone or with their partner.

Thematic Aspects of the Experience of Loving

Five themes were identified, all of which were defined in terms of contrasting aspects. When describing loving experiences, participants tended to focus primarily on positive rather than on negative aspects of the relevant theme(s). Despite this tendency, it was clear that loving experiences do not entail only positive themes. For example, participants often spoke of the

Table 8.1. *Situations Giving Rise to Awareness of Loving*

Situation	Frequency		Total Frequency
	Male	Female	
1. When with my mate, alone together.	2	7	9
2. When separated or away from mate.	4	5	9
3. When thinking, reflecting, or reminiscing about mate.	5	0	5
4. When family is together, or on special occasions.	2	2	4
5. When outdoors in a rural setting, in nature.	1	3	4
6. When touching, seeing, or physically close to mate.	1	3	4
7. At a gathering of friends, or with other couples.	1	3	4
8. When away from home together, on an outing.	1	3	4
9. When listening to romantic music.	2	1	3
10. When passing or returning to a nostalgic place.	1	2	3
11. When having sex, or sexually motivated.	1	2	3
12. When there are not other pressing matters, or things settle down.	2	1	3
13. When working or doing together.	2	1	3
14. When feeling sorry for mate.	0	1	1
15. When feeling upset or scared.	0	1	1
16. When talking on phone with mate.	0	1	1
17. When looked at by mate.	0	1	1
18. When reestablishing contact, or greeting.	0	1	1
19. When seeing an inspiring view.	0	1	1
20. When something bad has happened outside the home.	0	1	1
21. When mate is ill.	1	0	1
22. When mate is asleep and I'm awake.	1	0	1
23. When mate was pregnant.	1	0	1

importance of closeness and togetherness at the same time as they described a need for separateness or alone time. Absences from one another were described as "refreshing" and as increasing an appreciation for their partner.

Additionally, it is clear that the various themes are in a figure–ground relation to one another; they are all mutually interdependent and interrelated. (See Figure 8.1.) Respect and acceptance, for example, would be essentially meaningless in the absence of a realistic knowledge of the other. Nevertheless, knowing and respecting are two different focal experiences, each necessary for a fulfillment of the other. When one theme is figural in description, the remaining themes are best described as a ground, but not as absent.

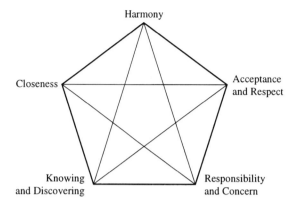

Figure 8.1. Interrelationships among major themes

Loving was described as figural in awareness at certain times and as a ground of awareness at other times. Most participants noted that an awareness of loving could occur at any time. What was most striking, however, is that virtually all participants described loving as related to the manner in which their relationships served as "a foundation" for their life. It seems to be precisely the capacity to "take love for granted," while turning attentions elsewhere, that facilitates returning to the relationship, becoming aware of various aspects of loving, and of appreciating and sharing experiences with one's partner. One participant noted, for example, that "we seem to have a lot to talk about, because we have both been going different ways." Another participant noted that "I don't believe that we could be very happy just being together all the time, because the things we like to do are so different. That brings a great deal to the relationship. It gives you a lot to talk about."

Theme I: Closeness. Being close involves a sense of interdependence and a desire to be and do together, along with a sense of affection, enjoyment, serenity, and satisfaction. With respect to bodily closeness, it involves passionate touching and sexuality. It involves a sense of engagement and joy, which also often entails feelings of appreciation. These feelings frequently are expressed physically, as in hugging and holding. Closeness also involves communicating and sharing, with a sense of companionship that includes experiencing the other as both lover and best friend.

Many participants noted that this kind of closeness comes from being with the other not only during special occasions but in ordinary times as well. Participants described a sense of shared history as well as of future hope and purpose. There is a recognition that both partners contribute to building an ongoing relationship and that they share a related sense of having gone through a great deal together. A sense of exclusivity and fidelity is present here, which does not imply that other relationships are not present or important but that this relationship takes priority. There is also a sense of being tested, and surviving, thereby yielding a bond between partners. Obstacles and uncertainties were experienced both as threats to be met and as opportunities for strengthening the relationship.

Related to this sense of stability was a tendency to experience growth and change as gradual and continuous. Participants described such experiences when they spoke of expectations for a shared future and an anticipation of shared pleasures. Loving relationships often were described with a sense of thankfulness and gratitude. The following statements exemplify the theme of closeness.

Our marriage has been overcoming a series of obstacles. She's a part of what I do and has always been. We've been together long enough to have seen significant change in each other. Changes so far have only enriched our relationship. There's more rites of passage to go through. What that says is that we'll be having a continuing sense of purpose, which enhances a relationship.

It's a feeling of contentment. A great deal of happiness of just being together.

I like him. I enjoy being with him. It's contentment. There still is excitement, but it's different. There's a relaxed being together. A companionship. There's a need to be close. . . . Lots of times I just need to touch him.

The opposite pole to the theme of closeness involves being separate and distant; as such, it involves discontinuity and, in the extreme, neglect and abandonment. To some degree, times of separation are inevitable and desirable. All participants discussed interactions between being together and being apart. A balance is necessary, with participants reporting that either too much togetherness or too much separateness is destructive to the relationship. The quality of companionship is also modified by each of the remaining categories: Closeness in the absence of respect, concern, or responsibility is a qualitatively different experience than being together in their presence. The following statements present some of the flavor of this thematic pole.

Times of separation and absence have always been times of reflection and times that have created intensity and anticipation in us, so they were times of absolutely realizing we had love for one another.

We were spending less and less time together. At first, there was a togetherness, and then all these stresses built up that kept on driving a wedge. [Having a child] brought us together for the first two years or so, but then things just started wearing down.

The first statement illustrates how separation may be healthy to a relationship, whereas the second illustrates separation as a consequence of failure to cope with problems and stresses.

The theme of closeness also was related to the manner in which loving changes. As one participant noted, "One way our loving is different from the way it was 10 years ago is that we have another 10 years of experiences together, both positive and negative, put into it." Participants described the changes they had been through and the crises they had weathered as related to an underlying stability, commitment, and sense of continuing through time and transformation. The degree of threat of continuity depends on the power of a disruptive event and on the perceived strength of the commitment. Responsibility is particularly relevant since commitment is something that one chooses to make or not make. The desire not to be committed may be experienced as a central threat to continuity.

I usually have to make a change [of partners] because our values are different. I have no committed love relationships. My own mixed feelings are why my relationships usually have a fixed time period. I change all the time. I can't decide if I don't want to be committed to somebody or not. I don't think in those terms really. In the future, there will hopefully be just more freedom still. Never restricted at all. Free to love anybody at any time I want to, and able to do it in a real fulfilling way. I'm more reluctant to love than a lot of people. I'm reluctant to be committed in love, I guess. Afraid, I guess. It's sort of a fear of stagnation.

Here, a sense of oneself as changeable and inconstant relates to a corresponding inconstancy in one's relationships.

Another factor affecting closeness concerned how members of the pair reported dealing with rivalry, anger, and disappointment. Although some participants stated that they did not get angry very often, the expression of anger was described as an important counterpoint to the expression of affection. A number of participants stated that inhibitions regarding the expression of anger related to diminished affection.

When I began to realize I had resentments, or that I was angry, I internalized it rather than trying to deal with it. Then I felt guilty because I had those feelings. It took about five years before I could express any kind of anger toward him. It's still a very difficult thing, but it's something we choose to go ahead and try to deal with when it crops up, rather than letting it get out of hand or ignore it. I think one of the things I caught as a child was that any expressions of anger equated to not loving.

Theme II: Acceptance and Respect. These aspects of loving begin with attraction or admiration. Genuine respect and acceptance, however, were described as based upon learning about and knowing the other as well as finding him/her admirable, capable, or unique. This may include a sense of taking pride in and appreciating the other's individual qualities as well as in finding him/her worthy of honor.

Respect implies both accepting and valuing the other and allowing him/her to be as he/she is. It entails accepting differences and extending consideration to the other and is based on a sense of wholeness in the other and in the relationship.

> Respect was always a big factor. We fight, but we never demean one another. We talk about actions, not persons. Even though she knows all my ugliness, she makes it plain she respects me, and it feels good. This lady knows me and hasn't thrown me out. I'm aware of being accepted and accepting. We both have a deep amount of respect, and my opinion is that is the foundation of long-term love. . . . She's quite a gal, and I feel good about her. She's made out of some real stuff.

Here, also, notice the simultaneous presence of other themes. There is a sense of mutual knowledge as well as the suggestion of the participant's awareness of his wife's concern for him and for their relationship. Despite an intertwining of themes, respect stands out as the dominant one.

The contrasting, or opposite, aspect to this theme involves being contemptuous and/or rejecting. All participants stated that there were things about their mates they did not like, yet overall they still found them worthy of respect. An important aspect of respect was described as necessarily entailing self-respect: If one is self-contemptuous, he or she will have difficulty admiring another. Accepting oneself and accepting another involves a realistic sense of what can be expected from one another, tolerance for some degree of imperfection, and a sense of the relativity of one's own perspective. The capacity to respect one's own and the other's various qualities, good and bad, and to accept each other as a whole, separate person, appears to be a cornerstone of loving. An inability or unwillingness to tolerate a certain degree of imperfection, either in oneself or in the other, leads to contempt and rejection.

> [My love] had changed because I had lost respect for him. He was fooling around with some girls at work. I still cared very deeply, but nothing like I had before.

> I'm so cut off from enjoying things that are there to enjoy all the time that it's not funny. That's because of the depths of disappointment I have. I feel tremendously disappointed! In myself, and other people. I can feel let down very easily. I have a very thin skin. My self-esteem rises and falls with every breath.

Theme III: Knowing and Discovering. This theme involves experiences of mutual sharing and expressing oneself openly. Listening and communicating define important aspects of this theme, although some participants described discovering things about each other by being together. Participants also described a sense of discovery about themselves and their partners. This sense of discovery was seen as contributing to a sense of perspective on the other and on oneself. The experience of discovery implies a certain openness to possibility and a certain willingness to be surprised. Participants described a sense of curiosity about their mates and an appreciation for "their mystery." They also recognized never knowing all there was to know about the other or about themselves. Openness to discovery was described as relating to an awareness of the other's separateness and individuality. Respondents also noted that one must feel confident enough to risk uncovering potentially unpleasant truths about oneself.

The contrasting pole to this theme involved experiences of stagnating and being ignorant. The extent to which one feels "ignorant" of the other (or of the self) contributed to a sense of interest in discovering more. If mates became bored and indifferent, or rigidly demanded that the relationship remain as it was or as they wished it to be, such a relationship was described as losing vitality. At these times, stagnation was figural.

I assumed so many things. I assumed I knew what people were thinking. I have to work at asking what you're thinking or feeling. Part of our problem was that we both had a different perception of marriage, and we never shared what that was. By the time it dawned on me that we should talk about that, it was too late. I covered up a lot, and I really realized what a mask I wore. I swear to never again wear a mask. I've got to live with myself first. I spent twenty-five years trying to be what somebody else wanted me to be, and by golly, I'm gonna be myself now, no matter what.

Here, one senses that closed communication led to an experience of stagnation. This participant suggests that neither she nor her mate took responsibility for communicating. For her part, she suggests that she "wore a mask," feeling that somehow it was safer to appear to be "what somebody else wanted" than to be herself.

Theme IV: Responsibility and Concern. This theme was described in terms of a sense of the priority and value of the relationship, along with a sense of realism about personal expectations. It entails owning one's responses and reactions and accepting disappointment without blaming the other person. At the same time, responsibility entails a willingness to do the work involved in being intimate and to tolerate the unpleasantness and confusion that may exist prior to attaining agreement or understanding. Responsibility was described as involving the facing of conflict and attempting to solve it rather than avoiding it.

Things for me that make it work are acceptance of, "Hey, this is what you need, so I'll take time to give it." I think we do that for each other. The other thing is knowing that a lot of what you need and want is ridiculous, and even accepting that in the other person, even if you think they're silly. Being able to laugh, both at yourself, at the situation, and at the other person, and accept that it really can be funny if looked at in a certain light, is real important.

The next two excerpts exemplify both the importance of being willing to work on the relationship and the experience of willfulness and exploitation as forms of irresponsibility. Willingness is a very different attitude from willfulness, which sometimes masquerades as responsibility. In willfulness, one is responding not to the other but to a private motive of one's own irrespective of the consequence for the other.

At the beginning, I may have fallen into that belief that we were meant for each other. But as our relationship has grown, I've gone back to my old way of thinking, that it's something we both want and we both work at. You don't fall in love. You make it. You have to work at it to get it. We put aside time for each other when there's something else we could be doing. If a heated issue comes up, we don't say things that are bad for the relationship. We both have a lot of discipline about not saying something that will hurt.

We would fight and then get along again. I was crazy. I don't know how we stayed together as long as we did. He started running around, and I found out. It just tore me apart, but we'd get back together, and it was like, "Let's see how bad we can hurt each other." It was awful. During this time, I met another guy. I was using this guy to make myself feel better because I was being treated so crummy by this other guy.

The thematic contrast to responsibility and concern was described as being irresponsible and indifferent and included blaming and being insensitive, intrusive, or exploitative. As with each of the other themes, an important consideration was described as balance. None of the present participants reported that either they or their partner were expected to accept responsibility all the time, although both were expected to accept it some of the time. Most participants, however, reported that blaming seldom solved problems and served more as an obstacle to genuine understanding and loving.

Responsibility was described as intrusive or controlling when divorced from respect. Some participants state that one aspect to responsibility involved telling their partner when they were unwilling to deal with an issue rather than avoiding it entirely. The other side of responsibility was described as involving exploitation, which was described as an intentionally deceptive use of the other for one's own purposes and without regard for their well-being. It was characterized as indifferent to consequence for the other and as an absence of concern. The following statements, respectively, exemplify caring and its absence.

I'm not trying to love as much to give me security as I'm trying to love because I believe it's the right thing to do, and I know that to the extent something is accomplished, I can see the benefit, not only for me, but for them. I'm not sure that I'm better at loving now, but I think and feel like I am. I know a little more about how to keep from hurting people.

I would hook up sexually with women, and it would be fun, but there were no romantic streamings. I can see now I had girlfriends who were in love with me. I felt a little guilty I didn't feel that way about them. I felt sexually attracted to them. I liked it, but I wasn't at all attached. When I moved, those relationships would end, and I wouldn't think twice about it. I would be surprised that they would be hurt. I was pretty cut off from those feelings.

An irresponsible exploitation of the other also implies an absence of reciprocity. Responsibility and concern were experienced as requiring balance and fairness, a sense of equal give and take and of active giving and receiving. Most participants acknowledged, however, that a part of loving involves recognizing those times when investment in the relationship is unbalanced. Thus, part of the stability in any loving relationship was described as involving an ability to absorb times of imbalance, with trust that balance and fairness would be restored. Participants stated that although a lack of mutuality may exist for periods of time, eventually this too balances out. In cases where it did not, relationships tended to be unhappy (or to end), as in the following examples.

Our pastor said there were two things that were needed in a marriage, and those were love and commitment. The next day I asked him to leave because I realized I didn't have either of those from him. I felt I had both for him still, but that was no marriage.

Everything I wanted she wanted. Everything she wanted I wanted. Our intentions were one. It was a comic book romance!

Theme V: Harmony. This theme was described in terms of feelings of blending or fitting together. It was described as involving getting along without conflict and with a tendency to agree. This agreeable quality was described as symmetrical or complementary. It is here that harmony was described as overlapping with experiences of closeness, although harmony was also characterized as going beyond feeling comfortable with one's partner. Although one aspect of harmony involves getting along with the other person, it also was characterized as growing into progressively broader and more inclusive relatedness with one another. It was described as a process related to discovery and was characterized by feelings of trust, security, and belonging.

Participants pointed out that they were able to take their relationships for granted and to turn their attentions elsewhere for a period of time. Safety and security were described as central to feeling that the relationship was strong enough to enable partners to be as they "really are" and to express anger and disagreement without feeling at risk. It was also described as a "sheltered feeling" based on a confidence in the other's willingness and ability to respond to one's own needs and wants and still be accepted "warts and all."

When you love, you don't feel ashamed when you normally would. The fear and threat are gone out of self-disclosure.

A sense of harmony implies an ongoing integration, within oneself, between partners, and with one's world. In fact, it is appropriate to think of harmony as the integration of all of the other themes since it relates to the process of being and becoming together through time and transformation. Participants described a sense of harmony during times of absence of stress or problems, or after stresses had been overcome. It was largely for these reasons that the theme of harmony was placed at the apex of Figure 8.1.

The other side of this theme was described as a self-consciousness characterized by mistrust, conflict, and constriction. Conflict often was described as precipitated by selfishness, whereas harmony was related to humility and peacefulness. One potential threat to harmony involves mortality and the absence of any guarantee for the future. All participants spoke of crises that had threatened their relationships, along with a current recognition of possible future threats. Most based their sense of security on having survived past threats and of having learned to feel confident of their own and of their partner's ability to overcome obstacles to continuity.

Awareness of mortality, however, was described as a significant ground of the relationship. The very fact that a loving relationship is "time limited" was described as increasing its value. Some participants spoke of a "sense of priorities" that an awareness of mortality provided to them. In this context, mortality contributes to security by offering a kind of meaning to relationship that is hard to imagine if there were no time limits. Here, the individual is aware of engaging in a relationship within the context of growing older, of passing through life transitions, and, therefore, of having to find meaning within a temporary relation to a wider world in which the person is but a part. Whereas recognizing one's place in the grand scheme of things can correspond to a feeling of harmony, it can also be frightening.

Every relationship we form we have to let go of at some point in time. Part of the way loss impacts the relationship is the realization that as good as our relationship is, and as well as we think we have it together, there are no guarantees. We've got the present. We assume we have a future, but we don't know how much. We know it's limited. My basic definition of faith is learning to live without guarantees, because I don't think there are any. There are times that can be very scary.

In another sense, harmony also was related to a feeling of completeness – that all is as it should be and that there are no pressing needs to be dealt with. All participants reported difficulty and conflict in their relationships. It is clear that harmony was not simply experienced as the absence of conflict. Rather, participants noted that how one understands and deals with conflict influences the way in which harmony is experienced.

One aspect of loving was described by participants as involving a meshing of boundaries between separate entities. At some point, the boundary between self and other may exhibit an easy fit, resulting in a temporary feeling of being in harmony with the loved other. At this point, the boundary between the couple and the wider world becomes figural, and the person experiences not the dissolution of a personal boundary but a redrawing of the boundary, suggesting that conflict may serve to set a context in which experiences of harmony become possible.

The kinds of settings that facilitate [awareness of loving] are when there is less stress. It's security and things going smoothly enough that there's not some big thing on your mind that's preventing it. Then you reach that nice feeling of oneness. Everything seems to fit together. For me, it's a relaxed, peaceful kind of feeling. It might be that it's less focused on your own self. You're losing yourself in what's going on around you. It's kind of nice because you feel a part of everything, instead of apart from everything. In those situations, there's that tie between yourself and your partner, and then it expands out from there. We're part of a humankind sort of thing, instead of just a me and him sort of thing. If it was just the two of us, I don't think we'd make it in the world. It takes other people sharing. The times we're likely to have problems are the times when it's focused in on how I felt at the moment. [Initially], I remember the whole world just being blotted out. It was just me and him, and that's the only people that existed. We were not in the shell very long, because he brings people in all the time. I suddenly had to share this person who was my focus with all these people. Right away I saw that, "Hey, this has got to be bigger than just you and me." But his family is so wonderful that it became very easy to share him, and then to share me with them. Part of loving him becomes loving the extension of him, all these people that are a part of his life. In that sense, loving is no longer just from that person. Still, he's the pivotal point, because it's the kind of person he is that causes these concentric rings to grow.

Gender Differences

Despite a good deal of literature suggesting gender differences in love and loving, there were few differences in this study between male and female participants. In terms of the total number of statements made in reference to the five themes, males made 544 statements, and females made 543. A remarkable balance also was present in terms of the number of references to each of the various themes made by participants of both sexes. All participants made at least one reference to each theme, with most making more than a single reference. In a study such as this, the significance of counting must not be accepted without question, since it is unreasonable to assume a direct correspondence between the number of times that a person refers to a certain theme and the importance of that theme. With this caveat in mind, no quantitative or qualitative information surfaced in the present set of interviews to suggest that certain aspects of loving were more crucial to the experience of loving for one gender than for the other.

Implications and Conclusions

From an existential-humanistic point of view, love has been described as presenting a solution to the problem of death, albeit not a completely satisfactory one. Loving, as described by the present set of participants, appears less an avoidance of death and more an affirmation of relationship based precisely on limitation and transitoriness. As such, it accords with May's (1969) assertion that love is always a blending of libido, eros, philia, and agape. According to May (and Fromm, 1956), responsibility is the fundamental theme, entailing a unity of love and will. This description accords nicely with the distinction between willingness and willfulness and with the emphasis placed by participants on "being willing." Willingness relates to agape and eros, since it tends to manifest itself in experiences of harmony and expansiveness that correspond both to a sense of spiritual oneness and to an "expanding circle" of relationship. Within this experience, the individual "reaches beyond" the self not in spite of but because of human limitation and mortality.

The theme of harmony also was located within a concern for one's own personal growth apart from the other: "If you lose your sense of purpose, you lose a lot of your worthwhileness in relationship to another. If I have things to do that matter, then I will still be fit for living with." This statement suggests that a reciprocal requirement for loving is one's involvement in a wider world (i.e., that one must participate in activities worth doing and that what one does makes a difference). It is the meaning of one's activities that influence (and in turn are influenced by) the meaning of one's relationships. Caring involves being willing to make a sacrifice, perhaps even sacrificing all that one is and has.

Loving is thus inseparably intertwined with one's relation to oneself.

The more you feel good about . . . who you are, the more you feel like, "Hey, it's good to be me." It's not that it's better to be me than anybody else. It's just that I know me, and it's good to be me. I'm not sure I've gotten that far yet, and I'm not sure I ever will, but I think your loving experiences in life go right along with that process. To the extent that you get there, I think that helps in your loving relationships.

This statement, and others like it, support Fromm's (1956) contention that how one feels about oneself makes possible the loving of another. To the extent that love is sought as a substitute or consolation for absence of favorable self-regard, its genuineness is to be questioned. By contrast, loving as a fulfillment of a balanced relationship with oneself and one's world accords well not only with Fromm's views but with the present set of interviews as well.

Psychoanalytic Approaches to Love

Overall, the emphasis of early psychoanalytic theory (Freud, 1914/1957) on the pleasure principle would appear inadequate to explain the experiences of loving described by present participants. Although it cannot be denied that pleasurable satisfactions attend to various loving experiences, it is only a cynical observer who would maintain that loving is "nothing but" sensual selfishness. A more adequate psychoanalytic perspective for understanding love and loving would seem to be found in object relations theories. Winnicott's (1965) paper on the capacity for concern clearly addresses the human capacity for taking care of other people – as one participant put it, "to care about the benefit not only for me but for them." Object relations theory shares with attachment theory a view of relationship as fundamental in contrast to the Freudian notion of primary narcissism. Present respondents were quite clear in noting that relationship is fundamental and that pleasure and pain are consequences rather than antecedents to relationship.

The present set of interviews suggest that relationship and not instinct is fundamental, but the question remains as to how loving is defined experientially. Most participants emphasized strongly that loving is not a unipolar experience entailing only affection, warmth, kindness, and concern. Rather, loving also involves the balancing of anger, coldness, cruelty, and indifference, which remain human possibilities even within loving relationships. Klein's (1937/1964) view would seem to apply here, since it is the integration of destructive tendencies into a balanced approach to others that enables loving to proceed. Loving is not a pure state attained once and for all; rather, it is better described as a continuing willingness to confront one's own negativity and to take responsibility for it.

From this perspective, loving is characterized not by the absence of hatred and destructiveness but by the manner in which one integrates and makes amends for the inevitable presence of a dark side. For Winnicott (1965), concern was the outcome of opportunities for reparation on the part of the growing infant that enables it to recognize a sense of bodily based selfhood. Concern implies a capacity to delay gratification and to relinquish fused relatedness. The alternative is to relate to another person who is recognized as an autonomous center of initiative and value. Such a transition marks the capacity to make the distinction between being loved and active loving.

One consequence of responsibly coping with conflict in a loving relationship was described by many participants as a sense of harmony with one's partner and the world. At first glance, harmony might appear to have a lot in common with what elsewhere has been labeled *symbiotic relatedness* and/or *primitive fusion*. In their descriptions of loving harmony, however, present participants emphasized a sense of comfort and belonging related not as much to a loss of boundaries as to a sense of a fitting together. Acceptance of separateness and the limitations that it imposes lead to the possibility of growing into a harmonious relationship with one's partner. The refusal to acknowledge separateness guarantees that one will not experience a comfortable "fitting in." Desperately clinging to a fantasy of perfect love appears to be the surest way of having no love at all. Periods of harmony were viewed as a temporary reward for the willingness to live within an imperfect, and somewhat transitory, world.

Gender and Loving

Descriptions secured from male and female participants exhibited no thematic differences in their description of loving experiences, although some minor variations could be noted. Despite this finding, one may ask how the men and women interviewed in the present study appear so similar in expressing relational concerns when so many authorities have led us to expect differences (Chodorow, 1978; de Beauvoir, 1952; Dion & Dion, 1973; Kephart, 1967; Rubin, 1973). Much of the prior literature devoted to gender differences has been concerned with the failure of men and women to establish or sustain intimacy. It is likely that a population of young, or never-married, or divorced individuals would yield greater gender differences than individuals now in continuing loving relationships. It is also possible that more participants were members of dual-career families in which greater equality is present than in "traditional" family constellations. Within this context, the conclusion seems to be that equality within basically symmetrical relationships tends to produce couples who emphasize many of the same qualities in describing loving.

It is also possible that social and cultural changes relating to the division of labor between the sexes, the increased opportunities for career development for women, and increasing male consciousness of emotional-relational dimensions of experience have tended to produce more congruent cross-gender descriptions despite some of the classic cross-gender distinctions reported in the social-psychological literature (i.e., Buss, 1988). In addition, it seems likely that in the most loving of traditional patriarchal relationships, mates had knowledge of and respect for one another, accepted responsibility (albeit different responsibilities), and expressed concern for one another. Loving may remain fundamentally the same, regardless of whether sex roles are symmetrical or hierarchial.

Relation of Present Findings to Social-Psychological Research

Many attempts to study the topic of love from a social-psychological perspective have focused on interpersonal attraction and mate selection. These are obvious topics to investigate using college students as participants. What attracts one person to another person may or may not relate to what produces a continuing loving relationship. A number of studies suggest that factors such as proximity, reciprocity of liking, and attractiveness "determine" who falls in love with whom. There are likely to be many other factors involved in the selection of one's mate, including the manner in which one attributes value to the other.

The factors that make a stranger desirable are likely to be qualities that can be easily perceived, whereas the subtleties involved in long-term relationships may take more time to discover (Murstein, 1986). The issue of subtlety seems to relate to a distinction between loving and being in love. For example, it has been shown (Driscoll, Davis, & Lipitz, 1972; Kinget, 1975; Tennov, 1979; Waller & Hill, 1951) that limits on the availability of a potential lover increase the desirability of that lover. Being passionately in love appears to involve tantalization (i.e., the implied promise of passion that requires an obstacle to its gratification). Consequently, the "reciprocity-of-liking rule" and the "least-interest hypothesis," while apparently contradictory, can both be true within the limits of their application. Some degree of reciprocity of liking must be present for interest to be generated in the first place. People who are unavailable may incite fantasy but tend not to incite a hope of consummation and, therefore, an intense desire. On the other side, ready availability presents little uncertainty and tends not to engage an individual in the process of discovering another person. There are unquestionably market factors present in assigning value, and virtually all participants in the present study perceived their partners as somehow unique and different from the crowd. Value consequently may be assigned in terms of uniqueness or difficulty of obtaining. Again, the issue of establishing a loving bond involves the integration of tendencies toward dependency and isolation: Too far in either direction ends the game.

Similarly, the perspective in this study of loving as an integration of polarities provides a way of understanding how some studies demonstrate that loving is facilitated by high self-esteem, whereas others demonstrate that low self-esteem increases receptivity to affection. Within the present context, self-esteem seems a relatively superficial evaluation based on an individual's apprehension of oneself as good yet not entirely self-sufficient. To the extent that self-acceptance entails no self-criticism, an individual is likely to behave "as if" he/she is totally self-sufficient, and others may feel they have nothing to offer. To the extent that self-criticism entails no self-acceptance, an individual is unlikely to believe in what others offer. Although not employing the same terms as the present analysis, the social-psychological analysis of the seemingly contradictory effects produced by variations in self-esteem on the need for, and pursuit of, romantic relationships may be characterized by a cancelling out effect involving self-esteem and self-assurance. Where the present analysis differs, however, is in locating "their effect" in the space between partners and not within the individual (see also Register & Henley, 1992).

Pursuing this difference one step further leads to the suggestion that partners in a loving relationship make contributions to one another that provide a fertile ground for the growth of mutual self-esteem. This involves mutual respect and also mutual recognition of each other's limitations. Loving entails the integration of human frailty and human strength, which do not exist as either/or categories but as an integrated ground from which relationship develops. From a position of strength, partners have something to offer to one another; from a point of frailty (or need), partners have the possibility of receiving something from one another.

Another question frequently considered in the social-psychological literature concerns the effect of similarities and differences in attitude and personality on the formation and strength of loving relationships. Again, seemingly conflicting results have been found. As long as research questions are phrased in either/or ways, conflicting results are likely. All participants in this study indicated that they had a lot in common with their mates at the same time as they recognized areas in which they differed. Certain aspects of attitude and personality exhibit similarity, and others do not. A view of loving couched in terms of co-defining polarities suggests that the viability of a relationship depends not on any specific similarity or difference but on an overall balance between the two. Too much similarity may result in boredom; too many differences, intolerable frustration. Some difference serves as a ground for dialogue, whereas some similarity means that things can be taken for granted. If everything has to be negotiated, there is likely to be little time to enjoy one another, whereas if everything is known in advance, there is likely to be little that is exciting.

Numerous studies have been concerned with evaluating various aspects of love and loving over short periods of time, but few have considered it over a longer period of time. Studies using questionnaire methods have developed so-called love scales, and for the most part, the factors that appear in this literature also emerged as themes in the present set of interviews. Thus, several researchers have recognized that the importance of sexual passion will vary with the stage and age of a loving relationship (Cimbalo, Faling, & Mousaw, 1976; Kinget, 1975; Lawson, 1981; Murstein, 1986; Reik, 1944; Sternberg, 1986; Williamson, 1966). A number also have identified different styles of loving, depending on which thematic concerns are dominant in the relationships (Lasswell & Lobsenz, 1980; Lee, 1976, 1977; Prasinos & Tittler, 1984; Sternberg, 1986, 1987). Although emphases vary, these studies reveal many of the same themes that emerged in the present one – namely, that respect, caring, intimacy, affection, tenderness, self-disclosure, security, generosity, tolerance, trust, appreciation, optimism, and harmony all are important aspects to loving relationships. Although all of these themes (factors in social science parlance) are important, the goal of the present set of interview was not to identify which feature "really" means which type of love but to describe an organized structure within which all of the themes would be viewed – not as separate factors but as integrated aspects of an overall pattern or Gestalt. When this is done, the need to decide which one is most important to which type does not seem quite so important or compelling a problem.

Loving and the Life Cycle

Sociocultural changes have influenced sex roles as well as the nature of loving. It is important to consider the relation of present results to what is usually termed *self* – that is, to the experience of personal continuity. Western Protestant tradition has it that "the self" is consolidated in late adolescence through a commitment to a relationship and to a vocation, and that the adequacy of one's "self" may be evaluated by the stability of one's commitments. As Erikson (1963) pointed out, however, identity is not something that is achieved once and for all. In less rapidly changing times, adaptation to the conditions of one's life tended to exhibit relatively more stability. In a technological age, the meaning of a reassuring sense of personal continuity (to use Erikson's phrase) has changed, and no one is ever independent of the historical context within which he or she lives. Swidler (1980) identified the new moral imperative as fidelity to personal development, and this theme was clearly present in a number of interviews. One participant, for example, noted that

Our thing is growth, and sometimes I feel like we're limiting each other in our growth with our love. It's warm, it's wonderful. It feels great! But sometimes I feel I need to be more on the edge. We're both into not being comfortable all the time, just as a way to grow and find out more things, and experience them. We want to grow, and so there's a freedom we give each other. I don't really want to grow apart, but I have to make sure I grow somehow.

Here, the primary fidelity is to one's own need to grow, and aspects of a loving relationship may even be sacrificed to this value. Many participants spoke of the importance of personal growth and development but reported experiencing this growth and development within the context of a relationship rather than as separate from it. Evidently, people can experience a relationship as facilitating or constricting their development throughout the course of life. The dual possibilities inherent in interpersonal life relate to Swidler's (1980) identification of the polar themes embodied within love as "choice versus commitment, rebellion versus attachment, self-realization versus self-sacrifice, and libidinal expression versus restraint."

A commitment is something that one chooses to reaffirm. Loving involves both sacrifice and self-realization, and it was not unusual for participants to report finding a degree of self-realization consequent upon a choice to make a sacrifice. To the extent that an individual maintains polarities as mutually exclusive, relational stability will be elusive. Making a commitment does not relieve one of the burden to choose any more than avoiding commitment protects one from stagnation. The creativity of loving lies in melding tendencies toward dependence and isolation in a continuous experience. The themes emerging from the present set of interviews exhibit a similar embodiment of apparent contradictions that, on closer analysis, emerge as complementary features of loving, features that entail integration and not exclusion. From this perspective, commitment is not as much a limitation on one's freedom as a fulfillment of it, and a lack of commitment is not as much a preservation of freedom as a paralysis of choice.

9

Falling Apart

In everyday language, we sometimes speak about ourselves and others as "falling apart." These experiences are described in terms of a loss of personal control combined with a more global sense of not exactly knowing where we are, who we are, or even if we are. These episodes also often involve experiences of tension and depression as well as a sense of being strangely out of tune with the ordinary flow of events and things. When this happens, the world becomes a strange place to the person, and he or she is unable to do anything in that world. It does not seem surprising, under these conditions, to characterize the experience as one of falling apart or cracking up, even if we are not exactly clear what it is that has fallen apart or cracked up.

Within the theoretical language of clinical psychology, but most especially that of psychoanalytic self psychology (Kohut, 1977), such experiences are frequently described in terms of a construct known as *fragmentation* or *annihilation anxiety*, with both terms referring to the fragmentation or annihilation of the personal self. As should be clear, episodes of falling apart are profoundly unnerving and interrupt the normal progress of a life. If a person is to get on with the rest of life, however, the episode and its related anxieties must be dealt with and resolved. The resolution to such episodes is thought to take place primarily within the context of a supportive environment, usually involving another person. Within this context, the suffering individual is enabled to overcome the disintegrative effects of anxiety and to reestablish a coherent and continuing sense of personal existence.

However unpleasant such incidents are experienced to be, not all theo-

This chapter is based on the unpublished doctoral dissertation *A Phenomenological Study of the Experience of Falling Apart* by Bruce Seidner, submitted to the University of Tennessee in 1986.

263

rists view them as necessarily undesirable, either at a personal or cultural level; in fact, some arguments have been raised in favor of the positive nature of disintegration (Dambrowski, 1964) as well as of a nonunified, or polycentric, experience of self (Hillman, 1975). Although definitely minority views, both Dambrowski and Hillman are concerned about the prevailing view of a human being as settled, orderly, and singular. In fact, Hillman (1975) writes as if psychology were required to "dethrone the dominant fantasy ruling our view of the world as ultimately a unity.... [This means that] instead of trying to cure pathological fragmentation we [should seek to] cure consciousness of its obsession with unity" (p. 41). One consequence to getting rid of such fantasies is to offer a view of human life that is fundamentally pluralistic and variable – an anarchy of selves rather than a single, centralized one.

A proper reading of Hillman, however, does not yield a fragmented experience of self as most desirable but as one in which the various modes of consciousness give rise to a continuously emerging effort at integration. Although not to be confused with what is usually meant by self, Hillman does note that rather than exalting breakdown for its own sake, his intent is to offer a "model of disintegrated integration." Using a political metaphor, he seeks a confederation of fragments, not a single central authority capable of bending time and history to local conditions. Thus, the self is to be freed from its obsession with unity but not obliterated.

Using a similar line of analysis, Dambrowski also describes the potentially salutary effect of falling apart. Although he recognizes that not all instances of falling apart are, or will be, beneficial, he still feels that such disintegrative experiences may serve to free the person for change. As such, some experiences of disintegration may become "the ground for the birth and development of higher psychic structure" (p. 5). Unlike Hillman, however, Dambrowski views disintegration as a positive event leading to a new and more creative self. It is not the unitary self that is at issue in Dambrowski, only that human beings sometimes need the energizing jolt of a disintegrative experience to move the "personality to a higher level (of functioning)."

Despite these opinions, the majority of psychologists are considerably less sanguine about instances of falling apart and tend to view such episodes as profoundly detrimental to the person undergoing them. For this reason, the study of falling apart has been most concerned with analyzing the nature and role of anxiety and personal confusion in such episodes. This joint focus derives from clinical encounters with individals in the midst of disintegrative incidents in which the presenting symptomatology reveals an anxious and disoriented individual unable to perform even the simplest of personal acts. Given this experiential base, it is a simple step to specify the major conceptual players as self and anxiety, and the major conceptual issue as one of specifying the relationship between self and anxiety as these intersect in episodes of falling apart.

The Concept and Experience of Self

Since the concept of self has such a long and complex history in philosophy and social science, it seems wise to begin with a relatively conventional definition. *Webster's Ninth Collegiate Dictionary* (1985) offers four definitions of *self* that are relatively unremarkable, and a fifth entry – "self as a combined form" – initiates an inset in the Dictionary of 213 *self*–other constructions beginning with *self-abasement* and ending with *self-worship*. Following this inset are slightly more than three complete pages of *self*–other word constructions that contain approximately 273 separate entries, give or take a few depending on how individual entries are counted. A careful examination of this latter set of entries reveals that about 60% relate to people (e.g., self-actualize, self-security, self-concept) and that the remaining portion relates to mechanical processes (self-governing; self-rising flour), thought (self-evident), or objects (self-belt; self-heal – a flower).

Since the Ninth Edition is a fairly complete one, it also contains a date for each entry – that is, "the earliest recorded use in English." Although many of the items are provided with specific dates (e.g., self-denial [1642]), others are specified by dates such as (14c), meaning before the 14th century. If an historical analysis is made of the 169 entries coded as "*self*–person" words, results indicate that 1 item was first recorded in the 15th century, 17 in the 16th century, 50 in the 17th century, 26 in the 18th century, 49 in the 19th century, and 26 in the 20th century. Although the purist could suggest that the last value ought to be prorated to 30 given the fact that the dictionary includes items only up to 1985, the conclusion seems to be clear that the introduction of *self*–person words reached its peak in the 17th and 19th centuries. So as to allay any fears that these results simply describe the rate at which new words came into the English language, a comparable century-by-century count was made for the 94 *self*–object words. Results here revealed what would seem to be a more normative and regularly increasing pattern: that is, with 2 new words appearing in the 16th century, 8 in the 17th century, 6 in the 18th century, 30 in the 19th century, and 47 (or 55, if prorated) in the 20th century. The two patterns are thus quite distinct: *self*–object words do not peak in the 17th and 19th centuries, as do *self*–person words, but progress in a fairly regular way from the 15th through the 20th century.

This simple numerical excursion through the history of *self*–person words suggests that Western culture has not always been equally concerned with the issue of what is meant by the term self. Two other, considerably more scholarly, analyses – one by Van den Berg (1961) and the other by Baumeister (1987) – come to the same historical conclusion: namely, the self as either an experience or concept has not always been equally salient in Western history. On the basis of his more philosophical-religious analysis, Van den Berg (1961) locates the solidification of what he calls the "inner self" in two separate individuals living two centuries apart: Martin Luther (1483–1546) and Jean Jacques Rousseau (1712–78). Van den Berg makes particular use of Luther's essay "About the Freedom of a Christian" in which Luther makes a crucial distinction between the "inner man" and the "outer man" and comes to the conclusion that the inner man is the more religiously pure. The case with Rousseau does not involve a search for purity, only for the affirmation of a self – "moi seul." As he writes in *The Confessions* (1787), "In this book is written what I have done, what I have thought, and what I have been." Van den Berg's historical reckonings lead him to conclude that two significant moments in the emergence of the Western self occurred in the 16th century and in the 18th century. Although not mentioned by Van den Berg, Descartes's *Cogito* (c. 1520) coincides with the first period of the self.

The second essay, by Baumeister (1987), is concerned not with the historical solidification of the self (concept) but with an attempt to determine "how the self became a problem." On the basis of a careful reading of a variety of literary and historical documents, Baumeister divides the relevant historical eras into seven separate phases, beginning with what he terms the *late Medieval period* (1000–1400) and ending with the *Recent Twentieth Century* (post-1945). For each of these periods, he considers the relevant literature under four headings: self-knowledge, self-definition, self-fulfillment, and relation of self to society. Without going too deeply into the subtleties of his analysis, it seems quite clear that the modern experience and concept of self has changed dramatically from the late Medieval period, where self-knowledge was "unproblematic," to the Puritan period, where self-knowledge was clouded by a deep concern with issues of self-deception, to the Modern (Freudian) period (from 1900–45), in which complete knowledge is impossible, to the later portion of the Modern period (1945–60), in which self-knowledge is defined by a quest for personal development.

Correlated with these themes of self-knowledge, the individual's relationship to the social order also changed. In the late Medieval period, the relationship was fixed and public, and the person was viewed as a link in

"The Great Chain of Being." During the Puritan period, the individual's task was to work for common and personal good, and success in these endeavors was believed to yield eternal salvation. During the early part of the 20th century, the relationship could be defined best as one of alienation combined with a need to evaluate the culture critically, sometimes even by muckraking. In the final half of this century, the relationship seems to have become one of accommodation – that is, of taking a stance toward society in which the individual alternates between recognizing his/her immersion in the society and attempting to assert an individual perception of it. The present-day self seeks fulfillment within the constraints imposed by the social context, sometimes finding a unique personal identity on the basis of "myth making."

A careful examination of Baumeister's "stages" indicates many more distinct phases in the 150-year period from 1841 to 1990 than in the 840-year period from 1000 to 1840. Perhaps this is inevitable, given the greater number of written sources available during this period combined with the fact that linguistically a secure sense of self did not develop until the late 16th century. Another possible way of thinking about these results, however, would be to suppress our interest in more modern concerns and see if, perhaps, some simpler plan would be sufficient to characterize Baumeister's analysis. From a careful reading of his article, it seems possible to conceptualize the development of self as having not seven, but two, distinct moments: one beginning in the 15th century and ending in the late 16th century (as both Van den Berg and Baumeister now suggest), and a second beginning in the 18th century and continuing on to the present. The first of these phases concerned issues of sin and salvation and eventuated in what could best be called the "religious self." The second of these concerned, and continues to concern, issues of individuality, alienation, and actualization (in that order) and speaks to the emergence of a more "secular self." This latter self, thus defined, seems a far more complex and troubled one than the religious self from which it evolved.

Regardless of whether we consider only European sources (as Van den Berg does) or primarily English and American ones (as Baumeister does), and whether we see two or seven stages, the overriding conclusion seems to be that the concept of self as revealed in novels, philosophical tracts, religious essays, literary criticism, and social science is one that always has to be contextualized by its sociohistorical situation. The idea and reality of self is thus an historically dependent one, and any attempt to view the self as having a universal and a-historical structure seems to have overlooked some rather compelling evidence suggesting that the late 20th-century concept has evolved over the course of at least 400 years of Western history.

The human self is thus not a fixed entity, and we must always be sensitive, as Van den Berg entitled one of his books, to "the changing nature of man" as an historical being.

If history provides one ground configuring what is understood and experienced as a normative self, it seems clear that culture must also have a significant impact. Although any text in cultural anthropology will provide numerous examples of the ways in which "self" is affected by social cultures, Fisher and Fisher (1993), in a section of their book entitled "The Relativity of the Self," make reference to experiences of self among the Maori of New Zealand and the Wintu Indians of northern California. In summarizing differences between the experiences of self in Western and Maori societies, they cite the somewhat playful statement "that if the self in Western societies is the driver of the car, it is, in Maori culture, simply a 'passenger' in one's body" (p. 153). In commenting on more general differences in experiences of self, Fisher and Fisher (1993) conclude that there "is great latitude as to the kind of self-structure a culture can require its participants to fashion. A culture can demand a self of practically zero magnitude or one, at the other extreme, of the overblown dimension common in the 20th Century West" (p. 153).

There is one final piece to the puzzle of self, and this concerns the issue of whether it is useful to talk about a single self (a self of selves as William James, 1890, put it) or whether it is more useful to consider self as a constantly shifting set of aspects and perspectives. Basing his approach on James, Pollio (1982) proposed that we consider the experience of self in terms of three different classes of experience: (1) a bodily aspect defined in terms of the unique pattern of intentions expressed by the nature and style of personal actions; (2) a social aspect defined in terms of experiences and actions in the context of interpersonal situations involving groups of people significant to the person such as friends, family, and/or work associates; and (3) a reflected or intellectual aspect defined in terms of James's distinction between the I and the me. Of these three aspects, the first two refer to unreflected aspects of personal existence – the I as knower or doer – whereas the third refers to the I-as-known or, more simply, the Me. I and Me, however, are not two different or even two closely interrelated phenomena: rather, for either the I or the Me to make sense, experientially or conceptually, there has to be both an I and a Me. If I and Me – or any of the other distinctions made such as between the body and social self – are viewed as distinct events, then we have missed the fact that all three are aspects (not elements) of an integrated Gestalt that is not only internally coherent but also coherently related to the major contexts defining human existence.

The original motivation for proposing a tripartite division was based on developmental data derived from a wide variety of sources concerning infants and children as they progressively come to adult status. So, for example, the development of the embodied aspects of the person were derived from facts such as the young child's ability to recognize itself in the mirror at age 1 and to develop a phantom limb only after age 6. The development of the interpersonal or social aspects of self were based on facts such as the young child's inability to use pronouns until at least 2.5 years of age as well as upon the inability of a child younger than 6 or 7 to play appropriately with other children in a game. Reflected aspects of self, on the other hand, would seem to have 4 to 6 years of age as a lower limit for the child's ability to answer a question such as "Who are you?" Combining those results with the notorious increase in so-called identity questions posed by the young adolescent leads to the conclusion that the development of self-reflection begins in the middle years of childhood and reaches an early peak in adolesence. As should be clear, issues of self-reflection (i.e., identity) continue to be raised over much of the complete life cycle.

Combining all of these findings suggests that the development and maintenance of a reassuring sense of personal self is a lifelong project. Although this project occasionally will produce periods of discomfort – the so-called identity crises described by Erikson (1963) – it is also clear that each resolution will serve to yield a new and more sensitively balanced Gestalt capable of effectively relating the person to his or her world. Developmental psychologists such as Piaget and Erikson tend to tie the various developmental achievements to specific ages; what seems more important is that developmental achievements are sensibily interrelated. That is, some aspects occur before others and provide the ground from which new and different aspects will emerge. Body and social achievements obviously interrelate: If an infant is unable to move in an oriented and intentional way, it would be unlikely to relate to others except as a recipient of their actions. The developing, intentional body–self thus is a prerequisite to the development of a movement toward other people and the subsequent development of the interpersonal aspects of the self. It also seems clear that once the child enters bodily into the social world, new movement skills will be taught by the other people with whom he or she now interacts. As before, there is a complex interaction between the body and the social selves that brings about a new and relatively stable personal organization appropriate to the child and his or her present situation.

The self emerges not only out of a continuing series of interactions among its aspects, combined with a continuing reflection on such interactions, but also on the basis of personal relationships to the world. For this reason, different situations always have the possibility of affecting the time of arrival of each stage, although probably not the order. Despite variations, there seems to be a reasonableness to the order in which various aspects of the person develop, and it is only out of such order that an infant comes to move more precisely from body to others, from others to society, and, finally, from society to various worlds of formalized reflection known as *knowledge*. It is this order that provides not only for the emergence of an organized Gestalt known as self but also for the possibility of such a self being able to organize new aspects of itself and of the world within which it must continuingly negotiate its place.

Anxiety and Self in Psychoanalytic Theory

The sense of relative coherence and possibility that both common sense and academic psychology call the *self* is sometimes experienced as incoherent, depleted, or profoundly stuck. If the disturbance is transitory, the person will get over it and continue on with his or her life. If, however, the disturbance is more profound, the person experiences disorganization or, more dramatically as the title of the present chapter suggests, an episode of "falling apart." When this happens, it seems quite proper to talk about the person as fragmented and disconnected from the supports provided by other people, the world, one's body, and one's history. Under this condition, the world can be described only as chaotic and unpredictable, a place where issues of continuity and, even, of continuing, are never far from hand.

When the clinician encounters individuals in the midst of such an episode, the person is usually characterized as suffering "overwhelming" or "crippling" anxiety. These descriptions seem apt not only in terms of the ways in which such individuals report feeling but also in terms of how they appear to an outside observer. It was (and is) in this light that therapists, beginning with Freud, came to consider to problem of anxiety as crucial to clinical practice involving individuals in the midst of such episodes. In fact, it seems fair to say that from his earliest clinical and theoretical papers, the nature and meaning of anxiety was central to all of Freud's work: "The problem of anxiety is a nodal point linking up all kinds of most important questions: a riddle, of which the solution must cast a flood of light upon our whole mental life" (Freud, 1917/1935). It is perhaps for this reason that no other aspect of Freud's theoretical musings evidenced such changes over time as he continued to expand and rework his understanding of the nature and effects of anxiety.

Broadly speaking, Freud's views on anxiety can be characterized in terms of two separate, but related, theories with the first very much grounded in his project for a scientific version of psychoanalysis (Freud, 1895/1966). In this biologically motivated work, Freud postulated that excess drive energies had an overexcitatory effect that could become toxic. Without some motoric discharge, the individual was thought to experience a traumatic effect of overwhelming anxiety. In this first theory, the basis for traumatic anxiety was the presence of undischarged libido. Although Freud (1917/ 1935) could ascribe no physical component to these predominately emotional experiences, he did think of them as constitutional: "When there is an accumulation of excitation or unused libido, the libidinal excitation vanishes and anxiety appears in its place" (p. 82).

Traditional drive theory conceptualized traumatic anxiety of the type involved in episodes of falling apart as an overstimulated state of the ego. In the face of such overstimulation, the ego attempts to cathect objects. Such cathexis serves to drain off excess energy, thereby allowing the ego to avoid traumatic anxiety. When there is no available object for purposes of drive discharge, as in infancy, libidinal energies were thought to become "toxic." This level of traumatic anxiety then becomes a developmental analogue for adult experiences of traumatic or annihilation anxiety.

As Freud's theories developed, the conceptual languages of ego psychology arose to supplement the language and concepts of early drive theory. Freud's new emphasis on the ego assumed the existence of a well-structured and relatively independent ego as a given in adult life. Under these conditions, anxiety was defined in terms of prototypic danger situations that were capable of overwhelming the ego and, thereby, of disrupting its integrative and synthesizing functions. Such anxiety situations were dependent upon various stages of development, with the earliest developmental anxiety concerning the loss of the love object, followed by anxiety over castration and, finally, by persecutions originating in the superego.

In Freud's second theory, anxiety was viewed as the outcome of conflict – or as a portent of conflict – between the often incompatible aims of the id, ego, and superego. Such conflict threatened to result in a dangerous or potentially traumatic situation that could be avoided by means of a lesser level of anxiety described as *signal anxiety*. This type of anxiety was viewed as allowing the ego to avoid a traumatic state in terms of more adaptive ego functioning as well as in terms of a defense that culminated in the inhibition of an impulse or in the formation of a symptom(s) (Freud, 1926/1959).

Much of the later psychoanalytic literature on anxiety attempted to replace Freud's first theory of anxiety with the second (Rangell, 1968). Many analysts (e.g., Strachey, 1959) take for granted that by moving to a structural model Freud replaced the first theory with the second. In fact,

Freud never was fully able to incorporate the existence of anxiety within the structural model (Rangell, 1968) and always reserved room for a somatic or constitutional etiology in certain types of anxiety-related phenomena observed in clinical practice. Because of these observations, he remained equivocal to the end about which of his two theories of anxiety he preferred, and he never arrived at his customary resolution of relevant theoretical problems.

Ego psychologists (e.g., Rangell, 1955, 1968), subscribing for the most part to the view presented in Freud's second theory, came to view anxiety as an outcome of conflict and typically underestimate its somatic component. Self psychologists, on the other hand, follow the intentions of Freud's first theory of anxiety much more closely. The British school of object relations (e.g., Fairbairn, 1952), and later self psychologists such as Kohut, (1977), are able to resolve Freud's dilemma on the basis of postulating pre-oedipal personality constellations. In the case of self psychology, for example, Kohut (1971, 1977) has proposed a line of narcissistic self-development that occurs alongside a line of interpersonal development. Thus, the problem of self-fragmentation, and correlatively the problem of self-cohesion, is given coequal status with the problem of how we relate to other people. Freud had not yet developed a theory that enabled him to understand the paradox of a patient who simultaneously presents the therapist with seemingly mature interpersonal relations and primitive and unstable self-development. In terms of self psychology, Freud's traumatic anxiety of the first type was recast as annihilation anxiety and characterized as a deficit in the structure of the self.

Annihilation anxiety concerns the fear of self-fragmentation as the most basic negative experience against which the entire person is arranged. Such anxiety is more fundamental than "structural" anxiety, which is developmentally more advanced and based upon conflict in interpersonal relating. Self psychologists describe the need for supportive relationships, termed *self–object relationships*, until relatively late in development. Such relationships mitigate annihilation anxiety by providing organization and support, thereby yielding feelings of self-cohesion, temporal stability, and positive emotions. Clearly, this line of thinking is also present in the writings of object relations theorists such as Winnicott (1958, 1965), who postulated the need for a holding environment, and Klein (1937/1964), who conceived of the mother as a protective shield for the developing infant.

In psychoanalytic self psychology, the establishment of self–object relationships is a requisite to normal development of the maturing self. Self psychology makes extensive use of Freud's structural model, but its salient contribution characterizes anxiety as an inability of the self to integrate its various representations due to deficit or developmental arrest (Kohut, 1977; Stolorow & Lachmann, 1980). In both object relations theory (Fairbairn, 1952) and self psychology (Kohut, 1977), the nascent self does not need another person (i.e., or object) for purposes of drive discharge; rather, the other person is needed to maintain one's sense of going-on-being as a self in relation to others. With this radical change in the psychoanalytic model of what it means to be human, the constitutional or drive model is deemphasized. Although self psychologists still make use of the structural model (and the concepts of conflict) for lesser anxieties, in accounting for annihilation anxiety they tend to emphasize the deficit model and to view the self as overwhelmed in the face of having to go on living without the supporting structure provided by the caretaking of other person(s).

Although not directly phenomenological, self psychology does attempt to cast falling apart in experiential terms. Although self psychology may be viewed as an outgrowth of psychoanalysis, there are salient differences in both theory and practice that differentiate them (Goldberg, 1983). Thus, whereas ego psychologists customarily advocate a conflict model, self psychologists more often advocate a deficit model to understand "falling apart." Some theorists, however, such as Gedo and Goldberg (1973) and Gedo (1979), have attempted to reconcile both lines of development and thereby to incorporate Freud's first and second theories of anxiety into a single model of development and pathology.

Anxiety and Self in Existentialism

The modern existentialist statement of anxiety begins with Kierkegaard in *The Concept of Anxiety* (1844/1980). Here, the fundamental ontological potential of anxiety arises as the individual faces possibilities and assumes responsibility for becoming who it is that he or she chooses to become. It is Kierkegaard's position that in becoming a person, the confrontation with anxiety is ever present as the individual wills and chooses new ways of being. One chooses to be with only one's aspirations, which in many cases are at odds with prevailing social values and pressures. Such a will to act defines one as an independent center of intention (i.e., as a self), and the responsibility for choosing to become that self rests squarely with the individual. May (1950/1977), in line with this view, defines anxiety as a diffuse apprehension cued by a threat to some value that the individual holds essential to being who it is he or she has chosen to be.

Unlike psychoanalysis, Kierkegaard did not articulate a concept of self or of anxiety in terms of natural science categories. His approach to human life operated largely in terms of an historical rather than a naturalistic ontology. For Kierkegaard, the self is relational in character; it is not a given but rather is the possibility for an ongoing dialectic. The self is further characterized as a dialectical relationship between the body/soul (i.e., as a psychosomatic unity of body/emotion) and the spirit or reflective consciousness (i.e., how it imagines or projects itself).

The individual, who necessarily is tied to the temporal and immediate, is not yet reflective enough to be considered a self by Kierkegaard. The first stirrings of self are constituted by relationships between the spirit, as it aspires to reflective awareness, and the body/soul as it exists in the world of everyday life. The self only emerges in relation to a reality that can transcend the actual. For Kierkegaard, the ultimate relationship by which the self can relate itself "to its own self" is in terms of its relationship to God. The relationship to God is a possibility; it represents the highest aspirations of the person projected and personified. This continual relationship to the possible, as opposed to the actual, is what characterizes selfhood for Kierkegaard.

Within this approach, selfhood is determined by what the self relates itself to. In selfhood, the self of Kierkegaard must continually relate itself to the transcendent without losing its relationship to the actual, and selfhood is always a becoming and is never complete in character. In despair, the self is without a balanced relationship between the possible and the actual; hence, alienation results. Selfhood is a potential that embodies our freedom. Because the self is a dynamic balance of the actual and the possible, the self can be lost.

Such loss comes about through inauthentic or nontranscendent relationships; then there is only dread. In the so-called demonic state, the self is related only to somatic aspects of the dialectic, and the spirit is ignored. Within the demonic mode, the self dreads the potential of freedom, not out of the innocence of a child who has yet to become but as an adult oriented toward unfreedom. Whereas fear has an object, the anxiety known as *dread* is objectless and can be viewed only as the concomitant of an existence in freedom. By not facing anxiety and becoming, one lives in the dread of freedom or in a "sickness unto death" (Kierkegaard, 1849/1980).

In *I and Thou* (1923/1970), Buber offers a different description of human existence in which the development of the I, in combination with two modes of consciousness, is described as a basis for both alienation and redemption. At the outset, Buber (1923/1970) establishes the nature of existence as a co-constituted relationship involving both a personal and worldly polarity. Within this context, the quality of relationship between the two polarities specifies the quality of human experiences of self. For Buber, relationships cannot be described by single words but only by relational ones, I–Thou and

I–It. In this sense, the I of human experience is twofold, and the possibility of I–Thou and I–It encounters yield the possibility of qualitatively different experiences of self.

We start life in relation, or as Buber (1923/1970) put it, in a "primal encounter." At first, "I consciousness is woven in relation to Thou." "I consciousness differentiates as that which reaches for, but is not, You." Thus, "the consciousness of the constant partner crystalizes the I consciousness" (Buber, 1923/1970). What Buber is referring to in these situations is that there is no such thing as an infant at this stage of development; only what in objective thought (or hindsight) may be called an-infant-and-a-mother-in-relation. As development proceeds, this relationship establishes the infant's reflexive relationship to him- or herself. Such development continues until one day the "bonds are broken and the I confronts its detached self as a You" (Buber, 1923/1970). The I subsequently "takes possession of itself and continues into relations in full consciousness." Thus, for Buber, "the individual person becomes an I through a You."

The I of the I–Thou does not describe a separate subject and object but rather an encounter of relation. The I that emerges from such encounters is relational and not bounded, and there is nothing "conceptual" about the experience of I–Thou as described by Buber. To encounter aspects of the world in their actuality – in full presentness – is to be in an I–Thou relation. Only when such a unity of relation is divided into a multiplicity of adaptive uses and concepts does the person enter into I–It relationships. The I–Thou relation is the most significant mode of being for Buber and may be experienced both in regard to animate and inanimate aspects of the world. If either are encountered as things of experience and/or of use rather than of presence, then the I of I–It is present.

"The I of the I–Thou is said with one's whole being" (Buber, 1923/1970), whereas the I of I–It is a part-experience based on the use of an object or in the duality of subject and object. The I of the I–It has no present quality, it is only past (experience). "The I of the I–It appears as an Ego and becomes conscious of itself as a subject of experience and use." Thus, "ego emerges with the force of an element when the primal experience has been split" (Buber, 1923/1970). The ego has no substance; it is functional but empty of the actual. As in Kierkegaard's conceptions of self, Buber's I is relational and dynamic, and the achievement of selfhood is never a finished event.

It is Heidegger's intention in *Being and Time* (1927/1962) to reveal and describe the fundamental nature of Being of which our particular historical being is but one possibility. *Dasein*, in his view, is an opening or location in which other people and the things of the world appear. For Heidegger, anxiety or dread (*Angst*) is especially suited to reveal the being of *Desein*.

This mode of attunement discloses fundamental insights not only into our being but into Being itself.

Anxiety reveals *Dasein* in its "throwness," or in the fact that we find ourselves in situations of precarious contingency. "Death, as the end of Dasein, is Dasein's own-most possibility, non-relational, certain and as such indefinite, not to be outstripped" (Heidegger, 1927/1962). In spite of our efforts to carve out a meaningful and familiar home in the world, the possibility of nonbeing is ever present. In basic agreement with Kierkegaard, anxiety or dread has no object, and we are anxious in the face of being-in-the-world as such. It is the "nothing and nowhere" of dread (anxiety); it is utter meaninglessness that is its primary ontological quality (Heidegger, 1927/1962).

Heidegger describes dread as a coloration of being, as a disclosure of the world rather than a feeling that one has. It is a relation to the world that encompasses being in all of its aspects but without the familiar feeling of being at home, and it is the metaphor of not being at home in the world that captures Heidegger's description of existential dread. To escape the feeling of not being at home in the world, the modern person "falls into" the situation of *Das Man*. By being absorbed into the reality of *Das Man*, personal existence preempts an openness to being with stereotyped forms of culture. To "fall" into conventional forms is to live inauthentically and is characterized as a flight of *Dasein* from itself. To experience dread is to face the possibility of meaninglessness and, thereby, to face and accept responsibility for the existence that one carves out.

Dread is not to be confused with fear, which always involves a specific person, object, or situation and which always is experienced as threatening my very specific being-in-the world. When we experience dread, according to Heidegger, we are not fleeing from anything definite but from dread itself. Such dread presents itself never in a specific form to confront my meaninglessness but always as an indeterminate accusation of inauthenticity. What I dread is the world itself, where and when it reveals itself as without meaning, as a nothingness. To deal with the overwhelming nature of dread, the human being sometimes is able to turn it into a more manageable experience of fear. By reacting to dread as a fear of some specific event or situation, the person is able to keep away from its fateful message and avoid its engulfing power.

Although this analysis leads Heidegger to conclude that all dread is an intimation of the final nothingness of death, and that only by accepting life as a being-toward-death is it possible to undertake the work of authentic existence, the important point for present purposes is in his evocative rendition of a world lived under the mood of dread. As with Kirkegaard,

Heidegger's description evokes for us the experience of overwhelming dread and offers a clear background for any attempt to understand more fleeting experiences of falling apart. Since the experience is a human one, it is important to heed Heidegger's view that it is only by experiencing dread, and living through it, that it is possible to defeat the pretense provided by conventional thought and action. Although the idea of falling apart may seem a threatening one, it may be the only way to come to terms with our world as our own (*eigentlich*, authentically).

It was with some of these understandings in mind that Fischer (1970, 1989) undertook a series of phenomenological studies concerning the human experience of anxiety. In this work, Fischer (1970, 1989) began by exhaustively attempting to survey both the world views and preconceptions of the major anxiety theorists in an attempt to achieve a new integration of their works. His main critique of prior work centered on the domains of experience that were selected and/or found unsuitable for study because of the investigator's preconceptions. Additionally, he noted a failure to differentiate the experience of the "other-being-anxious" from that of "anxious experiencing." In the former case, the person is studied as an object whose experience is questionable because it is "subjective" and must be objectified by the investigator. An additional problem arises when the investigator attempts to apply his or her own personal history of anxious experiencing to understand the "causes" of anxious experiencing in the other. In these situations, the subject is not permitted to describe the ways in which experience is personally configured but rather has his or her experiences recast in terms of what anxiety means for the investigator. The anxious experiencing of the person, as described by the person, has only rarely and coincidentally been presented in the psychological literature.

For these reasons, Fischer felt the need for a detailed and systematic pretheoretical descriptive analysis of anxious experiencing. To accomplish this task, he collected essays in college-level courses where students were asked to describe experiences of being anxious (Fischer, 1978). On the basis of these essays, Fischer came to describe the experiential structure of anxiety in terms of both a worldly pole – the "what" in the face of which one is anxious – and a more personal pole – the "about which" one is anxious. The event, the "what" in the face of which one is anxious, was described as the possibility of losing a chosen, lived, and/or planned-for world. The "about which" one is anxious was described as the becoming of the person one had chosen to be or had to be. For example, when students face an examination that is experienced as capable of deciding employment, and hence life choices, the what "in-the-face-of-which" they are anxious is the examination and the "about which" they are anxious is their ability to pass it. The world pole is the event of the examination, with its promise of the future lived-for-world. The personal pole is the participant's uncertain ability to pass the examination and thereby to become whom he or she wishes to become (i.e., an adequate person, able to realize his or her meaningful intentions).

Fischer's work is radically descriptive in intent, and he appeals to the reader's experience to judge the validity of his account. His analysis does not seek or imply a causal relationship nor does it develop an explanatory structure. In the case of the college student, for example, an examination is not construed as the cause of anxiety; rather, it is the manner in which the student is involved with and open to a situation that may or may not entail anxiety. Other possible ways of construing this situation could be to feel anger, annoyance, or despair.

In a different attempt at achieving an experiential understanding of anxiety, Fingarette (1963) employed the "fundamental" insights of psychoanalytic theory at the same time as he sought to rid it of its nonexperiential conceptual categories. Fingarette begins his analysis of anxiety by assuming that the disposition to seek a meaningful life is fundamental to human existence. To this end, meaning schemes are developed that have conceptual, motivational, and affective aspects. This proposal of a thrust toward meaning represents Fingarette's reconceptualization of the synthesizing functions of the (psychoanalytic) ego. It is his position that synthesis is not a function of the ego but is the ego itself. The "self," therefore, is not some internal structure that produces and integrates meaning; rather, it is the process by which we continuously strive to produce meaning in our lives. When the ego, construed as a meaning-producing process, fails in its synthesizing activity, meaninglessness and its concomitant, anxiety, arise. Fingarette maintains "that anxiety is the other face of the ego. It is not primarily an affect, one among many affects, which the ego must master; rather *it is* ego-disintegration." The ego neither produces nor experiences anxiety; rather, when an individual is unable to maintain, create, or manage meaningful action in the world, he or she lives the world anxiously.

The early psychoanalytic understanding of anxiety, as an overstimulation that becomes toxic, can now be reconceptualized as a failure in the person's efforts at integration rather than as an inability to discharge libido. This failure of integration is anxiety and, in existential terms, is defined by a lack of meaningfulness. The contexts and meanings that involve the person thus become the form that anxiety takes. Whereas Freud would have understood the infant's loss of its mother as separation anxiety and her unavailability as an object for drive discharge, Fingarette understands this anxiety as a loss of a meaning and context that cannot be integrated by the infant.

In other words, the infant has lost the holding environment in which meanings are produced and experienced (Winnicott, 1965).

The primary and constitutional emphasis that Freud ascribed to neurosis can now be understood in terms of the fundamental ontological possibility of anxiety – namely, as the other side of meaningful life. Fingarette thus achieves a unification of anxiety theory: Signal anxiety and traumatic anxiety differ only in the degree to which the ongoing work of synthesis (or meaningful living) is disrupted. For Fingarette, the potential for anxiety is an existential given and is counterpart to the potential for meaningful living. The forms of anxiety are attributable to the degree and fashion in which current meanings are (or are not) integrated by the person.

The Present Program of Research

To develop a thematic description of the human experience of falling apart, a series of 12 phenomenological interviews was conducted. Of the 12 participants, 8 were female and 4 were male. Ages ranged from 23 to 44. Educational levels also varied: One participant was a high-school graduate, 3 had approximately 2 years of college, and 8 had finished college and were completing or had completed advanced degrees in business, psychology, social work, or nursing. No attempt was made to select participants based on demographics, or even on the belief that they had sustained an experience of falling apart. In fact, 4 of the volunteers initially were unsure, as they put it, "if I have ever really fallen apart." The only criteria for participation were that the person volunteered for the study and was articulate and willing to be interviewed.

At the beginning of each interview, participants were encouraged to ask questions, and the collaborative nature of the research was emphasized. All interviews were as open-ended and neutral as possible; the interviewer tried to avoid imposing theoretical language and limited questions largely to an elaboration of the participant's language and experience. Following an initial introduction, each participant was told: "People have described the experience of falling apart. Does this way of talking about experience make sense to you? Have you had experiences you might describe this way?" Typically, participants began relating what they had experienced. Some, however, did not find the metaphor of falling apart meaningful and chose instead to use a different phrase such as "dissolving" or, in the local metaphor, "being all tore up."

Previous studies using phenomenological methods have attempted to reduce the text to what have been termed significant statements (e.g., Colaizzi, 1978). Because of the storylike form of the present interviews, this method did not seem appropriate, and a different mode of analysis, arising from the transcripts themselves, was developed. Since the obvious commonality across transcripts was their narrative form, the first step was to organize the various texts in order to make the narrative flavor of each interview more pronounced. This was done by abridging the transcript and by creating a narrative digest of the interview. This digest explicitly ordered the content of each transcript more overtly along the lines of a story – a story with a beginning, middle, and end (see also RAH).

In all of the interviews, participants repeated themselves, redescribing the same experiences and meanings at a number of different points in the dialogue. The tangents, stories within stories, and digressions in the interviews also were sorted along narrative lines. All aspects of a given narrative were then compared, and only the richest and most representative descriptions were kept. No new language was introduced, and consolidation was undertaken solely as an abridgment or digest of the interview text. Textual contradictions were not reconciled in order to avoid losing the dramatic and personal form of each interview. A careful attempt also was made to avoid interpretation during the process of summarizing individual narratives.

To organize these narrative digests further, the familiar literary conventions of setting, focal experience, and resolution were used to organize each interview. These categories were obvious in each of the various transcripts, and they allowed for the creation of narrative summaries. Although it can be argued that imposing a narrative framework on the present set of interviews is somewhat arbitrary, it seemed appropriate given the clear, narrative quality to all 12 interviews. Once initial narrative summaries had been prepared, they were further, and more specifically, categorized according to setting, focal experience, and resolution.

Finally, all narrative summaries were thematically considered within the context of an interpretive group. This stage in the analysis consisted of two steps: First, each narrative was described in terms of a series of summary statements describing its content; second, all statements were read and named by thematic meanings suggested by the text. Succinctly stating the content of all synopses was done next to allow group members not familiar with the text to arrive at a grasp of the narrative without having to read the complete interview. Thematizing content, on the basis of a limited number of empirically derived meanings, led to a structural description of the phenomenon. Once such a description was developed, it was read to members of the research group to secure their reactions to the specific intepretations made.

Table 9.1. *Narrative Structure Used to Describe Interviews*

Setting

The setting states the context of the experience as it emerged in the dialogue. It is the proximal ground or "when" of the experience of "falling apart."

Focal Experience

The focal experiences are those aspects of the narrative that were figural for the participants in the dialogue. It is what the participants came to talk about as the "what" or recurrent core of the experience of "falling apart."

Resolution

The resolution is what delimits the focal experience in time. In the course of the dialogue, participants also described how the focal experience changed over time. The experience in all cases came to a resolution or ending.

Everyday Experience

The everyday experience is the most inclusive ground for the present collection of dialogues. Of the 12 participants, 7 described their usual experience of daily living before, during, and after their description of the focal experience, its resolution, and setting.

When all members of the group were convinced that each summary captured the interview in a clear and useful way, an attempt was made to develop an overall thematic summary of all 12 interviews. The purpose of this step was to portray the situated meanings of the various narratives. As such, it was meant to retain the meanings derived from each of the interviews and, by extension, of each participant's experience.

In addition to these procedures, an informal follow-up meeting was arranged with each of the 12 participants to allow them to review thematic descriptions of their interview. Each participant was given his or her own narrative synopsis to read. In addition, thematic meanings and schematic summaries were presented to individual participants. At this time, each participant had an opportunity to provide feedback and/or to discuss present findings as they related to him or her.

Since all protocols exibited a narrative flow, present results were organized initially in terms of such a structure. The specifics of this structure are presented in terms of the four categories defined in Table 9.1. As may be seen, the structure is characterized by the categories of Setting, Focal Experience, Resolution, and Everyday Experience. It is within the context of these categories that the specific context of all 12 participant interviews are presented.

Setting

Table 9.2 presents the 20 specific settings within which all 12 participants located their narratives. On the basis of thematizing these situations, it was possible to define a single theme as crucial: The potential or actual loss of some person, place, or both (person and place). Given the open-ended structure of the interviews, it is impressive that all of the settings for falling apart could be described as involving the threatened or actual loss of an individual's usual life-world. As described in the present set of interviews, the major features of everyday life are people and places.

The category *People* was used to include experiences of falling apart in which the loss of important relationships through travel, divorce, or death was focal. All participants who described an actual loss discussed it in terms of losing ordinary meaningful interactions that they had experienced as anchoring their everyday lives prior to the loss. Even the threat of loss, through marital conflict, was found to occasion an experience of "falling apart" for some participants.

No less an important anchor for the world of everyday life is presented by the second category, *Place*. Although this category included such issues as geography, it speaks primarily to a nexus of meaningful and typically familiar relationships that were experienced in regard to places and objects described as part of everyday life. A home town, the color of one's room, an experience of "everything in its place," all were described as significant constants to an individual's world which, when lost, led the person to an experience of falling apart.

In thematizing the 20 settings described by participants, the situation for falling apart may be defined as one in which a threatened or actual loss of the familiar world of people, places, and relationships takes place. Such loss was described as overwhelming, and participants described feelings of being unanchored, helpless, and incapable of realizing customary actions such as thinking about, or doing, ordinary tasks.

Focal Experience

Table 9.3 presents the particulars of the focal experiences described by all 12 participants. These experiences were found to yield four themes: Crying/Pain, Lost (Losing), Alterations in Time, and Out of Control. The first theme, Crying/Pain, relates to the body as lived, in particular as it becomes figural in experiences of falling apart. Bodily tensions and stress, cramps, trembling, cold sweat, and sobbing or screaming all find their thematic place within the theme of Crying/Pain.

Table 9.2. *Settings Described by Participants*

Setting I: People

Participant 2:
1. He is on a date and wondering if he will be accepted by her.
2. He is in an examination and wondering if he can demonstrate his knowledge to the professor.

Participant 3:
3. She is in the process of being divorced.

Participant 4:
4. She is having significant problems with her mother-in-law and fears losing her husband.

Participant 5:
5. She is in an argument with her husband.

Participant 7:
6. She is losing her father through the parent's divorce.

Participant 9:
7. He is talking to an authority figure (coach or professor).

Participant 10:
8. He is trying to make sense of his father's erratic behavior.
9. He is finding out that his mother has cancer.

Participant 6:
10. She is being threatened by her dangerous ex-husband, who is demanding to see her.

Setting II: Place

Participant 8:
11. She comes home from elementary school to find her room painted a color "she hates."
12. She is in her car and sees headlights coming at her in the same lane.

Participant 9:
13. He is in his room, and it becomes unfamiliar.

Setting III: People and Place

Participant 1:
14. She has moved to a new place to begin graduate school, leaving behind important relationships.

Participant 2:
15. He is alone in his car and is afraid of becoming lost.
16. He is alone, thinking about the inescapability of death.
17. He is threatened with being sent away to military school.

Participant 10:
18. He is trying to understand why his girlfriend wouldn't come over during the snowstorm to spend the night; his brother and his girlfriend are together in the same apartment.

Participant 11:
19. She is on a new job, preceded by divorce, children going off to school, and the death of a close friend.

Participant 12:
20. He has moved to a new place to begin graduate school and has left his friends.

Table 9.3. *Focal Experiences Described by Participants*

Crying/Pain

Participant 1: She is aware of her body in anxious/uneasiness, stress, and depression. She is crying.

Participant 2: His body does not belong to him – heart pounding, palms sweating, panicked.

Participant 3: She is experiencing a higher level of anxiety and deep depression.

Participant 4: She is tense in the stomach, is nauseous, and has a pounding headache.

Participant 4: She is going to yell out.

Participant 5: She is frustrated and angry; there's a knot in her stomach, and nausea.

Participant 7: She is sobbing and nauseated.

Participant 8: She is crampy, moody, blah.

Participant 9: He experiences racing heart, butterflies in the stomach, and dry mouth.

Participant 10: He is crying and in anguish.

Participant 11: She feels frightened and is crying.

Participant 12: He is tight as a drum, scared; he has a physical sensation of cracking like an egg and is crying.

Lost (Losing)

Participant 1: She is disoriented and hanging on desperately to coherent information.

Participant 1: She is questioning her faith/relationship to God.

Participant 2: He does not know where he is, and terrible things could happen.

Participant 3: She is feeling totally lost.

Participant 3: She is aware that she could cease to be.

Participant 5: She feels rejected by her husband and is losing this relationship.

Participant 7: She is isolated and lonely.

Participant 8: There is an indefinite not knowing.

Participant 9: His body and everything is unfamiliar.

Participant 10: He is isolated and wondering why this (setting) has happened.

Participant 11: She is preoccupied and disconnected from people.

Participant 12: He is feeling unreal and disconnected.

Alterations in Time

Participant 2: There is no future and no past.

Participant 3: It is difficult to put time constraints on this experience.

Participant 6: It is hard to describe because it happens in such a short amount of time.

Participant 10: Time stands still; there is no future.

Participant 12: He doesn't know how long it lasted.

Out of Control

Participant 1: She can neither think nor do.

Participant 2: He can't think, and everything is out of proportion.

Participant 3: She fears becoming dysfunctional and having to be locked up.

Participant 4: She is going to flip out.

Participant 5: She can't control her thoughts; she is shaking and trembling.

Table 9.3. (*continued*)

Participant 6:	She is losing it, can't handle it, fearing screaming and beating everything up; becoming mentally disabled.
Participant 7:	She is unable to talk.
Participant 8:	She needs to do something but can't.
Participant 8:	Crying and screaming are her only options.
Participant 9:	He has lost control of thought and body.
Participant 10:	He can't do anything; it is a breakdown.
Participant 11:	She can't make decisions and feels overwhelmed.
Participant 12:	He does not want to be there but can't control it.

The second theme, Lost/Losing, portrays a feeling of being lost or of losing a sense of the familiar. In general, participants reported a sense of not being-at-home in their world. This experience is an important aspect to the phenomenon of falling apart and includes an experience of being confused and isolated, as well as a loss of the meaning of events and situations encountered.

The third theme, Alterations in Time, describes distortions in the experience of time as well as an inability to mark time in a conventional manner. Time is described as losing both its future and its past; participants also reported an experienced loss of temporal continuity, with time being described by the person as an "eternal present." Within the temporal domain, falling apart was described as an unconventional mode of being-in-time, which was described as a particular aspect of the more general loss of familiarity characterizing the total experience.

The fourth theme, Out of Control, speaks to a feeling of not being in control of one's life, behavior, or emotions. Participants reported fearing the expression of often violent impulses and/or extreme vulnerability and helplessness. Thinking and planning were described as unavailable, and the body was experienced as not responding to one's intention to speak or to do.

Even though each theme captures a significant aspect of falling apart, it is important to keep in mind that they are not isolated elements but interdependent aspects of the total experience. The theme, Alteration in Time, implies an experience of being lost because time serves as an important aspect of the way in which we carve out our day-to-day existence in the world. The theme of Alterations in Time, thus, also defines an aspect of the strangeness of the experience. As should also be clear, the theme of Crying/Pain interrelates with the themes of Control and Lost. The person is anything but comfortable when he or she experiences the life-world as failing to support personal action or even a personal future. Individuals who report experiences of falling apart are living in a world that seems out of control, unmanageable, and atemporal; they cry out as an embodied expression of their situation.

Taking all of these themes into account yields the following description of the focal experience of falling apart: The person in the midst of such an experience is confused and disoriented. Familiar meanings are lost, and the person does not feel anchored, grounded, or at-home. Relationships to other people and the usual sense of personal continuity in time are altered and strange. There is a preoccupation with the present, and the past and future are experienced as unavailable. The person feels isolated from other people, and there is a sense of being both out of control and helpless to do anything about the present situation. Customary and voluntary actions are not available, and the person reports experiences of panic, terror, rage, and depression. Bodily awareness of stress, tension, and pain also are figural for the person. There is no future and no way out, and the person experiences the possibility of nonbeing.

Resolution

In addition to describing specific experiences of falling apart, all 12 participants described the way in which each episode was resolved. The specific resolutions described by present participants are presented in Table 9.4. An examination of individual narratives revealed that all 12 resolutions could be described in terms of two themes: Reconnection and Reestablishing Control. Again it is interesting, given the latitude allowed by the interview format, to find such empirical agreement as to how experiences of "falling apart" resolve themselves. There is a symmetry between the ways in which episodes of falling apart are resolved and the settings and focal themes describing the experience. Thus, when there is a loss of familiar meanings and relationships in situations defining falling apart, the resolution phase is characterized by a reconnection and reestablishment of relationships and meanings. This symmetry also takes place in regard to the pattern of relationship between resolutions and focal experiences. Here reconnection and reestablishment of control proceeded along the lines of a return to a familiar time, of no longer feeling lost, of being in control, and of being comfortable in a bodily way.

The theme of Reconnection describes an interpersonal resolution to the experience of falling apart; that is, an interpersonal connection (or contact) was established and served to anchor the person who reported feeling lost

Table 9.4. *Resolutions Described by Participants*

Reconnection

Participant 1:	She contacts friends and goes to see a counselor.
Participant 2:	He seeks out an available person.
Participant 3:	She began talking to a friend and entered counseling.
Participant 4:	She expresses her feelings to her husband.
Participant 7:	She calls her fiancé over and cries.
Participant 8:	She likes to complain about it to someone.
Participant 9:	He goes to see his father or his grandparents.
Participant 11:	She was in treatment.
Participant 12:	He patted the dogs.

Reestablish Control

Participant 1:	She moves, cuts down at work, and affirms positive thoughts.
Participant 2:	He thinks about the future and the past.
Participant 4:	She cries and then tries to drop it (i.e., to stop thinking about the problem).
Participant 5:	She screams and then tries to face up to things in perspective.
Participant 6:	She catches hold of herself and rejects him.
Participant 7:	She goes to college and work to stay out of the house.
Participant 8:	She waits until the event is over to shake or cry.
Participant 9:	He can fight it off by paying attention to something ordinary.
Participant 10:	He has to break out and get away and/or he will think and write it.
Participant 11:	She decided to enter treatment.
Participant 12:	He cried rather than becoming pent up.

during the disintegrative episode. In this mode of relationship, the person serving to anchor the participant makes him- or herself available in a helpful and healing way. One finds a home port in the storm, and experiences of meaning and bodily comfort return.

The theme of Reestablishing Control speaks to the often stressful struggle to resolve the experience of falling apart through personal effort. Control was described as being reestablished after a "cathartic" session of crying, exercise, or some external distraction. In a few cases, even the decision to seek help as a first step toward resolution was described as an experience of reestablishing control. The overall meaning of this step was to emphasize how one's personal continuity and agency are reestablished on the basis of individual effort.

Taking all of these themes and their interrelationships into account yields the following general description of the way in which experiences of falling apart are resolved: The person reestablishes familiar anchors in the continuity of personal being and/or in an interpersonal connection in which someone listens to, talks to, understands, and/or helps the person in turmoil. In addition, the person may reassert self-initiated activity, either in the form of venting an emotion or by accepting the limits of his or her present situation.

Everyday Experience

In describing their experiences of falling apart, all participants described the world of everyday experience (Table 9.5) as the larger horizon within which to locate experiences of falling apart. Talking about one's everyday experience is quite a problem because it serves most often as a silent ground to other events emerging as figural. Despite the tendency of our everyday world to serve as ground, 7 of the 12 participants shared insights about the ongoing world of everyday reality that served as a counterpoint to previous themes characterizing the experience of falling apart.

One theme that emerged to characterize the familiar and comfortable cadence of one's usual being-in-the-world was that of "smoothness" or "synchrony." Within the theme of Synchrony, participants described feelings of comfort, relaxation, and at-homeness as well as a more general sense of things going smoothly and in synchrony with expectations.

A second theme that emerged concerned the almost effortless everyday competence with which we perform what we want to do or accomplish. Within this second theme, Competence, participants reported an unspoken confidence and sense of efficacy that pervades their every experience of living and acting in their worlds.

Taking both of these themes into account yields the following description of the way in which everyday life is experienced. The person feels a familiar sense of natural ease and competence. Feelings of order, security, and resilience occur, and reflection is figural only when some aspect of the world becomes problematic. In short, the person experiences him- or herself as competent and in synchrony with the requirements of everyday life.

Participant Feedback

After a summary narrative had been prepared for each participant, a follow-up interview was arranged. At this time, participants were provided with a narrative synopsis of their interview; in addition, they were presented with the general thematic meanings derived from all 12 interviews. Following this, they were asked to discuss their interview in light of the themes developed, and to let the interviewer know whether these themes did or did not accord with their understanding of the experience of falling apart.

Table 9.5. *Everyday Experiences Described by Participants*

Competence

Participant 1: She is able to manage the world the way she wants.
Participant 2: He is anchored and knows where he is, who he is, and what he's doing.
Participant 5: It doesn't usually bother her when things go wrong.
Participant 6: She tries to be emotionally controlled.
Participant 8: She plans her days and accomplishes goals.
Participant 9: He is able to think coherently and speak convincingly.

Synchrony

Participant 1: She has a sense of faith and calm.
Participant 2: He is in an activity with no element of self-reflection.
Participant 5: She is not tense, and everything is going smoothly.
Participant 9: He is aware of comfort and ease.
Participant 12: He feels himself, relaxed, and at-home.

The tenor of the follow-up interviews was complimentary and appreciative. Participants described feeling understood. None took issue with his or her specific synopsis, and all agreed both with the description of the course of events and its narrative rendering. Several participants spontaneously noted that both the interview and its follow-up had been positive experiences, and several expressed the hope that their material would be helpful in the treatment of people in crisis.

Implications of Present Results

The experience of falling apart was conceptualized in early psychoanalytic theory in terms of traumatic anxiety that was constitutionally based and depended upon infantile experiences of being unable to discharge libidinal energies (Freud, 1895/1966). When the individual experienced such anxiety as an adult, he or she was helpless to function as an ongoing entity. With the development of Freud's tripartite model of personality, however, anxiety was recast in terms of relations between id, ego, and superego (Freud, 1926/1959). In this rendering, anxiety became a signal of intrapsychic conflict arising from the incompatible aims characteristic of these psychic agencies.

Object relations theory and self psychology discuss anxiety in terms of the interpersonal nature of infantile and more mature forms of dependency (Fairbairn, 1952). Such dependency is seen as a normal stage in the development of a more independent and cohesive experience of self. The loss of a supportive interpersonal matrix before the establishment of relative independence was thought to occasion the most basic dread that can be experienced (Winnicott, 1958). Self psychology has developed this theme in terms of the need for self–object relations (Kohut, 1977), and traumatic anxiety is rendered by this theory in terms of the inability of an individual to maintain a cohesive sense of self. Beyond infancy, this state of affairs is thought to reflect an inability/failure to structure the experience of self adequately, thereby yielding a state of precarious selfhood that is easily disrupted.

In a more existential-phenomenological mode, Fischer (1970, 1971, 1978) has described the experience of anxiety in terms of a world pole, the "what" in the face of which one is anxious, and a subject pole, the "about which" one is anxious. One is anxious in the face of losing a life-world for which one has striven. One is anxious about being unable to achieve what one needs to achieve or who he or she wants/needs to be. In other words, one is anxious about an uncertain ability to realize one's meaningful intentions in the face of a threat to one's present or projected life-world.

It is often difficult to bridge differences between the various conceptual languages of psychoanalysis, let alone between psychoanalysis and existentialism. Fingarette (1963), however, has attempted to recast psychoanalytic insight in terms of existential ontology. In this attempt, he underscores the critical significance of the "synthesizing functions" of the ego in terms of the person's attempt to seek meaningfulness in his or her life. To this end, Fingarette characterizes the "self" not as an actor within some person but as the process of integration itself. This description accords well with other descriptions (e.g., Pollio, 1982) deriving from the position initially articulated by William James (1890).

It is somewhat confusing, however, to speak of a "self" acting meaningfully in the world where meaningful action is nothing other than what is usually meant by the person's actions and experiences. Schafer (1976, 1983) has attempted to clarify this issue in terms of his focus on personal narrative as the center of a person's intentional stance toward the life world. It should be clear by now that all theorists, whatever their orientation, view anxiety as a fundamental aspect of one's relationship to what is usually meant by self. That is, where there is meaningful living, there is the possibility of an experience of self, and where meaningful living is not possible or blocked, there is an experience of diffuse and objectless dread (Kierkegaard, 1844/1980; May, 1950/1977).

Given these considerations, the present research attempted to arrive at an empirically based thematic description of the experience of falling apart. To accomplish this task, 12 adult participants were recruited and interviewed individually. An analysis of the resulting interviews revealed that they could be characterized in terms of the narrative categories of setting, focal experience, resolution, and the world of everyday living. The use of these categories appeared to allow the experience of falling apart to emerge with surprising economy and univocality of expression. This occurred despite the fact that each of the 12 volunteers related an assortment of life experiences with obvious demographic and personal differences.

In all interviews, participants responded, first and foremost, with stories in which an unfolding sequence of events was apparent. The historian Hayden White (1981), in discussing the human tendency toward narrative, quotes Barthes (1977) as saying: "Narrative is simply there like life itself ... international, transhistorical, transcultural." He continues to note that narrative might well be considered a solution to a problem of a general human concern – namely, "the problem of how to translate knowing into telling, the problem of fashioning human experience into a form assimilable to structures of meaning that are generally human rather than culture specific." White then goes on to discuss the etymology of the word narrative, whose Sanskrit root (*gna*, to know) and whose Latin root (*narro*, to relate) point to the movement of meaningful experience into words. White makes the point that narrative is not out there as a thing to be seen but as a symbolic human form no less "objective" than biography or history, which use it to tell their story.

Narrative structure unifies personal experience and makes life sensible. In the context of history, the narrative is created by the historian – a peculiar sort of product having the form of an object yet not the ontological status of an object. In psychoanalysis, the issues raised by narrative have been discussed by Spence (1982) in terms of a distinction between historical truth (the "facts" of a life) and narrative truth (the unifying themes and patterns that the individual identifies as his or her specific life history). Although Spence affords a degree of objectivity to historical truth that might be questioned, his conception of narrative truth is in agreement with present results: Human beings describe their lives in terms of stories that both describe and create personal and social meanings. Since stories are created events, they express a world and, in so doing, allow both for a more ready personal assimilation and a clear intersubjective communication of the world created. Narrative facilitates the fusion of horizons (Gadamer, 1960/1975), which is the task at hand, and permits unique experiences such as those of falling apart to be shared and understood.

Thematic analysis of the present set of interviews suggests that narrative structure is as ordinary (everyday) as it is fundamental. The settings provided by participants for their experiences of falling apart could be described by the actual or threatened loss of either People, Place or both

People and Place together. The major themes defining focal experiences of falling apart were Crying/Pain, Lost (Losing), Alterations in Time, and Out of Control. All participants also described how episodes of falling apart were resolved; usually these were rendered in terms of the themes of interpersonal Reconnection and/or the Reestablishment of (personal) Control. Finally, most participants also described how these episodes differed from their everyday experiences – that is, when things were not falling apart. This aspect of their experiences may be rendered thematically in terms of the everyday experiences of Synchrony and Competence.

The setting for falling apart, then, is the threatened or actual loss of the familiar world of people and places, and their needed, co-defining structures. When such an event takes place, the world is experienced as overwhelming. As one participant put it: "I felt unanchored, helpless, and unable to go about ordinary activities such as thinking and doing ordinary tasks" – what Heidegger (1927/1962) might have described as the experience of not being at home in the world (*unheimlich*).

In describing the focal experience of falling apart, all participants reported being confused and disoriented. Familiar meanings were lost, and the person reported not feeling anchored, grounded, or comfortable. Relationships and the usual sense of a continuity in time also were described as altered. Participants reported a preoccupation with the present, such that past and future were experienced as unavailable. Interpersonally, participants reported feeling cut off and isolated. There also was a sense of being out of control and helpless, and the person reported experiencing agitation, terror, rage, and depression. Bodily awareness of stress, tension, and pain predominated, and many participants reported crying. All reported that at the moment of falling apart, there was seemingly no way out and that they felt headed toward nonbeing.

In the resolution phase of the episode, participants reported reestablished familiar anchors in terms of a continuity of personal being and/or of an interpersonal context in which they were listened to, talked to, understood, and helped. Some participants also reported reasserting self-initiated activity in the form of a venting of emotion or through an acceptance of the situation. Finally, the experience of falling apart was contrasted by some participants with more ordinary everyday experience in which they reported feeling a familiar sense of ease and competence. Feelings of order, security, and resilience colored awareness, and self-reflection only appeared as figural when something was experienced as problematic.

Relationships with other people and movement within significant places both provide basic anchors to the human life-world. The experience of an ongoing and cohesive sense of self, then, is fundamentally co-defined by interpersonal relationships to other people and by body relationships to familiar places – what could be termed the competent and synchronic experience of an intentional body-self combined with a competent and synchronic social-self (Pollio, 1982). The loss of relationships defining these experiences yields a loss of familiarity, an estrangement from the *Lebenswelt*. Although all alienations do not yield experiences of falling apart, falling apart is the starkest of such alienations. It is, in effect, an experience of being lost, and experiences of falling apart define a mode of being marked by a dissolution of relationship with the familiar. It is an agitated despair, an especially virulent incidence of what Kierkegaard called the "sickness unto death" (1849/1980).

The familiar world of people and place, in which one lives meaningfully and in synchrony with feelings of competence, also is lost. Fingarette (1963) defines this state of meaninglessness as anxiety, and as an antithesis to the meaningful and the familiar. In regard to Fischer's (1970) analysis of anxiety, it is no longer merely that the project of an ongoing intentional self is threatened; in an episode of falling apart, the experience of coherence itself is lost. One of the participants described this situation in the following terms: "Anxiety is just like a constant nagging kind of sensation to me . . . when I anticipate something bad is going to happen; . . . for me, the terror [of falling apart] was like the bad thing happening."

The experience of personal continuity – what is called *ego* in more clinical writings and *self* in more psychological writings – would seem best described as a special mode(s) of being marked by synchrony and competence in relationship with familiar settings of people and places. The situation of falling apart provides an opposite experience in which the lived body becomes figural as fragmented, constrained, or limited: *It* is in pain, *it* is crying, *it* is not experienced in vital engagement or as ground for intentional activity-in-the-world, and, finally, *it* is the location of stark emotions and tensions that fill the person with dread. In short, the body is experienced as completely different from its more everyday mode of being lived (see Chapter 3). As one participant commented; "I was tight as a drum . . . it's terrifying . . . it's a physical sensation of coming apart . . . it's not a metaphor."

The everyday experience of time (see Chapter 4) can be described in terms of tempo as well as in terms of changes and continuities that describe a becoming in time. Time can also be described as having a *now/never* structure as well as one of limits and choices. In the experience of falling apart, there is an alteration in the experience of each of these themes: Variations in tempo run from chaotic and fast to a perpetual now whose prior and future aspects have vanished as if they never existed. Since time is experienced as aberrant, there is an absence of both continuity/change and limits/choice, and the self that experiences falling apart is not the ordinary self, since the present "self" experiences only a now that threatens never to become a not-now. In episodes of falling apart, the person also experiences extreme limitations on his or her choice of activities; in fact, there is an absence of an ability to do ordinary things. A further alteration in the experience of time was noted in terms of participants' difficulty in "being on time." When time was mentioned, it was usually thematic in terms of an inability to mark time or even to tell how long a period of time the experience of falling apart lasted (i.e., "I don't know how long it lasted . . . I don't have any idea how it ended.").

Alterations in the experience of time also were clearly related to the theme of Lost/Losing. In fact, of all the themes, this one seems to capture the experience of alienation best. In Greek, *alienus* means a stranger, and the stranger is never at home where he or she now lives. Things only have meaning in relationship – in pointing to other things, other people, the world. Things do not have meaning in and of themselves, and the same is true for the experience of personal continuity. When there is alienation, the self is a stranger to the things (people and place) and intentions experienced as constituting it. In describing an experience at work, one participant said, "It was so confusing . . . I thought, what does this mean? . . . There were these little conflicting pieces of information there, and I couldn't do any-thing else, I had to get it straight." And later in the interview, "[It was] a crisis of faith, a crisis of what am I doing here? . . . how did God let this happen, I thought we had this straightened out." To experience a loss of familiar relationships, or one of being lost, is to experience being alien in what once was familiar geography.

Not only is there alienation, there is also a helplessness and a loss of bodily control, both of which make it impossible to engage the world intentionally. It is this quality of feeling out of control that differentiates the experience of falling apart from a more quiet contemplation of personal alienation. One is completely helpless even to entertain such ideas as alien-ation. Again this experience was commonly described by participants: "What I mean by chaotic . . . it's a process that's going wild like a train running down the tracks with nobody steering it or conducting it. . . . Then it would start to feel like I couldn't control it anymore and I was going to go stark raving mad."

If the experience of falling apart is one of being lost and of being out of touch with other people and one's body, then its resolution can only be described as one of being found. Relationships that were experienced as lost are renewed or replaced. Past and future return and unfold, and the person again experiences an ability to exist as a center of intentionality capable of undertaking and completing projects. Choices, and the limits they entail, are regained, tempo changes from random and chaotic to orderly and rhythmic, and the body is no longer experienced as constrained to a problematic objectification but as a competent intentional mode of interacting with the world.

These conclusions regarding the self have been anticipated to some degree by Edward Murray (1986) in his discussion of the experience of self that one has during the course of ordinary life events. In framing this discussion, Murray begins by locating such experiences within the ground of what he terms "scatteredness," or what we have termed "falling apart." To clear the way, he considers the theoretical work of both Hillman (1975) and Dambrowski (1964) concerning the potentially beneficial effects of falling apart – what the former calls "disintegrated-integration," and the latter calls "positive-disintergration." In commenting on these attempts to view the experience of falling apart in a positive light, Murray (1986) notes: "Thus, while seeming to extoll the disintegrative experience, they [Hillman and Dambrowski] actually see it as a furthering of the person's efforts at unity."

The reason "scatteredness," to use Murray's term, is so significant even to the ordinary experience of self has to do with the fact that conciousness is intentional and, "therefore, by definition, scattered among the objects of its experience." For this reason, it remains for the person to perform the more centripetal act of drawing together the scattered projects, objects, places, and people of experience and return them "to the center of my existence . . . to the mineness that brought them to consciousness, to the self that is their referent, and their home" (Murray, 1986, p. 205). The attainment of what each I, following lines suggested by historical period and social culture, will call my self, is thus an achievement that is neither given all at once nor one easily attained.

Murray's emphasis on the temporality of self harkens back both to Heidegger and to the present set of respondents. What was lost in "falling apart" was not only other people and significant places but a sense of the future, a sense of becoming. Since Heidegger early recognized temporality as a basic mode of existence, it seems clear that any sense of self must involve not only where we are now but also complex relationships to our complete unfolding in time as lived by each of us. Although not everyone (e.g., Merleau-Ponty, see Chapter 4) necessarily agrees with Heidegger that the privileged temporal domain is the future, the lack of any possibility of becoming clearly characterizes a broken or scattered existence. Becoming not only moves the present forward, it also enriches what has gone before and provides the possibility for integrating now with memories and antici-pation; *my* now with *my* memories and *my* anticipations.

Although the present set of interviews all stressed the significance of time, it is also important to note that participants were quite clear in emphasizing the role played by interpersonal relationships in resolving episodes of falling apart. When participants experienced being alienated and out of control, it was the empathic and interpretive action of other people that was described as helpful and restorative. Participants, having lost the possibility to create a cohesive experience of continuity on their own, turned to others who were there in relationship for them. Significantly, this experience also describes the structure of psychotherapy, and it might be said that relationship is the single most significant aspect of the therapeu-tic process. Both object relations theory and self psychology have described the need for relationship contexts in therapy; contexts that have been called the holding environment (Winnicott, 1958) or the self–object matrix (Kohut, 1971). On a day-to-day level, the experience of the self is a self-in-relation, and being out-of-relation is problematic. For Buber (1923/1970), a preponderance of I–It relationships defines a sterile, alienated, and despair-ing existence. On the other hand, Buber describes the I of I–Thou as relational and fulfilling. In terms of the present set of interviews, these concerns were described as feelings of synchrony and competence. It is important to note, however, that these relationships were described as in-the-world, not as internal or subjective events.

Psychoanalysis, with its intrapsychic perspective, has been inclined to view human relationships as internal to the psyche. Although this stance may provide a theoretically advantageous narrative, it does not accord with descriptions provided by the present set of participants. In fact, most were quite clear in noting that interpersonal relationships do not "exist" as "internal representations"; rather, they are worldly, and personal continu-ity is not the result of internalizing good or bad objects but living in an embodied way with familiar places and people. Intrinsic to this experience is the fact that both the people and the places of importance to me endure and, if they do change, change in ways that are sensibly coherent with present and former experiences. It is not so much that we "fall apart" as our world does not "hold us together."

There is, then, a fundamental reversal to be made in the con-ceptualization of self usually described in the clinical literature. Rather than viewing the self as an "ego" or as a "self-representation" – bounded by the skin, from the inside out – the self may more reasonably be described as supported and co-defined simultaneously from the outside-in *and* from the inside-out. In just this way does Heidegger (1927/1962) describe *Dasein* as a clearing through which being is disclosed. The self-world is defined by the contour of its clearing, and the experience that we label *self* is supported as much by the context of significant people and places as by those of time and body. The experience of self as revealed in the present set of interviews is a being-event that presupposes a relatively constant ground (or matrix) of relationships. Although there clearly are individual differences in the flexibility/resilience of this process, the ability to maintain a cohesive sense of self, one marked by the everyday experience of synchrony and competence, is to a large extent dependent on the presence of familiar anchors defined by people and place. Where living is meaningful, there is selfhood; where living is meaningless or inauthentic, there is the experience of an unknown dread that breaks through in periodic episodes of falling apart. The person is never an isolated sufficiency, and when the person's mode of being at home in the world fails, so too does the person.

10

The Meanings of Death in the Context of Life

Lawrence M. Ross

Death is a phenomenon that touches each human life. As human beings, we are faced at every moment with the possibility of our own death and with the death of those we love. The experience of life always serves as background to the meanings of death just as the meanings of death always serve as a background to those of life. This is the case whether death is experienced as a phenomenon that is meaningless, meaningful, or absent of meaning. According to Heidegger (1927/1962), human being-in-the-world is always a being-toward-death, and, insofar as this is the case, my experience of life is a testament to how I comport myself toward death. Perhaps it was for these reasons, not yet so clearly perceived, that Socrates sometimes described philosophy as "the study of death."

Every comprehensive religious and philosophical system must address the problem of how death is to be understood within the context of life. Both Hinduism and Buddhism contend that there is no personal self; therefore, there can be no personal death. Hinduism is based upon Being, or that which is changeless and eternal and, therefore, not subject to death. Buddhism is based upon a process of Becoming, which involves continual change thereby eliminating personal identity and the significance of personal death.

In the Judaic tradition, God's covenant with Israel promised a continuity of the Jewish nation, and individual death was always related to the larger context of the Jewish people. Individual death within the Christian tradition also involved a transformation. In earliest Christianity, the death of Jesus transformed the lives of his disciples; in later Christianity, the death of Jesus

This chapter is based on research originally reported in an unpublished doctoral dissertation entitled *The Experience of Death and Dying: A Phenomenological Study* by L. M. Ross, presented to the University of Tennessee in 1987.

represented a redemption of all mankind, and personal death became a point of transition toward an afterlife of reward.

In psychology, psychoanalysis initially characterized death anxiety as a derivative of other unconscious needs and fears. With the postulation of Thanatos, however, Freud characterized the wish for death as a wish for a return to the quiescence of inorganic existence. In existential thought, however, death anxiety is viewed as a basic and not a derivative aspect of the human condition. Since all being is a being-toward-death, the ever-present, certain-yet-indeterminate, potentiality for nonbeing is experienced as dread. In the face of dread, one musters courage thereby taking the possibility of my death into my life. Such courage transforms the meaning of death, and it is the certainty of personal death that guarantees my life as a process of unique becoming.

Complementing religious, philosophical, and psychological perspectives are more empirical ones. Such studies frequently crystallize around, and attempt to answer, such questions as: Is death anxiety a universal phenomenon? How do aging, religiosity, gender, and socioeconomic level correlate with attitudes toward death? Is the meaning of death changed as a consequence of repeated exposure to death? In general, the empirical study of such questions is correlational in nature and is conducted on the basis of standard social science methods such as attitude scales, projective tests, questionnaires and so on.

Views of Death

Religious Orientations Toward Death

Perhaps the most important context for studying the various ways in which the meaning of death may be grasped in the midst of life is that of religion. But not all religions deal with death (or life) in the same way, and it becomes important to describe the ways in which various religious traditions address this topic. As a starting point, P. T. Raju (1974), in a foreword to the book *Death and Eastern Thought*, points out that "when a philosophy regards personality as extending beyond life and death, it treats the subject of death more earnestly and positively. When the contrary view is taken, namely, that death puts an end to life and personality . . . death becomes an issue to be generally evaded." It is perhaps the hallmark of Eastern thought that the term *life* is never restricted to that span of years between birth and death. Instead, such thought assumes an endless series of births and deaths that the human being must suffer through until proper knowledge is obtained to break the cycle and reach enlightenment.

The Hindu Attitude Toward Death. Early speculations about an afterlife in Hindu thought pointed to "two paths for mortals – that of the Fathers – blessed ancestors – and that of the gods" (Holck, 1974). During this early period, there was already a belief in an independent and all pervading cosmic principle known as *Rta* that accounted for regularity and order in the universe. At this time, however, it was also believed that if one acted in compliance with Rta, then one would, after death, join Yama (the first man who died), the Fathers, and the gods.

Somewhat later Hindu views believed strongly in the power of the gods, and the importance of sacrifice as a religious activity ushered in the Brahman period (800 B.C.) in which the power of the gods was mitigated and then usurped by the power of sacrifice. During this period, both gods and men were seen as depending upon sacrifice for strength and survival (Holck, 1974). Thus, the power of men, or at least of one caste of men (the priests), was raised to that of the gods since it was believed that flawless enactment of a sacrificial ritual could compel the gods to yield to human demands.

The Brahmans (priests), whose position became increasingly exalted, soon performed rituals designed not only to live out one's full term of life but to sidestep death and become immortal – but not without a price, that of having to give up the body. Within the Brahman texts is a myth involving Prajapati (the lord of creatures), who taught the priests to perform the rituals necessary to obtain immortality. If they performed the proper ritual action (Karmana), or understood the sacred knowledge well enough, they were able to obtain immortal life. Although the doctrine of transmigration (Karma-samsara) did not become formalized until the later writings of the *Upanishads*, Brahman writings did suggest that those who are ignorant either of the sacred knowledge or of the proper acts will be required again and again to return to death.

These ideas came to fruition in the *Upanishads*, where sacrificial rituals were downplayed in favor of other modes of attaining liberation. In general, such liberation is attained only when the person is able to emancipate him- or herself from a perception of reality involving the duality of subject and object. If we cling to ignorance, we will be forced to continue to suffer endlessly in the cycle of life, death, rebirth, and redeath. According to the doctrine of Karma-samsara found in the *Upanishads*, the essential nature of human being is to be found in personal action, and good deeds and bad deeds result in rebirth as higher and lower forms, respectively. The form of rebirth ultimately matters little, however, since any rebirth is a result of ignorance, and we will continue to be reborn as long as our actions are motivated by a desire to produce consequences and/or we are attached to the results of our actions.

The culmination of Hindu thought, however, is found in the *Bagavad-Gita* (the Song of the Divine). In form, the *Gita* is a conversation between prince Arjuna and the god Krishna (the "embodiment" of Oneness). Arjuna is found on the battlefield, awaiting an upcoming battle in which many will be killed. He is sorrowed with regard to this prospect and wonders what course of action he should take. He says to Krishna, "We know not which is better for us, to conquer them or that they should conquer us." Krishna proclaims, "Whence came to you this weakness in this moment of crisis. It is ignoble, O Arjuna, and neither leads to heaven nor brings glory."

Krishna goes on to say that there was never a time when he (Arjuna) was not. "Of what is not, there is no coming to be, of what is, there is no ceasing to be. He who knows this, is indestructible, eternal, unborn, changeless." Krishna then continues: "Having regard to your own dharma [duty] you must continue. If you will not engage in this righteous battle, then having forsaken your particular dharma . . . you will incur sin. Your interest is in action alone, never in its fruits. Let not the fruits of action be what impels you, but do not let yourself be attached to in-action either. He who does not contribute to the continued movement of the wheel thus set in motion is evil, delighting in the senses he lives in vain."

These fragmentary passages capture the relevant aspects of Hindu thought concerning death (and life). Arjuna must engage in action because that is his dharma (duty). One's duty is part and parcel of the situation one is in, and one must act without regard to the fruits of that action. Thus, dharma, situation, and action define the unified context of experience, and Arjuna's sorrow over death can only be based on his attachment to the manifestations of the world and to his ignorance of the "One." Krishna reveals himself and Arjuna as manifestations of the "One" and, in so doing, reveals that death is illusory: That which is, always is; that which is not, can never come to be. Arjuna is neither the creator of his situation nor is he responsible for it. He is responsible, however, for action within that situation and, in fact, is bound to such action. Only when Arjuna is able to realize the Oneness of Being will liberation occur on the basis of proper, detached, and nonself-conscious action.

The Buddhist Attitude Toward Death. Both Hindu and Buddhist thought assume that an attachment to things is the cause of suffering and yields the recurring cycle of life and death. Both also believe that one must break this cycle to be liberated. Buddhism, however, rejected a belief in "The All" or "The One" as lying behind various manifestations or phenomena. Although both viewpoints agree that there is no personal self, except in ignorance,

Buddhists also deny the existence of a suprapersonal being that is eternal. As a consequence, there is no belief in Being, only in Becoming, and each moment is both a birth and a death.

The origin of Buddhism involves Prince Siddhartha Guatama, who for the first 29 years of his life, knew little of suffering. His first encounter with suffering was during a journey when he came across an old man. Prince Siddhartha asked his charioteer about the condition of this man, to which the charioteer replied that all men were subject to aging. On his second and third journeys, Siddhartha encountered a sick man and a dead man, respectively. He realized then that suffering was a basic condition of life and, at this point, undertook to engage in a life of austerity in the hope of purifying himself and of finding a release from suffering. Legend has it that while meditating, a woman offered him a meal. Siddhartha partook of this meal and thereby came to realize that is was not wrong to be happy and that health was necessary for the attainment of wisdom.

In Buddhist practice, there are two meditational contexts designed to overcome attachment to sensual striving and to realize the impermanence of all things (Amore, 1974). The first of these contexts is mindfulness of the inevitability of one's death, and the second involves meditation upon ten types of corpses in various states of decay. Meditation of this sort yields specific benefits; for example, meditating on a swollen corpse corrects lusting after bodily forms; meditating on a corpse cut in two corrects thinking of the body as solid or full; meditating on a worm-eaten corpse corrects thinking of the body as "mine."

In Japan, Buddhism focused on *mujo* (impermanence), which Lafluer (1974) pointed out "relativized death by making every moment a type of dying." Dogen (1200–54), a Japanese monk greatly influential in spreading Zen Buddhism in Japan, rejected the notion of becoming per se because it seemed to him that such an emphasis focused too strongly on emptiness, thereby negating the fullness of each moment. Instead, Dogen felt that one must simultaneously experience the complete discontinuity of each moment yet live in the fullness of that moment. He also believed that there was no nirvana apart from samsara; rather, nirvana is "seeing" that the samsaric realm is all that we have: At enlightenment, one does not stand apart from change; one becomes it. Relativizing life and death in this way allows one to transcend death as conceived in Western terms (i.e., as of a personal self) and makes it a cornerstone of Zen Buddhist philosophy and practice.

The Jewish View of Death. All religions must deal with at least two central questions: How did the universe originate, and what happens when a human being dies? In the Old Testament, a theory of origins is clearly presented in the book of Genesis. As part of the biblical narrative contained in the first two chapters, man (and woman) were given the choice of knowledge or immortality. In choosing knowledge, they chose mortality. In commenting on this choice, Carse (1980) points out that "with knowledge came death and . . . (the fact) that they . . . could no longer live in an eternal present with no anxiety. When God forced them from the Garden, He drove them into *time* [and] made them historical: forever drawn ahead by a future they could never finish, [and] by a past [in which] meanings are endlessly changing."

More important than death was the fulfillment of God's promises in life – promises and deeds that assured the continuity of His people. According to such a view, what can be expected from God will only be received in the context of life. The logic of Hebraic thought "counseled concentration and attention upon this life and world, for all hope was cut off about a better lot in the next" (Brandon, 1962). In pleading with God, it is apparent that Job's hope for an end to his suffering is in this world:

Are not my days few:
Cease then and let me alone, that I may take comfort a little,
Before I go whence I shall not return,
Even to the land of darkness and of the shadow of death
A land of thick darkness, is darkness itself;
A land of the shadow of death, without any order,
And where the light is as darkness.   (Job 10:20–22).

The land of darkness, to which Job refers, was known as *Sheol*. Sheol is characterized as the underside of creation and is sometimes also described as a place of forgetfulness:

Turn, O Lord, save my life;
    deliver me for the sake of thy steadfast love
For in death there is no remembrance of thee
    in Sheol who can give thee praise?   (Psalms 6:4)

Death is the antithesis of life, and many biblical passages indicate that we do not survive after death.

For there is hope of a tree, if it be cut down, that it will
    sprout again . . .
But man dieth and wasteth away:
Yea, man giveth up the ghost, and where is he?
As the river decayeth and drieth up;
So man lieth down and raiseth not.   (Job 14:10–12)

The concept of individual life after death was of little importance as long as God's promise to Israel continued to be fulfilled within the context of history. The severity of the destruction of the Kingdom of Judah, first by the Assyrians and then by the Babylonians, changed all of this. In 586 B.C., the Babylonians conquered the city of Jerusalem, destroyed the great temple, and drove the priesthood and the people into exile. Following 100 years of exile, the Jews returned to Jerusalem and restored the temple, which stood until 70 A.D. when it was destroyed for a second and final time by the Romans.

The impact of these events shook the foundations of Jewish thought and practice. For the first time, there was serious questioning of the continuity of the Jewish people and of the fulfillment of God's promise. The destruction of the temple also marked the end of the era of temple priests and ushered in a Rabbinic age in which primary interest was invested in the reading and interpreting of a written text (the Torah), a task that could be done anywhere and any time.

The threatened survival of the people greatly weakened the sense of their corporate existence and ushered in a concern for the individual. In so doing, the possibility of individual survival after death and judgment before God were raised. The apocalyptic writings, after the fall of the temple in 586 B.C., mark the beginning of the doctrine of resurrection, a doctrine that allows for the possibility of survival after death. Although such a doctrine represents a departure from previous eschatology, it is not as radical as it might seem. Resurrection is not a theory of immortality nor does it involve dualistic notions of an indestructible soul separate from the body. Rather, the doctrine of resurrection is in accord with the original postulation of psychophysical unity and, therefore, involves a reunion of body and spirit. In the Old Testament, there are only three scriptural references to this doctrine, chronologically in Isaiah 26:19; in Ezekiel 37:3,5,11,12; and in Daniel 12:12.

Underlying these passages, the movement of Hebraic thought may be seen. Isaiah, for example, provides the first mention of resurrection, suggesting that survival after death is not mere existence (as in Sheol) but is similar in form to life itself. Ezekiel uses the doctrine of resurrection to reestablish the promise of God to bring the person home in death to the land of Israel, which reviews the original covenant of nation over individual. Finally, Daniel presents the most radical departure from previous thought in stressing individual judgment in afterlife and in providing the first clear indication of immortality. By the time of the destruction of the Temple in 70 A.D., Jewish thought surrounding these issues was split into two schools. The Sadducees rejected a belief in resurrection and were faithful to the original postulation of no survival after death. The Pharisees, on the other hand, supported a belief in resurrection and maintained that only the souls of the good passed into another body whereas those of the evil were afflicted with eternal torment.

The Christian View of Death. The major view of death in the New Testament derives primarily from the synoptic gospels and those of John and Paul. The synoptic gospels of Matthew, Mark, and Luke portray Jesus as aligned with the Pharisees on the issue of resurrection. Matthew also takes great pain to trace Jesus' lineage back forty-two generations to Abraham, thereby characterizing him as "thoroughly human, born to a long line of mortals, of the most ordinary strengths and weaknesses" (Carse, 1980). Carse then goes on to say that "salvation here is not from history but in it. There is a strong sense of continuity with the whole history of the Jews."

Jesus' human qualities are amply portrayed in the synoptic gospels – for example, in the depiction of his emotional state when near death. Carse (1980) asserts that "curious is the fact that with all the references to his future resurrection, the Synoptic Gospels picture Jesus facing his own death with a range of emotions we might expect in any ordinary mortal." Luke (22:42) recounts the following prayer offered by Jesus: "Father, if thou will, remove this cup from me; nevertheless not my will, but thine be done." Matthew (27:46) reports Jesus' final words as "My God, why hast thou forsaken me?"

The synoptic gospels thus portray Jesus as historical, subject to the frailties of other men, and as expressing views on the nature of resurrection and judgment that echo other views in the Old Testament. Jesus' notion of resurrection never occupied a central place in his own teachings and often was used to counterpoint what Jesus emphasized as most important: the way one should live in this life. Significant difference between Jesus and his Jewish contemporaries concerned his special emphasis of the importance of "right living," which consisted of discipleship, repentance, and unconditional love. The extent to which Jesus deemphasized death relative to life may be seen in Matthew 8:22, where a disciple stated he would follow Jesus after burying his recently deceased father. To this Jesus replied, "Follow me, and leave the dead to bury the dead."

Whereas the synoptic gospels emphasized the human qualities of Jesus, John deemphasized such qualities:

In the beginning was the word
  and the word was with God
  and the word was God
He was in the beginning with God
  all things were made through him
  and without him was not anything made that was made.   (John 1:1–3)

Thus, for John, all that Jesus said and did during his lifetime was revelatory. In contrast to the synoptic gospels, John describes Jesus as separate from the Jews and makes no distinction between Pharisees and Sadducees. In fact, John places major emphasis on Jesus as the son of God, stressing that God may be known only through Jesus. What this came to mean is that one is free either to accept or reject Jesus; however, John cautions, "whoever does not see the light, that Jesus is the son of the Father, is a liar" (1 John 2:22). Those who *refuse* to see this light will live in darkness and will be in bondage to death.

John's understanding also does away with traditional views of resurrection and what happens to the believer after death. Instead, judgment, resurrection, and salvation all occur *in the moment* of acceptance or rejection of Jesus. There is no need to wait for the Kingdom of God because it is already at hand. This emphasis on the quality of present life is the main locus of agreement among the Old Testament, the synoptic gospels, and John. The problem for John is not that life ends but that it may be lived wrongly, and in so doing, one may already be condemned.

Whereas John equated death with willful ignorance, Paul equated it with violations of biblical law. In his interpretation of events, Paul drew heavily on the Garden of Eden narrative and asserted that God's original plan was for human life to be deathless. In breaking God's law, Adam condemned himself and all who descended from him to die. Thus, God's law guarantees our death, and our disobedience must be paid for. Paul argues that Jesus makes this payment and, in so doing, allows for the redemption and salvation of humankind. Unlike John, Paul interprets the coming of the Kingdom of God as an event in time for which one must wait.

Paul's gospel says little about what happens to the unfaithful. The first complete account of hell is given by John (Revelation 10), although it is not until Augustine that the more contemporary Christian views of Heaven and Hell emerge. According to Hick (1976), "Augustine's magisterial presentation of the Christian myth, the drama of creation, fall, salvation, heaven and hell dominated the imagination of the West for the next thousand years and more ... [and] his understanding of the final state of man became an authoritative statement about the afterlife." This final state includes the damned as embodied beings able to burn perpetually in literal flames and the blessed as embodied beings able to enter heaven.

The idea of an embodied afterlife, however, came to an end in the writings of Aquinas. In these writings, the soul was now separate from the body, judgment came immediately following death, and all human beings were destined for eternal life in heaven or hell. As Hick (1976) comments in regard to this change: "The broad development within Christianity consisted in a shift from earth to heaven (and hell), with divine judgment coming forward to the moment of each individual's death, and with a corresponding change in emphasis from body to soul."

Psychoanalytic Views of Death

A second context for the possible meanings that death might hold during life derives from various psychological theories, most especially those of psychoanalysis. Within psychoanalysis, the major position concerning death seems to be that one's personal death is subjectively inconceivable. Freud (1926/1959) specifically pointed out that it was impossible to imagine our own death, and whenever we do so, we are "still present as spectators." For this reason, any fear we may have of death must be a secondary derivative of other unconscious fears and thoughts. Fenichel (1945) put the matter quite directly: "It is questionable whether there is any such thing as a normal fear of death; actually, the idea of one's death is subjectively inconceivable and therefore probably every fear of death covers other unconscious ideas."

Freud, therefore, relegated a fear of death to developmental anxieties associated with what could be called "real development dangers" (Freud, 1926/1959). Carrying this analysis to its logical psychoanalytic conclusion, Freud reasoned that "nothing resembling death can ever have been experienced, or if it has, as in fainting, it has left no observable traces behind. I am, therefore, inclined to adhere to the view that the fear of death should be regarded as analogous to the fear of castration and the situation to which the ego is reacting is one of being abandoned by the protecting superego" (Freud, 1926/1959). The main significance to this point of view is that death anxiety is a secondary derivative of other anxiety-provoking situations and not a primordial condition of anxiety. As for death anxiety itself, Freud (1926/1959) noted that "the psychoanalytic school could venture the assertion that at bottom no one believes in his own death, or to put the same thing in another way, in his unconscious everyone of us is convinced of his own immortality."

Although death anxiety is not fundamental, Freud did postulate Thanatos as a fundamental instinct (1920/1950). For Freud, Thanatos operated on the "nirvana principle" in which the organism was thought to seek return to an inorganic state. Thanatos is, thus, more primitive than the pleasure principle, and on this basis, Freud was led to conclude that since the life instincts produce tension (whose release is felt as pleasure), they must be opposed to the pleasure principle and that "the pleasure principle seems actually to serve the death instincts." Freud went on to note that "if we are to take it as a truth that knows no exception that everything dies for internal reasons – becomes inorganic once again – then we shall be compelled to say that the aim of all life is death."

Later psychological views of death have been influenced by existential philosophy and tend to view death anxiety as a primary reaction concerned with the prospect of personal annihilation. As Becker (1973) put it: "The idea of death haunts the human animal like nothing else . . . It is the mainspring of human activity – activity designed largely to avoid the futility of death, to overcome it by denying . . . that it is the final destiny." If death anxiety is basic, the terror of nonbeing should begin very early. Rank believed that the fear of life and the fear of death arise simultaneously in the trauma of birth. "The inner fear which the child experiences in the birth process has already both elements, fear of life and fear of death, since birth on the one hand means the end of life (former life) and on the other also carries a fear of new life" (Rank, 1945).

These twin fears set limits to human existence and lead to the assumption that character structure is the means by which an individual attempts to minimize and balance them. Within this context, it is important to note the way in which Rank defines life and death; for Rank, death is experienced as an urge toward being engulfed, whereas life is experienced as an urge toward separation and/or individuation. He further believed that within the womb, the fetus and its environment function as a unity, and birth serves to bring about the death of this unity. To move toward life – toward individuation – previous integrative modes must be abandoned, and the individual person must continually "die" to be (re)born.

Basing his approach on Rank, Becker (1973) believed that a basic human urge is not toward individuation but toward cosmic specialness. "Man's desire is to stand out, to be the one in creation . . . he must desperately justify himself as an object of primary value in the universe . . . he must be a hero." At the same time as we yearn for uniqueness, we also yearn for cosmic merger, not only as a reflex to the terror of being alone but as a genuine desire to be part of some larger totality. Becker also believed that we attempt to balance these urges so as to minimize our fears and to allow society to provide us with a manageable feeling of heroism thereby effecting a compromise between urges for personal heroism and for feeling powerful as part of a larger totality.

Society is unable to succeed in this task and often provides meaning only at the cost of deadening the person. The meanings provided by society are contrived meanings and, therefore, as ridden with the contingencies of creatureliness as the individual human being. Our attempts at heroism ultimately are failures, no matter how hard we try. Unlike Freud, Becker believed that the child does not wish to usurp the power of the father or to be like the father; rather, the child hopes to evade death by becoming "the father of himself, the creator and sustainer of his own life" (Becker, 1973).

Ultimately, this project is doomed because the human being is unable to evade the contingency of the body. At the same time as our attempts at heroism fail, so too do our attempts at merger. For example, we may personify the universe in the form of a leader or a lover so as to satisfy the need for cosmic merger. This strategy will also result in failure since the other so personified is only human and, therefore, subject to decay. Wherever we turn, the solutions proposed by society fail and the individual person is left, on his or her own, to integrate the dual urges toward individuation and merger that define the human condition.

Existential Views of Death

Within existential thought, the major positions concerning death have been articulated primarily by Sören Kierkegaard and Martin Heidegger.

Kierkegaard. To understand Kierkegaard's views on death, it is necessary to locate them within the context of his more general views concerning human existence. For Kierkegaard, human existence is paradoxical, since every human being is "a synthesis of the infinite and the finite, the temporal and the eternal, freedom and necessity." Because of these polarities, human beings are anxious in their being; "if a man were a beast or an angel, he would not be in anxiety. Since he is a synthesis he can be in anxiety, and the greater the anxiety the greater the man" (Kierkegaard, 1844/1980).

Because we are a synthesis of animal and spirit, Kierkegaard speaks of "natural" death insofar as we are animals and "spiritual" death insofar as we are spirit. Natural death involves the "negating of the existing subject" and is always a present possibility and not a future event. The ever-present possibility of death, coupled with an alternation between being and nonbeing, serve as a potent source of dread. Although the fact that one must die is certain, the hour of death is unknown, and this too becomes a source of anxiety.

Since a "continuous endurance" of the thought of death is not pleasurable, one type of man – the immediate man – seeks security "under the cover of the crowd" and thinks about death in terms of cultural or religious platitudes. A second type of man, the speculative philosopher, also refuses to meet death on its own terms and evades the possibility of personal death by discussing death in general – as apart from personal existence. Of this attitude, Kierkegaard states that "the fact of my own death is not for me such a something in general, although for others the fact of my death may indeed be something of that sort. Nor am I for myself a something in general, although for others I may be a mere generality" (Kierkegaard, 1846/1941). To live authentically, as the immediate man and the speculative philosopher do not, the possibility of death "must be present everywhere in thought just as it is everywhere present in existence" (Kierkegaard, 1846/1941).

Spiritual death is described by Kierkegaard as "a sickness." In health, the person is a synthesis of polarities and attempts to maintain the tension between them. In sickness, there is a "disrelationship in a relation which relates itself to its own self and is constituted by another, so that the disrelationship . . . reflects itself infinitely in relation to the Power which constituted it" (Kierkegaard, 1846/1941). The self is not self-originating but is constituted by the Power, which is God. The relation of the self to itself and of self to God is a unitary phenomenon since human beings are a synthesis of paradoxical aspects. Sickness that involves a God relationship must therefore be to an infinite degree, and since the spiritual aspect of a person "cannot die," such sickness can only be experienced as a "sickness unto death (e.g., Kierkegaard, 1849/1980)."

Kierkegaard delineates three different forms of sickness unto death that one may go through until becoming authentically religious: aesthetic, ethical, and religious. Combining these "forms of sickness" with the immediate and reflective modes yields a number of possibilities. For example, the type of person described as the immediate aesthetic, seeks to maximize enjoyment, as for example, in taking pride in physical appearance. The reflective aesthetic knows that the moment of attaining pleasure is transient and so takes pleasure in approaching such a moment, moving toward it as long as possible without seizing it. The aesthetic man of either type "cannot die for he has not really lived; in another sense he cannot live, for he is already dead." The sickness unto death that characterizes such a person is the despair of willing not to be oneself.

A second class of person – the ethical person – equates decision with life and "becomes conscious of himself as this definite individual, with these talents, these dispositions . . . as a definite product of a definite environment" (Kierkegaard, 1847/1959). In living in the moment as a definite entity, such a person is subject to the despair of willing to be oneself. He or she is in despair because there is no realization that the self is always in the process of becoming and can never become "definite." Furthermore, the self is not constituted by itself, and in willing to constitute oneself, the ethical person wills to tear the self away from God who constituted it. Unfortunately, such a person is unable to do this because God is the stronger of the two and compels him to be the self he does not will to be (Kierkegaard, 1846/1941). The despair inherent in willing to be oneself is that in so doing one paradoxically wills not to be oneself.

Kierkegaard uses Socrates to exemplify the religious person. In *The Meno*, Socrates speaks approvingly of the doctrine of anamnesis: that is, Truth is present in each of us, and in the process of birth, we forget it. As opposed to the ethical man, who wills to be the Power that constitutes the self, Socrates "allows the eternal to show through his historical existence." A person holding this point of view posits that human beings are eternal and, therefore, death is eliminated because the historical self is eliminated. Kierkegaard maintains that this cannot be so; we must have an historical self, thereby moving religion to a different level in which the "Truth within us makes its appearance when an eternal resolve comes into relation with an incommensurable occasion" (Kierkegaard, 1844/1936). The "incommensurable" occasion of which Kierkegaard speaks is Jesus, and it is Jesus who represents the appearance of the eternal in fully human, historical form.

The paradox represented by Jesus cannot be comprehended by reason; it can be known only on the basis of "a leap of faith." The appearance of the eternal in human form means that the truth of this paradox is always in the process of becoming. The anxiety inherent in a self that is becoming, which alternates between being and nonbeing, which is a dynamic synthesis of animal and spirit, and which is the unitary relation that relates itself to God and man, becomes the "means of salvation in conjunction with faith" (Kierkegaard, 1844/1980). Anxiety, therefore, offers the possibility of freedom and enables the self, through faith, to become itself.

Heidegger. Although Heidegger is not a religious existentialist, many of his conclusions echo those of Kierkegaard. For Heidegger, Being is always a Being-in-time, and *Dasein*'s mode of being is always futural. As a potentiality-for-Being, *Dasein*'s being is anxious. Of all of *Dasein*'s possibilities, death is its "ownmost" possibility, for it is "the possibility of the absolute impossibility of *Dasein*. . . . As long as *Dasein* is, there is in every case something still outstanding that *Dasein* can be and will be. But to that which is outstanding, the end itself belongs (and the end of Being-in-the-world is death)" (Heidegger, 1927/1962). Thus, *Dasein*'s mode of being-in-the-world is always a Being-toward death.

To understand the full impact of this view, it is necessary to explicate some of the terms that Heidegger uses to characterize death.

1. Death is *Dasein*'s "ownmost possibility." Since it is death that assures *Dasein* of other possibilities, it follows that only death is able to make my

existence truly mine. Death as the end of *Dasein* guarantees *Dasein* as a finite and, therefore, a unique potentiality for Being.

2. Death is "nonrelational." Just as *Dasein* is uniquely mine, so too the end of *Dasein* is uniquely mine: "No one can take my dying away from me." One cannot experience death by watching others die; in this case, one is just "there alongside."

3. Death is "certain and indefinite." The certainty of death is not an empirical but an "apodictic" one existentially based on anxiety. The nothingness of dread uncovers for me the possible impossibility of my existence.

4. Death is "not to be outstripped." No one can escape death since *Dasein*'s existential character is as a Being-toward-death.

For Heidegger, death is *Dasein*'s ownmost possibility; nonrelational, certain, indefinite, and not to be outstripped. Each individual, however, is free to decide how he or she will comport him- or herself toward this existential certainty. At any given moment, one may live authentically, as a Being-toward-death, or one may attempt, inauthentically, to "flee in the face of death." It is important to note that there are no "authentic individuals" because authenticity must be constantly renewed. Inauthentic modes of being "await" or "expect" death as an event apart from life. In relegating death to *Das Man*, it becomes impersonal and "ambiguous." *Das Man* says "one of these days one will die too, but right now it has nothing to do with us" (Heidegger, 1927/1962).

Authentic modes of being anticipate death and maintain it as a possibility: "The closest closeness which one may have in Being-toward-death as a possibility is as far as possible from anything actual. The more unveiledly this possibility gets understood, the more purely does the understanding penetrate into it as the possibility of the impossibility of any existence at all" (Heidegger, 1927/1962). In this way, death is made conspicuous and personal, and in order to gain a freedom toward death, "*Dasein* must have courage in the face of such dread." Only if this is undertaken will the person be able to attain a wholeness in his or her potentiality for Being.

Empirical Research on Death

Although social science research dealing with the human understanding of death is vast (see, for example, reviews by Kurlychek, 1978; Lester, 1967; and Pollak, 1979), the majority of studies may be organized in terms of the following more or less independent topics:

1. Death acceptance vs. death denial,
2. Death attitudes related to age and aging,
3. Death anxiety related to personality (actualized or nonactualized),
4. Death attitudes related to real or imagined exposure to death,
5. Death attitudes related to religiosity, and
6. Death attitudes related to temporal experience and futurity.

Death Acceptance vs. Death Denial. Research in this area attempts to answer several important questions: Is the fear of death universal? Are defensive patterns operating in individuals who say they do not fear death? What is the nature of such defensive patterns, if they do occur? Do some individuals accept death more readily than others, and what acounts for acceptance rather than fear or denial? Many researchers (e.g., Sarnoff & Corwin, 1959; Boyar, 1964; Dickstein & Blatt, 1966; Templer, 1970; Dickstein, 1972) make the assumption that death anxiety is both universal and unitary (we all fear death in the same way) and that an absence of such fear can be due only to various forms of defensive functioning. Other researchers (e.g., Collett & Lester, 1969; Bell, 1975; Nelson & Nelson, 1975; Hoelter, 1979; Conte, Weiner, & Plutchik, 1982; Florian & Kravitz, 1983) also believe that death anxiety is universal but not unidimensional; that is, there are clear differences in what is feared – for example, a fear of death itself or a fear of dying, a fear of personal death or a fear of the death of a loved one.

Death Attitudes Related to Age and Aging. Many researchers (e.g., Christ, 1961; Conte et al., 1982; Jeffers, Nichols, & Eisdorfer, 1966; Kastenbaum & Costa, 1977; Kimsey, Roberts, & Logan, 1972; Lester, 1972; Pollak, 1977, 1979; Pollock, 1971; Rhudick & Dibner, 1961; Shneidman, 1971; Templer, 1971) report that attitudes toward death, such as anxiety, are unrelated to age. Other researchers (e.g., Feifel, 1956; Nelson, 1979; Scott, 1896) report a positive association between fear of death and aging, whereas still others report a decrease in death fear as one ages (Martin & Wrightsman, 1965; Nelson, 1979; Patton & Freitag, 1977; Robinson & Wood, 1985; Stevens, Cooper, & Thomas, 1980).

Death Anxiety Related to Personality (Actualized or Nonactualized). Distinguishing between people who demonstrate so-called actualizing tendencies – internal locus of control, high sense of competence, achievement, purpose, life satisfaction, independence – and those who demonstrate so-called non-actualizing tendencies – dependency, helplessness, depression, external locus of control, low sense of competence/achievement/purpose/

life satisfaction – has been an important variable in attempting to under-stand personal conditions that may account for death anxiety or death acceptance. In general, studies in this area indicate that self-actualizing individuals are less fearful and/or more accepting of death than nonself-actualizing people (e.g., Aronow et al., 1980; Bolt, 1978; Durlak, 1972a,b; Jeffers et al., 1966; Lester & Collett, 1970; Neimeyer & Chapman, 1980; Robinson & Wood, 1983; Shrut, 1958; Wesch, 1971; Wood & Robinson, 1982).

Death Attitudes Related to Various Types of Exposure to Death. The central questions involved in this area are: Do attitudes toward death and dying change as a consequence of exposure to the actual or imagined threat of self-death, the threatened or actual death of others, and/or to death-related discussions? In general, investigators have found that imagined exposure to death appears to increase preoccupation with thoughts of death (Bell, 1975; Feifel, 1956). There also is some evidence to suggest that such exposure is correlated with less reluctance to speak about death or to interact with the dying (Krieger, Epting, & Leitner, 1974). Studies involving actual exposure to death are almost unanimous in reporting increased death anxiety for a period of time following the death (Adam, Lohrenz, & Harper, 1973; Boyar, 1964; Lester & Kam, 1971; Livingston & Zimet, 1965; Patton & Frietag, 1977; Taylor, 1983). On the other hand, exposure to the potential death of oneself has been found to reduce death fear, increase one's sense of spirituality and/or specialness, and to influence a reorientation toward the meanings of life, including an enhanced focus on achieving one's goals, the importance of others, and the importance of the present moment (Dobson, Tattersfield, Adler, & McNicol, 1971; Druss & Kornfield, 1967; Hackett, 1972; Noyes, 1980, 1982; White & Liddon, 1972).

Death Attitudes Related to Religiosity. Correlational studies investigating relationships between religiosity and death anxiety have produced inconsis-tent results. Although most studies suggest that religiosity (or, at least, intrinsic religiosity) is associated with a reduced fear of death (Jeffers et al., 1966; Martin & Wrightsman, 1965; Minton & Spilka, 1976; Ross & Pollio, 1991; Stewart, 1975; Swenson, 1961; Templer, 1972), other studies have failed to find such a relationship (Christ, 1961; Feifel, 1974; Kalish, 1963; Templer & Dotson, 1970). Still other studies have found a positive relation-ship between religiosity and death anxiety (Feifel, 1956; Feifel & Nagy, 1981), and still other studies have found a curvilinear relationship where those who score low or high on religiosity scales report fearing death less than those who score in the middle (Leming, 1980; McMordie, 1981;

Williams & Cole, 1968). In most cases, it appears that a commitment to either a religious or a nonreligious stance is associated with lower death anxiety when compared with an intermediate, uncommitted religious stance. The question of whether religion is an adaptation to the fact of personal mortality or serves to deny or repress this fact, remains open. Feifel and Branscomb (1973) further suggest that it is necessary to distinguish between conscious and unconscious attitudes toward death acceptance. In their studies, for example, they found increased galvanic skin responses (GSR) to death-related words (in contrast to neutral ones) for both religious and nonreligious individuals, suggesting "a below conscious dread of death."

Death Attitudes Related to Temporal Experience and Futurity. There are two main questions in this area of study: Is the degree to which one fears death associated with one's future time perspective? Are different perceptions of time associated with different attitudes toward death? Although there have been only a few studies relating death anxiety to future time perspective, such studies have consistently indicated an inverse relationship between future time perspective and death anxiety (Bascue, 1973; Bascue & Lawrence, 1977; Dickstein, 1975; Dickstein & Blatt, 1966; Handal, 1969; Shrut, 1958). There results also suggest that high-scoring death-anxious people tend to live more in the present, to be more worried in general, to avoid thinking about the future, and to see themselves as not living as long as low-scoring death-anxious individuals.

The Present Program of Research

The topic of death is a complex one that has been pursued from a great many different perspectives. The one perspective that has been pursued infrequently is that of an individual human being attempting to describe the meanings that death might hold in his or her ongoing life. For this reason, the present study was designed to describe thematic aspects of an individual's present experience of death in light of the many possible ways in which human beings may, and do, report experiencing it. To accomplish this purpose, twenty-six adults were asked to participate in a phenomenological interview that began with the following request. "Think about an experience, event, or period in your life when you were particularly aware of death. Please tell me about it; how did you deal with it; has anything since that experience felt the same way?" If this request failed to yield a conversation, a further question was asked: "Under what circumstances are you most and least aware of death?"

Participants in this research included twelve male and fourteen female adults ranging in age from twenty-five to fifty. Thirteen of the participants were recruited from local church study groups; the remaining participants were recruited from graduate classes in psychology and education. All participants volunteered following a brief description of the study. It is important to note that participants reflect a narrow range of individuals when compared to the general population. Unlike many prior studies, which used randomization procedures, participants were selected for their willingness to participate in a lengthy personal dialogue about the meaning of death for them. Consequently, participants, for the most part, were better educated than the statistically average person (20 had at least a master's degree); they also fell within a relatively narrow range of age and socioeconomic status.

Modes of Experiencing the Meanings of Death

To provide an overall sense for the present set of interviews, Figure 10.1 was constructed. The outer dashed line represents the meanings of life as a context against which the various modes of experiencing death become figural. Whenever death is figural in any capacity, the ground to this experience was the current meanings of life to the participant.

The outermost circle is labeled Phenomenally Distant Aspects of Experiencing and refers to those aspects of experience that are general and abstract rather than specific and personal. There is an "as-if" quality to these concerns; they are experienced as conceptual beliefs, values, and attitudes rather than as core aspects of who one is. Participants described three categories having such as-if qualities:

1. Cognitive and social beliefs and concepts,
2. Attitudes toward the dying process, and
3. Values for which one would sacrifice one's life.

The first of these categories involved abstract ideas about death (i.e., whether one believes death is the end of all experiencing, etc.). One participant discussed his general belief in the following terms:

Death is a fulcrum point. In what we call *life* here, death is the end of life, and then we bounce into afterlife.

Attitudes toward the dying process involve ideas and opinions about how one would, or would not, like to die. For example, participants frequently noted that they would like to die quickly and painlessly or that they

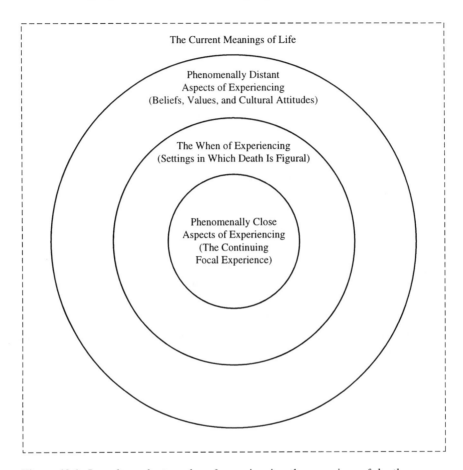

Figure 10.1. Interdependent modes of experiencing the meanings of death

would like to know when they were going to die in order to tie up loose ends and/or visit significant others. The following excerpt points to a wish to have enough time to deal with the fact of dying:

> I would want to know I was dying and have time to come to terms with it . . . come to terms with the reality of the body dying. I want an opportunity to live that through in an immediate sense. If it happens in small enough doses, it will feel like I have some control over it.

Values for which one would sacrifice one's life point more toward the meanings of life than those of death. In this mode, participants discussed those aspects of life for which they would be willing to die (e.g., to save the

life of a loved one). This mode of experiencing was characterized as phenomenally distant since it concerned events that were not likely to take
place:

I do not believe in the importance of dying for your country . . . I do believe that
there are other things more important than life. I wouldn't be a member of a fascist
organization just so I could continue living. I'd rather die than have to live my life
under their jurisdiction and rules. There are things that are more important than
your own personal life . . . your values.

Returning again to Figure 10.1, the next circle concerns an enumeration
of various real or projected settings in which death is figural. The When of
Experiencing was located between the phenomenally distant and close
aspects of the experience since it serves as the setting in which death is
figural and inextricably links together all remaining aspects of experiencing
death. An example follows:

I had to deal with the fact of being very close to death in Vietnam, it coming at any
time and not really being able to do a lot about it. I lived in constant fear during
those rocket attacks. There wasn't much you could do about it – you were at their
mercy.

The larger setting in which death was figural in this excerpt involves
the participant's potential death in Vietnam. The more specific setting
involved the realization that he was not able to do anything about his
situation.

The innermost circle of Figure 10.1 is labeled Phenomenally Close Aspects of Experiencing and may be characterized in terms of two interdependent modes of experiencing: immediacy and perceived consequences. The
immediacy of experience was described as an actual, imminent, or potential
experience of death of self or other. The perceived consequences were
described as involving the ways in which this experience continues to be
focal in one's life. Perceived consequences also were described as dealing
with the ways in which people continue to be changed by the experience of
death and/or by the ways in which the meaning of this experience changes
over time.

Examples of the immediacy of experience would be feeling shocked or
numbed by the death of a close relative, missing him, crying, being unable
to concentrate, and wandering aimlessly. An example of perceived consequence would be continuing to miss this person over the course of many
years. In addition, such experiences also lead to realizing how precious
relationships are and of seeing relationships as more important in one's life
than one had previously thought. One participant described his immediate
feelings with regard to his grandfather's death as follows:

Table 10.1. *Themes and Subthemes in the Experience of Death*

I. *Death Perceived as Meaningless*
   (against the meanings of life)
   A. Death as a barrier
   B. Death as a loss of meaning
   C. Death as an intrusion upon prior meanings
   D. Death as a condition that overrides or obscures the meanings of life

II. *Death Perceived as Meaningful*
   (in relation to the meanings of life)
   A. Death as an escape from conditions that override or obscure the meanings of life
   B. Death as something one attempts to control
   C. Death as an appeal to life's meanings
   D. Death as a reinstatement/transformation of meaning

III. *Death Perceived as Absence of Meaning*
   (neither meaningful nor meaningless; as cut off from the meanings of life)
   A. Death perceived in a passive mode as an absence of meaning
   B. Death rendered in an active mode as an absence of meaning

---

I was surprised how quickly and readily tears came to my eyes, and I thought maybe my grandfather is in heaven or whatever, but he's not available to me anymore.

Another participant described some of the perceived consequences of her father's death:

My father's death shook the whole family's foundation and we were not a close extended family. His death left a huge hole in things. Family get-togethers would be flat. And I realize what an enormous impact he had on people and how many people felt his death.

Themes Characterizing the Focal Experience of Death

After sorting through all of the individual protocols, it was found that three major themes were sufficient to characterize the structure of all 26 interviews; Table 10.1 presents a summary of these results. As may be noted, each major theme is composed of a number of subthemes. So, for example, the first and second themes each contain four subthemes, whereas the third theme contains only two subthemes.

Beginning with Theme I – Death Perceived as Meaningless (against the meanings of life) – we note the following four subthemes:

A. As a barrier,
B. As a loss of meaning,

C. As an intrusion upon prior meanings, and
D. As a condition that overrides or obscures the meanings of life.

For each subtheme, death is experienced as meaningless insofar as it opposes or disrupts the meanings of life. Subtheme A, death as a barrier, refers to the ways in which death puts an end to various meanings of life – for example, being with others, having control, accomplishing things – or to the inherent limits associated with death – for example, the inability to know when one will die or if there is an afterlife.

There are some things where no matter how calm you are, how controlled you are, how well you plan – there is nothing you can do about it. There were feelings of frustration and anger tied to that lack of control.

Subtheme B, death as a loss of meaning, involves the experience of a survivor who, immediately following the death of a loved one, experienced a transient state of confusion, disorientation, and aimlessness.

I would go to the grocery store and wander about aimlessly. Emotionally, I was upset enough that I couldn't concentrate on anything.

Subtheme C, death as an intrusion upon prior meanings, points to the ways in which participants described how death disrupts and changes one's life. Such intrusions involve unwanted changes in role relationships, in mood (becoming angry or despairing), and so on. The following example points to an intrusion upon prior meanings and involves a perceived loss of self-confidence following the sudden death of a brother:

When you're young, you feel invincible, like there's nothing you're not in control of. This was a situation where someone with all the confidence in the world would be unable to have control. Frankly, from that point on, I was never quite as confident as I was before.

Subtheme D points to the ways in which emotional and/or physical suffering are conditions that repudiate the meanings of life. One participant described her mother's illness in the following terms:

We learned that my mother had cancer so bad that they couldn't do much with it. My mother was an extremely active person, and I knew she didn't like television and was not going to feel like reading. She liked to do arts-and-crafts kinds of things, and I knew she was not going to be able to do those things. There was regret that she wouldn't be able to fulfill her dreams and anger that it [getting cancer] happened when everything was going for her the way she wanted.

The second major theme – Death Perceived as Meaningful (in relation to the meanings of life) – is also comprised of four subthemes:

A. Death as an escape from conditions that override or obscure the meanings of life,

B. Death as something one attempts to control,

C. Death as an appeal to life's meanings, and

D. Death as a reinstatement/transformation of meaning.

The common thread uniting the four subthemes is that the meanings of death in some way complement, continue, or enhance the meanings of life.

The first subtheme – that of death as an escape from conditions that override or obscure life's meanings – involves viewing death as meaningful when it puts an end to the perceived meaninglessness of suffering. It is an escape from conditions that override life's meanings; in this case, death is characterized as a meaningful relief both by the sufferer and the survivor.

I had my right lung removed, and I was near death and very aware of that – all hooked up to some machine. I was in a lot of pain, which even the morphine shots could not relieve. And I thought why can't it just be over with now and I would be without pain.

Subtheme B refers to the ways in which people prepare for or attempt to postpone death. In this sense, the meanings of life are enhanced in relation to the meanings of death. Participants reported preparing by making out a will, by becoming more acquainted with death through study, by "eating right" to enjoy a long full life, and so on. One participant embraced the notion of personal mortality by enrolling in class:

I had a course on death, and it fascinated me for a long time. It was an experiential class, and there was an emphasis on talking about death and embracing the idea that you are going to die, that you're mortal. A lot of moves and exercises we did were geared to that.

Subtheme C concerns those conditions that lessen the sting of death – for example, dying when one feels completed or fulfilled, dying in old age, dying peacefully and/or painlessly. One such mitigating factor involves the dying person's acceptance of his or her own imminent death.

My mother was having a bout with cancer, and she said she was ready to die – that she'd accomplished everything she wanted and had a great sense of peace. So it definitely influences your feeling about death – how your loved ones feel about it.

Subtheme D involves various modes of transcendence. These may come about through the strength of one's religious beliefs or through personal confrontation with the inevitability of "my death." One can transcend death as a meaningless event by taking it into one's life, thereby making life more significant. In the following example, the reality of death brings to the fore the importance of engaging with others:

When my grandfather died, I turned around right in front of everybody, but I didn't care which was very unusual for me, and went over to my grandmother and took her hand and told her to have strength, which was both for her – by reaching out to her, and inviting her to reach out to me. It was a gesture that seemed like a caring and right thing to do but which also served to do something with these emotions of Oh, yes I do care, more than I realized.

Death may also influence or transform the way one lives:

I typically tended to be future oriented. As I see the effect of death on people's lives, the more I realize that's a fallacious way to arrange one's life. I need to be more aware of what's happening in the present. In other words, death is changing my experience of time.

Faith or religion was described as another mode of transcending the experience of death as a meaningless event:

My faith has grown to a point where I accept the inevitability of my own and others' death. Without religion I would have to wonder what the purpose of mine or anyone else's life would mean – if there was no afterlife. Religion provides us with purposefulness. . . . I see death as a road to understanding – calm and peaceful.

The third major theme deriving from the present set of interviews was that of Death Perceived as an Absence of Meaning – in other words, as cut off from the meanings of life. This theme was comprised of two subthemes:

A. Death perceived in a passive mode as an absence of meaning, and
B. Death rendered in an active mode as an absence of meaning.

In the case of subtheme A, death was described as alien or far away. It was perceived as outside of one's life, as not having an effect on that life, or as having little personal significance:

What struck me most was the lack of feeling about the death, the lack of meaning to his death. He was just a grandfather who I didn't spend a lot of time with.

Another participant said:

Well, in childhood, at least until my father died, I remember thinking death was completely alien. . . . As far as I was concerned, it just did not concern me and mine.

Subtheme B, on the other hand, was described as involving an active distancing from the expected impact of death through denial or avoidance. Examples included purposely avoiding a funeral, denying the possibility that a loved one undergoing a serious operation might die, and so forth.

One individual described how he distances himself from thoughts of his own death:

When I read about someone dying in an accident, you tend to say: This guy was asking for it and I'm not, so I don't have to worry about it even though it's happening to people everyday. I suppose it's a way of distancing myself.

General Discussion

The purpose of the present set of interviews was to describe the ways in which the phenomenon of death is experienced and thought about in the midst of life. If the present structure is to be useful in describing such experiences, it should be possible to relate the various themes to previous discussions of the meaning of death in religion, psychoanalysis, philosophy, and empirical psychological research.

Relationship to Religious Thought

Hindu thought culminates in the *Upanishads* and the *Bagavad-Gita*, and these works postulate that the ignorant person must suffer an endless series of births and deaths as long as he or she remains attached to the fruits of his or her actions. Reincarnation is something not to be wished for since it only continues suffering, or those conditions that obscure the meaning of life. The enlightened person, however, is liberated from the cycle of life and death. By eliminating the personal self, and consequently personal death, later Hindu thinkers relegated death to an absence of meaning since for the enlightened person death is an illusion based upon ignorance.

Much of what has been said with regard to later Hindu thought also applies to Buddhism. Before Siddhartha became the Buddha, he lived a sheltered life. During this period, death was absent of meaning, alien, and distant. In his journeys, Siddhartha discovered aging, sickness, and death. He came to understand these conditions as suffering (or as conditions that obscure life's meaning), and this new understanding intruded upon his previous beliefs; death and suffering were now no longer seen as absent of meaning but as against the meanings of life.

Upon becoming enlightened, the Buddha understood that suffering is perpetuated by ignorance and attachment. The Buddha also saw that all existing things are impermanent and that the universe is in a process of becoming. In this way, the Buddha came to the conclusion that since everything is in a process of becoming, there can be no personal self and hence no personal death. Like Hinduism, Buddhism relegated personal death to an absence of meaning because it can only be a fiction based on ignorance.

Japanese Buddhism focused on *mujo* (impermanence), which "relativizes death by making each moment a type of dying" (Lafleur, 1974). Death perceived as the transient nature of all things led to an appreciation of aesthetics and to an appreciation of the fullness of each moment. Such a view transformed death from an experience of barrier to one of a meaningful source of beauty and potential creativity.

The Judaic view of death is based on the premise that life is historical and that God's covenant with Israel involves the destiny of a nation and not that of an individual. Silberman (1969) points out that "viewed in this way, death, though no less the dissolution of the individual, lost its ultimacy, for the corporate entity, the nation of Israel, endures." Symbolic immortality through the continuity of the nation is a meaningful transformation of individual death: One symbolically lives on as part of the larger whole.

Some passages in the Old Testament indicate that human existence does not survive death; others indicate that it continues to exist in a diminished form – in Sheol. Based on either account, the death of an individual is viewed as a barrier to the meanings of life. In the former case (where the human being does not survive), death is a barrier to continued being; in the latter case (where human existence is weak and lacking vitality), death is a barrier to meaningful human action.

According to the synoptic gospels, Jesus' views on life and death were similar to the prevailing Hebraic tradition and stressed the meanings of life as he saw them: discipleship, repentance, and unconditional love. Keck (1969) states that for Jesus, "death is not an obstacle to faith in God or something that must be overcome – it is a qualifier of man's existence and as such makes life so precious that there is no equivalent for it." In this way, death is meaningful because it transforms the meanings of life. In the synoptic gospels, the fact of Jesus' death did not so much transform personal existence after death as it did one's existence during life. Jesus' death offered meaning within life: from person to person and from generation to generation. In addition, Jesus, and/or the meaning of Jesus' life, was transformed (immortalized) through disciples who practiced what Jesus preached.

According to the Gospel of John, Jesus as the Son of God constitutes a truth that one is free to accept or reject at any moment. According to John, in accepting the truth of Jesus, one is immediately transformed and resurrected in one's present bodily being. Eternal life is not everlasting life, nor is resurrection a phenomenon that occurs after death. One may have eternal life (knowledge of the absolute Truth of Jesus) and yet still die. In other words, death becomes meaningful through the acceptance of "absolute truth" in life. Those who refuse to accept Jesus are already dead, and their living constitutes a meaningless existence.

In the Gospel of Paul, death is transcended because the faithful share not only in Jesus' life but in his death. Death is now made meaningful on the basis of a transformation: A physical body dies, and a spiritual existence is raised. It is only through the death of Jesus that life and death are reinstated with meaning. Paul believes that "for as by [the sins of] a man came death, by a man has come also the resurrection of the dead. For as in Adam all die, so also in Christ shall all be made alive." Although Paul, John, and the synoptic evangelists interpret the meaning of Jesus' death differently, all agree that through Jesus death is meaningful because it entails a transformation for the faithful and a continuation of meaninglessness for the unfaithful.

Relationship to Psychoanalytic Thought

Within the context of psychoanalysis, personal death must be absent of meaning because it is "subjectively inconceivable" (Fenichel, 1945). Instead, Freud postulated that death anxieties are derived from prior encounters with realistic dangers, which have the force of making one's anxiety about death meaningless. This view also suggests that death anxiety may bring about a more permanent disruption in life's meanings since such anxiety yields a loss of personal power as well as negative emotional states such as depression or helplessness. In addition, death anxiety may be equated with barriers to life's satisfactions. Since death anxiety derives from developmental anxieties, it is associated with anxieties arising from potentially unmet needs along the course of development. For example, as the infant develops, he or she comes to recognize mother as a need-satisfying object. Death anxiety in this phase would derive from a fear of losing mother's love – thereby leaving the infant's oral needs unmet – which would be experienced as a barrier to the satisfaction of such needs.

Although death anxiety is not viewed as a fundamental human instinct, Freud did postulate the existence of Thanatos (the death instinct). This instinct was characterized as a fundamental unconscious wish for a return to an inorganic, tensionless state of being. Thus, Freud (1920/1950) was forced to conclude that "the aim of all life is death" and, in so concluding, paradoxically transforms death into a meaningful aim of life (i.e., as an urge toward the quiescence of inorganic existence).

Relationship to Existential Thought

Since human existence is continually in the process of becoming, one's being-in-the-world is always a being-toward-death regardless of whether or not one chooses to acknowledge this fact. Since death is certain yet indefinite, one's "being-toward-death is essentially anxious" (Heidegger, 1927/ 1962). One may comport oneself toward this possibility in one of two ways: authentically or inauthentically. Inauthentic being evades death, perceives it as absent of meaning, and relegates it to *Das Man*. In terms of the present study, some individuals who described death as absent of meaning viewed themselves as "passive" in relation to death (i.e., as choosing not to think about it). Other participants described more "active modes" of not dealing with death in which they actively kept away from sick people or funerals. Although experientially there is a difference between "active" and "passive" modes (of dealing with death), both refuse to link the death of others, or the idea of death, to "my death."

Authentic comportment toward death anticipates death in the acknowledgment of one's being as a being-toward-death. Authentic being musters courage in the fact of anxiety associated with acknowledging this possibility and, in this way, takes death into life. When death is acknowledged as one's "ownmost" possibility, it serves to individualize one's life by freeing one to choose authentically between possibilities. In addition, it also serves to transform death into a possibility that suffuses life with freedom and meaning.

Relationship to Empirical Research

Empirical research has been concerned with a great many different issues concerning the human reaction to death. Some of these studies have dealt with the degree to which an individual accepts or denies death, some with the role of religion, and some with the experience of time. To organize the implication of present results for empirical research, the same six headings used to organize prior research will again be used to structure the present discussion.

Death Acceptance vs. Death Denial. One group of researchers (Boyar, 1964; Dickstein, 1972; Dickstein & Blatt, 1966; Handal, 1969; Lester, 1967; Sarnoff & Corwin, 1959; Templer, 1970) who have attempted to study the human reaction to death have made the following three assumptions about death anxiety: It is universal, it is unitary, and its absence is due to defensive maneuvers. Taken together, these assumptions suggest not only that we all fear death but that we all fear it in the same way. A second group of researchers (Collett & Lester, 1969; Conte et al., 1982; Florian & Kravitz, 1983; Hoelter, 1979; Nelson, 1978; Nelson & Nelson, 1975) also assumes that death anxiety is universal and that any absence of such anxiety is due to defensive mechanisms such as repression or denial. In addition, these investigators assume that death anxiety is a multidimensional, and not a unidimensional, phenomenon. A third and final group of researchers (Kurlychek, 1976; Ray & Najman, 1974; Stout, Minton, & Spilka, 1976; Swenson, 1961, 1965) make a different set of assumptions – namely, that death anxiety is not a universal phenomenon, that it is multidimensional, and that the absence of death anxiety may be due either to defensive maneuvers or to various modes of acceptance.

Part of the difficulty in determining whether or not death anxiety is universal concerns a lack of clarity in distinguishing among the terms *death anxiety*, *death fear*, and *death concern*. Technically speaking, death anxiety (dread) arises only in the face of "no-thing," whereas death fear only arises in the face of "some-thing." Death concern, on the other hand, may include any of a number of feelings, such as anger, despair, and worry, and in this sense must conceptually encompass both death anxiety and death fear.

After sorting through these terms, present results suggest that at the experiential level, all individuals report some concern regarding either the death of oneself or of one's significant others. Only a few individuals, however, reported being specifically anxious and/or fearful of their own death. Death concern included such issues as feeling guilty about not being able to take care of one's family after one dies, feeling angry that life is so short, feeling anxious about the possibility of nonbeing, and feeling fearful about the unknown process of death.

Despite these concerns, participants also reported being concerned with the meaning of death and with accepting it as a personal possibility. When this took place, death was described as a completion, a chance to engage with deceased loved ones in an afterlife, or as a relief from an existence of pain and suffering. Present results thus suggest that death anxiety is not a universal phenomenon, although a concern with death is. One may manifest both death concern and acceptance since death is a complex phenomenon, and conscious acceptance of death need not be equated with repressed death anxiety. These findings are in accord with those of Weisman and Hackett (1961), who feel that individuals can both be accepting of death and view it as an appropriate closure to their lives.

Part of the difficulty that prior research has had in dealing with issues of death acceptance or denial concerns the issue of method; that is, most prior investigators asked participants to complete a series of rating scales. Generally speaking, rating scales constrain respondents by providing them only preformed statements to rate, and no attempt is made to secure additional information about the respondent's specific understanding of the topic or the alternative. Any attempt to describe the way(s) in which various items fit together generally involves factor-analytic procedures to determine the overall structure. The method of human dialogue used in the present study, however, allows for a much greater range of individual expression, such that the participant – rather than some abstract pattern of mathematical covariation – determined what went with what in his or her unique experience. Even when prior investigators have attempted to evaluate unique aspects of a person's experience of death, such results have not been integrated into a meaningful structure of the total experience.

Results of the present study thus do not confirm the assumptions of previous empirical studies that assume that death is a unitary phenomenon and/or that the absence of death anxiety is due to defensive operations. Indeed, anxiety is not the only possible reaction to death; depending on context, one might feel relieved, depressed, angry, or helpless. To say that one is anxious in the face of death gives relatively little information about the individual's specific experience. Rather, we must attempt to describe what the person is anxious of and what he or she does in the face of such anxiety; for example, we may be fearful about dying before having accomplished what we wanted to accomplish. In the face of this fear, we might pursue life goals more earnestly, thereby increasing feelings of accomplishment and decreasing our fears of death.

Death Attitudes Related to Age and Aging. Within this area of research, the primary question has been about relating death anxiety to age. Results of some studies indicate no correlation between death anxiety and age; other studies report that death anxiety increases as people age; and still other studies find that death anxiety decreases as people get older. The great majority of studies involve cross-sectional methods, and what present results suggest most clearly is that any specific experience of death is always individual and unique. Under this reading, the question of whether individuals in some demographically defined age group experience more or less death anxiety becomes a potentially irrelevant one. A more relevant question would seem to concern the way in which each person's experience of death changes as he or she ages, as well as the possible ways in which an individual's experience of both life and death change as a function of age.

Aging was described by present participation in many different ways. For those who considered it as "running out of time," death was characterized as a barrier to life's meanings. For those who described it as allowing them to attain their goals and dreams, death was described as a completion. In those cases where aging was associated with pain and suffering, death was viewed as a welcome relief. The way in which one understands aging influences how one perceives death, just as how one views death influences how one views aging.

Death Attitudes Related to Personality (Actualized or Nonactualized). The relevant question here concerns the degree to which one's personal mode of actualization relates to the experience of death. Investigators have offered four hypotheses:

1. Individuals who are highly actualized (e.g., have internal locus of control, high sense of competence, achievement, vitality, etc.) will accept death because they are capable of integrating "my death" into "my life" as a completion.
2. Individuals who are highly actualized will be anxious about death because they will be incapable of perceiving it except as a barrier to continued actualized living.
3. Individuals who are nonactualized will be anxious about death because they feel incomplete, and death will eliminate any possibility for completion.
4. Individuals who are nonactualized will accept death as a release from suffering.

Results of previous empirical studies are mixed (Farley, 1971; Nehrke, Bellucci, & Gabriel, 1978); each hypothesis has been confirmed by some investigators and not by others. Once again, such a pattern of findings is to be expected since each hypothesis is mutually exclusive and serves to bring to light different ways of experiencing the meaning of death. The present study reveals that some participants who reported a sense of having accomplished a great deal and of having good relationships with others reported accepting death with equanimity: For them, death was described as a meaningful completion. Individuals who reported feeling that their lives had not been meaningful (or as meaningful as they would have liked) reported experiencing death as a barrier to the possibility or hope of meaningfulness in contrast to their present sense of meaninglessness. Finally, some individuals who reported suffering from conditions that obscure meaning – such as bodily deterioration – described death as a meaningful escape from a meaningless existence.

Thus, there can be no one-to-one correlation between personal modes of actualization and the way one experiences death. In taking the stance that one's experience of death depends on one's level of actualization, previous investigators have assumed that actualization automatically determines the experience of death. Present results suggest that the experience of life grounds the experience of death – and vice versa – and that the meanings of life and death do not exist as separate "factors" but as a unique experiential gestalt. As such, all four hypotheses seem to describe possible reactions for specific individuals regardless of their specific personality characteristics.

Death Attitudes Related to Various Types of Exposure to Death. The key question here is whether attitudes toward death and dying change as a function of exposure to death, whether such exposure is imagined, imminent, or actual. In general, previous results suggest that attitudes often (but not always) change following exposure to death; for example, Taylor (1983) reports that students who suffered early parental loss generated more death themes in compositions than those who had intact families. Furthermore, those who suffered early parental loss tended to see death as "long ago in the past or as an abstract representation." Other researchers found that the death of a close friend increased thoughts of personal mortality. Noyes (1980, 1982) reports that individuals who have had near-death experiences may undergo any of a number of changes in attitude including a reduced fear of death, a reorientation with regard to the meanings or preciousness of life, a greater sense of helplessness, and so on.

Results deriving from the present set of interviews again concur with prior findings – namely, that exposure to death, be it imagined, imminent, or actual, changes an individual's understanding of both death and life in many ways. Exposure to death may make it more immediate and significant in one's life. As such, it may be perceived as an intrusion that serves to change relationships, increase one's sense of helplessness, and influence one's faith or belief system. Exposure also may either bring home the experience of death as a barrier to life's meanings or demonstrate its transformative possibilities. As present participants described situations in which they were forced to confront the inevitability of personal death, or were required to work through the death of a significant other, the meanings of life became more salient. Within the present set of interviews, some participants reported that exposure to death served to establish new priorities in their lives, whereas others reported attempting to render death absent of meaning by denying it or by viewing it as abstract and general. In all cases, however, an exposure to death was taken up by the individual in such a way as to be congruent with other aspects of his or her own unique perceptions of the meanings of both life and death.

Death Attitudes Related to Religiosity. The relevant question here is whether religiosity decreases death anxiety. Correlating religiosity with death anxiety has produced inconsistent results, with some studies indicating no relationship, others a negative relationship, others a positive relation, and still others, a curvilinear relationship. Although correlational studies of this type have produced inconsistent results, most studies do indicate that strong religious conviction, accompanied by frequent participation in a variety of religious activities, is associated with lowered death anxiety. This finding can be understood in terms of present themes in the following way: Those individuals who manifest genuine faith transform death into a meaningful point of transition to an afterlife of reward. Under such a transformation, one's identity and meaning continue in the afterlife, thereby mitigating any personal anxiety associated with nonbeing. Despite the comfort afforded by this view, some individuals did report other types of death concerns – for example, leaving loved ones behind.

A few earlier studies have indicated that religious individuals fear death more than nonreligious ones. These findings may be understood as fighting the barriers in preparing for death. If an individuals is afraid of the possibility of nonbeing, or of eternal punishment, he or she might turn to religion as a way of dealing with such modes of meaninglessness. Under these conditions, religion is used strategically in an attempt to transform death into something meaningful. Although religion may provide the possibility for transformation, strategic use of religion does not automatically guarantee that the person will be able to accept its teachings or its comfort.

Finally, a few studies have reported a curvilinear relationship between death anxiety and religiosity. As stated previously, many highly religious individuals view death as a meaningful transformation. On the other hand, many nonreligious people, who hold a strong belief that death is the end of existence, may experience death as meaningful through an authentic confrontation with nonbeing, thereby enhancing the meanings of life and making death more meaningful. Those who describe themselves as moderately religious, however, may be unable to perceive death as meaningful and therefore will dwell on the meaninglessness of death. Such a state of affairs would account for greater anxiety among the moderately religious than among either the nonreligious or the very religious.

Death Attitudes Related to Temporal Experience and Futurity. The relevant question in this area is whether death anxiety influences future time perspective. In general, investigators report that individuals who manifest a great deal of death anxiety tend to live more in the present, to be more worried about time, and to avoid projecting themselves into the future. In terms of present results, such findings may be understood in the following way: Individuals with high death anxiety perceive death as meaningless. As a way of dealing with such potential meaninglessness, they cling rigidly to the present. As time moves on, however, the barrier to meaning represented by death comes to loom progressively larger, thus yielding a situation in which it would make sense for the person to live in the present and to avoid projecting him- or herself into a future where death would be certain. If death can be experienced only as a barrier, a loss, an intrusion, or a condition that obscures life's meanings, the future can be filled only with dread until the person is able to come to some accommodation with his or her fate as a mortal human being.

Implications for Treatment

No attempt has been made to validate or repudiate various philosophical or religious renderings of death. Such understandings do not seem a matter for empirical research representing, as they do, the deepest fears, values, and aspirations of different cultures, religions, and individuals. Although there is much to be learned from empirical evaluations of all of human experience, there are some issues that cannot be resolved by empirical methods, and one is required to be silent in their presence. Such silence is not to be construed as ignorance but respect for the difficult task that each of us faces in regard to death.

Through phenomenological interviewing, however, an individual's unique perspective on death may be seen in light of the many possible ways in which human beings can and do experience death in the midst of life. Since a phenomenological interview is designed to allow for a sympathetic understanding of personal experience, it offers a means of describing how an individual who suffers from death anxiety differs from someone who does not. Results of the present study suggest that individuals who seek professional help do so because they focus primarily on the meaninglessness of death rather than on its transformative possibilities. If this is the case, treatment should involve understanding and working through the specific type(s) of meaninglessness involved. In addition, the person can be made aware of the various ways in which an authentic confrontation with death may serve to enrich his or her experience of life.

It follows that treatment should begin by having the clinician attempt to determine which aspect(s) of meaninglessness are problematic for the person, and which aspect(s) of meaningfulness could be helpful in resolving such issues. For example, suppose that a female patient who has been married for many years comes into treatment when she learns that her husband is dying of cancer. In counseling her, the clinician discovers that she is afraid to be alone and that she tends to depend upon her husband for emotional support and understanding. Within the context of the present thematic structure, this individual would seem to be experiencing death both as a barrier to engaging with her husband and as an intrusion upon prior meanings.

Identifying these specific themes as aspects of her situation should provide a specific direction toward which treatment could work so as to help her reinstate possible sources of meaning in her life. Such reinstatement could be done in a number of ways; for example, although the absence of her husband will be felt acutely, the patient may come to understand that her husband continues to live on in her memories as well as in the ways he has influenced her. Identifying barriers to engagement as an area of concern should allow the patient to prepare for her husband's death and to cherish the remaining time that they have together. By engaging with her husband during this time, she should be able to avoid undue guilt or regret that could further disrupt the meanings of her life after his death. Since engaging with her husband is one of the meanings of life that she emphasizes most strongly, this loss could also be ameliorated by encouraging her to reach out to other significant individuals.

The point to this example is not to provide a specific clinical technique but to describe some of the ways in which the present thematic structure may be used to identify and clarify problematic issues concerning the topic of death. Reinstatement of meaning (though it can be accomplished in any number of ways) must specifically address those aspects of meaninglessness that serve as a source of distress to the specific person presently sitting with the clinician. When this is done, some of the impending trauma may be mitigated by reinstating the problematic aspect of death back into the midst of life. Although the death of a loved one cannot be overcome, it can be made more meaningful to the suffering person now experiencing death as intrusive, alienating, and meaningless.

PART IV

The Phenomenology of Everyday Life

11

Toward an Empirical Existential-Phenomenological Psychology

Could there possibly be such a thing as an empirical existential-phenomenological psychology? Aside from the articulatory problems such a linguistic mouthful might cause, this approach would also seem to require contemporary psychology to give up, or at least strongly modify, certain long-held beliefs and practices. For one, there is the issue of content: No longer could psychology be described as the disciplined study of behavior; it would now have to become the disciplined study of behavior and experience or, even more radically, experience and behavior. Second, there is the issue of method: No longer would a quantitative evaluation of disinterested observation in special situations be criterial; now a new and more qualitative emphasis would be placed on dialogue, narrative, and interpretation as these affect descriptions of the extralaboratory worlds of everyday life. Finally, there is the issue of biology: An existential-phenomenological psychology deriving from Merleau-Ponty would, of necessity, have to reconfigure the significance of biological fact and theory for psychology. As such, it would seem to call into question all contemporary attempts at what is usually termed *reductionism*.

Although it is possible to view each of these considerations as asking psychology to give up something it now holds dear, a more productive way of thinking about the relationship between existential phenomenology and contemporary psychology is in terms of a series of issues to be confronted rather than a set of injunctions to be followed. If such a turn is taken, four questions emerge of significance for any dialogue between contemporary psychology and existential phenomenology. Each of these questions deals with a longstanding concern in psychology, and our present purpose is not to solve these issues but to raise them once again, this time from a different perspective.

337

1. What do we mean by behavior, and how is what we mean by behavior related to what we mean by experience?
2. What methods should we use to describe in a rigorous way empirically relevant aspects of experience?
3. What should be the relationship of biology to existence; that is, is it possible to take biological facts into account without viewing them as causative?
4. What new perspectives on consciousness does the present orientation yield that could not be derived from existing theories and methods?

If such a thing as empirical existential-phenomenological psychology is to be a viable enterprise, it must say something of significance about each of these topics, something that is worth the cost of asking contemporary psychology to reconsider not only its procedures but its premises.

Human Behavior and Human Experience

Human beings do things – they behave – and with the exception of Skinner, few psychologists seem to have considered behavior as interesting in its own right. Rather, most take a more methodological stance in which behavior is significant primarily in terms of what it points to rather than in terms of what it might mean. The cognitive psychologist, for example, considers behavior as providing entry into the more significant, but hidden, realm of mental process. Much of early cognitive psychology, especially in its linguistic mode, was interested in establishing the reality of theoretical constructs such as rules, transformations, and language acquisition devices. More recent work is no less interested in mental phenomena; this time, the theoretical lexicon is one of frames, scripts, schemas, and holograms.

Much of early behavior theory also espoused a methodological behaviorism, and systems as simple as Guthrie's or as complex as Hull's viewed behavior as an observable indicator pointing to the psychological organization of habitual actions and their successive combinations and permutations. For such theories, the maze and memory drum became the psychological equivalent of the chemist's test tube in which the operation of hypothetical laws took place over putatively real networks of interconnections. Historically, it is significant to remember that Pavlov viewed the conditioned response as a way of probing the nervous system – a "psychic secretion" he called it. Psychoanalysts also were not particularly interested in what people did; rather, behavior was epiphenomenal to the real drama played out among shadowy actors performing on the interior stage of the psyche.

The only psychological system to be interested in what organisms did in their world was radical behaviorism. For Skinner, there was no doubling of the world, no inner world, however defined, in contrast to a more observable outer one. Everything an organism did took place in some environment, and Skinner, at his best, presented a descriptive analysis of behavior as behavior-in-the-world. Although the system is stridently third-person, there were times when behavior was playfully described from a more first-animal perspective, as in Skinner's famous description of the pigeon in a missile (1960).

Skinner also dealt with time differently from most other psychologists. Unlike the early and continuing traditions of methodological behaviorism, which atomized time into units called *trials*, Skinner consistently evaluated behavior within the context of a continuous temporal flow. From this perspective, the rate and temporal pattern at which a behavior was performed by a single animal was crucial – not the speed of reaction nor the percentage correct, across a group of subjects, over a collection of experimenter-defined events called *trials*. Rates, and changes in rate, characterized behavior – not some abstract movement that occurred only once an "internal" connection had been established. In his own way, Skinner evidenced a concern for intentionality, context, and the continuity of time unique among empirical psychologists. Although some may denigrate the system as simplistic because it concerns "performance" and not "learning" or "cognition," such criticism reflects an allegiance to a more Cartesian perspective rather than to an appreciation for the situatedness of organismic activity (i.e., for the situatedness of existence).

Aside from Merleau-Ponty (1942/1963), who had a few kind words to say about Skinner's behaviorist ancestor John B. Watson ("In our opinion, when Watson spoke of behavior he had in mind what others call existence" [p. 226]), few psychologists or philosophers seem to appreciate Skinner's significance for existential psychology. In a classic paper, however, Kvale and Greness (1967) compared Skinner to Sartre and came to the then-surprising conclusion that once terminological differences were overcome, a striking resemblance could be seen. Although Skinner is not an existential phenomenologist and Sartre is not a radical behaviorist, it is informative to discuss Skinner in existential terms and Sartre in behavioral ones. Despite an undeniable difference between the existential and behavioral traditions – such as the latter's insistence on a third-person, physicalistic description of both organism and world as absolutely necessary to its project – their points of similarity are equally noteworthy and undeniable. Skinner and Sartre both share in the rejection of an inner agency that directs outer action, an emphasis on the dialectical relationship between individuals (or individual organisms) and their surrounding worlds, and a desire to describe behavioral phenomena rather than to explain them by referring to hypothetical, internal mechanisms. Perhaps most importantly, however, both agree that the human being is defined by what the person does, not by what he or she thinks about doing, would like to do, or plans to do. For both Skinner and Sartre, it is action-in-the-world that matters; accordingly, both sought to purge psychology of the Cartesian legacy in which "I think" defines what "I am."

Radical behaviorism is not the only psychological system to have considered the psychological significance of what organisms do in their world. Here, we also must consider the contributions of Edward Tolman (1932), who attempted a *descriptive* characterization of behavior from a rigorous third-person point of view. Depending on how one reads Tolman, his description emphasized three, four, or five different characteristics. Paraphrasing his list produces the following points: (1) Behavior is always directed toward some specific aspect of the situation; (2) behavior always takes place in a given context and involves a mutual exchange between some organism and relevant aspects of its setting; and (3) behavior is always an affair of the whole organism engaging its environment. Although Tolman used words such as *purposive*, *wholistic*, and *molar* to characterize behavior, it is possible to characterize his approach as (1) intentional, (2) situated, and (3) in-the-world.

Perhaps the clearest maxim to describe the role of behavior in a phenomenological approach to psychology was offered by Snygg and Combs (1949) and associates (e.g., Combs, Richards, & Richards, 1976), and the maxim was this: "Read behavior backwards." Through this phrase, researchers are required to engage in "a continuous process of observing, inferring, testing, observing, inferring, testing" until they "come closer to an accurate appraisal of the meanings existing for other people which affect their functioning" (Combs et al., 1976, p. 378). Since the observer is "outside" the field of the person being observed, he or she should be able to see (or infer) more of the figure/ground patterns that define the situation for the actor than might be true for the actor him- or herself.

Although Snygg and Combs view "inference" as a crucial ingredient to "reading behavior backwards," Romanyshyn and Whalen (1989) have stressed differences between inferring and interpreting the meaning that human events have to, and for, human beings. The root meaning of *to infer* is "to bring into"; the root meaning of *to interpret* is "to mediate or negotiate between." In terms of the meaning of a behavioral act, *to infer* means to "present something that is not yet there, whereas *to interpret* means to read something that by definition is there" (p. 26). To infer the meaning of behavior is to look beyond the behavior to its cause, physiological substate, or mental schema; to interpret the meaning of behavior is to stay with a specific example of contextualized behavior until it forms a sensible ensemble from which a meaning emerges by which it is understood. With this meaning of *meaning* in mind, it seems clear that we should replace the verb *to infer* by the verb *to interpret* in the advice offered by Snygg and Combs.

Interpreting the meaning of carefully observed behavior, although not specifically mentioned by name, was made most credible, and used to great advantage, by Piaget in his descriptions of the sensory-motor world of the infant. Although Piaget's descriptions become progressively more theory-laden (and motivated by Cartesian considerations) as they approach adult cognition, his descriptions of the early worlds of childhood are both phenomenologically revealing and derived from nonverbal behaviors produced by an infant and interpreted by Piaget. A careful reading of Piaget's methods clearly suggests that he is engaged in a (behavioral) dialogue with the infant. Although Piaget used a more linguistic approach in dealing with older children, the earliest work involved a behavioral dialogue in which Piaget set questions in environmental terms and the infant answered in behavioral ones. Piaget's work demonstrates that it is possible to engage in dialogical research without language and, furthermore, that the results of such dialogue may be used in describing the first-person world of the other.

A different domain in which behavior, rigorously observed and intepreted, has been used to provide insight into what the person is experiencing concerns the phonological description of language, most especially in the distinction between phonetic and phonemic descriptions. In the former case, phonetic description is person-, language-, and context-free – in short, a third-person catalogue of differences that can be detected by a skilled observer in the stream of sound regardless of the language considered. As such, it is precisely correct for no specific language and least wrong for all languages. Phonemic description, on the other hand, requires the co-participation of a native speaker/listener and thereby yields that minimal set of sounds making a difference to the informant. Considered in this way, phonemic methodology defines a behaviorally based, first-person procedure requiring interaction between an outside observer and the person whose language is of interest, and phonemic description provides a catalogue of significant sounds as heard and produced by speakers of a specific language.

It is possible to generalize this usage as, indeed, cultural anthropology does in its distinction between "-etic" and "-emic" descriptions of culture.

This analogy, which derives from the linguistic concepts of phon*etic* and phon*emic* description, is meant to suggest that the anthropological observer is free to describe the meaning of objects, words, and actions as these are for individuals in the culture (or subculture) or from the point of view of some detached, outside observer. In both the cultural and linguistic cases, it is clear that although inquiry starts with -etic description, -emic description is a second, and more significant, moment in the anthropologist's understanding of the culture in question.

Köhler (1947) approached the issue of what the behavior of another person might mean to an observer in a slightly different way. Although acknowledging that inference is sometimes helpful in describing what someone else's behavior might tell us about his or her phenomenal world, he argued against placing too much credence in such reconstruction. Rather, Köhler proposed that behavior is a perceptual form that reveals itself directly and does not require us to have had a similar experience to know what it means:

> Do we never understand others as beings who are extremely different from ourselves? The characteristic manliness of Douglas Fairbanks used to impress me very much, although unfortunately I could not offer anything comparable. On the other hand, sometimes I see in the face of another person unpleasant greed in a version for which I hardly have counterparts in my own experience. . . .
>
> The problem of social understanding does not directly refer to behavior (as a physical fact). It refers to perceptual facts which one person experiences in contact with other persons; for, both the bodies and the behavior of such other persons are given to the first person as percepts and changes of percepts. (pp. 130–131)

The discussion of behavior seems to yield several conclusions, the most significant of which is that behavior exhibits many of the same properties as experience: Both are intentional, both are centered on certain focal events, both are situated and context-sensitive, and (in Skinner's hands at least) both take place within the framework of continuous time. A second conclusion is that it is often possible to describe an individual's first-person world on the basis of what he or she does as well as in terms of what he or she talks about. Finally, the present discussion suggests that it is incorrect to separate behavior and experience; rather, both are better construed as aspects of a reversible figure in which both participate dialectically. As Merleau-Ponty (1942/1963) noted, this dialectic is quite properly called *existence*, thereby suggesting that behavior-and-experience form a unity whose figural aspect is determined by our perspectival view of the person, either as actor or as an object of observation.

Under this rendition, a description of the first-person field may be attained by emphasizing behavior *and/or* experience according to the possibilities of the situation, the person, the topic, and the researcher attempting the task. To come now to the question of whether there is a significant role for behavior in existential-phenomenological psychology, the answer must be an affirmative one, especially if behavior is viewed as situated meaningful action and not as abstract movement performed in response to contrived settings. Empirically minded psychologists may have to relinquish their interest in behavior-as-indicator; they need not, however, give up their interest in behavior-as-life.

Existential Phenomenology and the Question of Method

As early as 1970, Giorgi was warning psychologists about the pernicious effects of an excessive concern with methodology. Although he was chiding psychology for choosing its methods in advance of its phenomena, the fact is that for existential phenomenology to become an empirical discipline, it does need to develop, or select, procedures that are capable of yielding insights into its unfolding subject matter. Such concerns seem to be at the heart of attempts by existential-phenomenological researchers (e.g., Polkinghorne, 1989; see Chapter 2 of the present book) to systemize their methods and modes of reporting results. The outcome of such a critical look is not to yield a single method as "the" method of existential-phenomenological research but to sensitize phenomenological researchers to the concerns of colleagues not quite as familiar (or comfortable) with their methods.

With this caution in mind, the method of dialogue seems to provide a useful path toward phenomenological description and interpretation. Dialogue is not the only method, but it does provide a reference point for alternative linguistic procedures such as written narratives, self-reports, cued recalls, or sets of questions concerning the "what" of some significant experience. Each of these methods may be used in the presence or absence of other more standard procedures such as behavioral observation (which, as noted, can be construed and conducted as a special type of dialogue), attitude questionnaires, and personality, projective, or intelligence tests. In all cases, the aim is the same: to describe the first-person world of individuals serving as co-participants in the research.

Although no specific phenomenological procedure, aside from dialogue, has an extensive history, some have been used more frequently than others, thereby permitting an assessment of relative values and limitations. Probably the three most frequently used methods are thought sampling, cued recall, and narrative description. Since the first two were named by cognitive rather than existential-phenomenological psychologists, they tend to sound more Cartesian than they are in empirical use. In both cases, the procedures were designed to allow the researcher to gain insight into what co-participants were aware of during or shortly after participation in certain situations or tasks. These procedures stand in contrast to the more extensive phenomenological interview, which takes place in no special temporal relationship to the events of interest.

In the thought-sampling method, the investigator interrupts individuals as they go about their ordinary activities to ask them what they are aware of at that moment. The most extensive and programmatic studies of this genre are by Klinger (1981; Klinger, Bartoc, & Mahoney, 1976) in which beepers were given to a group of student volunteers. Once students were accustomed to wearing beepers, Klinger sent out a signal on a random basis that cued subjects to write down what they were aware of at that time. Since the researcher did not want the participant's life to be totally "beeped," the person was allowed a certain number of hours per day off the beeper. The major names (and papers) in this area are Klinger (1981), Hurlburt (1980), and Hurlburt, Leach, Leach, and Saltman (1984). In addition to work by Klinger, Hurlburt, and their associates is correlated research conducted by Csikszentmihalyi, Larson, and Prescott (1977), which concerns self-reports of the activities engaged in by adolescents during an ordinary week. Finally, there is the more recent attempt by Miller (1993) to describe the thoughts of students engaged in critical writing tasks, specifically in regard to metaphoric transformations that do or do not find their way into the student's written work.

Pollio and his associates (Pollio, 1984; Pollio & Swanson, 1995; Hunt & Pollio, 1995) have also used a variant of this procedure in studying what college students report being aware of during lectures or when listening to comic records. In one study (Pollio, 1984), for example, students were interrupted at random times during an ongoing lecture and asked to write down "what you were aware of just before the bell sounded." Although this procedure produced a great deal of educationally significant information (for example, across a large number of undergraduate classes, only 61% of student protocols contained responses that were on-target with respect to the instructor or lecture content), more significant results emerged from simultaneously sampling student awareness and student behavior. In the simplest case, self-reports provided by students were coded into the two categories of on- and off-target. At the same time, behavioral records were made of what students did during the 30-second period immediately preceding the self-report, and these records also were coded into the categories of on- and off-target.

Table 11.1. *Classification of Self-Reports and Behavioral Observations*

Behavioral Record	Self-report		Totals
	On-target	*Off-target*	
On-target	.64	.29	.93
Off-target	.03	.04	.07
Totals	.67	.33	1.00

Source: From Pollio, 1984.

Table 11.1 presents the results of this two-way classification of self-reports and behavioral observations. In the best of all possible worlds, the two diagonal cells – on/on and off/off – would add to close to 100%, and the researcher could then use (as lecturers do) student behavior as an index of student awareness (self-report). As may be seen, one of the four cells, Behavior-on/Self-Report-off, violates this simple pattern; in fact, about 29% of the cases fell in this cell. What these data reveal, at a minimum, is that looking on-target does not always cooccur with self-reports that are on-target as common and pedagogical sense as well as methodological behaviorism would seem to require.

One way to conceptualize these results concerns viewing self-reports as providing a first-person perspective on the situation. Similarly, it is possible to describe behavior as providing a third-person perspective. Behavior and self-report thus provide simultaneous but different points of view on the same event. From an existential-phenomenological perspective, it is reasonable to consider self-reports as describing a "me-for-me" perspective and behavioral records as describing a "me-for-you" or, more generally, a "me-for-someone-else" perspective. Although social scientists typically prefer the latter of these perspectives, it should be clear that observation yields only a part of the picture.

Rather than becoming mired in a debate over which procedure yields data more accurately reflecting the situation, it seems wiser to determine what – if any – coherent relationships obtain between the two perspectives. Both forms of data capture unique aspects of the event, and both seem able to enhance understanding. Once we recognize the possibilities in considering both perspectives, it seems clear that both are likely to have their own unique histories and contemporary contexts – contexts and histories that sometimes overlap and sometimes do not. Whether we consider the 29% of items falling in the on/off cell of Table 11.1 to indicate *politeness* ("I'm bored but will try not to let the instructor see it"), *strategy* ("I want a good grade and won't show I'm bored"), or *consideration* ("I don't want to hurt the instructor's feelings"), the general methodological point seems to be that the conscientious researcher must take both behavior and self-reports into account whenever possible.

In the cued-recall procedure, to come now to a second procedure used in phenomenologically motivated research, the investigator begins by record-ing some significant situation such as a psychotherapy interview on tape. Once recorded, the tape is then played back in the presence of one or more participants (see, for example, the work of Bradley, 1993; Clark & Peterson, 1986; Hector, Bradley, Daigle, & Klukken, 1990; Shavelson & Stern, 1981; Shavelson, Webb, & Burstein, 1986). As a concrete example, consider the situation in which a teacher is videotaped as he or she teaches a class. Once the tape has been recorded, the investigator then replays the tape and asks the teacher to stop the tape whenever he/she "remembers what he/she was aware of at that moment in the classroom." The researcher also has the option of stopping the tape and of asking for a report whenever significant events occur on the tape (i.e., a question, a smile, excited discussion) or whenever the researcher notes that the participating instructor changes his or her behavior during the recall session itself (i.e., by smiling, wincing, becoming excited, etc.). Whenever the tape is stopped, the researcher asks questions of the following sort: "What were you aware of at that point?" "Can you tell more about that moment in the class?"

In clinical training and practice a variant (actually an ancestor) of the cued-recall process, called *interpersonal process recall* (IPR), has been used as a research procedure for evaluating the teaching and process of psycho-therapy (Kagan, 1975). Although IPR has been most widely used as a training procedure in counseling psychology, it also has been used to de-scribe and evaluate counselor interventions (Elliot, 1986; Powell & Hector, 1987) and reactions to such interventions (Bradley, 1993; Hector et al., 1989). Structured measurement formats have frequently been used for data collection, but they often are complemented by free-response formats (Elliot, 1986) in order to exploit the richness of information provided by the technique.

Although cued-recall, IPR, and self-report procedures seem to have a good deal of empirical utility in relating behavior to experience and vice versa, their major drawback is that they do not, by themselves, readily allow for a thick, rich description of the phenomenon in question. If descriptions such as those presented in preceding chapters are desired, the use of more linguistically motivated procedures such as interviews or written narratives seem more useful. Although it is possible to derive themes from self-report procedures of the types described (see Hunt & Pollio, 1995), the resulting themes are far less detailed than those deriving from dialogic or narrative procedures.

To provide a comprehensive account of current phenomenological methods, we still need to describe narrative procedures of the type used in many prior studies such as those conducted by Fischer on the experience of being anxious (1970, 1974, 1978, 1989). In this research, co-participants were asked to "please describe in as much detail as possible a situation in which you were anxious. To the extent that you can, please include in your description or characterization how you came to realize you were anxious . . . as well as what you experienced and did while you were anxious."

These instructions generally produced lengthy narratives presenting an extended description of some situation characterized as an anxious one by the participant. Once a narrative was secured, the researcher attempted to recapture the meaning of being anxious as revealed in the story. Basically, Fischer (1989) describes his procedure as involving a series of four steps or reflections:

In the first, each subject's description, which may be elaborated in the context of a follow-up interview, is regarded as a story that characterizes his or her involvement with the phenomenon of being anxious. I read and reread the description or story asking, "What's happening here? . . . What are the global units of that unfolding?" When I had realized a sense of those units – I refer to them as scenes – I mark them off with brackets on a copy of the subject's description.

When I delineated the scenes of the description, I again reflect upon them and attempt to state their respective meanings, but now from my own perspective; that is, from the perspective of a researcher who is trying to comprehend the subject's lived through experience of being anxious.

In the third [phase], I utilize the meanings of the scenes in an effort to synthesize an answer to the question: What was the psychological meaning of being anxious as it was experienced and lived by this subject in this situation? This answer is referred to as a *situated structural description*.

In the fourth and final reflection I ask: What is the psychological meaning of being anxious as a possibility that human beings may live and experience? My answer, which is called a *general structural description* of being anxious, has been realized by constructing and comparing over 25 situated structural descriptions, always looking for that which seems essential to all of them, even if present less articulately in some. (p. 134)

Thus, the procedure involves an initial reflection that divides the protocol into a series of scenes or incidents and a latter set of reflections that explicitly take place from the perspective of the researcher, first in more general terms and later in terms of his or her perspective as a psychologist. A final description is attained by reflecting on a number of situated scenarios deriving from a number of different protocols. The general situated description, which is usually couched in thematic as well as in narrative terms, presents the researcher's interpretive description of what the experience of being anxious is like for him and for his set of co-participants.

A variant on the narrative method, which is less time-intensive and derives from dialogical interview procedures, proceeds in terms of two sequential questions to be answered, in writing, by co-participants. The first of these questions is: "Please think of some times or situations in which you were aware of X – that is, about some phenomenon such as being in a role, thinking about language, etc." The second question asks the co-participant to "please select one of these situations and describe, in as much detail as you choose, your experience in that situation."

Answers given in response to the second question provide the basic content of the research, although responses to the first question also may provide useful information. So, for example, in a study concerning the experience of social role by college-age students, Beier and Pollio (1994) discovered that most of the role situations listed – being a son or daughter, trying to impress someone, being a student – concerned age-appropriate concerns of participants. The major results of this study, however, were presented in terms of thematic patterns; for the study of roles, the relevant thematic pattern is presented in Figure 11.1. As may be seen, the themes include three levels: first, the experience of a proper form to the role; second, an experience of how well I fit the role or how well others perceive it fits me; and finally, the experience of being hyperaware of other people, myself, and my body.

Although this description does not do justice to the richness of participant protocols, it does indicate that it is possible to develop a nontrivial thematic structure from the less extensive protocols of a large number of co-participants, as from the more extensive protocols of a smaller number of phenomenological interviews. The questionnaire procedure was designed to provide a condensed version of the phenomenological interview and, where the question is reasonably straightforward, seems to provide a useful alternative to the more extended interview format. Where the topic is likely to be complex and/or to require a great deal of clarification by the participant, dialogic interviews seem to be the more useful procedure. It should also be noted that once written protocols are produced by the questionnaire procedure, group interpretation may be used to develop a thematic structure of the phenomenon.

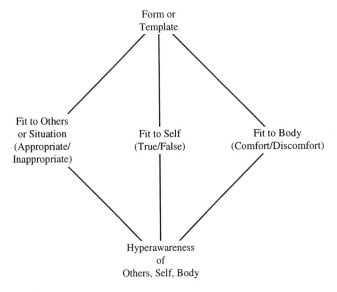

Figure 11.1. Schematic diagram of thematic structure (from Beier & Pollio, 1994)

A Small (Hermeneutic) Caveat Concerning Method

Many of the methods used to describe significant human phenomenon in existential terms are linguistic in nature. Hermeneutic analyses of the type described by Heidegger (1927/1962) and carried forward by Gadamer (1960/1975) have been concerned with explicating relationships between linguistic events (texts) and the ways in which these are interpreted. Hermeneutic approaches to understanding invariably characterize it in terms of two mutually implicative aspects: historicity and circularity (Gadamer, 1960/1975). Historicity emphasizes that understanding is a temporally finite process contextualized by preunderstandings manifested in the interpretive situation. Circularity implies that for understanding to take place, sociohistoric preunderstandings must be applied to the text at hand while simultaneously not remaining closed onto themselves.

Whenever something is interpreted as something, the interpretation will be founded essentially upon fore-conception. An interpretation is never the presuppositionless apprehending of something presented to us. . . . All interpretation operates in this foreunderstanding. Any interpretation which is to contribute to understanding must already have understood what is to be interpreted. . . . But if we see this (interpretive) circle as a vicious one and look for ways of avoiding it, even if we just sense it as an inevitable imperfection, then the act of understanding has been misunderstood from the ground up. . . . What is decisive is not to get out of the circle but to come into it in the right way. This circle of understanding is not an orbit in which any random kind of knowledge may move. It is not to be reduced to the level of a vicious circle, or even of a circle which is merely tolerated. In the circle is hidden the possibility of the most primordial kind of knowing. We genuinely take hold of the possibility only when, in our interpretation, we have understood that our first, last, and constant task is never to allow our fore-conception to be presented to us by fancies and popular conceptions, but rather to make the scientific theme secure by working out these fore-structures in terms of the things themselves. (Heidegger, 1927/1962, *Being and Time*, Section 32)

The caveat that hermeneutic theory offers to any analysis of language-based texts is as follows: Interpretation always depends upon the actions of historically finite beings who are unable to achieve an absolute perspective in coming to their interpretations. Thus, a human being and not some metaphysical framework is ultimately responsible for what is taken as knowledge. Any so-called objective method of analysis remains a human construction that is as historically and culturally bound as any other, natural science included (Merleau-Ponty, 1945/1962). Under this rendition, knowledge must be characterized as an ongoing dialogue in which new understandings are attained in relevant sociocultural contexts. The process is neither arbitrary nor preordained. Worldly facts always may be understood differently and, in the process, yield new meanings. Interpreters understand texts only in terms of categories and perspectives available to them on the basis of a culturally mediated (linguistic) tradition. In holding that there is no understanding outside of language, justifiable preunderstandings and interpretations are not themselves objective; although a justifiable interpretation must be demonstrable in terms of textual details, it is comprehensible only in terms of an extratextual tradition.

From a hermeneutic perspective, therefore, any existential-phenomenological study is one whose interpretations are informed by the philosophical tradition of existential phenomenology. This framework serves as a general preunderstanding that, when applied to a specific text, gives rise to a new understanding not reducible to the initial preunderstanding. Understanding reflects a fusion of horizons between the researcher and his or her participants. Through this fusion, the existential concerns present in participant descriptions are made thematic, although it must clearly be kept in mind that a fusion of horizons only occurs in a zone of ambiguity that is not to be reduced to the antinomy of objective fact or subjective construction. The task is to say something meaningful without attempting to elevate it to the level of atemporal truth.

The Perspectival Meanings of Reductionism

Wolfgang Köhler's book *Gestalt Psychology* (1947) ends with the following sentence: "At this point, just as at many others, it seems to be the natural fate of Gestalt Psychology to become Gestalt Biology." For the reader who has gone through Köhler's extraordinary book, it is both a surprising *and* an expected denouement: surprising because of Köhler's brilliant rejection of atomistic notions in psychology and biology, expected because of his insistence on the doctrine of isomorphism. Although isomorphism, as either fact or conjecture, has always been problematic to psychological theory, it did have an interesting implication in the hands of Gestalt psychology – namely, that the structures of perception could be used to specify the necessary structures of brain function. If perceptual events operated wholistically, so Köhler's argument went, so too must the corporeal structures of brain tissue.

In its positive light, isomorphism freed psychology to pursue its task without being overly constrained by a central nervous system that seemed to be composed of a mosaic of elements – a situation at variance with the more wholistic patternings of perceptual and other psychological events. Isomorphism also implied that a unified theory of the sciences must cut in two directions: Findings in biology, physics, and other natural sciences could no more constrain what was thinkable in psychology, sociology, and political science than the other way round. In fact, the second implication is more congenial to Gestalt theory – namely, if a fact of psychology contradicted what was known in biology, it was biology that needed to reconsider its facts at least as much, if not more, than psychology. If there were to be cross-disciplinary influences, the logic of Gestalt psychology suggested that they should go in the macro to micro direction rather than vice versa.

The most direct manner in which to grasp what this might mean for psychology is contained in an analysis on reductionism by Luria in the volume, *The Oxford Companion to the Mind* (Gregory, 1989). Following Vygotsky, Luria notes that to study a complex phenomenon, the scientist has to preserve its essential features. What this means is that "one must be able to describe their rules [of operation] without the loss of any individual characteristics." Thus, it is possible to reduce H_2O to H and O. When we look at some of the properties of H in isolation, we discover it burns; when we look at some of the properties of O in isolation, we note that it is necessary for something to burn. The main phenomena – H_2O – exhibits neither of these characteristics, suggesting that "in order not to lose the basic features of water, one may split it into units [H₂O] but not [make those units] into elements." For Luria, as for Vygotsky, the task is one of discovering the proper level for describing the phenomenon of interest. Any attempt to reduce a phenomenon to units appropriate to a different level is viewed as destroying the phenomenon.

All of this, of course, was known to Gestalt psychology. Köhler's last sentence, however, was meant to go further in order to join up with a more general view of what a proper relationship should be like between psychology and its most adjacent neighbor, biology: "It seems to be the natural fate of psychology to become biology." Within mainstream psychology, the belief always has been that psychology ultimately would give precedence to its more distinguished neighbor(s) in the natural sciences, and this was not a problem but a desirable state of affairs. Somehow psychology did not feel that it had anything valid to say unless it ultimately could be cast into the languages of biology, physics, or chemistry. Although this strategy is most obvious in sociobiological theories of mind and behavior, even Skinner, who never liked appealing to absent gods, felt that the final description of psychological phenomena must be in physical language. As with Köhler, Skinnerian psychology would ultimately have to become Skinnerian biology.

Perhaps the most revealing locale in which the issue of biological reductionism emerged was psychoanalysis. Early in his career, Freud could never quite decide whether to describe phenomena in quasi-biological terms or in more humanistic-literary ones. While Freud was postulating drives and libido, he also was characterizing human problems in terms of the myth and drama of Oedipus. Was biology or drama destiny for the human being? Freud wavered in his answer, as have most psychologists concerned with the therapeutic endeavor, and the question to be set by an existential-phenomenological approach is to provide a way out of the reductionist box that renders unto biology what is biology's and unto psychology what is psychology's.

How is this to be done? One way is to clarify the term *reductionism* itself. The word *reduction* not only occurs across scientific disciplines but in phenomenology itself. Indeed, Husserl sought to discern transcendental essences on the basis of what he called the *phenomenological reduction*. Although Merleau-Ponty (1945/1962) notes that the most important lesson taught by the attempt at phenomenological reduction is the impossibility of such a reduction, the desire to arrive at something more essential seems to have motivated Husserl's use of this term in phenomenology. In ordinary usage, reduction connotes a process of somehow making an object into something smaller. As used by biologists and phenomenologists, reduction has no such connotation; in fact, reduction in both biology and phenomenology refers to an attempt to purify something. This usage, which is less frequent in English, is also much closer to its etymological meaning, which derives from the Latin words *re* and *ductare* – to lead back to, where the implication is to "lead back to some origin."

Under this reading, it is clear that what is at issue in both biological and/or philosophical reduction is an attempt to lead us back to some domain that is not necessarily smaller but more essential. For Husserl, it meant moving away from the presuppositions of prior philosophies; for psychology, it meant moving molar behavior (or experience) back to the (more primary) domains of biology, chemistry, physics, and so forth. Freud was uncertain in his reductive tendencies and could never decide whether to lead his analysis of the human psyche back to medicine, biology, literature, drama, or development or to an eclectic domain seemingly able to incorporate all of these concerns known as *psychoanalytic theory*.

Freud's dilemma suggests a way of approaching what reductionism could lead psychology back to. Here, the answer would seem to be: to whatever the psychologist views as most significant for illuminating the phenomenon under consideration. In the same way as no single method is appropriate to all psychological phenomena, so too must we recognize the significance of multiple interpretive contexts. There is no context-free understanding of phenomena. Rather, we must always accept that any understanding is perspectival and that a context-free description, understanding, or explanation is not possible for phenomena falling within the purview of psychology. Investigator and phenomena co-select the relevant disciplinary contexts of interpretation, and the belief that physical (or biological) description is true, in some final sense of the term, must be dismissed as the only valid goal of psychological description.

Such freedom of choice may be viewed as promoting conceptual disorder or chaos. Merleau-Ponty (1945/1962) suggests a different interpretation – namely, that the psychologist is a perpetual beginner and must take nothing for granted about what is or is not a proper approach to the study of human existence. Phenomenological psychology, like phenomenological philosophy, may temporarily find itself in biology, literature, poetry, or drama and be no less revealing than if it temporarily found itself in any or all of these disciplines at once. This state of affairs suggests that psychology does not have to decide a priori that it is important to interpret its phenomena in terms of biology; rather, what seems a better strategy is to explore those conditions under which psychology and biology yield concordant and discordant interpretations of specific phenomena. Biology is never irrelevant to psychology, but neither is history, literature, or poetry; all must be coordinated for the psychologist to clarify points of discordance as well as points of agreement. The freedom afforded by such an approach to reductionism is meant to release psychology not from the relevant aspects of other disciplines but from the constraint that human existence ultimately must be explicated on the basis of only one system of thought or one method of inquiry. The research psychologist need no longer worry about giving something up when room is made for phenomenological thought in psychology. All phenomenology asks of psychology is that it focus on its phenomenon at least as much as on its neighbors. The task is to say something meaningful, whether such meaning is to be construed in biological terms or in terms of some other relevant interpretive framework.

Experience Revisited: Some New Descriptions and Relationships

The first, and probably still most psychologically astute, description of human consciousness was provided by William James (1890, 1899) at the end of the last century. As may be remembered, what James called the *stream of thought* was described in terms of a set of interrelated characteristics. Although much of his discussion was couched in seemingly dualistic language – "Now we are seeing; now we are hearing; now recollecting, now expecting; now loving, now hating; and in a hundred other ways we *know* our *mind*s to be alternately engaged" (James, 1892, p. 154; italics added) – the overall impression is more in tune with phenomenology than cognitive psychology. At its best, James's description offered a clear appreciation for unreflected, first-person experience that was concerned as much with what it was about as well as how it moved and selected among its variegated objects. For one of the few times in the history of philosophy or psychology, human experience was convincingly rendered in terms of experientially relevant principles.

Similar to the majority of his contemporaries in both philosophy and psychology, James used the term *consciousness* to describe his topic, although such a term seems too abstract to capture the headlong flow of human experience that was James's more immediate content. For this reason, the term *experience* seems the proper one for describing our first-person dealings with the world. The term *consciousness*, on the other hand, seems better reserved for more philosophical or scientific usage – that is, where a specific attempt is made to describe the general structures of human experience in an abstract and schematic way.

With this understanding, it is possible to reiterate, with significant elaboration, the three major characteristics offered in Chapter 1 as criterial for a first-person description of human experience:

1. It is intentional.
2. It is constantly changing yet sensibly continuous.
3. It is contextual.

Intentionality

In its original use in phenomenological philosophy, the intentional nature of human experience simply meant that human beings never experience experience, and that all experiencing requires a phenomenal point of reference. Experience is always relational, suggesting that the human being is never a self-contained entity searching for something to understand, look at, or consider. Rather, experience always takes place in relation to something other than itself, and it is only meaningful to describe our social, temporal, and embodied experiences as relating me to the social and natural worlds without ever implying that I could experience anything – experience included – independent of just such a pattern of ongoing relationships.

All of this, of course, was known to Husserl, Heidegger, and Merleau-Ponty; there is nothing new in characterizing human existence as a network of relationships perpetually directed toward but never fully encompassing a content other than itself. Merleau-Ponty, in fact, approvingly ended his *Phenomenology of Perception* (1945/1962) with the following quote from St. Exupéy: "Man is a network of relationships and these alone matter to him." What does raise the possibility of saying something new about intentionality, however, takes place when an attempt is made to describe intentionality prior to its thematization as a foundational postulate of phenomenological philosophy – that is, to describe it as an experience rather than as a concept whose structure is assumed to be known. If this is done, we note that the focal objects of experience invariably are more compelling and definite than the person for whom they are figural; that is, one pole in every intentional relationship is experienced as better articulated and more definite than the other.

Consider the case of what ordinarily is called *perception*: here, the object perceived is always better defined and more compelling than the perceiver, with the latter often experienced as an uncertain and ill-defined presence. Similar contrasts apply to any experience described in intentional terms: There is always some aspect of the first-person field that is clearer and more definite than some second aspect of that same field, which is more ambiguous and ill-defined. One locale in which this difference occurs most clearly concerns the experience of looking at oneself in the mirror. Within this context, the I-seen-in-the-mirror is clearly different from the I-who-sees-in-the-mirror, with the difference being that the mirror-I is clear, stable, and well bounded, and the I-that-sees, if figural at all, is vague and unstable.

If we accept the human experience of what is figural as more distinct than the I for whom it is figural, whatever definition of I is attained must depend upon the structuring provided by the focal object and the field within which it is situated. It appears that Buber (1923/1970) was correct in describing the I as a fundamentally relational being-event that assumes a different meaning and configuration depending on its mode of relating to the world. Such openness and variability lead to the further possibility that the changing nature of experience is not a contingent aspect of human existence but one fully comprehensible within a phenomenological description of intentionality itself. When we move from the concept of intentionality to the experience of intentionality, we note an asymmetrical relationship in which the noetic pole is considerably more indeterminant and open than the noematic one.

Descriptions that explore the phenomenal experience of intentionality are few and far between. One of the most engaging is provided in an essay by D. E. Harding entitled "On Having No Head." This essay was excerpted in Hofstadter and Dennett's book *The Mind's I* (1981) and appears in a section entitled "A Sense of Self." Harding's essay begins with his discovery that experientially he has no head: "It was something absurdly simple. . . . I stopped thinking (and came to the conclusion that) to look was enough." When Harding did look, he found "khaki trouserlegs terminating downward in a pair of brown shoes, khaki sleeves terminating sideways in a pair of pink hands, and a khaki shirtfront terminating upward in absolutely nothing whatever."

And what was the emotional impact of this "discovery"?

It was all, quite literally, breathtaking. I seemed to stop breathing altogether, absorbed in the Given. Here it was, this superb scene, brightly shining in the clear air, alone and unsupported, mysteriously suspended in the void, and (and this was the real miracle, the wonder and delight) utterly free of "me," unstained by any observer. Its total presence was my total absence, body and soul. Lighter than air, clearer than glass, altogether released from myself, I was nowhere around.

Yet in spite of the magical and uncanny quality of this vision, it was no dream, no esoteric revelation. Quite the reverse: it felt like a sudden waking from the sleep of ordinary life, an end to dreaming. It was self luminous reality for once swept clean of all obscuring mind. It was the revelation, at long last, of the perfectly obvious. It was a lucid moment in a confused life-history. It was a ceasing to ignore something which (since early childhood at any rate) I had always been too busy or too clever to see. In short, it was all perfectly simple and plain and straightforward, beyond argument, thought, and words. There arose no questions, no reference beyond the experience itself, but only peace and a quiet joy, and the sensation of having dropped an intolerable burden.

In commenting on this piece, Hofstadter (1981) muses on the unspoiled and childlike nature of Harding's essay and discovery. Hofstadter, however, feels offended "at an intellectual" level and seems initially unable to conceive how anyone "can sincerely entertain such notions without embarrassment." After going on for a few more paragraphs, he begins to sense the significance of the step that he, along with the rest of Western philosophical thought, took by repudiating the importance of direct experience: "But this stepping outside of myself is a gigantic and self-denying step that serves to replace much direct knowledge I have of myself." Although Hofstadter senses the paradox, he is unable to resolve it, because he is unable to get past the fact that "he has a head," and comes to the conclusion that his "self" is a "there-being" and not a thing. Under an empirical evaluation of the experience of intentionality, we are again led to the correctness of Heidegger's description and to the power of his observation: Self and *Dasein* are not the same, and both imply a different understanding of what it is to be a human being.

Temporality

Variability is an essential aspect to human experiencing, and this "fact," now revealed by a phenomenological and literary description of intentionality, seems to provide an empirical basis for the second major characteristic of consciousness – namely, that it is both constantly changing and sensibly continuous. This aspect of experience is captured in James's image of the stream as well as in his description of consciousness as consisting "of an alternation of flights and perchings."

Whereas the stream metaphor captures the general sense of James's description, the flight-and-perchings metaphor is meant to capture distinctions between the transitional and substantive aspects of consciousness. James, in fact, concluded his discussion of this metaphor by explicitly making a contrast between what he termed the *focus* and *fringe* of experience. In this way, he described an early appreciation for what later Gestalt writers would term the *figure/ground* structure of human experience, a psychological structure having application considerably beyond its original use in relation to perceptual events. In fact, in the hands of Gestalt social psychologists such as Kurt Lewin and Solomon Asch, the concept of figure/ground was generalized to include the total relational matrix within which human life is lived and reflected upon. It is this latter sense – as well as in the somewhat more limited one used by Gestalt perceptual theory – that the notion of ground has been used in the present analysis. What is new to this analysis, however, is that three of the major existential grounds – body, time, and others – have been articulated on the basis of first-person dialogues, thereby making it possible not only to assert that a figure/ground structure characterizes human experience but also to describe potential patterns among the major grounds, including the ground of world not explicitly thematized in the present set of studies.

Before getting to this task, however, one significant implication to the figure/ground structure of human experience must be made, and this concerns the possibility that the continuity of experience and, through it, of personal existence, is provided by the continuity of its grounds rather than by the continuity of a self-sustaining entity known as *consciousness*. Consciousness is relational in the most profound sense of the term, and any attempt to locate it in the person (as James sometimes seems to do and most contemporary psychologists regularly do) misses a potentially deeper relationship between the intentional and figure/ground aspects of human existence. Only if the continuity of experience is carried by the grounds of consciousness, and not by some segregated bearer of consciousness, is it possible to answer James's celebrated question (1890) as to how Peter and Paul know who is Paul and who is Peter when both awake after a night's sleep, surgery involving anesthetic, being hit on the head, a mystical experience, or, in short, after any one of a number of cases in which there is a break in the continuity of personal existence.

The simplest answer is that Paul experiences Paul and (Peter, Peter) not only on the basis of remembering which "stream" is which – as James suggested – but, more importantly, on the basis of his (their) reimmersion into the continuing grounds of his (their) everyday life. As empirical results concerning the experience of falling apart reveal (see Chapter 9), such experiences occur primarily when the grounds defining personal existence shift radically, not when consciousness, conceived as some structure known as *self* or *ego*, disintegrates or decomposes. What we experience as our "self" is provided with continuity on the basis of its continuing situatedness within the relatively unchanging grounds of world, body, time, and others and not vice versa. To use the Jamesian metaphor once more: The stream of consciousness is not to be located within the person but in relationships to the various grounds contextualizing personal existence.

The reassuring sense of personal continuity that we experience, to use Erikson's (1963) description of identity, is sustained and supported by the major grounds of human existence. In nontechnical language, we may say that time supports the continuity of personal existence in terms of memories and projects, body supports it in terms of habit and brute corporeality, other people support it in terms of individuals significant to us as well as in terms of our sociocultural milieu, and the natural world supports it in terms of objects, places, and natural contexts. Personal existence (identity, ego, self, I) is also sustained by our reflections on each of these domains as well as by the reflections of others, both in our immediate world and in our history. The self, to choose one term among many, is not an independent agent but is always and already a contextually held "there-being" (*Da-sein*), continuously in flux and continually delimited by encounters with otherness of any and all kinds. It is neither a transparent knower nor an executive homunculus.

Contextuality

The first and foremost observation to make about the contextual nature of human consciousness is that it consists of four major grounds: time, body, others, and world. In each of the preceding chapters, one or all of these grounds was spontaneously mentioned by participants having no prior knowledge of existential philosophy nor specifically asked about them in describing personal experiences of quite disparate topics. Although such observations do not prove that body, time, others, and world exhaustively provide the contexts within which human events and situations assume their experiential shape, they do suggest that these grounds regularly contextualize experiences as different from one another as being in love and being lonely or falling apart and making amends. In addition, such findings also encourage a search for potential patterns of relationship among the grounds themselves in the hope that such patterns will allow us to describe more precisely the ways in which they serve to support the experience of personal continuity so frequent in descriptions of significant human topics.

As a start, consider the major themes characterizing the human experience of the human body: Vitality and Activity (engagement), Instrument and Object (corporeality), and Expression and Appearance (interpersonal meaning). As must be the case, each theme in the experience of body only emerged as figural against the more inclusive domains of others, time, and world, and we should expect comprehensible relationships between specific themes of embodiment and one or another of these grounds. The thematic experience of body as interpersonal, for example, provides a clear case in point – namely, that this aspect of the human experience of the human body must be grounded by interrelatedness to and with other people. Both subthemes defining the general theme of interpersonal meaning require another person (or persons) to perceive the body as appearance, expression, or both.

A second theme of embodiment, Vitality and Activity, yields a focus on engagement with the world as a relevant ground. In describing this theme, respondents reported being primarily aware of the physical world, with little attention paid to the corporeal body per se. Experiences of vitality and activity seem to concern personal absorption in the world and, while the person may sometimes experience bodily activity directly, the overall impression is of being caught up in the world or in some ongoing project of that world.

The final theme characterizing experiences of the body was that of Instrument and Object. Not only does this theme imply that the body is experienced as a separate and enduring object but also as a mode of doing, as an instrument enabling us to accomplish present and future projects. Both aspects of this theme implicate time not only in the obvious sense that objects endure and projects are temporal but also in the more subtle sense that skillful use of an instrument requires synchronizing ourselves with the requirements of the instrument and the task. This meaning was expressed by one of our participants, originally a dancer and now a professor of dance, who noted in describing a dancer's body as his instrument: "It's all a matter of getting the movements in the right sequence, at the right tempo."

Turning now to experiences of lived time, it is possible to relate various themes of temporal experience to the grounds provided by body, world, and others. A relatively clear case is afforded by the theme of Tempo, a theme characterized by contrasting experiences of change in speed and regularity. Returning to specific examples used by participants to express this theme reveals that Tempo often emerged as figural against the ground of bodily events:

I've got a fast metabolism, and I'm constantly on the move.
My husband is slow and even tempered.

In both cases, Tempo was described in terms of a contrast between two or more embodied experiences, suggesting that the body grounds this aspect of lived time in the same way as lived time grounds certain aspects of bodily experience (i.e., those concerned with doing).

A second theme characterizing lived time is that of Limits and Choices. Although this theme entails a focus on doing, its major focus is on the limits imposed by the temporal organization of contemporary social and interpersonal life. Not only did participants report being aware of the need to coordinate project deadlines; they also were aware of needing to schedule their day, week, or year so as not to violate social convention or interpersonal relationships. Being late, being early, or being on time are not neutral events; all have clear meanings in regard to our relations with other people. In addition, socially significant temporal markers such as birthdays, anniversaries, graduations, and holidays were experienced as exercising a limit on what the person could do during that specific period as well as expressing a significance to the other person if left unobserved. As should be clear, age norms exist that define (i.e., limit) what is socially expected at any given point in life.

A final pair of temporal themes concerned experiences of Change-and-Continuity and its somewhat more fragmented counterpart, Now or Never. At its most basic, Change-and-Continuity refers to instances of people or things changing yet remaining the same. Included within this theme are experiences we have with significant other people – children with parents, parents with children, old friends and classmates with one another, and so on – as well as with changes taking place in the natural world as ordinary as day and night or as complex as the changing topography of our landscape. Experiences of change and continuity also derive from bodily experiences: Although aches and pains partially define the subtheme of body as object, they also provide bodily instances of change and continuity. Experiences of now/never also may be explicated in terms of body (as when I am dieting), others (who aren't satisfying me), and world ("Why isn't what I want here now?").

Similar to the domain of body, the major themes defining the human experience of time exhibit clear relationships to one another and to all remaining domains. Although some relationships are more obvious than others, what is clear is that the grounds encompassing our experiences are themselves sensibly organized. We come to our experiences of time in terms of body, world, and others just as we come to our experience of body, world, and others in terms of our experiences of time.

The experience of others was defined by three themes: Connection (proximity and synchrony), Benefit (satisfaction and annoyance), and Comparison (similarity and difference). The most obvious way in which one of these themes relates to one or more of the remaining grounds concerns that of Connection. Both subthemes in which experiences of connection were figural described it in terms of *distance* (near and far) or in terms of being in or out of *synchrony* with someone else. The first subtheme is an embodied, world-oriented one, whereas the second is a more temporal one. To be near someone depends upon embodied experiences of worldly space; to be in synchrony with someone builds upon lived experiences of time. Both experiences are lacking when we confront a barrier to relating, as in cases of being lonely (see Chapter 6), making amends (Chapter 7), or dealing with the death of a loved one (Chapter 10). The experiences of disjuncture, barrier, and distance attendant on these experiences all attest to the significance of synchrony and closeness as metaphors of human connection, especially as these take place in intimate relationships (see

Chapter 8). These and other considerations suggest that world, time, and body provide crucial reference points for interpersonal connection in the same way that experiences of interpersonal connection provide reference points for experiences of lived time and/or lived space.

The remaining themes defining the human experience of other people concern issues of Benefit (satisfaction and annoyance) and Comparison (similarity and difference). The role of the body in the case of Benefit seems clear: Experiences of benefit often are embodied in nature, and we regularly describe relationships as comfortable or soothing and annoying or irritating. The role of time in relation to this theme is a bit more complex, although experiences of benefit were described as evincing a concern with a present or future reaction that someone else has or will have in response to what I do or did. The theme of Comparison also was described as taking place within a complex ground composed of both time and body. Another person may be experienced as similar (or different) in relation to me or to other people, in terms of his or her actions as well as in terms of predictions I make concerning how he or she will react in some specific situation. Although other relations may be described, the important point is that, similar to each of the remaining grounds, our experience of other people always implicates one or another aspect of these grounds as the proper context for our more figural experiences of other people.

A final ground to human experience is that of world or more precisely, the world of things, place, and nature. Although the present set of studies made no attempt to describe the thematic structure of these domains, it is clear that any approach emphasizing being-in-the-world as a significant aspect must accept a groundedness in the physical world as given. Within an existential approach, the human experience of the natural world is unreflectedly given to us by our movements, our experiences of changes and stability, and by our attempts to mark out various portions of the world as our own. Just as the worlds of body, time, and others contextualize our experiences of nature, things, and place, it should be clear that the natural world provides a significant ground for each of the other major contexts of human life.

But what is the nature of this "world" when considered phenomenologically? It seems clear that it cannot be the world given to us by physical science any more than it can be a solipsistic representation contained entirely in consciousness. These positions are, of course, philosophical positions, and the nature of phenomenological psychology is to look not to philosophy but to experience in defining what is to be meant by its terms and concepts. When Merleau-Ponty attempts to describe the natural world and things, he does so by way of our perceptions of things and the natural world. Although there may be hallucination and illusion in that world, he concludes that "what is certain for us is that there is a world. To ask oneself whether the world is real is to fail to understand what one is asking, since the world is not a sum of things which might always be called into question, but the inexhaustible reservoir from which things are drawn. . . . The world is the invariable framework of all illusion and disillusion: I know myself only insofar as I am inherent in time and in the world" (1945/1962, pp. 344–5).

As in all things phenomenological and existential, the person and the world co-constitute each other, and while philosophy or natural science may make one or another description of the world most significant, what must not be lost sight of is the undeniable presence of a world that is certain and co-determinate with us. Heidegger's concept of "throwness" seems most relevant here; we are thrown into a world that both supports and limits our projects. The play on words which reveals that project (*entwurf*) and thrown (*geworfen*) are both derived from the same verb is as profound as it playful – to have a world, one must project oneself forward, a move indicating a certain confidence in the continuity and changeability of the world and the person. Far from being an "alien" presence, person and world co-determine each other even if Western thought is sometimes able to envision only one of these coordinates as existing independently of the other. The world, therefore, is as ambiguous as the being for whom it sets a context and a horizon.

Some Further Thematic Similarities

Although preceding paragraphs have attempted to describe points of similarity among the major existential contexts that yield quite reasonable relationships, a few additional ones seem uniquely significant for psychology. Consider the thematic pair *first/slow* (tempo) in regard to time and the pair *similarity/difference* (comparison) in regard to other people. Both themes refer to a perceptual encounter – comparison in the case of people, tempo in the case of time. Is there a similar perceptual aspect to body? Here, the relevant theme seems to be Expression and Appearance, or that theme concerned with the body as a perceptual event for someone else. Although the specific nature of the perceptual encounter is different in each domain, what is similar is that regardless of whether we are concerned with time, body, the world, or others, a significant aspect of our experience is perceptual in nature.

Returning one final time to the various themes characterizing the major grounds, it is possible to relate the bodily theme of Instrument and Object to the temporal theme of Limits and Choices. Both themes refer to experiences of personal activity: in one case, of using the body to achieve a specific goal; in the second case, of choosing to perform some action and of accepting the limit that what was done precludes what might have been done. Within the domain of others, the relevant theme is that of Benefit – where other people are experienced in terms of their differential reactions to what we did (or did not) do. In all three cases, there is a thematic awareness of personal action or what in more ordinary terms would be called *behavior.* Regardless of whether we are concerned with body, time, or others, a significant aspect to our experience concerns our present, past, or projected actions in specific worldly situations.

Perhaps, paradoxically, this final set of similarities suggests that had psychology begun with an unprejudiced description of its content as experienced, it would have arrived at a discipline emphasizing both behavior and perceptual experience. Romanyshyn (1978) seems to have had something of this in mind when he suggested that psychology be construed as the disciplined study of "behavior-and-experience" so as to emphasize their inseparability. The relationship between the two, however, is not one of "cause and effect, nor even of manifest to latent content, but rather . . . [as a] reversible figure of psychology." Romanyshyn thus suggests that we are free to emphasize one or the other (or both) aspect as significant, provided we never lose sight of the fact that they are inseparable facets of a single field of existence.

One consequence to considering behavior-and-experience as the content matter of psychology was noted in regard to studies using contemporaneous self-reports and behavioral observations. What was then suggested on methodological grounds – that interpretive priority *not* be given to one or the other perspective – may now be set within a more extended framework of what behavior-and-experience means for a psychological observer and for the person serving as his or her research subject. From this more inclusive framework, rendering existence as behavior-and-experience stresses that there are no situation-free observations any more than there are isolated subjects or investigators.

This last, seemingly methodological, point leads to what must be the most general conclusion to be drawn from an existential-phenomenological approach to psychology – namely, that human experience and human behavior only emerge within the ground of an ongoing network of relationships invariably encompassing experiences of time, body, others, and world. Within the context provided by this complexly interwoven field, focal events and actions assume a specific form only in terms of limits and supports provided by that field. In every specific case, the focal event (or action) emerges in conjunction with a more variable and ill-defined aspect of the field that historically has been termed *person, self, ego,* or, more simply, *I.* Within the present context, the I can be thought of only as a relational event, always and already defined by ongoing relationships with its field and never a segregated unity unto itself.

This conclusion suggests that the chief gain of an existential-phenomenological approach to psychology is to offer a way of uniting those contemporary approaches emphasizing an objective or behavioral view with those stressing a more subjective or mental perspective. This synthesis can be achieved by recognizing that human existence always takes place in context, never in the interior of an impregnable self or cogito. As Merleau-Ponty (1945/1962) put it in his famous answer to the question, "What is phenomenology?":

Probably the chief gain from phenomenology is to have united extreme subjectivism and extreme objectivism in its notion of the world or rationality.... To say that there exists rationality is to say that perspectives blend, perceptions confirm each other, and meaning emerges. But it should not be set in a realm apart, transposed into absolute spirit, or into a world in the realist sense. The phenomeno-logical world is not pure being, but the sense which is revealed where the paths of my various experiences intersect, and also where my own and other people's inter-sect and engage each other like gears.... The phenomenological world is not the bringing to explicit expression of a pre-existing being, but the laying down of being. [It] is not the reflection of a pre-existing truth ... [but] the act of bringing truth into being. (p. xx).

This answer, offered to a philosophy concerned about relinquishing cherished beliefs, also seems applicable to psychology. What existential phenomenology offers to psychology is the possibility of overcoming the split between mind and body, spirit and world, and subjective and objective knowledge not by denying one in favor of the other but by demonstrating they are interrelated moments of a more dynamic and interconnected total-ity – that of contextualized human existence forever committed to a world it can never totally comprehend but toward which it is continually directed. Only if such interconnectedness is acknowledged will it be possible for psychology to pursue its overriding aim: to describe human existence in a way that is methodologically rigorous and conceptually attuned to the complexity of its topic – the nature and meaning of ongoing human life.

References

Aanstoos, C. (1986). Phenomenology and the psychology of thinking. In P. Ashworth, A. Giorgi, & A. de Koning (Eds.), *Qualitative research in psychology* (pp. 79–116). Pittsburgh: Duquesne University Press.

Adam, K. S., Lohrenz, J. G., & Harper, D. (1973). Suicidal ideation and parental loss: A preliminary research report. *Canadian Psychiatric Association Journal, 18*, 95–100.

Ainsworth, M. D. (1985). Patterns of attachment. *Clinical Psychologist, 38*, 27–29.

Ainsworth, M. D. (1989). Attachments beyond infancy. *American Psychologist, 44*, 709–716.

Amato, J. (1982). *Guilt and gratitude: A study of the origins of contemporary conscience.* London: Greenwood Press.

Ames, L. B. (1946). The development of the sense of time in the young child. *Journal of Genetic Psychology, 68*, 97–125.

Amore, R. C. (1974). The Letendix philosophical systems. In F. H. Holck (Ed.), *Death and Eastern thought.* Nashville: Abingdon Press.

Anderson, C. A., Horowitz, L. M., & French, R. (1983). Attribution style in lonely and depressed people. *Journal of Personality and Social Psychology, 45*, 127–136.

Anderson, P. F. (1983). Marketing, scientific progress, and the scientific method. *Journal of Marketing, 47*, 18–31.

Anderson, P. F. (1986). On method in consumer research: A critical relativist perspective. *Journal of Consumer Research, 13*, 155–173.

Arendt, H. (1958). *The human condition.* Chicago: University of Chicago Press.

Arlow, J. A. (1986). Psychoanalysis and time. *Journal of the American Psychoanalytic Association, 34*, 507–528.

Aronow, E., Rauchway, A., Peller, M., & DeVito, A. (1980). The value of self in relation to fear of death. *Omega, 11*, 37–44.

Asch, S. E. (1951). Effects of group pressure upon the modification and distortion of judgments. In H. Guetzkow (Ed.), *Groups, leadership and men.* Pittsburgh: Carnegie University Press.

Asch, S. E. (1956). Studies of independence and conformity: A minority of one against a unanimous majority. *Psychological Monographs, 70* (9, Whole No. 416).

Atchley, R. C. (1982). The aging self. *Psychotherapy: Theory, Research and Practice, 19*, 388–396.

Atwood, G. E., & Stolorow, R. D. (1984). *Structures of subjectivity: Explorations in psychoanalytic phenomenology.* Hillsdale, NJ: Analytic Press.

Bach, S. (1980). Self-love and object-love: Some problems of self and object constancy, differentiation and integration. In R. Lax, S. Bach, & J. Burland (Eds.), *Rapprochement: The critical subphase of separation-individuation.* New York: Aronson.

Bardis, P. D. (1971). Erotometer: A technique for the measurement of heterosexual love. *International Review of Sociology, 1,* 71–77.

Bardis, P. D. (1979). The kinetic-potential theory of love. In M. Cook & G. Wilson (Eds.), *Love and attraction: An international conference.* New York: Pergamon Press.

Barthes, R. (1977). Introduction to the structural analysis of narratives. In *Image, music, text* (Stephen Heath, Trans.). New York: Hill and Wang.

Barnes, H. (1956). Introduction. In J.-P. Sartre (Ed.), *Being and nothingness.* New York: Philosophical Library.

Barry, W. A. (1970). Marriage research and conflict: An integrative review. *Psychological Bulletin, 73,* 41–54.

Baruch, G., & Barnett, R. C. (1983). Adult daughters' relationships with their mothers. *Journal of Marriage and Family, 45,* 601–606.

Baruch, G., & Brooks-Gunn, J. (1984). *Women in midlife.* New York: Plenum Press.

Bascue, L. (1973). Relationship of time orientation and time attitudes to death anxiety in elderly people. *Dissertation Abstracts International, 34,* 866–867.

Bascue, L. O., & Lawrence, R. E. (1977). A study of subjective time and death anxiety in the elderly. *Omega, 8,* 81–90.

Baum, M. (1971). Love, marriage and the division of labor. *Sociological Inquiry, 41,* 107–117.

Baumeister, R. F. (1987). How the self became a problem: A psychological review of historical research. *Journal of Personality and Social Psychology, 52,* 163–176.

Becker, E. (1971). *The birth and death of meaning.* New York: Free Press.

Becker, E. (1973). *The denial of death.* New York: Free Press.

Beebe, B., Stern, D., & Jaffe, J. (1979). The kinesthetic rhythm of mother–infant interaction. In A. Siegman & S. Felstein (Eds.), *Of speech and time: Temporal patterns of interpersonal context.* Hillsdale, NJ: Lawrence Erlbaum.

Beier, B., & Pollio, H. R. (1994). A thematic analysis of the experience of being in a role. *Sociological Spectrum, 14,* 257–272.

Belenky, M. F., Clinchy, B. M., Goldberg, N. R., & Tarule, J. M. (1986). *Women's ways of knowing: The development of self, voice and mind.* New York: Basic Books.

Belk, R., Sherry, J. F., & Wallendorf, M. (1988). A naturalistic inquiry into buyer and seller behavior at a swap meet. *Journal of Consumer Research, 14,* 449–470.

Belk, R., Sherry, J. F., & Wallendorf, M. (1989). The sacred and the profane in consumer behavior: Theodicy on the Odyssey. *Journal of Consumer Research, 16,* 1–38.

Bell, B. D. (1975). The experimental manipulation of death attitudes. *Omega, 6,* 199–205.

Bell, R. R. (1971). *Marriage and family interaction* (3rd ed.). Homewood, IL: Dorsey Press.

Bellah, R. N., Madsen, R., Sullivan, W. M., Swidler, A., & Tipton, S. M. (1985). *Habits of the heart.* Berkeley, CA: University of California Press.

Berger, P. L., & Luckmann, T. (1966). *The social construction of reality.* Garden City, NY: Doubleday.

Bergson, H. (1896/1991). *Matter and memory* (N. Paul & W. Palmer, Trans.). New York: Zone Books.

Bernard, J. (1972). *The future of marriage.* New York: Bantam.

Bernikow, L. (1982). Alone: Yearning for companionship in America. *The New York Times Magazine,* Aug. *15,* 24–34.

Bernstein, R. J. (1986). From hermeneutics to praxis. In B. Wachterhauser (Ed.), *Hermeneutics and modern philosophy.* Albany, NY: State University Press of New York.

Berscheid, E., Dion, D. D., Walster, E., & Walster, G. W. (1971). Physical attractiveness and dating choice: A test of the matching hypothesis. *Journal of Experimental Social Psychology, 7,* 173–189.

Berscheid, E., & Fei, J. (1977). Romantic love: Sexual jealousy. In G. Clanton & L. Smith (Eds.), *Jealousy* (pp. 101–109). Englewood Cliffs, NJ: Prentice Hall.

Bleicher, J. (1980). *Contemporary hermeneutics.* London: Routledge & Kegan Paul.

Bolt, M. (1978). Purpose in life and death concern. *The Journal of Genetic Psychology, 132,* 159–160.

Boss, M. (1979). *Existential foundations of medicine and psychology.* New York: Jason Aronson.

Bowlby, J. (1958). The nature of the child's tie to his mother. *International Journal of Psycho-Analysis, 39,* 350–373.

Bowlby, J. (1977). The making and breaking of affectional bonds: Aetiology and psychopathology in the light of attachment theory. *British Journal of Psychiatry, 130,* 201–210.

Bowman, C. C. (1955). Loneliness and social change. *American Journal of Psychiatry, 112,* 194–198.

Boyar, J. I. (1964). *The construction and partial validation of a scale for the measurement of the fear of death.* Unpublished doctoral dissertation, University of Rochester, Rochester, NY.

Boyden, T., Carroll, J. S., & Maier, R. A. (1984). Similarity and attraction in homosexual males: The effects of age and masculinity–femininity. *Sex Roles, 10,* 939–948.

Bradley, K. M. (1993). *A phenomenological investigation of participant's experiences of positive events in the therapy process.* Unpublished doctoral dissertation, University of Tennessee, Knoxville, TN.

Bradley, N. C. (1947). The growth of the knowledge of time in children of school age. *British Journal of Psychology, 38,* 67–78.

Bragg, M. E. (1979). A comparative study of loneliness and depression. *Dissertation Abstracts International, 39,* 6109B.

Brandon, S. G. F. (1962). *Man and his destiny in the great religions.* Manchester, England: Manchester University Press.

Brandt, L. W. (1968). The phenomenology of the self-concept. *Existential Psychiatry, 6,* 422–432.

Buber, M. (1957). Guilt and guilt feelings. *Psychiatry, 20,* 114–129.

Buber, M. (1923/1970). *I and thou* (W. Kaufmann, Trans.). New York: Charles Scribner's Sons.

Buchwald, C., & Blatt, S. J. (1974). Personality and the experience of time. *Journal of Consulting and Clinical Psychology, 42,* 639–644.

Burnam, M. A., Pennebaker, J. W., & Glass, D. C. (1975). Time-consciousness, achievement-striving, and the Type A coronary prone behavior pattern. *Journal of Abnormal Psychology, 84*, 76–79.

Buss, D. M. (1988). The evolutionary biology of love. In R. Sternberg & M. Barnes (Eds.), *The psychology of love* (pp. 100–118). New Haven, CT: Yale University Press.

Buss, D. M. (1989). The evolution of human intrasexual competition: Tactics of mate attraction. *Journal of Personality and Social Psychology, 54*, 616–628.

Button, E. J., Fransella, F., & Slade, P. D. (1977). A reappraisal of body perception disturbance in anorexia nervosa. *Psychological Medicine, 7*, 235–243.

Byrne, D. (1971). *The attraction paradigm.* New York: Academic Press.

Byrne, D., Clore, G. L., & Smeaton, G. (1986). The attraction hypothesis: Do similar attitudes affect anything? *Journal of Personality and Social Psychology, 51*, 1167–1170.

Byrne, D., Ervin, C. R., & Lambert, J. (1970). Continuity between the experimental study of attraction and "real life" computer dating. *Journal of Personality and Social Psychology, 16*, 157–165.

Calabresi, R., & Cohen, J. (1968). Personality and time attitudes. *Journal of Abnormal Psychology, 73*, 431–439.

Calder, B. J., & Tybout, A. M. (1987). What consumer research is. *Journal of Consumer Research, 14*, 136–140.

Caporeal, L. R. (1989). Mechanisms matter: The difference between sociobiology and evolutionary biology. *Behavioral and Brain Science, 12*, 17–18.

Carse, J. P. (1980). *Death and existence: A conceptual history of human mortality.* New York: John Wiley & Sons.

Casper, R. C., Halmi, K. A., Goldberg, C., Eckert, E. D., & Davis, J. M. (1979). Disturbances in body image estimation as related to other characteristics and outcome in anorexia nervosa. *British Journal of Psychiatry, 134*, 60–66.

Cattell, R. B., & Nesselroade, J. R. (1967). Likeness and completeness theories examined by 16 personality factor measures on stable and unstable married couples. *Journal of Personality and Social Psychology, 7*, 351–361.

Cespi, A., & Horbener, E. S. (1990). Continuity and change: Assortive marriage and the consistency of personality in adulthood. *Journal of Personality and Social Psychology, 58*, 250–258.

Chapple, E. D. (1940). Personality difference as described by invariant properties with individuals in interaction. *Proceedings of the National Academy of Sciences, 26*, 10–16.

Chodorow, N. (1978). *The reproduction of mothering: Psychoanalysis and the sociology of gender.* Berkeley, CA: University of California Press.

Chodorow, N. (1980). Gender, relation, and difference in psychoanalytic perspective. In H. Eisenstein & A. Jardine (Eds.), *The future of difference* (pp. 3–19). Boston: G. K. Hall & Co.

Christ, P. E. I. (1961). Attitudes toward death among a group of acute geriatric patients. *Journal of Gerontology, 16*, 56–59.

Cimbalo, R. S., Faling, V., & Mousaw, P. (1976). The course of love: A cross-sectional design. *Psychological Reports, 38*, 1292–1294.

Clark, C. M., & Peterson, P. L. (1986). Teacher's thought processes. In M. Wittrock (Ed.), *Handbook of research on teaching* (pp. 255–295). New York: Collier-Macmillan.

Clarke, A. C. (1952). An examination of the operation of residential propinquity as a factor in mate selection. *American Sociological Review, 27*, 17–22.

Colaizzi, P. F. (1978). Psychological research as the phenomenologist views it. In R. Valle & M. King (Eds.), *Existential-phenomenological alternatives for psychology* (pp. 48–71). New York: Oxford University Press.

Colarusso, C. A. (1979). The development of time sense – from birth to object constancy. *International Journal of Psychoanalysis, 60*, 243–251.

Colarusso, C. A. (1987). The development of time sense: From object constancy to adolescence. *Journal of the American Psychoanalytic Association, 35*, 119–144.

Colarusso, C. A. (1988). The development of time sense in adolescence. *Psychoanalytic Study of the Child, 43*, 149–197.

Colarusso, C. A. (1991). The development of time sense in the young adult. *Psychoanalytic Study of the Child, 46*, 125–144.

Collett, L. J., & Lester, D. (1969). The fear of death and the fear of dying. *The Journal of Psychology, 72*, 179–181.

Combs, A. W., Richards, A. C., & Richards, F. (1976). *Perceptual psychology: A humanistic approach to the study of persons.* New York: Harper & Row.

Conger, J. J. (1981). Freedom and commitment: Families, youth, and social change. *American Psychologist, 36*, 1475–1484.

Conte, H. R., Weiner, M. B., & Plutchik, R. (1982). Measuring death anxiety: Conceptual, psychometric, and factor-analytic aspects. *Journal of Personality and Social Psychology, 43*, 775–785.

Cottle, J. T. (1967). The circles test: An investigation of perception of temporal relatedness and dominance. *Journal of Projective Techniques and Personality Assessment, 31*, 58–71.

Cottle, J. T. (1968). The location of experience: A manifest time orientation. *Acta Psychologia, 28*, 129–149.

Cottle, J. T. (1969). Temporal correlates of the achievement value and manifest anxiety. *Journal of Consulting and Clinical Psychology, 33*, 541–550.

Crisp, A. H., & Kalucy, R. S. (1974). Aspects of the perceptual disorder in anorexia nervosa. *British Journal of Medical Psychology, 45*, 395–405.

Csikszentmihalyi, M., Larson, R., & Prescott, S. (1977). The ecology of adolescents and experiences. *Journal of Youth and Adolescence, 6*, 281–294.

Csikszentmihalyi, M., & Rochberg-Halton, E. (1981). *The meaning of things: Domestic symbols and the self.* Cambridge: Cambridge University Press.

Dambrowski, K. (1964). *Positive disintegration.* Boston: Little, Brown & Co.

Dapkus, M. A. (1985). A thematic analysis of the experience of time. *Journal of Personality and Social Psychology, 49*, 408–419.

Davis, S. (1990). Men as success objects and women as sex objects: A study of personal advertisements. *Sex Roles, 23*, 43–50.

de Beauvoir, S. (1952). *The second sex.* New York: Alfred A Knopf.

de Beauvoir, S. (1970/1973). *The coming of age* (P. O'Brian, Trans.). New York: G. P. Putnam's Sons.

Denner, B., Wapner, S., McFarland, J., & Werner, H. (1963). Rhythmic activity and the perception of time. *American Journal of Psychology, 76*, 287–292.

de Rivera, J. (1981). *Conceptual encounter: A method for the exploration of human experience.* Washington, DC: University Press of America.

de Tocqueville, A. (1830/1969). *Democracy in America* (G. Lawrence, Trans.; J. Mayer, Ed.). New York: Doubleday.

Deutsch, H. (1944). *The psychology of women* (Vol. 1). New York: Grune & Stratton.

Dewald, P. A. (1972). *Psychoanalytic process.* New York: Basic Books.

Dickie, J., & Stroder, W. H. (1974). Development of mirror image responses in infancy. *Journal of Psychology, 88,* 333–337.

Dickstein, L. S. (1972). Death concern: Measurement and correlates. *Psychological Reports, 30,* 563–571.

Dickstein, L. S. (1975). Self report and fantasy correlates of death concern. *Psychological Reports, 37,* 147–158.

Dickstein, L. S., & Blatt, S. J. (1966). Death concern, futurity and anticipation. *Journal of Consulting Psychology, 30,* 11–17.

Dilling, C. A., & Rabin, A. I. (1967). Temporal experience in depressive states and schizophrenia. *Journal of Consulting Psychology, 31,* 604–608.

Dilthey, W. (1883/1958). Einleitung in die Wissenschaften. In *Gesammelte Schriften* (Vol. 1). Leipzig: Teubner.

Dion, K. K., & Dion, K. L. (1975). Self-esteem and romantic love. *Journal of Personality, 43,* 39–57.

Dion, K. L., & Dion, K. K. (1973). Correlates of romantic love. *Journal of Consulting and Clinical Psychology, 41,* 51–56.

Dion, K. L., & Dion, K. K. (1988). Romantic love: Individual and cultural perspectives. In R. Sternberg & M. Barnes (Eds.), *The psychology of love* (pp. 264–289). New Haven, CT: Yale University Press.

Dittes, J. E. (1959). Attractiveness of group as a function of self-esteem and acceptance by group. *Journal of Abnormal and Social Psychology, 59,* 77–82.

Dobson, M., Tattersfield, A. E., Adler, M. W., & McNicol, M. W. (1971). Attitudes and long term adjustment of patients surviving cardiac arrest. *British Medical Journal, 3,* 207–212.

Doob, L. (1971). *Patterning of time.* New Haven, CT: Yale University Press.

Dreyfuss, V. H. (1982). *Husserl, intentionality, and cognitive science.* Cambridge, MA: MIT Press.

Driscoll, R., Davis, K. E., & Lipitz, M. E. (1972). Parental interference and romantic love: The Romeo and Juliet effect. *Journal of Personality and Social Psychology, 24,* 1–10.

Druss, R. G., & Kornfield, D. S. (1967). The survivors of cardiac arrest. *Journal of the American Medical Association, 201,* 75–80.

Durlak, J. A. (1972a). Measurement of the fear of death: An examination of some existing scales. *Journal of Clinical Psychology, 28,* 545–547.

Durlak, J. A. (1972b). Relationship between individual attitudes toward life and death. *Journal of Consulting and Clinical Psychology, 38,* 463.

Dymond, R. (1954). Interpersonal perception and marital happiness. *Canadian Journal of Psychology, 8,* 164–171.

Eckhoff, T. (1974). *Justice: Its determinants in social interaction.* Rotterdam: Rotterdam University Press.

Eddy, P. D. (1961). *Loneliness: A discrepancy within the phenomenological self.* Unpublished doctoral dissertation, Adelphi College, New York.

Eisemann, M. (1984). Contact difficulties and the experience of loneliness in depressed patients and non-psychiatric controls. *Acta Psychiatrica Scandinivaca, 70,* 160–165.

Elder, G. H. (1969). Appearance and education in marriage mobility. *American Sociological Review, 34,* 519–533.

Elliot, R. (1986). Interpersonal process recall (IPR) as a psychotherapy process research method. In L. Greenberg & W. Pinsof (Eds.), *The psychotherapeutic process: A research handbook* (pp. 503–527). New York: Guilford Press.

Ellis, A., & Harper, A. (1961). *Creative marriage.* New York: Stuart.

Ericsson, A. K., & Simon, H. A. (1984). *Protocol analysis: Verbal reports as data.* Cambridge, MA: MIT Press.

Erikson, E. (1956). The problem of ego identity. *Journal of the American Psychoanalytic Association, 4,* 56–121.

Erikson, E. (1963). *Childhood and society* (2nd ed.). New York: W. W. Norton.

Erikson, E. (1968). *Identity, youth and crisis.* New York: W. W. Norton.

Evans-Pritchard, E. E. (1940). *The Nuer.* London: Clarendon Press.

Fairbairn, W. R. D. (1952). *Psychoanalytic studies of the personality.* London: Routledge & Kegan Paul.

Farley, G. A. (1971). An investigation of death anxiety and the sense of competence. *Dissertation Abstracts International, 31,* 7595.

Federn, P. (1926). Some variations in ego-feeling. *International Journal of Psycho-Analysis, 7,* 434–444.

Federn, P. (1952). *Ego psychology and the psychoses.* New York: Basic Books.

Feifel, H. (1956). Older persons look at death. *Geriatrics, 11,* 127–130.

Feifel, H. (1974). Religious conviction and fear of death among the healthy and terminally ill. *Journal for the Scientific Study of Religion, 13,* 353–360.

Feifel, H., & Branscomb, A. B. (1973). Who's afraid of death. *Journal of Abnormal Psychology, 81,* 282–288.

Feifel, H., & Nagy, V. T. (1981). Another look at fear of death. *Journal of Consulting and Clinical Psychology, 49,* 278–286.

Feingold, A. (1988). Matching for attractiveness in romantic partners and same-sex friends: A meta-analysis and theoretical critique. *Psychological Bulletin, 104,* 226–235.

Fenichel, O. (1945). *Psychoanalytic theory of neurosis.* New York: W. W. Norton.

Fingarette, H. (1963). *The self in transformation.* New York: Harper & Row.

Fiore, A., & Swenson, C. H. (1977). Analysis of love relationships in functional and dysfunctional marriages. *Psychological Reports, 40,* 707–714.

Fischer, C. S., & Phillips, S. L. (1982). Who is alone? Social characteristics of people with small networks. In L. Peplau & D. Perlman (Eds.), *Loneliness: A sourcebook of current theory, research and therapy.* New York: Wiley-Interscience.

Fischer, W. F. (1970). *Theories of anxiety.* New York: Harper & Row.

Fischer, W. F. (1971). The faces of anxiety. In A. Giorgi, W. Fischer, & R. von Eckartsberg (Eds.), *Duquesne studies in phenomenological psychology* (Vol. 1). Pittsburgh: Duquesne University Press.

Fischer, W. F. (1974). On the phenomenological mode of researching being-anxious. *Journal of Phenomenological Psychology, 4,* 405–423.

Fischer, W. F. (1978). An empirical-phenomenological investigation of being-anxious: An example of being-emotional. In R. Valle & M. King (Eds.), *Existential-phenomenological alternatives for psychology* (pp. 166–181). New York: Oxford University Press.

Fischer, W. F. (1989). An empirical-phenomenological investigation of being anxious: An example of the phenomenological approach to emotion. In R. Valle & S. Halling (Eds.), *Existential-phenomenological perspectives in psychology* (pp. 127–136). New York: Plenum Press.

Fisher, S. (1970). *Body experience in fantasy and behavior.* New York: Appleton-Century-Crofts.

Fisher, S., & Cleveland, S. E. (1958). *Body image and personality.* New York: D. VanNostrand Company.

Fisher, S., & Fisher, R. L. (1993). *The psychology of adaptation to absurdity: Tactics of make believe.* Hillsdale, NJ: Lawrence Erlbaum Associates, Inc.

Florian, F., & Kravitz, S. (1983). Fear of personal death: Attribution, structure and relation to religious belief. *Journal of Personality and Social Psychology, 44,* 600–607.

Fraisse, P. (1963). *The psychology of time.* New York: Harper & Row.

Freedman, B. J. (1974). The subjective experience of perceptual and cognitive disturbances in schizophrenia. *Archives of General Psychiatry, 30,* 333–337.

Freud, S. (1895/1966). Project for a scientific psychology. In J. Strachey (Ed. & Trans.), *The standard edition of the complete psychological works of Sigmund Freud* (Vol. 1, pp. 283–387). London: Hogarth Press.

Freud, S. (1905/1938). Three contributions to the theory of sex. In A. Brill (Ed. & Trans.), *The basic writings of Sigmund Freud* (pp. 553–629). New York: Random House.

Freud, S. (1905/1953). Three essays on the theory of sexuality. In J. Strachey (Ed. & Trans.), *The standard edition of the complete psychological works of Sigmund Freud* (Vol. 7, pp. 135–243). London: Hogarth Press.

Freud, S. (1912/1963). The most prevalent form of degradation in erotic life. In P. Rieff (Ed.), *Sexuality and the psychology of love* (pp. 58–70). New York: Crowell-Collier.

Freud, S. (1914/1957). On narcissism: An introduction. In J. Strachey (Ed. & Trans.), *The standard edition of the complete psychological works of Sigmund Freud* (Vol. 14, pp. 67–102). London: Hogarth Press.

Freud, S. (1917/1935). *Introductory lectures on psychoanalysis* (J. Riviere, Trans.). New York: Liveright.

Freud, S. (1920/1950). *Beyond the pleasure principle* (J. Strachey, Trans.). London: Hogarth Press.

Freud, S. (1921/1955). Group psychology and the analysis of the ego. In J. Strachey (Ed. & Trans.), *The standard edition of the complete psychological works of Sigmund Freud* (Vol. 18, pp. 65–143). London: Hogarth Press.

Freud, S. (1925/1963). Some psychological consequences of the anatomical distinction between the sexes. In P. Rieff (Ed.), *Sexuality and the psychology of love* (pp. 183–193). New York: Crowell-Collier.

Freud, S. (1926/1959). Inhibitions, symptoms and anxiety (A. Strachey & J. Strachey, Trans.). In J. Strachey (Ed.), *The standard edition of the complete psychological works of Sigmund Freud* (Vol. 20, pp. 77–174). London: Hogarth Press.

Freud, S. (1931/1961). Female sexuality. In J. Strachey (Ed. & Trans.), *The standard edition of the complete psychological works of Sigmund Freud* (Vol. 21, pp. 225–243). London: Hogarth Press.

Friedman, M. (1965). Introductory essay. In M. Buber, *The knowledge of man* (pp. 11–58). London: George Allen & Unwin Ltd.

Fromm, E. (1941). *Escape from freedom.* New York: Holt, Rinehart & Winston.

Fromm, E. (1955). *The sane society.* New York: Holt, Rinehart & Winston.

Fromm, E. (1956). *The art of loving.* New York: Harper & Row.

Fromm-Reichmann, F. (1959). Loneliness. *Psychiatry, 22,* 1–15.

Gadamer, H.-G. (1960/1975). *Truth and method* (G. Barden & J. Cumming, Trans.). New York: Seabury.

Gaev, D. M. (1976). *The psychology of loneliness.* Chicago: Adams Press.

Gardner, H. (1985). *The mind's new science.* New York: Basic Books.

Gedo, J. (1979). *Beyond interpretation: Toward a revised theory for psychoanalysis.* New York: International Universities Press.

Gedo, J., & Goldberg, A. (1973). *Models of the mind.* Chicago: University of Chicago Press.

Gerardi, D. L. (1986). Replication of the phenomenology of loneliness in the therapeutic dyad. In S. M. Natale (Ed.), *Psychotherapy and the lonely patient.* New York: Harrington Park Press, Inc.

Gergen, K. (1985). The social constructionist movement in modern psychology. *American Psychologist, 40,* 266–275.

Getsinger, S. H. (1976). Sociopathy, self actualization, and time. *Joural of Personality Assessment, 40,* 398–402.

Gibson, J. J. (1979). *The ecological approach to visual perception.* Boston: Houghton Mifflin.

Gifford, S. (1960). Sleep, time and the early ego. *Journal of the American Psychoanalytic Association, 8,* 5–42.

Gilligan, C. (1980). In a different voice: Women's conceptions of self and of morality. In H. Eisenstein & A. Jardine (Eds.), *The future of difference* (pp. 274–317). Boston: G. K. Hall & Co.

Gilligan, C. (1982). *In a different voice: Psychological theory and women's development.* Cambridge, MA: Harvard University Press.

Giorgi, A. (1970). *Psychology as a human science.* New York: Harper and Row.

Giorgi, A. (1975). An application of phenomenological method in psychology. In A. Giorgi, C. Fischer, & E. Murray (Eds.), *Duquesne studies in phenomenological psychology* (Vol. 2). Pittsburgh: Duquesne University Press.

Giorgi, A. (1983). Concerning the possibility of phenomenological research. *Journal of Phenomenological Psychology, 14,* 129–170.

Giorgi, A. (1989). Learning and memory from the perspective of phenomenological psychology. In R. Valle & S. Halling (Eds.), *Existential-phenomenological perspectives in psychology* (pp. 99–112). New York: Plenum Press.

Glass, D. C., Snyder, M. L., & Hollis, J. F. (1974). Time urgency and the Type A coronary prone behavior pattern. *Journal of Applied Social Psychology, 4,* 125–140.

Goethals, G. W. (1973). Symbiosis and the life cycle. *British Journal of Medical Psychology, 46,* 91–96.

Goffman, E. (1959). *The presentation of self in everyday life.* Garden City, NY: Doubleday.

Goldberg, A. (1971). On waiting. *International Journal of Psychoanalysis, 52,* 413–421.

Goldberg, A. (1983). *The future of psychoanalysis.* New York: International Universities Press.

Goldman-Eisler, F. (1952). Individual differences between interviewers and their effect on interviewees' conversational behavior. *Journal of Mental Science, 98,* 660–671.

Goldstein, K. (1939/1963). *The organism.* Boston: Beacon Press.

Gordon, S. (1976). *Lonely in America.* New York: Simon and Schuster.

Gorman, B. S., & Wessman, E. A. (1977). *The personal experience of time.* New York: Plenum Press.

Gregory, R. L. (1989). *The Oxford companion to the mind.* Oxford: Oxford University Press.

Grene, M. (1982). Landscape. In R. Bruzine & B. Wilshire (Eds.), *Phenomenology: Dialogues and bridges* (pp. 55–60). New York: State University of New York Press.

Guntrip, H. (1969). *Schizoid phenomena, object relations and the self.* New York: International Universities Press.

Hackett, T. P. (1972). The Lazarus complex revisited. *Annual Review of Internal Medicine, 76,* 135–137.

Hagan, T. (1986). Interviewing the downtrodden. In P. Ashworth, A. Giorgi, & A. de Koning (Eds.), *Qualitative research in psychology.* Pittsburgh: Duquesne University Press.

Hale, C. (1993). Time dimensions and the subjective experience of time. *Journal of Humanistic Psychology, 33,* 88–105.

Handal, P. J. (1969). The relationship between subjective life expectancy, death anxiety and general anxiety. *Journal of Clinical Psychology, 25,* 39–42.

Hartgenbusch, H. G. (1927). Gestalt psychology in sports. *Psyche, 27,* 41–52.

Hartog, J., Audy, J. R., & Cohen, Y. A. (Eds.). (1980). *The anatomy of loneliness.* New York: International Universities Press.

Hatfield, E., & Sprecher, S. (1986). Measuring passionate love in intimate relationships. *Journal of Adolescence, 9,* 383–410.

Hattis, R. P. (1965). Love feelings in courtship couples: An analysis. *Journal of Humanistic Psychology, 5,* 22–53.

Head, H. (1920). *Studies in neurology.* London: Oxford University Press.

Hector, M. A., Bradley, K. M., Daigle, S. L., & Klukken, P. G. (1990, August). *The phenomenological analysis of psychotherapy process using videotaped assisted recall.* Paper presented at the annual meeting of the American Psychological Association, Boston, MA.

Heidegger, M. (1927/1962). *Being and time* (J. Macquarrie & E. Robinson, Trans.). New York: Harper & Row.

Hick, J. (1976). *Death and eternal life.* San Francisco: Harper & Row.

Hillman, J. (1975). *Revisioning psychology.* New York: Harper & Row.

Hinkle, D. E., & Spora Kowski, M. J. (1975). Attitudes toward love: A re-examination. *Journal of Marriage and the Family, 37,* 764–767.

Hirschman, E. C. (1986). Humanistic inquiry in marketing research: Philosophy, method, and criteria. *Journal of Marketing Research, 13,* 237–249.

Hoelter, J. W. (1979). Multidimensional treatment of fear of death. *Journal of Consulting and Clinical Psychology, 47,* 996–999.

Hoffer, W. (1952). Development of the body ego. *Psychoanalytic Study of the Child, 5,* 18–23.

Hoffman, L. R. (1958). Similarity of personality: A basis for interpersonal attraction? *Sociometry, 21,* 300–308.

Hofstadter, D. R. (1981). Reflections. In D. R. Hofstadter & D. C. Dennett (Eds.), *The mind's I* (pp. 30–33). New York: Basic Books.

Hofstadter, D. R., & Dennett, D. C. (1981). *The mind's I.* New York: Basic Books.

Hojat, M. (1983). Comparison of transitory and chronic loners on selected personality variables. *British Journal of Psychology, 74,* 199–202.

Holbrook, M. B., Bell, S., & Grayson, M. W. (1989). The role of the humanities in consumer research: Close encounters and coastal disturbances. In E. Hirschman (Ed.), *Interpretive consumer research.* Provo, UT: Association for Consumer Research.

Holbrook, M. B., & Grayson, M. (1986). The semiology of cinematic consumption: Symbolic consumer behavior in *Out of Africa. Journal of Consumer Research, 13,* 374–381.

Holck, F. H. (1974). *Death and Eastern thought.* Nashville: Abingdon Press.

Horney, K. (1937). *Neurotic personality of our time.* New York: W. W. Norton & Company, Inc.

Hortocollis, P. (1974). Origins of time: A reconstruction of the ontogenetic develop-ment of the sense of time based on object relations theory. *Psychoanalytic Quarterly, 43,* 243–260.

Hortocollis, P. (1983). *Time and timelessness.* New York: International Universities Press.

Hunt, J., & Pollio, H. R. (1995). What audience members are aware of listening to the comedy of Whoopi Goldberg. *International Journal of Humor, 8,* 135–154.

Hurlburt, R. T. (1980). Validation and correlation of thought sampling with retro-spective measures. *Cognitive Therapy and Research, 4,* 235–238.

Hurlburt, R. T., Leach, B. C., & Saltman, S. (1984). Random sampling of thought and mood. *Cognitive Therapy and Research, 8,* 263–275.

Husserl, E. (1913/1931). *Ideas: General introduction to pure phenomenology* (W. Gibson, Trans.). New York: Collier Books.

Husserl, E. (1954/1970). *The crisis of European sciences and transcendental phenom-enology: An introduction to phenomenological philosophy* (D. Carr, Trans.). Evanston, IL: Northwestern University Press.

Huston, T. L. (1973). Ambiguity of acceptance, social desirability, and dating choice. *Journal of Experimental Social Psychology, 9,* 32–42.

Ihde, D. (1979). *Experimental phenomenology.* New York: Paragon Books.

Ingram, D. H. (1979). Time and time-keeping in psychoanalysis and psychotherapy. *American Journal of Psychoanalysis, 39,* 319–328.

Izard, C. E. (1963). Personality similarity and friendship: A follow-up study. *Journal of Abnormal and Social Psychology, 66,* 598–600.

Jacobs, L., Berscheid, E., & Walster, E. (1971). Self-esteem and attraction. *Journal of Personality and Social Psychology, 17,* 84–91.

Jacobs, M. (1968). The shifting existence of western man: An introduction to J. H. Van den Berg's work on metabletics of the human body. *Humanitas, 4,* 25–74.

James, W. (1890). *The principles of psychology* (2 vols.). New York: Holt.

James, W. (1892). *Psychology, briefer course.* New York: Holt.

James, W. (1899). *Talks to teachers on psychology: And to students on some of life's ideals.* New York: Holt.

Janet, P. (1877). Une illusion d'optique interne. *Rev. Philosophique, 1,* 497–502.

Jaspers, K. (1932/1969). *Philosophy* (Vol. 2) (E. Ashton, Trans.). Chicago: Univer-sity of Chicago Press.

Jeffers, F. C., Nichols, C. R., & Eisdorfer, G. (1966). Attitudes of older persons toward death. *Journal of Gerontology, 16,* 53–56.

Johnson, M. (1987). *The body in the mind: The bodily basis of meaning, imagination, and reason.* Chicago: University of Chicago Press.

Jonas, H. (1965). Life, death and the body in a theory of being. *Review of Metaphys-ics, 19,* 3–23.

Jones, W. H., Freeman, J. A., & Goswick, R. A. (1981). The persistence of loneli-ness: Self and other determinants. *Journal of Personality, 49,* 27–48.

Kafka, J. S. (1972). The experience of time. *Journal of the American Psychoanalytic Association, 20,* 650–667.

Kagan, N. (1975). Influencing human interaction: Eleven years with IPR. *Canadian Counsellor, 9,* 74–97.

Kalish, R. A. (1963). An approach to the study of death attitudes. *American Behav-ioral Scientist, 9,* 68–70.

Kassarjian, H. J. (1977). Content analysis in consumer research. *Journal of Con-sumer Research, 4,* 8–18.

Kastenbaum, R. (1965). The direction of time perspective: The influence of affective set. *Journal of Genetic Psychology, 73,* 189–201.

Kastenbaum, R., & Costa, P. T. (1977). Psychological perspectives on death. *Annual Review of Psychology, 28,* 225–249.

Katz, A. M., & Hill, R. (1958). Residential propinquity and marital selection: A review of theory, method, and fact. *Marriage and Family Living, 20,* 327–335.

Keck, L. E. (1969). New Testament views of death. In L. Mills (Ed.), *Perspectives on death.* Nashville: Abingdon Press.

Keen, E. (1970). *Three faces of being: Toward an existential clinical psychology.* New York: Appleton-Century-Crofts.

Kephart, W. M. (1961). *The family, society, and the individual.* Boston: Houghton-Mifflin.

Kephart, W. M. (1967). Some correlates of romantic love. *Journal of Marriage and the Family, 29,* 470–474.

Kerchoff, A. C., & Davis, K. E. (1962). Value consensus and need complementarity in mate selection. *American Sociological Review, 27,* 295–303.

Kerlinger, F. (1986). *Foundations of behavioral research.* New York: Holt, Rinehart and Winston.

Kestenberg, J., Marcus, H., Robbins, E., Berlowe, J., & Buelte, A. (1971). Development of the young child as expressed through bodily movement. *American Psychoanalytic Association Journal, 19*(4), 746–764.

Kierkegaard, S. (1844/1936). *Philosophical fragments* (D. Swenson, Trans.). Princeton: Princeton University Press.

Kierkegaard, S. (1844/1980). *Concept of anxiety* (W. Lowrie, Trans.). Princeton: Princeton University Press.

Kierkegaard, S. (1846/1941). *Concluding unscientific postscript* (D. Swenson & W. Lowrie, Trans.). Princeton: Princeton University Press.

Kierkegaard, S. (1847/1959). *Either/Or* (D. Swenson & L. Swenson, Trans.). Garden City, New York: Doubleday.

Kierkegaard, S. (1849/1980). *The sickness unto death* (H. Hong & E. Hong, Trans.). Princeton: Princeton University Press.

Kimsey, L. R., Roberts, J. L., & Logan, D. I. (1972). Death, dying and denial in the aged. *American Journal of Psychiatry, 129* 161–166.

Kinget, G. M. (1975). *On being human.* New York: Harcourt Brace Jovanovich.

Kir-Stimon, W. (1977). "Tempo-statis" as a factor in psychotherapy: Individual tempo and life rhythm, temporal territoriality, time planes, and communications. *Psychotherapy: Theory, Research, and Practice, 14,* 245–248.

Klein, M. (1928). Early stages of the oedipus conflict. *International Journal of Psycho-Analysis, 9,* 167–180.

Klein, M. (1933/1975). The early development of conscience in the child. In *Love, guilt and reparation & other works* (pp. 248–257). London: Delacorte Press.

Klein, M. (1937/1964). Love, guilt, and reparation. In M. Klein & J. Riviere (Eds.), *Love, hate, and reparation.* New York: W. W. Norton.

Klinger, E. (1981). Modes of normal conscious flow. In K. Pope & J. Singer (Eds.), *The stream of consciousness* (pp. 226–258). New York: Plenum Press.

Klinger, E., Bartoc, S. G., & Mahoney, T. W. (1976). Maturation, mood and mental events: Problems and implications for adaptive processes. In G. Serben (Ed.), *Psychotherapy of human adaptiveness* (pp. 95–112). New York: Plenum Press.

Knapp, R. H., & Garbutt, J. T. (1958). Time imagery and the achievement motivation. *Journal of Personality, 26,* 426–434.

Koff, E., & Kiekhofer, M. (1978). Body-part size estimation in children. *Perceptual and Motor Skills, 47,* 1047–1050.

Koffka, K. (1924). *The growth of mind* (R. M. Ogden, Trans.). New York: Harcourt.

Koffka, K. (1935). *Principles of gestalt psychology.* New York: Harcourt Brace & World.

Kohlberg, L. (1981). *Essays on moral development: The philosophy of moral development* (Vol. 1). San Francisco: Harper & Row.

Köhler, W. (1947). *Gestalt psychology.* New York: New American Library.

Kohut, H. (1971). *The analysis of the self.* New York: International Universities Press.

Kohut, H. (1977). *The restoration of the self.* New York: International Universities Press.

Kohut, H. (1984). *How does analysis cure?* Chicago: University of Chicago Press.

Kolnai, E. (1977). *Ethics, value and reality: Selected papers of Aurel Kolnai.* London: Athlone Press.

Koppitz, E. M. (1968). *Psychological evaluation of children's human figure drawings.* New York: Grune & Stratton.

Kreiger, S. R., Epting, F. R., & Leitner, L. M. (1974). Personal constructs, threat and attitudes towards death. *Omega, 5,* 299–310.

Kubie, L. C. (1975). Disturbances of the body image. In S. Arieti (Ed.), *American handbook of psychiatry: Vol. 4. Organic disorders and psychosomatic medicine.* New York: Basic Books.

Kuhn, T. S. (1970). *The structure of scientific revolutions* (2nd ed.). Chicago: University of Chicago Press.

Kuhs, H. (1991). Time experience in melancholia: A comparison between findings based on phenomenology and experimental psychology. *Comprehensive Psychiatry, 32,* 324–329.

Kurlychek, R. T. (1976). Level of belief in afterlife and four categories of fear of death in a sample of 60+ year olds. *Psychological Reports, 38,* 228.

Kurlychek, R. T. (1978). Assessment of attitudes towards death and dying: A critical review of some available methods. *Omega, 9,* 37–47.

Kurtz, S. A. (1988). The psychoanalysis of time. *Journal of the American Psychoanalytic Association, 36,* 985–1004.

Kvale, S. (1983). The qualitative research interview: A phenomenological and a hermeneutical mode of understanding. *Journal of Phenomenological Psychology, 14,* 171–196.

Kvale, S., & Greness, C. E. (1967). Skinner and Sartre. *Review of Existential Psychology and Psychiatry, 7,* 128–150.

Laban, R. (1947). *Effort.* London: McDonald & Evans.

Lafluer, W. R. (1974). *Japan.* In F. Holck (Ed.), *Death and Eastern thought.* Nashville: Abingdon Press.

Laing, R. D. (1961). *Self and others.* London: Tavistock.

Laing, R. D. (1965). *The divided self.* Baltimore: Penguin Books.

Lakoff, G. (1987). *Women, fire, and dangerous things.* Chicago: University of Chicago Press.

Laplanche, J., & Pontalis, J. B. (1973). *The language of psychoanalysis.* New York: W. W. Norton.

Lasch, C. (1979). *The culture of narcissism: American life in an age of diminishing expectations.* New York: W. W. Norton.

Lasswell, M. E., & Lobsenz, N. M. (1980). *Styles of loving.* Garden City, NY: Doubleday.

Lauer, J., & Lauer, R. (1985, June). Marriages made to last. *Psychology Today*, 22–26.

Laurence, L. T. (1980). A phenomenological investigation of professed marital satisfaction: Interviews with happily married people. *Dissertation Abstracts International, 41*, 3896B.

Lawson, D. M. (1981). A study of the relationship between love attitudes and marital adjustment through seven stages of the marital life cycle. *Dissertation Abstracts International, 42*, 1337A.

Lecomte du Nouy (1936). *Le temps et la vie*. Paris: Gallinard.

Lee, J. A. (1976). *Lovestyles*. London: Dent.

Lee, J. A. (1977). A typology of styles of loving. *Personality and Social Psychology Bulletin, 3*, 173–182.

Leiderman, P. H. (1980). Pathological loneliness: A psychodynamic interpretation. In J. Hartog, J. Audy, & Y. Cohen (Eds.), *The anatomy of loneliness*. New York: International Universities Press.

Leming, M. R. (1980). Religion and death: A test of Homans' thesis. *Omega, 10*, 347–364.

LeShan, L. (1952). Time orientation and social class. *Journal of Abnormal and Social Psychology, 47*, 589–592.

Lester, D. (1967). Experimental and correlational studies of the fear of death. *Psychological Bulletin, 67*, 27–36.

Lester, D. (1972). Studies in death attitudes: Part two. *Psychological Reports, 30*, 440.

Lester, D., & Collett, L. (1970). Fear of death and self-ideal discrepancy. *Archives of the Foundation of Thanatology, 21*, 130.

Lester, D., & Kam, E. G. (1971). Effects of a friend dying on attitudes toward death. *The Journal of Social Psychology, 83*, 149–150.

Levi-Strauss, C. (1958). *Anthropologie structurale*. Paris: Plon.

Levine, M., & Spivak, G. (1957). Incentive, time conception, and self-control in a group of emotionally disturbed boys. *American Psychologist, 7*, 110–113.

Levy, S. J. (1981). Interpreting consumer mythology: A structural approach to consumer behavior. *Journal of Marketing, 45*, 49–62.

Lewis, M. M. (1937). The beginning of reference to past and future in a child's speech. *British Journal of Educational Psychology, 7*, 39–56.

Lincoln, Y. S., & Guba, E. G. (1987). *Naturalistic inquiry*. Beverly Hills, CA: Sage.

Linn, L. (1955). Some developmental aspects of the body image. *International Journal of Psycho-Analysis, 36*, 36–42.

Livingston, P. B., & Zimet, C. N. (1965). Death anxiety, authoritarianism and choice of specialty in medical students. *Journal of Nervous and Mental Disease, 140*, 222–230.

Loucks, S. (1974). The dimensions of loneliness: A psychological study of affect, self-concept and object-relations. *Dissertation Abstracts International, 35*, 3024B.

Loucks, S. (1980). Loneliness, affect and self-concept: Construct validity of the Bradley Loneliness Scale. *Journal of Personality Assessment, 44*, 142–147.

Luft, J. (1969). *Of human interaction*. Palo Alto, CA: National Press Books.

Luria, A. (1989). Reductionism. In R. L. Gregory (Ed.), *The Oxford Companion to the Mind* (pp. 675–676). Oxford: Oxford University Press.

Lyons, J. (1973). *Experience: An introduction to a personal psychology*. New York: Harper & Row.

Maccoby, E., & Jacklin, C. (1974). *The psychology of sex differences*. Stanford, CA: Stanford University Press.

Mahler, M. (1972). On the first three phases of the separation-individuation process. *International Journal of Psychoanalysis, 53*, 333–338.

Mahler, M. S., & McDevitt, J. B. (1982). Thoughts on the emergence of the sense of self with particular emphasis on the body self. *American Psychoanalytic Association Journal, 30*, 827–848.

Mahler, M., Pine, F., & Bergman, A. (1975). *The psychological birth of the human infant*. New York: Basic Books.

Main, M., Kaplan, N., & Cassidy, J. (1985). Security in infancy, childhood, and adulthood: A move to the level of representation. *Monographs of the Society for Research in Child Development, 50* (1–2), 66–104.

Marcel, G. (1960). *The mystery of being*. Chicago: Gateway.

Martin, D., & Wrightsman, L. S. (1965). The relationship between religious behavior and concern about death. *The Journal of Social Psychology, 65*, 317–323.

Maslow, A. H. (1950). Self-actualizing people: A study in psychological health. *Personality, 1*, 11–34.

Maslow, A. H. (1970). *Motivation and personality* (2nd ed.). New York: Harper & Row.

May, R. (1958). The origins and significance of the existential movement in psychology. In R. May, E. Angel, & H. Ellenberger (Eds.), *Existence*. New York: Basic Books.

May, R. (1969). *Love and will*. New York: W. W. Norton.

May, R. (1950/1977). *The meaning of anxiety*. New York: W. W. Norton.

May, R. (1978). Preface. In R. S. Valle & M. King (Eds.), *Existential-phenomenological alternatives for psychology* (pp. iv–viii). New York: Oxford University Press.

May, R. (1983). *The discovery of being*. New York: W. W. Norton.

May, R., & Yalom, I. (1984). Existential psychotherapy. In R. J. Corsini (Ed.), *Current psychotherapies* (pp. 354–391). Itasca, IL: F. E. Peacock.

McAnany, P. (1977). Restitution as idea and practice: The retributive prospect. In B. Galway & J. Hudson (Eds.), *Offender restitution in theory and action* (pp. 15–31). Lexington, MA: Lexington Books.

McConville, M. (1978). The phenomenological approach to perception. In R. S. Valle & M. King (Eds.), *Existential-phenomenological alternatives for psychology* (pp. 94–118). New York: Oxford University Press.

McCracken, G. (1988). *Culture and consumption: New approaches to the symbolic character of goods and activities*. Bloomington: Indiana University Press.

McGrath, J. E., & Brinberg, D. (1983). External validity and the research process: A comment on the Calder/Lynch dialogue. *Journal of Consumer Research, 10*, 115–124.

McKellar, W. (1968). *Experience and behavior*. Harmondsworth, England: Penguin Books.

McMordie, W. R. (1981). Religiosity and fear of death: Strength of belief system. *Psychological Reports, 49*, 921–922.

Melges, F. T., & Freeman, A. M. (1977). Temporal disorganization and inner–outer confusion in acute mental illness. *American Journal of Psychiatry, 134*, 874–877.

Menninger, K. (1942). *Love against hate*. New York: Harcourt Brace Jovanovich.

Merleau-Ponty, M. (1942/1963). *The structure of behavior* (A. Fisher, Trans.). Boston: Beacon Press.

Merleau-Ponty, M. (1945/1962). *The phenomenology of perception* (C. Smith, Trans.). London: Routledge & Kegan Paul.

Merleau-Ponty, M. (1964/1968). *The visible and the invisible* (A. Lingis, Trans.). Evanston, IL: Nortwestern University Press.

Merleau-Ponty, M. (1970). *Themes from the lectures at the College de France, 1952–60* (J. O'Neill, Trans.). Evanston, IL: Northwestern University Press.

Miklisanski, J. (1947). The law of retaliation and the Pentateuch. *Journal of Biblical Literature, 66*, 296–300.

Miles, M. B., & Huberman, A. M. (1984). *Qualitative data analysis: A source book of new methods.* Beverly Hills, CA: Sage.

Miller, H. (1993). Metaphoric components of composing processes. *Metaphor & Symbolic Activity, 8*, 79–96.

Miller, M. (1964). Time and the character disorder. *Journal of Nervous and Mental Disease, 138*, 535–540.

Minton, B., & Spilka, B. (1976). Perspectives on death in relation to powerlessness and form of personal religion. *Omega, 7*, 261–268.

Mitchell, S. A. (1988). *Relational concepts in psychoanalysis.* Cambridge, MA: Harvard University Press.

Modaressi, T., & Kenny, T. (1977). Children's response to their true and distorted mirror images. *Child Psychiatry and Human Development, 8*, 94–101.

Moore, D., & Schultz, N. R. (1983). Loneliness at adolescence: Correlates, attributions, and coping. *Journal of Youth and Adolescence, 12*, 95–100.

Morris, J. (1983). Time experience and transference. *Journal of the American Psychoanalytic Association, 31*, 651–675.

Morris, P. S. (1982). Some patterns of identification and otherness. *Journal of the British Society for Phenomenology, 13*, 216–226.

Moss, D. M. (1982). Distortions in human embodiment: A study of surgically treated obesity. In R. Bruzine & B. Wilshire (Eds.), *Phenomenology: Dialogues and bridges* (pp. 253–68). New York: New York University Press.

Moustakas, C. E. (1961). *Loneliness.* Englewood Cliffs, NJ: Prentice-Hall.

Moustakas, C. E. (1972). *Loneliness and love.* Englewood Cliffs, NJ: Prentice-Hall.

Murray, E. L. (1986). *Imaginative thinking and human existence.* Pittsburgh: Duquesne University Press.

Murstein, B. I. (1972). Physical attractiveness and marital choice. *Journal of Personality and Social Psychology, 22*, 8–12.

Murstein, B. I. (1986). *Paths to marriage.* Beverly Hills, CA: Sage.

Murstein, B. I. (1987). A clarification and extension of SVR theory of dyadic pairing. *Journal of Marriage and the Family, 49*, 929–933.

Murstein, B. I., & Christy, P. (1976). Physical attractiveness and marriage adjustment in middle-aged couples. *Journal of Personality and Social Psychology, 34*, 537–542.

Myers, E. L. (1985). Special possessions: Their characteristics, meaning, and developmental function throughout life. *Dissertation Abstracts International, 46*, 961B.

Namnum, A. (1972). Time in psychoanalytic technique. *Journal of the American Psychoanalytic Association, 20*, 736–750.

Natale, S. M. (1986). *Psychotherapy and the lonely patient.* New York: Harrington Park Press, Inc.

Natsoulos, T. (1988). Gibson, James, and the temporal continuity of experience. *Imagination, Cognition and Personality, 7*, 351–376.

Nehrke, M. F., Bellucci, G., & Gabriel, S. J. (1978). Death anxiety, locus of control and life satisfaction in the elderly: Toward a definition of ego integrity. *Omega*, *8*, 359–369.

Neimeyer, R. A., & Chapman, K. M. (1980). Self/ideal discrepancy and fear of death: The test of an existential hypothesis. *Omega*, *11*, 233–240.

Nelson, L. D. (1978). The multidimensional measurement of death attitudes: Construction and validation of a three-factor instrument. *The Psychological Record*, *28*, 525–533.

Nelson, L. D. (1979). Structural conduciveness, personality characteristics and death anxiety. *Omega*, *10*, 123 133.

Nelson, L. D., & Nelson, C. C. (1975). A factor analytic inquiry into the multidimensionality of death anxiety. *Omega*, *6*, 171–178.

Nelson, W. M., & Groman, W. D. (1978). Temporal perspective from the Gestalt therapy assumption of present centeredness. *Psychotherapy: Theory, Research, and Practice*, *15*, 277–284.

Nerviano, V. J., & Gross, W. F. (1976). Loneliness and locus of control for alcoholic males: Validity against Murray Need and Cattell trait dimensions. *Journal of Clinical Psychology*, *32*, 479–484.

Neugarten, B. L. (1968). *Middle age and aging*. Chicago: Unviersity of Chicago Press.

Newell, A. (1982). The knowledge level. *Artificial Intelligence*, *18*, 87–127.

Newman, M. A. (1972). Time estimation in relation to gait tempo. *Perceptual and Motor Skills*, *34*, 359–366.

Nisbett, R. E., & Wilson, T. D. (1977). Telling more than we can know: Verbal reports on mental processes. *Psychological Review*, *84*, 231–259.

Nisenbaum, S. (1984). Ways of being alone in the world. *American Behavioral Scientist*, *27*, 785–800.

Noyes, R. (1980). Attitude change following near-death experiences. *Psychiatry*, *43*, 234–241.

Noyes, R. (1982). The human experience of death or what can we learn from near-death experiences? *Omega*, *15*, 25–35.

O'Grady, K. E. (1981). The development and validation of a measure of romantic love. *Dissertation Abstracts International*, *41*, 3584B.

O'Guinn, T. C., & Faber, R. J. (1989). Compulsive buying: A phenomenological exploration. *Journal of Consumer Research*, *16*, 147–157.

O'Leary, K. D., & Smith, D. A. (1991). Marital interactions. *Annual Review of Psychology*, *42*, 191–212.

O'Shaugnessy, J. (1985). A return to reason in consumer behavior: An hermeneutical approach. In E. Hirschman & M. Holbrook (Eds.), *Advances in consumer research* (Vol. 12, pp. 305–311). Provo, UT: Association for Consumer Research.

Otto-Apel, K. (1985). Scientistics, hermeneutics, critique of ideology: An outline of a theory of science from an epistemological-anthropological point of view. In K. Mueller-Vollmer (Ed.), *The hermeneutics reader* (pp. 321–346). New York: Continuum.

Packard, V. (1972). *A nation of strangers*. New York: David McKay Company, Inc.

Paloutzian, R. F., & Janigan, A. S. (1986). Interrelationships between religiousness and loneliness. In S. M. Natale (Ed.), *Psychotherapy and the lonely patient*. New York: Harrington Park Press, Inc.

Parsons, R. D., & Wicks, R. J. (1986). Cognitive pastoral psychotherapy with religious persons experiencing loneliness. In S. M. Natale (Ed.), *Psychotherapy and the lonely patient*. New York: Harrington Park Press, Inc.

Pattison, E. M. (1965). On the failure to forgive or to be forgiven. *American Journal of Psychotherapy, 19*, 106–115.

Patton, J. F., & Freitag, C. B. (1977). Correlational study of death anxiety, general anxiety and locus of control. *Psychological Reports, 40*, 51–54.

Peplau, L. A., & Perlman, D. (1982). *Loneliness: A sourcebook of current theory, research and therapy.* New York: Wiley-Interscience.

Pepper, S. (1942). *World hypotheses: A study in evidence.* Los Angeles: University of California Press.

Peter, J. P., & Olson, J. C. (1983). Is science marketing? *Journal of Marketing, 47*, 111–125.

Piaget, J. (1927/1969). *The child's conception of time* (A. Pomerans, Trans.). New York: Basic Books.

Pine, F. (1978/1980). On the expansion of the affect array: A developmental description. In R. Lax, S. Bach, & J. Burland (Eds.), *Rapprochement* (pp. 217–233). New York: Aronson.

Plessner, H. (1961/1970). *Laughing and crying* (J. Churchill & M. Grene, Trans.). Evanston, IL: Northwestern University Press.

Plugge, H. (1970). The ambiguity of having and being a body. *Human Inquiries, 10*, 132–139.

Polkinghorne, D. E. (1989). Phenomenological research methods. In R. Valle & S. Halling (Eds.), *Existential-phenomenological perspectives in psychology* (pp. 41–60). New York: Plenum Press.

Pollak, J. M. (1977). *Relationships between psychoanalytic personality pattern, death anxiety and self actualization.* Unpublished doctoral dissertation, Boston College, Boston, MA.

Pollak, J. M. (1979). Correlates of death anxiety: A review of empirical studies. *Omega, 10*, 97–121.

Pollio, H. R. (1982). *Behavior and existence.* Monterey, CA: Brooks/Cole Publishing.

Pollio, H. R. (1983). Notes toward a field theory of humor. In J. Goldstein & P. McGhee (Eds.), *Handbook of research in humor* (pp. 323–351). New York: Springer-Verlag.

Pollio, H. R. (1984). *What students think about and do during college lectures.* Knoxville, TN: Teaching-Learning Issues, Learning Research Center.

Pollio, H. R. (1990). The stream of consciousness since James. In M. Johnson & T. Henley (Eds.), *Reflections on* The Principles of Psychology: *William James after a century* (pp. 271–294). Hillsdale, NJ: Lawrence Erlbaum Associates.

Pollio, H. R., & Swanson, C. (1995). A behavioral and phenomenological analysis of audience reactions to comic performance. *Humor International, 8*, 5–28.

Pollock, G. (1971). On time, death and immortality. *Psychoanalytic Quarterly, 40*, 435–446.

Powell, J. H., & Hector, M. A. (1987, August). *Client perceptions of counselor self-disclosing and self-involving statements.* Paper presented at the annual meeting of the American Psychological Association, New York City, NY.

Prasinos, S., & Tittler, B. I. (1984). The existential context of lovestyles: An empirical study. *Journal of Humanistic Psychology, 24*, 95–112.

Price, D., Barrell, J. E., & Barrell, J. J. (1985). A quantitative-experiential analysis of human emotions. *Motivation and Emotion, 9*, 19–37.

Priest, J. (1980). *Governmental and judicial ethics in the Bible and rabbinic literature.* New York: KTAV Publishing House.

Radloff, L. S. (1977). The CES-D scale: A self-report depression scale for research in the general population. *Applied Psychology Measurement, 1*, 385–401.

Raju, P. T. (1974). Foreword. In F. H. Holck (Ed.), *Death and Eastern thought.* Nashville: Abingdon Press.

Rangell, L. (1955). On the psychoanalytic theory of anxiety. *Journal of the American Psychoanalytic Association, 3,* 389–414.

Rangell, L. (1968). A further attempt to resolve the "problem of anxiety." *Journal of the American Psychoanalytic Association, 16,* 371–405.

Rank, O. (1931). *Psychology and the soul.* New York: Perpetua Books.

Rank, O. (1936). *Will, therapy and truth and reality.* New York: Alfred A. Knopf.

Rank, O. (1945). *Will, therapy and truth and reality.* New York: Alfred A. Knopf.

Ray, J., & Najman, J. (1974). Death anxiety and death acceptance: A preliminary approach. *Omega, 5,* 311–315.

Register, L. M., & Henley, T. B. (1992). The phenomenology of intimacy. *Journal of Social and Personal Relationships, 9,* 467–481.

Reik, T. (1944). *A psychologist looks at love.* New York: Rinehart.

Rhudick, P. J., & Dibner, A. S. (1961). Age, personality and health correlates of death concern in normal aged individuals. *Journal of Gerontology, 16,* 44–49.

Ricoeur, P. (1976). *Interpretation theory.* Fort Worth, TX: Texas Christian University.

Riesman, D., Glazer, N., & Denny, R. (1961). *The lonely crowd: A study of the changing American character.* New Haven, CT: Yale University Press.

Robinson, P. J., & Wood, K. (1983). Fear of death and physical illness: A personal construct approach. *Death Education, 7,* 213–228.

Robinson, P. J., & Wood, K. (1985). The threat index: An additive approach. *Omega, 15,* 139–144.

Rogers, C. R. (1961). *On becoming a person.* Boston: Houghton Mifflin.

Romanyshyn, R. (1977). Phenomenology and psychoanalysis: Contributions of Merleau-Ponty. *Psychoanalytic Review, 64,* 211–223.

Romanyshyn, R. (1978). Psychology and the attitude of science. In R. Valle & M. King (Eds.), *Existential-phenomenological alternatives for psychology* (pp. 18–47). New York: Oxford University Press.

Romanyshyn, R., & Whalen, B. J. (1989). Psychology and the attitude of science. In R. Valle & S. Halling (Eds.), *Existential-phenomenological perspectives in psychology* (pp. 17–39). New York: Plenum Press.

Rook, K. S. (1984). Promoting social bonding: Strategies for helping the lonely and socially isolated. *American Psychologist, 39,* 1389–1407.

Rook, K. S., & Peplau, L. A. (1982). Perspectives on helping the lonely. In L. A. Peplau & D. Perlman (Eds.), *Loneliness: A sourcebook of current theory, research and therapy.* New York: Wiley-Interscience.

Roos, P., & Albers, R. (1965). Performance of alcoholics and normals on a measure of temporal orientation. *Journal of Clinical Psychology, 21,* 34–36.

Ross, L. M., & Pollio, H. R. (1991). Metaphors of death: A thematic analysis of personal meanings. *Omega, 23,* 291–307.

Rowe, J. A., Halling, S., Davies, E., Leifer, M., Powers, D., & van Bronkhorst, J. (1989). The psychology of forgiving another: A dialogical research approach. In R. Valle & S. Halling (Eds.), *Existential-phenomenological perspectives in psychology* (pp. 233–244). New York: Plenum Press.

Rubenstein, C. M., & Shaver, P. (1982). The experience of loneliness. In L. A. Peplau & D. Perlman (Eds.), *Loneliness: A sourcebook of current theory, research and therapy.* New York: Wiley-Interscience.

Rubin, Z. (1970). Measurement of romantic love. *Journal of Personality and Social Psychology, 16,* 265–273.

Rubin, Z. (1973). *Liking and loving: An invitation to social psychology*. New York: Holt, Rinehart & Winston.

Rubins, J. L. (1964). On the psychopathology of loneliness. *American Journal of Psychoanalysis, 24*, 153–166.

Ruiz, R. A., & Krauss, H. H. (1967). Test–retest reliability and practice effect with the Shipley Institute of Living scale. *Psychological Reports, 20*, 1085–1086.

Sacks, O. (1984). *A leg to stand on*. New York: Summit.

Sacks, O. (1985). *The man who mistook his wife for a hat*. New York: Summit.

Sadler, W. A. (1978). Dimensions in the problem of loneliness: A phenomenological approach in social psychology. *Journal of Phenomenological Psychology, 9*, 157–187.

Sager, C. J., & Hunt, B. (1979). *Intimate partners: Hidden patterns in love relationships*. New York: McGraw-Hill.

Sardello, R. J. (1978). A phenomenological approach to memory. In R. Valle & M. King (Eds.), *Existential-phenomenological alternatives for psychology* (pp. 136–151). New York: Oxford University Press.

Sarnoff, I., & Corwin, S. M. (1959). Castration anxiety and the fear of death. *Journal of Personality, 27*, 374–385.

Sartre, J.-P. (1943/1956). *Being and nothingness: An essay on phenomenological ontology* (H. Barnes, Trans.). New York: Philosophical Library.

Sartre, J.-P. (1957). *Existentialism and human emotions*. New York: Philosophical Library.

Sartre, J.-P. (1960/1963). *Search for a method* (H. Barnes, Trans.). New York: Vintage.

Schafer, R. (1976). *A new language for psychoanalysis*. New Haven, CT: Yale University Press.

Schafer, R. (1983). *The analytic attitude*. New York: Basic Books.

Schafer, S. (1970). *Compensation and restitution to victims of crime*. Montclair, NJ: Patterson Smith.

Schilder, P. (1935/1950). *The image and appearance of the human body*. New York: International Universities Press.

Schill, T., Toves, C., & Ramaniah, N. (1981). UCLA Loneliness Scale and effects of stress. *Psychological Reports, 49*, 257–258.

Schlater, J. A., Baker, A. H., & Wapner, S. (1974). Age changes in apparent arm length. *Bulletin of the Psychonomic Society, 4*, 75–77.

Schlipp, P. (1967). *The philosophy of Martin Buber*. London: Cambridge University Press.

Schry, E. (1978). *Van den Berg's approach to "unconscious" events*. Unpublished paper, Duquesne University.

Schutz, A. (1932/1967). *The phenomenology of the social world* (G. Walsh & F. Lehnert, Trans.). Evanston, IL: Northwestern University Press.

Schwartz, A. E. (1979). Androgyny and the art of loving: *Psychotherapy: Theory, Research and Practice, 16*, 405–408.

Scott, C. A. (1896). Old age and death. *American Journal of Psychology, 8*, 67–122.

Searle, J. (1982). What is an intentional state. In H. Dreyfuss (Ed.), *Husserl, intentionality, and cognitive science* (pp. 259–276). Cambridge, MA: MIT Press.

Secord, P. F., & Jourard, S. M. (1953). The appraisal of body-cathexis: Body cathexis and the self. *Journal of Consulting Psychology, 17*, 343–347.

Seeman, M. V. (1976). Time and schizophrenia. *Psychiatry, 39*, 189–195.

Shallis, M. (1982). *On time: An investigation into scientific knowledge and human experience.* New York: Schocken Books.

Shavelson, R. J., & Stern, P. (1981). Research on teachers' pedagogical thoughts, judgments, decisions, and behavior. *Review of Educational Research, 51,* 455–498.

Shavelson, R. J., Webb, N. M., & Burstein, L. (1986). Measurement of teaching. In M. Wittrock (Ed.), *Handbook of research on teaching* (pp. 80–86). New York: Macmillan Publishing Co.

Sherif, M. (1936). *The psychology of social norms.* New York: Harper.

Sherry, J. F., & Carmago, E. G. (1987). "May your life be marvelous": English language labelling and the semiotics of Japanese promotion. *Journal of Consumer Research, 14,* 174–188.

Shneidman, E. S. (1971, June). You and death. *Psychology Today,* 43–45, 74–80.

Shontz, F. (1969). *Perceptual and cognitive aspects of the body experience.* New York: Academic Press.

Shostrom, E., & Kavanaugh, J. (1971). *Between man and woman: The dynamics of intersexual relationships.* Los Angeles: Nash.

Shrut, S. D. (1958). Attitudes toward old age and death. *Mental Hygiene, 42,* 259–266.

Silberman, L. H. (1969). Death in the Hebrew Bible and apocalyptic literature. In L. Mills (Ed.), *Perspectives on death.* Nashville: Abingdon Press.

Simmel, M. (1958). The conditions for the occurrence of phantom limbs. *Proceedings of the American Philosophical Society, 102,* 492–500.

Simmel, M. (1966). Developmental aspects of the body scheme. *Child Development, 37,* 83–96.

Skinner, B. F. (1960). Pigeons in a pelican. *American Psychologist, 15,* 28–37.

Skinner, B. F. (1974). *About behaviorism.* New York: Alfred A. Knopf.

Slade, P. D., & Russell, G. F. M. (1972). Experimental investigation of bodily perception in anorexia nervosa and obesity. *Psychotherapy and Psychosomatics, 22,* 359–363.

Slater, P. (1970). *The pursuit of loneliness: American culture at the breaking point.* Boston: Beacon Press.

Smith, E. E., & Medin, D. L. (1981). *Categories and concepts.* Cambridge, MA: Harvard University Press.

Smith, J. S. (1981). The development of love relationships and progress toward marriage: The Colorado courtship study. *Dissertation Abstracts International, 42,* 2605–2606B.

Snygg, D., & Combs, A. W. (1949). *Individual behavior: A new frame of reference for psychology.* New York: Harper & Row.

Soloveitchik, J. B. (1984). *Soloveitchik on repentance* (P. Peli, Ed.). New York: Paulist Press.

Spence, D. (1982). *Narrative truth and historical truth.* New York: W. W. Norton & Company.

Spence, D. (1987). *The Freudian metaphor: Toward paradigm change in psychoanalysis.* New York: W. W. Norton.

Sperry, B., Ulrich, D. N., & Staver, N. (1958). The relation of motility to boys' learning problems. *American Journal of Ortho-Psychiatry, 28,* 640–646.

Spiegel, D. (1981). Man as time keeper. *American Journal of Psychoanalysis, 4,* 5–14.

Sprecher, S., & Hatfield, E. (1982). Self-esteem and romantic attraction: Four experiments. *Recherches de Psychologie Sociale, 4,* 61–81.

Sroufe, L. A. (1979). The coherence of individual development. *American Psycholo-*

gist, 34, 834–841.

Steck, L., Levitan, D., McLane, D., & Kelley, H. H. (1982). Care, need, and conceptions of love. *Journal of Personality and Social Psychology, 43*, 481–491.

Stern, D. (1983). The early development of schemas of self, other, and "self with other." In J. D. Lichtenberg & S. Kaplan (Eds.), *Reflections on self psychology.* Hillsdale, NJ: Analytic Press.

Sternberg, R. (1986). A triangular theory of love. *Psychological Review, 93*, 119–135.

Sternberg, R. J. (1987). Liking versus loving: A comparative evaluation of theories. *Psychological Bulletin, 102*, 331–345.

Stevens, S. J., Cooper, P. E., & Thomas, L. E. (1980). Age norms for Templer's Death Anxiety Scale. *Psychological Reports, 46*, 205–206.

Stewart, D. W. (1975). Religious correlates of the fear of death. *Journal of Thanatology, 3*, 161–164.

Stiles, D. B., & Smith, H. (1977). A film technique for assessing children's self-estimation of body size under static and dynamic conditions. *Perceptual and Motor Skills, 45*, 1275–1282.

Stokes, J. P. (1985). The relation of social network and individual difference variables to loneliness. *Journal of Personality and Social Psychology, 48*, 981–990.

Stolorow, R. D., & Lachmann, F. M. (1980). *Psychoanalysis of developmental arrests.* New York: International Universities Press.

Stout, L., Minton, B., & Spilka, B. (1976, April). *The construction and validation of multidimensional measures of death anxiety and death perspectives.* Paper presented at the Convention of the Rocky Mountain Psychological Association, Phoenix, AZ.

Strachey, J. (1959). Editor's Introduction. In *The standard edition of the complete psychological works of Sigmund Freud.* New York: W. W. Norton.

Strasser, S. (1967). Phenomenologies and psychologies. In N. Lawrence & D. O'Connor (Eds.), *Readings in existential phenomenology.* Englewood Cliffs, NJ: Prentice Hall.

Strober, M. (1981). The relation of personality characteristics to body image disturbances in juvenile anorexia nervosa: A multivariate analysis. *Psychosomatic Medicine, 43*, 323–330.

Sullivan, H. S. (1953). *The interpersonal theory of psychiatry.* New York: W. W. Norton & Company, Inc.

Swenson, C. H. (1961). Love: A self report analysis with college students. *Journal of Individual Psychology, 17*, 167–171.

Swenson, C. H. (1972). The behavior of love. In H. Otto (Ed.), *Love today: A new exploration.* New York: Association Press.

Swenson, C. H. (1973). A scale for measuring the behavior and feelings of love. In J. Pfeiffer & J. Jones (Eds.), *The 1973 annual handbook for group facilitators.* Iowa City: University Associates.

Swenson, C. H., & Gilner, F. (1964). Factor analysis of self report statements of love relationships. *Journal of Individual Psychology, 20*, 186–188.

Swenson, W. M. (1961). Attitudes toward death in an aged population. *Journal of Gerontology, 16*, 49–52.

Swenson, W. M. (1965). Attitudes towards death among the aged. In R. Fulton (Ed.), *Death and identity.* New York: Wiley.

Swidler, A. (1980). Love and adulthood in American culture. In N. Smelser & E. Erikson (Eds.), *Themes of work and love in adulthood* (pp. 120–147). Cambridge, MA: Harvard University Press.

Taylor, D. A. (1983). Views of death from sufferers of early loss. *Omega, 14*, 77–81.

Templer, D. (1970). The construction and validation of the Death Anxiety Scale. *Journal of General Psychology, 82*, 165–177.

Templer, D. (1971). The relationship between verbalized and nonverbalized death anxiety. *The Journal of Genetic Psychology, 119*, 211–214.

Templer, D. (1972). Death anxiety in religiously very involved persons. *Psychological Reports, 31*, 361–362.

Templer, D., & Dotson, E. (1970). Religious correlates of death anxiety. *Psychological Reports, 26*, 895–897

Tennov, D. (1979). *Love and limerence: The experience of being in love.* New York: Stein & Day.

Tharp, R. G. (1963). Psychological patterning in marriage. *Psychological Bulletin, 60*, 97–117.

Thompson, C. J. (1989). The role of context in consumers' category judgments: A preliminary investigation. In T. Srull (Ed.), *Advances in consumer research* (Vol. 16, pp. 542–547). Provo, UT: Association for Consumer Research.

Thompson, C. J. (1990). Eureka! and other tests of significance. In N. Goldberg, G. Gorn, & R. Pollay, *Advances in consumer research* (Vol. 17, pp. 25–30). Provo, UT: Association for Consumer Research.

Thompson, C.J., Henley, T. B., & Meguiar, T. M. (1989, March). Phenomenological methodology. Paper presented at the Southeastern Psychological Association, Washington, DC.

Thompson, C. J., Locander, W. B., & Pollio, H. R. (1990). Putting consumer experience back into consumer research: The philosophy and method of existential-phenomenology. *Journal of Consumer Research, 16*, 133–146.

Tillich, P. (1963). *The eternal now.* New York: Charles Scribner & Sons.

Tolman, E. C. (1932). *Purposive behavior in animals and men.* New York: Appleton-Century-Crofts.

Tysk, L. (1984). Time perception and affective disorder. *Perceptual and Motor Skills, 58*, 455–464.

Valle, R. S., & Halling, S. (1989). *Existential-phenomenological perspectives in psychology.* New York: Plenum Press.

Van den Berg, J. H. (1952). The human body and the significance of human movement: A phenomenological study. *Philosophy and Phenomenological Research, 13*, 159–183.

Van den Berg, J. H. (1961). *The changing nature of man.* New York: W. W. Norton.

Van den Berg, J. H. (1972). *A different existence: Principles of phenomenological psychopathology.* Pittsburgh: Duquesne University Press.

Veerhusen, D. L. (1979). The effect of the reciprocation of love and liking on the career of the premarital dyad. *Dissertation Abstracts International, 39*, 7544–7545A.

von Uexkull, J. (1934/1957). A stroll through the worlds of animals and men. In C. Schiller (Ed.), *Instinctive behavior.* New York: International Universities Press.

von Witzleben, H. D. (1958). On loneliness. *Psychiatry, 21*, 37–43.

Wachterhauser, B. R. (1986). History and language in understanding. In B. Wachterhauser (Ed.), *Hermeneutics and modern philosophy.* Albany: State University of New York Press.

Wallach, M. A., & Bordeaux, J. (1976). Children's construction of the human figure. *Perceptual and Motor Skills, 43*, 439–446.

Waller, W., & Hill, R. (1951). *The family.* New York: Dryden.

Walster, E. (1965). The effect of self-esteem on romantic liking. *Journal of Experimental Social Psychology, 1*, 184–197.

Walster, E., Walster, G. W., & Berscheid, E. (1978). *Equity: Theory and research.* Boston: Allyn & Bacon.

Wapner, S., & Werner, H. (1952). Toward a general field theory of perception. *Psychological Review, 59*, 324–338.

Watts, F. N., & Sharrock, R. (1984). Fear and time estimation. *Perceptual and Motor Skills, 59*, 597–598.

Weeks, D. G., Michela, J. L., Peplau, L. A., & Bragg, M. E. (1980). The relations between loneliness and depression: A structural equation analysis. *Journal of Personality and Social Psychology, 39*, 1238–1244.

Weisman, A. D., & Hackett, T. P. (1961). Predilection to death: Death and dying as a psychiatric problem. *Psychosomatic Medicine, 23*, 232–256.

Weiss, R. S. (1973). *Loneliness: The experience of emotional and social isolation.* Cambridge, MA: MIT Press.

Welkowitz, J., Cariffe, G., & Feldstein, S. (1976). Conversational congruence as a criterion of socialization in children. *Child Development, 47*, 269–279.

Werner, H. (1957). *Comparative psychology of mental development.* New York: Follett Publishing Company.

Werner, H., & Wapner, S. (1949). Sensory-tonic field theory of perception. *Journal of Personality, 18*, 88–107.

Wertz, F. (1983). From everyday to psychological description: Analyzing the moments of a qualitative data analysis. *Journal of Phenomenological Psychology, 14*, 197–242.

Wesch, J. (1971). Self actualization and fear of death. *Dissertation Abstracts International, 31*, 6270–6271B.

White, H. (1981). The value of narrativity in the representation of reality. In W. J. T. Mitchell (Ed.), *On narrative* (pp. 1–25). Chicago: University of Chicago Press.

White, R. L., & Liddon, S. C. (1972). Ten survivors of cardiac arrest. *Psychiatry in Medicine, 3*, 219–225.

Whorf, B. L. (1956). *Language, thought and reality.* Cambridge, MA: MIT Press.

Williams, R. L., & Cole, S. (1968). Religiosity, generalized anxiety and apprehension concerning death. *The Journal of Social Psychology, 75*, 111–117.

Williamson, R. C. (1966). *Marriage and family relations.* New York: Wiley.

Winch, R. F. (1958). *Mate selection: A study of complementary needs.* New York: Harper & Row.

Winch, R. F., Ktsanes, T., & Ktsanes, V. (1954). The theory of complementary needs in mate selection: An analytic and descriptive study. *American Sociological Review, 19*, 241–249.

Winnicott, D. W. (1958). *Through paediatrics to psychoanalysis.* New York: Basic Books.

Winnicott, D. W. (1965). *The maturational process and the facilitating environment.* New York: International Universities Press.

Winograd, T., & Flores, F. (1987). *Understanding computers and cognition.* New York: Addison-Wesley.

Wittgenstein, L. (1953). *Philosophical investigations* (G.E.M. Anscombe, Trans.). New York: Macmillan.

Wolf, W. (1957). *No cross, no crown.* Garden City, NY: Doubleday.

Wood, K., & Robinson, P. J. (1982). Actualization and the fear of death: Retesting an existential hypothesis. *Essence, 5*, 235–243.

Wyrick, R. A., & Wyrick, L. C. (1977). Time experience during depression. *Archives of General Psychiatry, 34,* 1441–1443.

Yarnold, P. R., & Grimm, L. G. (1982). Time urgency among coronary prone individuals. *Journal of Abnormal Psychology, 91,* 175–177.

Yates, S. (1935). Some aspects of time difficulties and their relation to music. *International Journal of Psychoanalysis, 16,* 341–354.

Young, J. E. (1982). Loneliness, depression and cognitive therapy: Theory and application. In L. Peplau & D. Perlman (Eds.), *Loneliness: A sourcebook of current theory, research and therapy.* New York: Wiley-Interscience.

Zaner, R. M. (1966). The radical reality of the human body. *Humanitas, 2,* 73–87.

Zaner, R. M. (1981). *The context of self, a phenomenological inquiry using medicine as a cue.* Athens, OH: Ohio University Press.

Zelkind, I., & Sprug, J. (1974). *Time research: 1172 studies.* Englewood Cliffs, NJ: Scarecrow Press.

Zilboorg, G. (1938, January). Loneliness. *Atlantic Monthly,* 45–54.

Name Index

Subject Index

agape, 235–6, 256–7
alienation, 141, 165–6, 185, 208, 294–5
  religious experience and, 193–4
aloneness, 157–90
  experiential themes of, 177–84
  forms of loneliness, 171–5
  phenomenological views of, 166–9
  psychopathology and, 158–62, 170–1, 185–
    90
anorexia, 72–3, 86
anxiety, 99–100, 117–18, 313–14
  death and, 307–8, 325–30
  fragmentation of self and, 263–5, 272–9
  loneliness, relations to, 161–2
  temporal orientation and, 100
Aristotelian view of the body, 61

behaviorism, 5, 31, 338–43, 352
Being and Nothingness, 11
Being and Time, 275
biological determinism, 63–4, 125–7, 338–9
body, 6–10, 359–60
  age identity and, 83–4
  body image, 68–71, 84–6
  body-in-time, 106–13
  experience of falling apart and, 282–3
  figure/ground relations and, 65–6
  gender differences in body experiences,
    87–8
  intentionality and, 67–8
  "lived" body, experiential themes of, 77–92
  personality and, 73–4
  phantom limb phenomena, theoretical
    analyses of, 71–2, 87
  phenomenological metaphors of, 67–8
  sexuality and, 63–4, 83–4
bracketing, processes of, 47–9

Cartesianism, 3–6, 10–11, 16, 30–1, 90–3,
  340–1

subject–object dualism, 3–5
  view of the body, 62–3
Christianity, 194–6, 223–4, 266, 305–7, 310–
  11
Cognitive psychology, 4–5, 30–1, 338–9
The Coming of Age, 57
consciousness as an interior monologue, 20–
  2, 26
content analysis, 37–40
cued recall procedures, 345–6

dasein (being-in-the-world), 5, 7, 10, 116–17,
  136–8, 359–65
  authenticity (good faith) versus
    inauthenticity (bad faith), 101–4, 168–9,
    213–15, 309–12
  being-toward-death and, 298–9, 311–12,
    325–6
  dread and, 274–8, 292–7
death, 114–15, 122, 274–5, 298–334
  aloneness and, 167
  Buddhism and, 301–2, 323–4
  Christianity and, 305–7, 324–5
  empirical research on, 312–15
  existential views of, 308–12, 326
  Hinduism and, 300–1, 323
  Judaism and, 302–5, 324–5
  psychoanalytic views of, 307–8
  meaning of, phenomenological themes,
    319–23
Death and Eastern Thought, 299
depression, 160–2, 187–8, 263–4
dialogue, as a methodological paradigm, 28–
  56, 337–8, 343–9
  open versus restricted dialogues, 34–6
dieting, 79, 83, 86, 112

ego, 63–4, 161–2, 232, 271–2, 278, 289–
  90
eros, 235

398